Praise for
Frontier Justice

"Andy Lamey tackles this timely and critical debate with an intellect and a passion that are formidable. *Frontier Justice* could, quite possibly, have a lasting effect on policy in Canada and elsewhere."

—*The Globe and Mail*

"Lamey has produced a superb and immensely readable work."
—Doug Saunders, *Literary Review of Canada*

"A page-turner . . . *Frontier Justice* shows that a more just treatment of refugees is possible, if we want it."

—*Ottawa Citizen*

"*Frontier Justice* provides what the debate over asylum and refugee claims so desperately needs: fresh thinking and historical perspective. Here is a wonderful writer tackling a subject, and a debate, as big as his talent."

—Paul Wells, *Maclean's*

"A book that pulses with intellectual curiosity and energy. . . . A calm, lucid voice in a debate often sidetracked by terrorist panic and hypocrisy about human rights."

— *The Chronicle Herald* (Halifax)

"Rivalling the film Casablanca for drama and romance is the refugee story of philosopher Hannah Arendt's escape from

Germany in 1933 and her reunion with her second husband after the invasion of France. Without passport or visa, Arendt managed to cross the border through a house that had its front door in Germany and back door in Czechoslovakia. Later, while in Paris, she met another German refugee and married him. They were separated after being interned but met again in the south of France. Lamey tells this story as a way of exploring the plight of the modern refugee and Arendt's own position on the 'impossibility of human rights' for refugees, inspired by what she experienced and witnessed during the war. It's a powerful introduction to a discussion of the contemporary refugee crisis."

—*The Age* (Australia)

FRONTIER JUSTICE

THE GLOBAL REFUGEE CRISIS
AND WHAT TO DO ABOUT IT

ANDY LAMEY

ANCHOR CANADA

For Kirsty

978-0-385-66255-0

Library and Archives Canada Cataloguing in Publication
is available upon request

Cover and text design by Paul Dotey
Cover image: Steve Ryan/Getty Images
Printed and bound in the USA

Published in Canada by Anchor Canada,
a division of Random House of Canada Limited
Visit Random House of Canada Limited's website:
www.randomhouse.ca

10 9 8 7 6 5 4 3 2 1

Every civilized people on the face of the earth must be fully aware that this country is the asylum of nations, and that it will defend the asylum to the last ounce of its treasure, and the last drop of its blood.

—*The Times* (London), February 28, 1853

CONTENTS

CONTENTS

PREFACE

THIS IS A BOOK ABOUT ASYLUM. The refugees referred to in its subtitle are the ones found at the frontiers of liberal states, people who make a special claim of entry in order to avoid persecution. Refugees in this situation have obvious similarities with people stranded in refugee camps in the developing world. First and foremost, both groups share a desire not to be sent back to a place where their lives could be in danger. The treatment of the two groups has also often risen and fallen together. As I note in the chapters to come, when Western states have introduced policies curtailing the protection they extend to asylum-seekers, it has often inspired governments in Asia and Africa to invoke harsh measures against refugees seeking to cross or already inside their own borders.

In addition to their similarities, however, the two types of refugees also have important differences. The needs of people seeking asylum can usually be met at the level of migration law. What they normally require is for Western states to recognize that they are not like other immigrants, and should be allowed to restart their lives in a strange new country. In regard to refugees in camps, relocation abroad is sometimes the best way to meet their needs. But not all residents of refugee camps want to be resettled in the West. Many would prefer instead to go home. The best way to help camp populations, therefore, will often be not through immigration law, but through humanitarian aid and diplomacy aimed at ending the crisis that sent them into exile.

The situation of refugees warehoused in camp is an important subject, and nothing would please me more than if this book caused readers to take a heightened interest in refugees in general. But a book that tried to solve every problem faced by refugees would not only be more complicated, but much longer, than the one I have tried to write. Sheer manageability is the main reason why I have focused on the issue of refugees seeking asylum. The second reason, as we will see, is that extending justice to them is difficult enough.

The book argues that there is an important relationship between the treatment of refugees and human rights. That relationship can be seen by noting the difference between a sufficient and a necessary condition. If this book that says so much about human rights says little about human rights issues not involving refugees, it is not because I am under the delusion that addressing the situation of refugees is a sufficient condition of ensuring human rights are respected. Obviously there are many ways human rights are violated, including many ways that do not involve refugees. But as I argue in Chapter One, it is a necessary condition of human rights having political force that refugees in particular be able to exercise them. If we cannot ensure at least that much, it calls into question the force and effectiveness of rights that are supposed to extend to all humanity. I try to show how human rights can meet this challenge, not because it is the only obstacle to human rights, but because it is a fundamental one.

This book does not say anything about the philosophical foundation of human rights. This is deliberate. Human rights have long been endorsed by different people for different reasons. There are a number of terms for this kind of agreement, whereby people who disagree at the level of first principles come together behind a shared political project. The most colourful label may be one used by economists, who sometimes refer to coalitions of Baptists and bootleggers, named after two groups in the United States who supported prohibition of the sale of alcohol. The doctrine of human rights is the biggest Baptist-bootlegger coalition in history, in that it has now been endorsed by a huge variety of philosophical, religious and cultural traditions. It is reasonable to debate any given justification for human rights, but there is a difference between this philosophical task and the more practical one of showing how rights might be respected in practice. It is this more down-to-earth project I try to accomplish in this book.

In this regard I take my inspiration from the authors of the Universal Declaration of Human Rights. In the lead-up to the Declaration's adoption in 1948, the United Nations consulted with thinkers from around the world regarding what rights to include. Jacques Maritain, a French philosopher involved in the drafting, noted that the intellectuals the UN consulted disagreed profoundly on the theoretical foundation of human rights. "At one of the meetings," Maritain wrote, "someone expressed astonishment that certain champions of violently opposed ideologies had agreed on a list of those rights. 'Yes,' they said, 'we agree about the rights but on condition that no one asks us why.'" This book seeks to create a similar consensus around a particular framework for upholding human rights, whether or not every reader agrees with my ultimate rationale for those rights.

ONE

THE PHILOSOPHER IN EXILE

In March of 1933, German politicians voted to grant their new chancellor, Adolf Hitler, the power to govern with impunity. Members of the Nazi party physically attacked parliamentarians before the vote to influence its outcome, but this terror campaign, it soon turned out, was nothing next to what would follow. It was suddenly normal for critics of the government to be beaten in the street. The most outspoken anti-Nazi activists became the first victims of the newly established concentration camp system, at the same time as anti-Semitic decrees expelled Jews from the civil service and other positions. In response to the wave of persecution, thousands of people began to flee the country. Among them were a young Jewish woman and her mother, who, shortly after the initial anti-Jewish laws were passed, left their home in Berlin for the last time.

The frightened women made their way south to the Erzgebirge mountain range, which marked Germany's frontier with Czechoslovakia. Neither one had a passport or visa. They were familiar, however, with a German exile group in Prague, which had set up a network of safe houses for escaping Jews and leftists. Armed with this knowledge, the two Berliners went to the mountain town of Carlsbad, where they sought out a kindhearted family who could provide them with a simple yet invaluable means of avoiding the border patrol: the house they lived in had its front door in Germany and its back door in Czechoslovakia. The two fugitives were taken in by their benefactors while it was light out, offered dinner, and released into the night. When their feet touched Czech soil, two things happened. They became refugees. And they set in motion a major episode in the history of human rights.

The escaping Jews were Hannah Arendt, then twenty-six, and her mother, Martha Beerwald. Why was their flight from fascism so remarkable? The answer has to do with Hannah Arendt's later transformation into one of the great political thinkers of the twentieth century. Arendt's philosophy was influenced by her experience as a refugee. So perhaps the best place to start in understanding Hannah Arendt, and seeing what we can learn from her about human rights, is by retracing the steps of her journey. As we will see, it is a journey that has much in common with that of refugees even today.

Arendt did not stay long in Czechoslovakia. After sending her mother to the relative safety of East Prussia (from where she would again flee the Nazis five years later), Arendt continued on to Switzerland and then to France, where she was reunited with her husband. Günther Stern, a communist and friend of the famous playwright Bertolt Brecht, had fled Germany several months in advance of his wife and mother-in-law. He was prompted to do so after Brecht had an address book confiscated by the Gestapo, which Stern feared would shortly result in the arrest of everyone whose name it contained. Now, in Paris, he and his wife were part of a wave of twenty-five thousand German refugees, 85 percent of them Jewish, who had poured into France, a greater number than that received by any other country.

Arendt's exile in Paris was not a happy time. Even before they became refugees, she and her husband had many differences. When it came to politics, for example, she never shared his commitment to communism. (Before the Nazis came to power, in fact, she was barely interested in politics at all, and always dated her political awakening to the rise of Hitler.) Now Arendt and her husband had little to unite them save the hardscrabble urgencies of refugee existence. When Stern left Paris for New York in 1936, his marriage to Arendt had long been over in all but name.

Things were hardly better for Arendt on a political level. The arrival of the German refugees, even though they represented a minuscule portion of France's population, was regarded in France as a major crisis. To be sure, there were people who spoke out on the refugees' behalf. They included not only French Jews but Socialists, liberals, left-wing Catholics and a few stray conservatives. But throughout the 1930s, these partisans of "hospitality," to use the term they most frequently invoked, had to engage in a fierce political battle with conservative and centre-left politicians, rank-and-file union members (union leaders tended to be pro-refugee) and business groups, all of whom filled the air with cries of "France for the French!" and denounced the Jews as economic parasites and "undesirables."

France's refugee crisis came to a head at the end of the decade. By this point Arendt's personal situation had improved somewhat: she was employed by a French Jewish charity and had managed to have her mother join her from Prussia. There was even a new man in her life, another German (albeit non-Jewish) refugee named Heinrich Blücher. But after Hitler's annexation of Austria in 1938, which sent another wave of desperate Jews into France, the political situation of every refugee in Paris deteriorated. France introduced repressive laws making admission much more difficult. Jews who were already present were barred from holding certain jobs or were sent back to Germany. Others were turned away at the border. A mood of despair spread through the Jewish community, and many refugees chose suicide. After a Polish Jew living in Paris shot a German embassy official, the Nazis responded with *Kristallnacht*—the night of broken glass— burning and looting Jewish homes, shops and synagogues across Germany. Anti-refugee voices in France were already alleging a Jewish conspiracy to drag France into a needless war with Germany; *Kristallnacht*, perversely, was taken as evidence for this view and resulted in calls for harsh reprisals against refugees. Paris's Jews lived in terror of what would happen next.

The answer came in the fall of 1939. Hostilities between France and Germany had now formally begun (albeit in the form of the phony war, before the bombs began to fall), and France ordered that all German men with suspicious political back- grounds be interned. It didn't matter that Heinrich Blücher and thousands of others had fled Germany precisely because they were Communists, and so would be the last people on earth to engage in pro-Nazi activities. Blücher was sent to a labour camp in a small French village, sleeping with two dozen other men in a barn that left them exposed to the constant cold rain, where he soon became ill.

Through desperate lobbying, Arendt managed to secure Blücher's release (a friend of hers tracked down the widow of a police prefect who agreed to serve as his guarantor). When Blücher returned to Paris he and Arendt married. But instead of a honeymoon, they had to contend with a new internment order—one that now included most German women. Four months after their wedding, Arendt and her husband reported to separate sports stadiums in Paris. Arendt was made to sleep on the stone bleachers of the Winter Velodrome alongside other Jewish women branded "enemy aliens." Every time a plane passed overhead they feared it was a German bomber come to end their lives. Finally, after a week, Arendt and the other female refugees were taken to a camp near Gurs, a town in southwest France. Constant rains had turned the camp into a muddy swamp. Although inmates were not forced to work, the residents kept themselves busy emptying the latrines and engaging in other chores to stave off depression.

During her internment, with the war situation growing worse, and not knowing whether she would ever see her husband again, Arendt was overcome with thoughts of killing herself. It was something many other camp residents considered. At one point, there was talk among the refugees of committing suicide en masse, as a form of protest against the way they had been treated by the French government. But the inmates soon decided that this would only please their captors. As Arendt later wrote, "When some of us suggested that we had been shipped there *pour crever* [to be snuffed out] in any case, the general mood turned suddenly into a violent courage of life."

Several weeks after Arendt's arrival in Gurs, German troops invaded Paris. All communications broke down and the camp descended into chaos. Many women decided to stay, afraid to leave the one place their husbands would at least know to look for them. When Gurs later came under the jurisdiction of the collaborationist Vichy government, most of these inmates were handed over to the Nazis for extermination. Arendt was lucky: she had somewhere she could go. The same Paris friend who had secured Heinrich Blücher's release, a wealthy German exile, was renting a house near the southern French town of Montauban. Arendt could reach it by travelling on foot and hitchhiking.

Montauban was in total confusion when Arendt arrived. Many homes had been left empty in the panic of war, and the mayor had chosen to express his opposition to the new Vichy government in northern France by turning empty buildings over to former internees. As a result, thousands of refugees were streaming into Montauban from all across France. They slept on empty floors, dragging in every mattress they could find, creating conditions almost as crowded and cramped as in the camps they had just escaped.

It was against this backdrop that Hannah Arendt had one of the happiest experiences of her life. One day she found herself on the main avenue of Montauban. There, amid piles of mattresses, furniture and garbage, she saw her husband walking down the street. Blücher's camp had been evacuated when the Nazis took Paris, and he had joined the great migration of people—travelling on bicycles, in the backs of trucks, on foot with everything they could carry—streaming into unoccupied southern France. Surrounded by crowds of refugees scavenging for scraps of food and tobacco, others seeking word of missing loved ones, Arendt and Blücher fell into a deep embrace. There would be other hurdles still to come. They would have to go to horrendous lengths to obtain visas. They would only narrowly avoid arrest. But from that moment forward, Hannah Arendt redoubled her "violent courage of life." Travelling with her husband, and followed shortly by her mother, she reached the safety of the United States in 1941.

What can we learn by looking back at Hannah Arendt's experience today? Luck clearly played a major role in her eventual escape to safety, such as her chance meeting with her husband in southern France. Arendt and Blücher were also fortunate to marry when they did. Shortly after their ceremony, wartime conditions made obtaining a French marriage licence next to impossible. The special emergency visas Arendt and Blücher eventually obtained were given only to single people or to couples who could produce a licence. Unmarried couples had to choose which of them would stay behind and hope for some other opportunity of escape. Yet although these and other details were specific to Arendt's case, she is not the only person fleeing persecution whose survival has been due to chance. Many refugees continue to make it to safety after just barely catching the right flight or running from their homes at the last possible minute. In this and other ways, Arendt's experience calls to mind the situation of people still seeking asylum today.

Arendt took flight from an anti-Semitic campaign that eventually became the worst genocide of all time. This made her a quintessentially modern refugee. Not because every refugee is necessarily fleeing genocide, but because before the Armenian genocide of 1915, refugees of this kind did not exist. Today we have been taught by events in Cambodia, Bosnia and Rwanda not to be surprised when genocide or its cousin, ethnic cleansing, drive yet another group of refugees across yet another border. But even today, crises of this kind are exacerbated by the inability of outsiders to reckon with evil. When refugees from genocide come forward to recount their experiences, they are often initially met with skepticism. Arendt herself was one of the first people to point out the inverse relationship between persecution and believability. "The very immensity of the crimes," she wrote, "guarantees that the murderers who proclaim their innocence with all manner of lies will be more readily believed than the victims who tell the truth."

If a refugee is often running from events that are literally incredible, the challenges he faces in escaping can be, by contrast, all too banal. Recall that when Arendt and her mother left Germany, they had no travel documents. This wasn't because they were absent-minded, or left in a hurry. It was because they faced the same dilemma anyone does who flees persecution by her own government. If the authorities are out to kill you, they are unlikely to process your passport application. (Even travelling to a foreign consulate to obtain a visa can sometimes be impossible: governments have been known to kill dissidents who make public a desire to flee abroad.) Today, legitimate asylum-seekers who cross borders by land often still arrive without papers. And with the rise of the jet age, when air travel without identification is next to impossible, it has also become common for genuine refugees to reach the safety of the West by travelling on fake passports.

Then there is the question of why Arendt and her family did not seek asylum in Switzerland or some other nearby country, but continued on to France. Beginning in 1933 and for several years afterwards, Switzerland did admit refugees, but always on the understanding that, as with Arendt, they were merely passing through and would not seek asylum in Switzerland itself. As time wore on, however, and the situation of German Jews worsened, Swiss officials became increasingly concerned that Switzerland not be, in the words of a Swiss police official, "saturated with Jews." So in 1938 the Swiss government sealed its borders and, when thousands of desperate refugees arrived, forcibly returned them to the Nazis.

In the context of the 1930s, Switzerland's policies were unremarkable. We do not like to think about it now, but during the Great Depression anti-Semitism was not confined to Nazi Germany. All Western countries eventually closed their doors to Jewish refugees. This was the main reason so many at first fled to France. As the historian Vicki Caron notes, geographic proximity to Germany and other factors certainly played a role in France's refugee influx. "Most important, however, was the fact that France had not yet implemented immigration restrictions, in sharp contrast to Great Britain or the United States."

If we can be grateful that Western states are no longer in the grip of an anti-Semitic conspiracy, the situation of France in 1933 nonetheless illustrates an enduring aspect of refugee politics, namely that the number of asylum-seekers a country receives is influenced by the policies of other refugee-receiving states. Many commentators on refugee issues, not to mention government policy-makers, have a tendency to focus on their own country in isolation. This can cause them to overlook the full range of factors that do and do not bring asylum-seekers to their shores. There have been situations, for example, where one country has deliberately made its asylum program less welcoming in the hope of attracting fewer refugee claimants, only to see the number of applications go up instead—because neighbouring countries have simultaneously made their own policies even harsher. Rather than solve any problems, the result is a race to the bottom that puts the needs of refugees at risk.

Finally, the refugee debate that took place in France can teach us something. On the one side there were those such as the French police officer who wrote in 1933 that German Jews "will soon constitute groups of discontented and violent exiles: veritable ghettos from the moral point of view, as well as the point of view of hygiene!" Today we recoil from the prejudice in this remark, and read with relief the words of those who spoke out for refugees. A typical representative was the minister of the French government who told the chamber of deputies that it was "an honour for our nation to remain loyal to the generous tradition of hospitality on which it has always prided itself." And yet, as fundamentally opposed as these viewpoints were, they also had something in common.

To suggest that the presence of Jews or any other foreigners represents a menace at the level of "hygiene" is to see them as a form of contamination. France will be infected by their presence. But note that a similar standard is employed—albeit in a much more humane way—in the suggestion that France will fail to live up to its "generous tradition of hospitality." Only this time, France will be damaged by *not* welcoming refugees. Extending back to the French Revolution and beyond, France had long seen itself as a great and magnanimous nation that took in political exiles in times of need. If France does not live up to this tradition in regard to German refugees, the politician was arguing, it will in a way fail to be itself, cease to be truly French.

In short, both sides in France's refugee debate invoked a vision of national identity. This is especially worth recalling today, when refugees have become subjects of international law, and there is a tendency to approach refugee issues in dry, legalistic terms. Make no mistake, international refugee conventions are an important development since Arendt's time. But laws do not interpret themselves, and different countries have implemented the same treaty in very different ways. To understand these differences, we need to broaden our focus beyond the law and take into account issues of national self-understanding. As we will see, refugee debates in many countries hinge not only on the question, How should we treat these strangers who need our help? All too often, they hinge on a much more emotional question. Who are we?

These are only some of the lessons we can learn by looking back at one of the worst refugee crises of all time. But there is another lesson, the one Arendt herself drew. It was contained in *The Origins of Totalitarianism*, the 1951 book that made Arendt's name. *Origins* was Arendt's attempt to comprehend the central political events of her lifetime, notably the rise of fascism and Stalinism, which Arendt considered philosophically indistinguishable. The book ranges over many other topics, however, and includes a chapter that may be the most widely read essay on refugees ever published.

Arendt wrote of the unprecedented refugee crisis Europe experienced in the aftermath of World War I, a time when many international borders were being redrawn. In the nineteenth century, eastern and central Europe had been dominated by four imperial dynasties that ruled over many different nationalities and language groups: the Hapsburgs of Austria-Hungary, the

Romanovs of Russia, the Ottomans of Turkey and the Hohenzollerns of Prussia. World War I caused all four empires to implode and be replaced by states that, most often, embodied the aspirations of a particular nationality. Parts of the Austro-Hungarian Empire, for example, were divided into the new states of Hungary and Austria. Latvia, Estonia and Lithuania similarly achieved independence from Russia. Poland, which had been partitioned by Prussia, Austria-Hungary and Russia, became an independent nation for the first time since 1795.

Many of the new countries' borders were finalized only after warfare with their neighbours. But even when new states did not engage in protracted fighting, they saw enormous flows of people cross their frontiers; ethnic Germans who had lived in Poland and elsewhere poured into Germany, Bulgarians went to Bulgaria, Hungarians to Hungary and so on. To get a sense of the enormous numbers of refugees travelling in all directions, we need only recall that 320,000 Armenians had fled to Europe (and the Middle East) to escape the Turkish genocide, just as hundreds of thousands of Jews were simultaneously driven out of eastern Europe by a wave of pogroms—and all this occurred while a million people were fleeing the Russian Revolution and millions more were displaced by the Great War itself.

Arendt noted that many asylum-seekers from this period received the same treatment as did refugees of her generation. A large number were denied entry to countries they attempted to enter, while others were forcibly expelled. The new democracy of Hungary, for example, sealed its borders so tightly that hundreds of people were trapped for months, and in some cases years, inside the train stations where they arrived. The United States and Canada introduced highly restrictive immigration policies, choking off an important avenue of escape. Even when refugees did make it across a border, they were often unable to obtain work or residency papers, and so lived a precarious existence made up in equal parts of poverty and fear of deportation. Many were herded into camps, much like Arendt had been, where dysentery and cholera were a constant menace. The result was that, according to one estimate, in 1926 there were still 9.5 million refugees stranded across Europe.

Arendt pointed out what a new phenomenon this was. Before World War I, refugees numbered in the thousands, not the millions. The rise of nationalism was a major contributing factor to the appearance of refugees in massive numbers. Eastern and Central Europe's division into nation-states was the culmination of a long process that had begun over a century before, according to which Europeans saw themselves not as members of villages, cities or estates, but nations. Nationalist logic says everyone should speak the same language and observe the same customs. This new thinking not only drove millions of people from their homes but it meant that if they sought refuge in another state, unless it was one that housed their own national culture, they could expect to find themselves again unwelcome—and sometimes even people who did share the culture of the majority were still turned away.

Yet Arendt's purpose in recalling Europe's first mass refugee crisis was not merely to offer a historical discussion. Indeed, her essay eventually leaves history behind and soars into the realm of philosophy. Because for Arendt, what the experience of refugees ultimately showed was the impossibility of human rights.

Arendt drew a common distinction between the rights of citizens and the rights of human beings as such. As citizens, we are entitled to the protection of our own government. A refugee is someone who loses that protection and all the entitlements that go with it. When such people show up at the border of a new country, they cannot assert the same rights as people who live there, such as the automatic right of entry. All refugees can appeal to is their sheer humanity, and the moral claims that are supposed to extend from it.

But in practice, Arendt bitterly pointed out, simply being a human being entitled refugees to nothing. Between the wars, even when refugees were not turned away at a border, or interned in camps where they died of disease, or driven to such despair that they took their own lives; even when refugees received enough scraps of charity to simply stay alive, they lived in a state of rightlessness. There was little they could do on their own behalf except keep running, until they found some country that would absorb them. But those sorts of decisions—to admit refugees, to let them work, to effectively treat them like citizens—were not decisions refugees themselves had any influence over. What decent treatment refugees did receive was due to acts of pity extended at the discretion of receiving states. Refugee "rights" never entered into it.

This was the case even in countries that had inscribed in law the principle of human rights. Since the eighteenth century, intellectuals and politicians such as Thomas Jefferson and the Marquis de Lafayette, representatives of the American and French revolutions respectively, had proclaimed their belief in the Rights of Man, as human rights were first called. This is the view that "every man is born with inalienable and indefeasible rights," as Lafayette put it. Yet even in wealthy advanced nations where this idea was the foundation of the legal system, there were no rights for refugees. As Arendt scathingly remarked, "The Rights of Man, supposedly inalienable, proved to be unenforceable— even in countries whose constitutions were based on them— whenever people appeared who were no longer citizens of any sovereign state."

The conclusion Arendt ultimately drew concerned the nature of rights. Rights, she argued, are not something we obtain simply by being born. Rather, we acquire rights through our membership in a political community. In the modern world, this means being a member of a sovereign state. And despite the rhetoric of "universal human rights," states do not equally uphold the rights of every human being on earth. Rather, they grant overwhelming priority to enforcing the rights of their own citizens. Refugees are human beings who are in essence citizens of nowhere. Which is to say, they are human beings with no rights worth speaking of.

Arendt summed up her view in a famous passage in which she says the very idea of human rights is nothing more than an abstraction:

> The conception of human rights, based upon the assumed existence of a human being as such, broke down at the very moment when those who professed to believe in it were for the first time confronted with people who had indeed lost all other qualities and specific relationships—except that they were still human. The world found nothing sacred in the abstract nakedness of being human. . . . [Refugees knew] that the abstract nakedness of being human was their greatest danger.

Today, when human rights have become the moral currency of our time, passages such as this can be hard to read. But to understand how Arendt could lash out at the idea of human rights, I would point to her own experience as a refugee. Perhaps more than anything, Arendt's attack on human rights was an attack on the hypocrisy she saw everywhere around her. France and other countries proclaimed their belief in human rights—not rights for citizens, or Frenchmen, or Christians, but rights for *human beings*—at the same time as she and countless other refugees were treated with contempt. The ultimate explanation of the interwar crisis of asylum, Arendt concluded, was the simple fact that the world is divided into states. In a political universe founded on national sovereignty, truly universal human rights are an impossibility. The refugee turned away at the border of a liberal state is the human embodiment of this philosophical contradiction. In Arendt's words, "It was a problem not of space but of political organization."

As this sentence is written, the world is again grappling with the issue of asylum. Debates over refugee issues, often acrimonious, have become a part of political life in many Western countries. Australia triggered an international incident in 2001 when it forbade a Norwegian freighter carrying several hundred asylum-seekers from landing on its shores. Even before the September 11 massacre, the United States became so concerned about terrorists posing as refugees that it introduced a sweeping asylum reform, one so restrictive that one observer has said it "essentially wipes out asylum as we know it." In 1993 Germany took the extraordinary step of amending its constitution to reduce the number of refugee applications it receives. Across Europe, the flip side of European nations' opening their borders to each other has been an unwelcoming attitude toward everyone else, to the point that refugee advocates now refer to Fortress Europe. Twice in recent years concerns over refugee flows have contributed to military action. The 1999 intervention of the North Atlantic Treaty Organization in Kosovo was partly motivated by the desire of nearby states to avoid an influx of displaced Kosovars. Following a coup in Haiti, U.S. President Bill Clinton gave as a reason for the 1994 invasion that restored Jean-Bertrand Aristide to power the need "to secure our borders."

It was not supposed to be this way. In the aftermath of World War II, when Europe was once again awash with displaced people, the United Nations introduced two measures to deal with refugees. One was the 1951 Convention Relating to the Status of Refugees, or the Refugee Convention for short, which defined a refugee as someone with "a well-founded fear of being persecuted for reasons of race, religion, nationality, membership of a particular social group or political opinion." By signing it, Western countries pledged not to return a genuine refugee to danger. The UN also established a High Commissioner for Refugees, the UNHCR, an office that would provide direct assistance to displaced people around the world.

Both the Refugee Convention and the High Commission have proven to be indispensable innovations. In hindsight, however, they seemed most successful during the Cold War. Not only was this a time when the global refugee population was comparatively small, falling from 15 million in the late 1940s to 2.9 million by 1975, but the defining asylum-seekers of this period were defectors from the Soviet bloc. Defectors often received a welcome reception in the West, partly out of genuine humanitarian concern, but also because Western governments wanted to score a PR victory in the struggle against communism.

Just how powerful this combination of motives could be was evident during the Hungarian crisis of 1956, when the Soviet Union suppressed a democratic revolution in its Eastern European satellite. By sheer coincidence, the Hungarian government had cleared the barbed wire and land mines along its border with neutral Austria a mere three weeks earlier. As a result, 180,000 Hungarians were able to escape, a figure that, when combined with the 20,000 more who went to Yugoslavia, represented 2 percent of the total Hungarian population. UNHCR, working closely with Western governments, quickly coordinated one of the most successful refugee operations of all time. Unlike the lingering refugee crises that lasted for years after both world wars, more than 150,000 Hungarians were granted permanent asylum in thirty-five Western countries within six months, an incredible achievement.

In the late 1970s, however, the international refugee situation began to change. Their numbers started to climb again, to the point that in 2009 there were over 11 million. If we add people displaced within their own country and similar groups who also receive aid from to the United Nations High Commissioner for Refugees, the total rises to 31 million. This is down from 1992, when the global population of displaced people was even higher, but clearly refugees are an enduring fact of political life. The late 1950s to the late 1970s seem the exception in a ninety-year period that has seen Western countries grappling with one major refugee crisis or another since the World War I events described by Arendt.

But it is not just that there are more refugees today than there were thirty years ago. The increase in sheer numbers has coincided with what has been called "the globalization of asylum." The spread across the developing world of airports and cheaper air travel has made it increasingly easy for people fleeing civil strife and persecution in places like Sri Lanka, Iraq, Afghanistan and Somalia to reach Europe and North America. In the early 1970s, the total number of asylum claims made in Western European countries never averaged more than 13,000. In the year 2000, the same countries received 412,700 asylum applications. This has given rise to a widespread concern across Western countries that they are or will shortly be inundated by people from the Third World filing asylum claims not to escape persecution, but to move to a country with a higher standard of living. In response, rich nations have introduced a host of measures aimed at making it difficult to claim asylum. Airlines and shipping companies are fined when they transport people without proper documents. Residents of poor countries increasingly require visas to travel to rich ones, and must pass inspection with migration officers posted in overseas airports. Even if they do make it to a Western country, asylum-seekers are often denied work or detained. That is, when they are not summarily expelled at the border or sent back on the next flight.

Such measures are increasingly the norm even in countries that have signed the Refugee Convention. The result is that to some observers, refugees have once again come to symbolize the gap between the rhetoric and the reality of human rights. As was the case after World War I, Western governments today announce their commitment to the moral worth of human beings while giving the back of their hand to refugees who show up at their borders. In the words of Matthew Gibney, a leading refugee expert at the University of Oxford, "liberal democratic states publicly avow the principle of asylum but use fair means and foul to prevent as many asylum seekers as possible from arriving on their territory where they could claim its protections." Gibney's phrase to describe the overall asylum situation today is "organized hypocrisy." It has a familiar ring.

Against this backdrop, it is not hard to see why Arendt's pessimistic view of human rights still attracts adherents. They note that more than two hundred years after the declaration of the Rights of Man, ninety years after the refugee crisis that followed World War I, fifty years after the Universal Declaration of Human Rights, we still have not been able to uphold meaningful rights for refugees. It seems a little late in the day to reply that, while the principle is a good one, we are still casting about for a way to implement it. For Arendtians will in turn reply that after a certain point, impossible ideas become bad ideas. If instead we stopped speaking of human rights altogether, it might or might not improve the lot of refugees. But it would at least have the virtue of intellectual honesty.

Such a cynical argument is not the one I want to make. According to Arendt, "the very phrase 'human rights' became for all concerned—victims, persecutors, and onlookers alike—the evidence of hopeless idealism or fumbling feeble-minded hypocrisy." By that standard, I wish to be counted among the most feeble-minded hypocrites and the most hopeless idealists. For I believe there are good reasons to be more optimistic about human rights than Arendt was.

One reason concerns the nature of rights. Some of the most scathing passages in Arendt's discussion occur when she zeroes in on the idea of inalienable rights and subjects it to merciless criticism. "No such thing as inalienable human rights existed," she flatly declares. In Arendt's view, a right is only truly inalienable if it is always upheld in practice. But surely that's not what anyone really means by saying rights are "inalienable." After all, murder has been a fact of life since societies began, but no one would take this to mean we should not speak of a right not to be killed. Saying rights are inalienable expresses a belief in the inalienable moral worth of human beings. Because we hold this belief, we condemn some practices, such as sending a refugee back to danger, no matter how often they occur. That is very different from claiming such practices are never going to happen—the impossible standard a right has to meet before it can be "inalienable" in Arendt's terms.

Another way to say this is that there is a difference between rights understood in a moral rather than a legal sense. If we think of human rights as a moral concept, we are unlikely to concede that such rights cease to exist simply because they are often not upheld in practice. Indeed, it's precisely because the moral worth of human beings is all too easy to violate that people began speaking of rights in the first place. The Rights of Man were originally used to condemn institutions, such as despotic rule and slavery, that were widespread, ancient and entrenched. Invoking the notion of rights against such institutions was a way of expressing revulsion at the situation of serfs and slaves, and a means of inspiring people to change those situations. So even before we get to the question of how to enforce rights in law, the idea of human rights performs the important task of expressing the judgment we want the law to uphold. In other words, it is precisely because we live in a world of human rights violations that human rights have value as a moral ideal.

However, even if we do distinguish between moral and legal rights, we still face a problem. Most people who believe in human rights want them to be more than talking points or diagnostic tools. We also want rights to be respected in practice. Rather than eliminating the problem Arendt identified, therefore, distinguishing between moral and legal rights transforms it. The problem is no longer to outline how human rights might be said to exist in the case of refugees. The problem is to show how their human rights might be *enforced*. Meeting this challenge requires far more than distinguishing between moral and legal rights. It requires showing how refugees seeking asylum might have their rights recognized in a world of sovereign states, something Arendt thought was impossible. I certainly agree with her that it is difficult. But outlining how we can meet the challenge she left us with is the central project of this book.

To some people this will not seem like much of a challenge. Someone who embraces an open borders view, for example, will be tempted to dismiss it. Advocates of open borders believe immigration controls should be abolished. From this point of view, the fact that liberal states police their borders and turn many people away is a contingent rather than necessary feature of those states. Get rid of immigration controls, an open borders advocate will say, and Arendt's challenge disappears. For what she really highlighted is not an inevitable tension between national sovereignty and human rights, but one more reason not to stop anyone at the border, refugee or otherwise.

This response does not really get around the problem. For one thing, the open borders view is controversial. It is at least arguable that human beings need to live in communities that exercise some form of entry control to maintain themselves. Moreover, we currently live in a world in which states guard their right to enforce their borders very zealously, and there is no sign of them giving up this aspect of their sovereignty any time soon. Even if the open borders view turns out to be correct, therefore, it will still mark a significant contribution to human rights to show how those rights might be enforced in a world of border enforcement, which is to say, in the world in which we live.

Open borders advocates are not the only people likely to pooh-pooh Arendt's challenge. So might someone who doubts refugees are worth singling out for special treatment. Although the laws of most Western states place refugees in a separate category from other migrants, not everyone is convinced this is a good idea. "The legal distinction between 'refugees' and 'immigrants' is phony," the distinguished journalist Michael Kinsley once wrote. Kinsley asks us who we would rather be: a starving peasant in the developing world or someone living under an oppressive political regime like the former Soviet Union. The answer, of course, is neither. But if that is so, why do we treat the two cases differently when it comes to immigration law? Why do we distinguish between economic and political motives for entering a new country?

Kinsley is surely right that there are people in such desperate economic circumstances that their lives are in danger, just as much as the average refugee's life is threatened by persecution. But the problem with Kinsley's objection can be seen by asking what people in dire economic circumstances really need. Take his example of someone facing starvation. In countries with food shortages, the poorest of the poor do not have the resources to emigrate. Moreover, there are usually far better ways to assist them than to go through the expensive process of flying them to the West. As Matthew Gibney puts it, "in the case of victims of famine or natural disasters, it is easier for outside parties to deal with the threats people face by exporting assistance or protection (food, building supplies, clean water) to people where they are than to arrange access to asylum." In the case of someone whose life is threatened by her own government, by contrast, it makes sense to give her priority in the immigration queue, as there are few other ways we can lend her assistance.

A third and final reason not to take Arendt's challenge seriously is because one doubts that the situation facing refugees is especially grim. Certainly there are limits to the parallels between refugees in Arendt's time and those of today. But some enduring problems remain. To see what they are, we need to look at what happens to asylum-seekers in the United States, Australia and Europe. As we will see, if the record of these countries is anything to go by, we are still living in an Arendtian universe. One in which there are many rights for citizens, but few for human beings.

TWO

AMERICAN LAVALAS

HAROLD KOH SAW REFUGEES in his nightmares. It started happening after his visit to United States Naval Station Guantánamo Bay. Located at the southeast edge of Cuba, the Guantánamo base occupies 117 square kilometres (including the water surface of the bay itself) and has a fluctuating population of roughly eight to ten thousand people, made up of American military personnel, their families and support staff. In geographic terms the base is the size of a small city; measured by population, it is closer to a small town. The people Koh had come to see, however, were not members of the normal base community. They were refugees whose presence at Guantánamo was due to forces—military forces primarily, but also political and historical ones—over which they had no control.

"The downtown part of Guantánamo looks like a military base," Koh says, "but then you drive out to this fairly desert-like environment." Koh is a law professor, and in October of 1992 he travelled to Guantánamo with two other lawyers, three

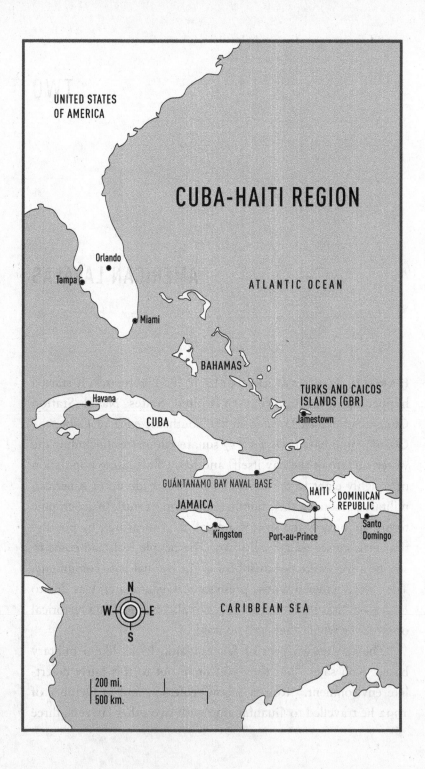

law students and three interpreters. The purpose of their trip was to meet with a group of approximately three hundred Haitian refugees who had been apprehended on the high seas as they attempted to reach the United States, and were now being held at Guantánamo. Koh's group had legally represented the Haitians for seven months, but to date had been able to meet with a only handful of their clients. Early on the day of the legal team's arrival, they were taken to a vast military hangar, where they were able to meet all the Haitians for the first time. But the location of the meeting had been chosen by the base authorities, and Koh wanted to see where the Haitians actually lived. As a result, Koh and another lawyer, Michael Ratner, were soon taken for a jeep ride. After passing a McDonald's, Baskin-Robbins and other familiar landmarks, their driver took them through several miles of arid land, turned a corner, and came to a stop in front of a remote group of buildings separated from the rest of the base by a checkpoint and guard towers.

More than mere curiosity was behind the lawyers' desire to see where their clients lived. The American government had told the attorneys that the Guantánamo detainees were housed in a "humanitarian" facility. As soon as the lawyers saw the refugees' living conditions, however, they realized the government had not been telling the truth. "There was no way you could go to that camp," Ratner recalls, "[and] say it was humanitarian. It's not even within my vocabulary. I came back calling it Dante's ninth circle of Hell."

The Haitians were crowded into single-room dwellings made of concrete blocks, inside of which they had hung sheets to create a semblance of privacy. Garbage bags were taped over chicken-wire windows in an unsuccessful attempt to keep the huts from flooding with rain. The air was filled with the constant roar of jets as well as gunshots from a nearby target range, and the stench of filthy portable toilets was impossible to miss. The refugees would later show their lawyers a two-foot-long banana rat they had caught. It was merely one of many oversized Caribbean pests, rodents and insects alike, that came into the camp at night and crawled over the refugees as they slept. Seeing such conditions for the first time, the attorneys suddenly realized how it was that a child born at Guantánamo had recently caught pneumonia and died.

Koh describes what he saw at Guantánamo as "a rights-free zone." It is a description Hannah Arendt would have understood. Much like Arendt and the other women held at the French camp at Gurs, the Guantánamo detainees would debate the idea of collective suicide. As an outside observer, Koh experienced a less severe, but still unsettling, form of distress. For months after his trip, he had nightmares in which he was officially responsible for turning back refugees. In his dreams, Koh saw himself organizing and executing the deportation of Haitians on a wide scale, to the one country where their lives would be in danger.

In reality, Koh and Ratner represented the Haitians' best chance for freedom. Working alongside many other attorneys and an army of law students, not to mention the refugees themselves, the two attorneys set in motion a sprawling legal odyssey, one that would eventually reach the Supreme Court of the United States. The lawsuit they initiated raised many complex issues, several of which changed as the litigation evolved. At its core, though, was an attempt to bring human rights law to bear on a controversial border-control practice now used by countries as far away as Australia: interdiction at sea. A disturbing question the Haitian refugee case and its aftermath raise is whether human rights can be enforced beyond dry shore. Or must we accept the view, long put forward by maritime chroniclers, that the ocean is a lawless wilderness; a place where people have always been able to do things that are forbidden on land?

The United States takes in more refugees than any other

industrialized country. Between 1946 and 1994 it admitted more than three million people seeking protection. Yet there has long been one group of asylum-seekers who have called into question the United States' status as a country of first asylum. In the early 1970s, visitors to Florida's eastern coast began to report the steady arrival of Caribbean fishing boats. The people on board made an incongruous sight during tourist season, when Florida's luxury beaches were teeming with wealthy sunbathers. One description of events at a beach just north of Miami in 1972 gives a vivid account of what an early landfall looked like: "Vacationers, slick with suntan lotion, gazed uncomprehendingly at the unpainted, battered fishing smack riding low in the water among the sleek white cabin cruisers. So crowded with black people, the small boat looked like a cartoon of Washington crossing the Delaware. The boat ran right in on the surf and grounded on the white sand beach, spilling black people. Dressed in rags, they carried little baskets and bundles, and spoke a strange, mellifluous language."

The language the boat people were speaking was Creole, the majority language of Haiti. Mired in chronic poverty, Haiti was then under the dictatorial rule of Jean-Claude Duvalier, known as Baby Doc, who had inherited his position as head of state from his father, François "Papa Doc" Duvalier. Under the Duvaliers, who presided over Haiti from 1957 to 1986, violence was a regular part of political life. Papa Doc, in particular, pioneered new methods of terror, which were often carried out by his private militia, the Tontons Macoutes, named after a bogeyman in Haitian folklore. After Baby Doc came to power he made cosmetic reforms, such as giving the Macoutes a new name. But he preserved their methods, which included leaving corpses of the government's critics hanging in public places.

Haiti's educated classes began fleeing the country almost as soon as Papa Doc came to power. In the 1960s and 1970s the elites were followed by poorer Haitians, who lacked the means to travel by air and took to the high seas in whatever boats they could build or find. The most common route of travel was across the Windward Passage, the 80-kilometre-wide body of water between Haiti and Cuba, then northwest along the Cuban coast, before finally crossing the Florida Strait to the United States.

Throughout the 1970s, a few thousand Haitians reached the United States this way every year. But in 1980 the number of Haitians arriving by boat spiked to almost 25,000. The same year, Fidel Castro announced that he would not stop anyone who left Cuba via the port of Mariel. Cuban Americans launched a flotilla of boats in response, eventually bringing 125,000 of their family members to Florida. The Mariel Cubans included several thousand criminals and psychiatric patients who, though relatively few in number, came to define the Mariel refugees in American public opinion. Combined with the strain on Florida's social services that came with so many people landing at once, the boatlift's overall result was a widespread perception that the border was unguarded. After losing his bid for re-election in 1980, Jimmy Carter cited Mariel as an important reason for his defeat: "The refugee question has hurt us badly. It wasn't just in Florida, but it was throughout the country. It was a burning issue. It made us look impotent."

It was with these events fresh in mind that Carter's successor introduced a policy to stem the flow of people coming to Florida. However, the migrants who would be most affected were not Cubans, who could count on Florida's large Cuban-American voting bloc to speak up for their interests, but Haitians. In 1981 the administration of Ronald Reagan signed an agreement with Jean-Claude Duvalier's regime that allowed the U.S. Coast Guard to interdict boats carrying undocumented Haitians and return them to Haiti.

Reagan administration officials said that the Haitian boat

people were merely looking to improve their standard of living. Economic migrants have few rights under international law: no nation is legally obliged to take a special interest in their welfare. Refugees, however, are a different story. In fact, the year before the Reagan-Duvalier interdiction agreement came into effect, the United States had incorporated the Refugee Convention into its domestic law. That meant the American government was obliged to never return a refugee to a situation where he or she had "a well-founded fear of persecution." This put the government in a dilemma, as it was determined to stop the stream of boats from Haiti, yet did not want to be seen as violating the refugee-protection standard it had just pledged to uphold.

The administration's solution was to conduct interviews with the Haitians at sea. After a boat coming from Haiti was intercepted, the passengers would be brought on board Coast Guard cutters. Speaking through interpreters, U.S. Immigration officials would conduct interviews on the helicopter decks and administer a questionnaire that included the following questions:

Why did you leave Haiti?

Have you belonged to any organization in Haiti?

Have you done anything in Haiti which you believe will result in problems for you if you return?

Have you ever been detained or sent to jail in Haiti?

Have you or your family been mistreated by the authorities in Haiti?

After carefully reviewing the Haitians' responses, Coast Guard personnel were to take those who showed a credible fear of persecution to the United States, where they would be allowed to make an application for asylum. The rest would be sent back to Port-au-Prince, the Haitian capital.

Interdiction was controversial from the beginning. Critics charged that the policy was racist, as Haitians were the only group singled out for such treatment. In response to this and other criticisms, administration officials invariably pointed to the on-board interviews as evidence that interdiction was conducted in a fair and humane way. As the U.S. attorney general put it in 1982, "We have taken careful steps to deal with possible asylum claims by those met at sea . . . I am confident that these procedures will insure that nobody with a well-founded fear of persecution is mistakenly returned to Haiti."

In 1989 the Lawyers Committee for Human Rights, an advocacy group based in New York, grew concerned that the interdiction program was not meeting the minimal safeguards the government claimed. The group sent a delegation to Haiti to conduct interviews with repatriated Haitians on the main pier in Port-au-Prince and elsewhere. Returned Haitians described numerous problems with the Coast Guard's procedures. Among the most serious was the fact that on-deck interviews were conducted by untrained Immigration personnel, who had no knowledge of refugee or asylum issues, and who spent very little time with each Haitian, sometimes only two minutes, including translation time. Many interviews were also done within sight or hearing distance of other Haitians. Returned interviewees told the human rights lawyers that they were too afraid to say anything about persecution with people listening in, as anything they said might get back to the authorities in Haiti.

Then there were the questions themselves. Immigration officials told the Lawyers Committee that they "ordinarily asked all of the questions [from the questionnaire] but sometimes found it too time consuming to write down all the answers." When the lawyers obtained the actual questionnaires used to interview one group of 182 Haitians, they discovered that only the following inquiries were put to them:

What is your name?

Where were you born?

What is your date of birth?

What is your current address?

Why did you leave Haiti?

What kind of work do you do?

In response to the question "Why did you leave Haiti?" some interviewees gave answers that indicated they had left in fear for their lives. "Cannot live," said one, "no parents; cannot help five children; lost two kids by gun fire; brother in law killed." Another stated: "Cannot work after finishing school; people being set on fire; cannot return to Port-au-Prince; lost three brothers; spent three years in prison for nothing; cannot go back to Port-au-Prince." Yet even when such information was volunteered, the people who spoke of such concerns were summarily returned to Haiti.

The Lawyers Committee published its findings in 1990. They noted that of the 21,461 Haitians who were intercepted in the first nine years of interdiction, a mere six were taken to the United States. "Of these," the attorneys wrote, "two had lived in the United States before and were presumably somewhat familiar with U.S. legal procedures and three were relatively well-educated teachers able to articulate their claims." The Lawyers Committee conservatively estimated that the government had returned "at least hundreds of refugees" to danger.

In the eyes of many, the Lawyers Committee had revealed the real purpose of the interviews: not to identify genuine refugees, but to add a procedural fig leaf to a cynical and callous policy. Partly in response to the committee's criticisms, Immigration officials introduced new interview guidelines in 1991. Consequently, the number of Haitians admitted to the United States rose slightly, to 3 to 5 percent of those interviewed each month. But even after this small change, major problems still remained. "It's no place to do an interview," one asylum officer said in 1992 of the Coast Guard cutters' decks. "The sun is a killer and the wind makes it impossible to write. Papers are curling up under twenty- to thirty-knot winds." He added: "There is just no privacy, scarcely the illusion of privacy. . . . We were shoulder to shoulder with migrants while interviewing somebody else. It's the worst possible place to do an interview."

Interdiction continued to attract criticism even after the changes brought about by the Lawyers Committee report. The program was widely seen as treating human beings as disposable. In the words of one member of Congress, the on-board screening process was "analogous to a fish-processing ship out there that processes the fish, keeps the keepers, and throws away the rest." Such was the debate leading up to the 1992 presidential campaign, when an untested candidate from Arkansas made a bold campaign pledge. If he were elected, he would abolish interdiction for good. It was a promise that would have fateful consequences, but not the ones Bill Clinton intended.

In 1992 Michael Barr was a third-year law student at Yale University. After the U.S. government won a legal challenge to its interdiction program, Barr says he was "totally and completely morally outraged." He identified with the Haitians and what was being done to them. As he puts it, "I'm Jewish and my father came to the United States in a boat in the '40s, [so] I just sort of immediately connected to what the Haitians were experiencing as they fled persecution." Soon Barr found himself discussing the situation of Haitian refugees with a half-dozen law school classmates. Their conversations gave rise to a mad thought: What if we put together our own legal challenge to interdiction? What if we persuaded our professors to help us take the U.S. government to court? Thus did a small group of law students begin what has aptly been called "the most important refugee case of the later half of the twentieth century."

When Barr and his fellow students came up with the idea of a lawsuit, they were reacting to a series of events that had started in Haiti two years before. In 1990, Jean-Bertrand Aristide won Haiti's presidential elections, making him the first Haitian leader to come to power democratically in over thirty years. Aristide was a charismatic former priest who spoke on behalf of Haiti's poor majority, and he had long denounced the country's dictators from his pulpit. When Aristide ran for president he called his political movement Lavalas, a Creole term variously translated as "torrential rain" or "wave," which is used to describe the heavy floods that occur during Haiti's rainy season. Lavalas conjured up the image of a cleansing wave rising up from Haiti's slums to wash away the country's political corruption. If that has never quite happened in modern Haitian history, in his early days Aristide came closer than any other leader, dramatically reducing the number of extrajudicial executions and similar abuses from the Duvalier era.

In September 1991, the Haitian military, with which Aristide had long been at odds, overthrew the Lavalas government. Under Aristide, the number of people fleeing Haiti by boat had slowed to a trickle; under the subsequent military regime, which would eventually kill more than five thousand people, boat departures exploded. Haitians took to sea in whatever craft they could find or quickly throw together. As one American Immigration official stationed on a Coast Guard ship said at the time, "I saw bed sheets tied to masts still covered with fresh tree bark . . . You wouldn't go out in a tiny pond in these boats." To Barr and his peers, the desperation of the Haitians was obvious, as was the injustice of the interdiction policy, which now involved returning unprecedented numbers of people to violent persecution.

The same year as the Haitian coup, thousands of miles to the north in New Haven, Connecticut, Yale Law School established the Lowenstein International Human Rights Clinic. Law school clinics are training programs that allow students to take part in cases featuring different areas of the law. When the coup began,

Yale's human rights clinic was taught by Harold Koh and Michael Ratner, two attorneys who, while they shared an interest in human rights, had arrived at the Lowenstein Clinic along very different paths.

Koh was the more academic of the two, the one who most resembled the traditional image of a bookish, button-down law professor. Koh had honed his prodigious intellect studying at Harvard and Oxford, and before getting involved in the clinic, he had spent his time quietly producing learned papers and monographs on less than incendiary, even subdued, topics ("My specialty before the lawsuit was international business transactions," Koh notes). Far from a firebrand or tenured radical, Koh had spent several years in the 1980s serving in the Justice Department under Ronald Reagan.

If Koh was a Spock figure, calm and cerebral, Michael Ratner was Scotty, fiery and outspoken. As a law student during the Vietnam era, he had participated in a student takeover of Columbia University, during which police waded through crowds of demonstrators, beating Ratner and other protestors as they went. When the Haiti lawsuit began, Ratner was commuting to Yale from Manhattan, where he worked as a civil rights attorney with the Center for Constitutional Rights, a prominent advocacy group. The legal equivalent of an old-fashioned rabble-rouser, Ratner had more than once launched a lawsuit he had no hope of winning, simply in order to draw attention to an injustice and, in his words, "help create a climate [for change] in the community."

Koh's and Ratner's different approaches to the law was crystallized during a speech Ratner gave at Yale when the first President Bush was in power. According to Laura Ho, a former law student involved with the litigation, "he talked about how Bush had blood up to his elbows, and Harold was like, 'Oh my god.' Harold Koh was more within the system, and Michael Ratner was more a lefty constitutional lawyer." According to Ho and other students, it was precisely because Koh and Ratner had such different approaches that they made an engaging teaching team, attracting many students to their clinic.

One of the Yale clinic's first cases had been a lawsuit against former Haitian dictator Prosper Avril, which the clinic had brought on behalf of six Haitian torture victims. Through their involvement in the Avril case, the two Lowenstein professors, as well as their students, came to take a keen interest in Haiti. As Ratner has put it, "We had personal ties to a number of the democratic leaders endangered by the coup . . . we simply wanted to save as many refugees as possible."

What the Yale team wanted to save the refugees from was something they had heard was happening at Guantánamo Bay. The unusual arrangement of an American military base on Cuban territory is a legacy of the 1898 Spanish-American War, during which U.S. marines captured the bay and brought it under U.S. control. After the war, when the victorious United States had a strong hand in Cuban affairs, it forced the smaller country to sign a treaty that allowed the United States to maintain a naval base at Guantánamo for as long as it likes. (The arrangement is an ongoing source of frustration in Cuba: Fidel Castro once called Guantánamo "a dagger plunged into the Cuban soil.")

Guantánamo is just across the Windward Passage from Haiti, and when thousands of people began fleeing Haiti in the wake of the 1990 anti-Aristide coup, the Coast Guard began taking interdicted Haitians to the large military facility. Over the course of the next eighteen months, more than thirty-six thousand Haitians would pass through the naval base. The interviews that had long been conducted on Coast Guard cutters were now done at Guantánamo instead. As before, any Haitian who was "screened out," or deemed not to have a credible fear of persecution, was sent back to Haiti without recourse.

To the Yale team, the mere fact that the flawed interdiction policy was still in effect was itself cause for concern. But through speaking with relatives of people detained at Guantánamo and Haitians hired to work as translators, the students started picking up rumours about mysterious "second interviews." Some people who passed the credible-fear test—that is, likely refugees— were singled out for an additional round of interrogation, during which their claims to be fleeing persecution were judged according to a more difficult standard of proof. It wasn't entirely clear what was happening to people who failed to meet that standard, or why they were being singled out for second interviews in the first place. When the lawsuit began, all that the Yale students had to go one were whispers that it had something to do with HIV.

One of the first things Koh and Ratner did after signing on for the case was to reach out for help, both outside and inside the law school. If they were going to beat the government in a court of law, they would need to find outside lawyers, particularly those with immigration and refugee experience. Within Yale, Koh sought help from every student he could find, whether they were enrolled in the human rights clinic or not. The result was that "Team Haiti," as the students began to call themselves, quickly grew to include seventy lawyers and law students (before the case was over, the number of students involved would rise to over 100).

Elizabeth Detweiler, a first-year student, joined Team Haiti almost by accident. One day she was working in Yale's immigration clinic (a separate entity from the one dealing with human rights) when the professor running the class made a surprise announcement. The Haitian Refugee Center, an advocacy organization in Miami, needed help processing the asylum claims of Haitians who were being brought from Guantánamo to Florida. Were any students willing to go down to Florida and help out? "The law school is willing to cover your plane ticket," he added.

Detweiler and several other students instantly shot up their hands. "We were like, 'Yeah! We'll go!'" she says. The students were not the only ones excited by the idea of a Florida trip. When Harold Koh found out that Detweiler and nine other students would soon be accompanying their professor to interview Haitians, he gave them a list of questions to ask about what exactly was happening at Guantánamo, which he hoped would result in valuable information for the lawsuit.

Detweiler and the others checked in to the Budget Inn located in the city's Little Haiti neighbourhood, where many of the refugees were temporarily located. The students found the Haitian Refugee Center in a state of total chaos. Of the 15,000 Haitians who had fled Haiti since the coup, 5,700 had been admitted to the United States. But they still had to file an asylum claim. That would require an attorney, and the Refugee Center had access to only five lawyers. Detweiler and her classmates set out to provide what assistance they could. Huddled around dining tables and using whatever translators were at hand, they began conducting interviews that lasted late into the night.

Detweiler's group quickly discovered what was really going on in Cuba. As Detweiler notes of the Haitians, "They hadn't felt listened to on Guantánamo, and they were eager to tell us what was happening." The interviewees explained that when each Haitian was taken to Guantánamo, he or she was given an HIV test. This had revealed a small percentage of positive cases— together with their family members (not all of whom were HIV-positive), they numbered roughly three hundred. During their interviews, some of the HIV-positive Haitians had demonstrated a credible fear of persecution. Yet unlike other Haitians whose claims of persecution were deemed credible and who were taken to the United States, members of the HIV group instead had to undergo a second interview, which was harder to pass, and which inevitably saw people who failed forcibly returned to Haiti.

Detweiler could hardly believe what she was hearing. It was bad enough that the Coast Guard was sending back thousands of Haitians who did not meet the credible-fear standard. Now it turned out that a second scandal was occurring at Guantánamo. It involved only a few hundred Haitians rather than thousands, but that did not change the fact that it was a scandal. The three hundred Haitians in the HIV group had passed the credible-fear test, and so had met the difficult standard the U.S. government was using to identify refugees, and yet the government was going ahead and returning members of that group anyway. To Detweiler and the other students at the Budget Inn, there was something especially brazen about the way the government was treating the HIV group of Haitians.

Tory Clawson, one of the students who went to Miami, was struck by the fact that that first-year law students were handling asylum claims, which were potentially a matter of life and death. But after the students were told what was happening at the second interview stage at Guantánamo, she says, "suddenly we saw we were part of something else that was even bigger . . . What was happening was so terrible, and we wanted to figure out a way to intervene."

A valuable piece of information the students gleaned from the Haitians at the Budget Inn was a description of Guantánamo and its daily rhythms. That knowledge would allow the legal team to rebut an argument they anticipated the government would make (correctly, it turned out), claiming that allowing lawyers onto Guantánamo would disrupt the military's activities. If Guantánamo was big enough to house a McDonald's and a Baskin-Robbins, the Yale attorneys would counter, it was big enough to withstand the presence of a few civilian lawyers. But the real challenge for the students in Miami would be to find a Haitian who knew enough of the second interviews to swear out an affidavit.

Detweiler, Clawson and the others would have to act quickly: when they arrived in Miami, Koh and Ratner were already on the eve of their first court appearance. The purpose of the hearing was to obtain a temporary restraining order, or TRO, that would put an immediate, albeit brief, halt to repatriations. That would give the legal team enough time to obtain an actual injunction, which would prevent repatriation until their case had been heard in its entirety. The attorneys wanted to get into court as soon as they could in order to save as many refugees as possible. But with the TRO hearing drawing closer, it was far from certain that they had enough evidence to convince a judge.

If they did not get enough evidence it would not be for lack of trying. In the three weeks since Michael Barr and his classmates had first discussed a lawsuit, the Lowenstein students had engaged in a whirlwind of activity. Koh had appointed Barr and the other third-years who had first approached him to be captains of legal squads, each taking ownership of a different aspect of the case. The students scrambled to bring themselves up to speed on everything from the precise legal status of Guantánamo to the medical needs of pregnant women with HIV (of which there were several at Guantánamo). As the TRO hearing drew near, the students also worked non-stop to research and write a legal brief that would present an airtight case against the government's actions.

"It was way higher intensity than I think anyone had experienced," says Barr. "We were working all the time. We would work until two in the morning on a draft legal argument and go over to Koh's house. He would get up, he'd edit the brief from two to five, we'd get three hours sleep, he'd meet us in the clinic at five, and we'd revise the draft and get comments from people. It was just around the clock. I slept on couches, people were sleeping all over the place . . . it was just a totally intense full-court press."

One area where the students' youthful dedication paid off was in finding outside help. They managed to obtain co-counsel in human rights organizations such as the American Civil Liberties Union and the San Francisco Lawyers' Committee for Urban Affairs (attorneys who, like the Yale professors themselves, would work on the case for free). Throughout the case, lawyers from these and other organizations with distinguished civil rights records would play a crucial role in shaping the litigation, both inside and outside the courtroom.

The initial breakthrough by an outside attorney came from one who, at first glance, made an unlikely human rights crusader. Joe Tringali was a partner at the Manhattan law firm Simpson Thacher and Bartlett. Over 120 years old and with offices in London, Tokyo and Hong Kong, Simpson Thacher's list of clients includes such venerable financial institutions as J. P. Morgan and Chase Manhattan. Yet in addition to the mergers and acquisitions cases that are common to white-shoe New York law offices, Tringali's firm also does a fair amount of pro bono work. It was in this capacity that Tringali agreed to devote himself to the Haiti case after his firm was approached by Michael Barr, who had spent a summer articling there.

Unlike many other lawyers who signed on to the lawsuit, Tringali had no experience with refugee law. So early in the litigation, to bring himself up to speed, he studied a previous Haitian refugee case. While doing so, he made a discovery that helped the Yale team remove the equivalent of a legal albatross that was hanging around their necks.

The albatross in question was a case called *Haitian Refugee Center v. Baker*. The same Haitian Refugee Center that had invited the Yale students to Miami had taken the first Bush administration to court immediately after the Haitian coup. The administration's initial response to the coup had been to condemn the military's action and to stop repatriation. In November of 1991, however, two weeks after the flow of boats began, U.S. officials announced that repatriation would resume. The Haitian Refugee Center initiated its suit the next day precisely to prevent that from happening.

Baker was why the government began taking interdicted Haitians to Guantánamo in the first place. The Refugee Center's lawyers had successfully obtained an injunction preventing the Coast Guard from sending anyone back to Haiti until their case was decided. The government thus had a choice: it could either admit Haitians to the United States or find somewhere else to send them. Michael Ratner and other observers have suggested that the administration did not want to admit large numbers of Haitians to the States because the election campaign of 1992 was not far off, and Florida would figure, as ever, as a battleground state. Sending Haitians to Guantánamo was thus a way for the administration to keep them out of sight and out of mind while it fought off the Refugee Center's legal challenge.

That the use of Guantánamo was intended to address the needs of the administration rather than the Haitians themselves was evident from the beginning. "They were keeping Haitians on the top of Coast Guard cutters where the sun was beating down on them twenty-four hours a day," says Ira Kurzban, the lead attorney for the Haitian Refugee Center, who visited Guantánamo during this time. "They were trying to force them to give up their fight for political asylum and go back. You had people living on top of cutters with their small children." Eventually, the base authorities allowed people off of the cutters and moved them into Guantánamo itself, housing them in what Kurzban remembers as "horrible, squalid camps."

The government went to extraordinary lengths to fight off the Refugee Center's lawsuit, to the point that the solicitor general himself, Kenneth Starr, appeared in a Miami court to square off against Kurzban. "There are three instances in history in the

United States where the solicitor general went to a district court and argued the case on behalf of the United States government," Kurzban says. "This is one of them." According to Kurzban, Starr's unusual move was an attempt to subtly apply pressure. "No question about it, it was to intimidate the judge: 'Now here I am, I'm the solicitor general speaking on behalf of the president of the United States, and I'm here in district court.'"

Starr is today best known for his activities as independent prosecutor under Bill Clinton, in which capacity he issued his controversial Starr Report, documenting Clinton's affair with Monica Lewinsky. At the time of *Baker* Starr was already a prominent figure who was being spoken of as potential Supreme Court material. Kurzban, for his part, had been widely hailed in publications such as *Newsweek* and *Esquire* as one of the United States' leading immigration lawyers, and he had achieved prominence in his own right as counsel for the Aristide government. The two veteran attorneys engaged in a titanic legal battle that reverberated up and down the American judicial system. After Kurzban won his injunction, Starr had it overturned on appeal. Kurzban won another injunction from the original court on remand—only to again lose it on appeal. Eventually Kurzban asked the Supreme Court to settle the matter. But in February of 1992 it declined to hear the case (the fate of most requests the court receives). The government was once again free to treat Haitians as it saw fit. This was the outcome that had so disappointed Michael Barr: in effect, he had asked Koh and Ratner to somehow triumph where Kurzban's formidable effort had failed.

Joe Tringali took the *Baker* record with him on a train ride from New York to Baltimore, where he was going to visit a close friend in the hospital. Like the other members of the Yale team, he sympathized with Kurzban's efforts to challenge the repatriation policy. But precisely because *Baker* touched on many of the same questions as the Yale case, it now posed a problem. Team

Haiti could not bring forward a suit that was essentially a retrial of *Baker*. Indeed, the legal team could be punished for launching a "frivolous" lawsuit if a judge decided their case was too similar to the previous one. Rather than walk into a courtroom and make the best arguments that came to mind, they would have to make their best arguments *and* show how they addressed a situation that was fundamentally different from *Baker*.

This was a tall order. But as Tringali's bumpy train car hurtled toward Baltimore, he spotted something in the *Baker* papers that brought him up short. It was a passage in a document the government had filed when the Supreme Court was deciding whether to hear the case: "Under current practice, any aliens who satisfy the threshold standard are to be brought to the United States so that they can file an application for asylum."

The key word was "any." To the uninitiated it would appear to be one unremarkable adjective. But to Tringali's methodical eye, it might as well have been highlighted in fluorescent yellow. In effect, the administration had promised the Supreme Court that it would take all Haitians who displayed a credible fear of persecution to the U.S. But it wasn't doing that with the HIV-positive refugees singled out for second interviews. The change in government policy, Tringali immediately realized, meant that the Yale lawyers were addressing a new situation, one that did not exist during *Baker*.

Tringali shared his discovery with his fellow attorneys shortly after returning to New York. "Everybody thought it was a great thing for us to have," Tringali says, "because it was so contradictory to the [government's] position. They had represented to the Supreme Court that they were going to do one thing, and now they were doing something else. We thought it was something we were going to be able to use to our advantage."

If Tringali's *Baker* find was Team Haiti's first breakthrough, it was soon followed by another. A fringe benefit of Tringali's involvement was that the Yale team had access to his firm's New York offices. The day before the TRO hearing was to be held in a Brooklyn court, Koh and a half-dozen students travelled from Yale to Simpson Thacher and Bartlett and set up a war room in one of the firm's spacious conference rooms. They were joined there by Michael Ratner, who helped them finalize all the material they would present the next day. It was while working there late at night on borrowed computers and eating takeout food that the legal team received a leaked copy of an internal government document—one that made public for the first time exactly what was going on at Guantánamo.

The document was a memorandum from the Immigration and Naturalization Service, the agency responsible for the interdiction interviews. To this day, former members of Team Haiti are tight lipped about who gave them the Rees memo (so-called because it was written by Grover Rees, general counsel for the INS), stating only that they received if from a third party who worked outside the administration. Whoever it was, Team Haiti had clearly found their Deep Throat. The Rees memo was doubly damaging to the government, both for what it said and for when it was written.

The memorandum revealed that the government's justification for second interviews was a U.S. law that barred most immigrants with HIV from applying for admission to the country. The law, which was introduced in 1987, has long been controversial. Indeed, in 1990 various public health organizations recommended it be struck down, on the grounds that HIV is not spread by casual contact, the policy's purported justification. In response, conservative groups such as the Christian Action Network of Forest, Virginia, initiated a mail campaign, sending their members letters that began by asking, "Are there not enough homosexuals with AIDS in the United States that we now need to import more?" Lawmakers in Washington soon received more than thirty-five thousand letters supporting the ban, with the result that it was still on the books at the beginning of the 1992 presidential campaign. (Bill Clinton and Al Gore announced that they would lift the ban if they won, but once in office they reversed themselves, and it remained in effect until 2009.)

A key aspect of the HIV ban is that it has always allowed for exceptions. For one thing, it had never been applied to foreigners who made asylum claims. Nor had it previously applied to interdicted Haitians who passed the credible-fear test: they had previously been taken to the United States regardless of their HIV status. Finally, the government could always issue a waiver, which would allow any HIV-positive foreigner entry to the country.

Given these facts, citing the HIV rule seemed to the Yale lawyers not so much a rationale as a rationalization. As Ratner puts it, the administration was claiming it had to "keep the HIV people in Guantánamo because of the so-called exclusion rule . . . But of course there were always ways you could waive that. The administration, the attorney general, has a right to waive it. So it wasn't like that barred them." As Ratner and other members of Team Haiti point out, even leaving aside all of the loopholes in the HIV exclusion rule, there is a difference between not admitting people to the United States and forcibly returning them to a place where their lives are in danger.

The Rees memo was dated February 29, a mere five days after Kenneth Starr had indicated to the Supreme Court that "any aliens who satisfy the [credible-fear] standard" would be taken to the United States. Team Haiti thus had in its hands an incriminating document that revealed the administration had gone back on its word almost as soon as its lawyers were down the Supreme Court's marble steps.

The legal team scrambled to incorporate the Rees memo into its court papers. They were still at it at three in the morning, with only six hours to go before their hearing, when another document came spiralling off the fax machine. The first-year students in Miami had found a refugee who could testify about the second interviews. Lacking a printer, they had hurriedly transcribed the testimony by hand on a yellow legal pad ("I was deemed to have the best handwriting," Tory Clawson recalls) and faxed it from the tiny office of the Budget Inn. Given that it was the middle of the night and no notary public was open who could certify it as an affidavit, they had to send it on simply as an affirmation.

Third-year student Lisa Daugaard was in the Simpson Thacher office when the Miami fax came through. Of all the students who worked on the case, Daugaard may have been the most devoted: she would continue to work on the lawsuit after she left law school. According to Daugaard, a strange sense of elation came over her as she read the fax.

It wasn't because of the grim procedures that it described taking place on Guantánamo. Rather, it was the realization that she wasn't the only one who had become consumed by the Haiti case, putting in so many hours that her grades, not to mention her chance of graduating, were now in jeopardy. Tory Clawson, Elizabeth Detweiler and the other first-years in Miami were throwing their law degrees away too, not resting until they got what the lead attorneys needed.

"It was really a great feeling to get [the affirmation]," Daugaard says, "because it was the first instance of the dynamic among all the people working on the case that continued to the very end, which was, you know, I'm going to totally destroy the whole rest of my life, which would be completely useless if everyone else weren't doing the same thing. It wouldn't make any sense for me to do this crazy thing by myself; I need you to be doing it too." In that spirit, when the challenge of taking on the government seemed overwhelming, Daugaard and the others would repeat a slogan Koh had shared with them: They're an army, we're a family.

The affirmation confirmed something the students had heard from other sources: Haitians who were made to undergo second interviews were not allowed to speak with a lawyer. Of all the information and documents Team Haiti obtained at the beginning, this would prove the most crucial.

According to the Rees memo, the second interviews at Guantánamo were to be "identical in form and substance, or as nearly so as possible," to asylum interviews in the United States. That was why second interviews were being conducted according to a higher standard of proof: Haitians were being asked to demonstrate a well-founded fear of persecution, the same standard employed in asylum hearings within the United States itself. But asylum-seekers who made it to the United States had the right to consult with a lawyer—hence the human floodtide that overwhelmed the Haitian Refugee Center and the original reason for the Yale students' Miami trip. But at Guantánamo, the government was preventing the Haitians from consulting an attorney. This was not an abstract difference. The lawyers working on the Haitian lawsuit, among others, were willing to go to Guantánamo and represent the Haitians for free if need be.

There was no longer any question of the Yale lawsuit overlapping with *Baker*. Koh and Ratner could mount an entirely separate challenge, one they raced to finalize as dawn approached. For the time being they would put off any direct attack on the overall interdiction program or the HIV detention policy. Instead, their opening salvo would emphasize the issue of access to lawyers. They would argue that it was wrong for the government to conduct second interviews without granting the Haitians access to legal counsel—counsel that the Yale attorneys would themselves be willing to provide.

The lawyers settled on this approach for several reasons, one of which was their belief that black, HIV-positive foreigners who did not speak English could expect little sympathy in public opinion. The legal team reasoned that they would be doing the Haitians no favours by emphasizing their HIV status or their desire to enter the United States. Focusing on the right to a lawyer, by contrast, "was asking for something 'as American as apple pie,'" as Ratner puts it. If the strategy worked, it would also have the advantage of granting the lawyers access to Guantánamo to consult with their clients—and potentially obtain more evidence to mount a challenge to the larger repatriation policy.

Bleary-eyed and physically exhausted, but intellectually energized by their discoveries, Koh and Ratner, together with Daugaard and her fellow students, headed to Brooklyn to appear in the chambers of Judge Sterling Johnson Jr. As they had anticipated, the government's lawyers argued that the case was simply a repeat of *Baker* and so a waste of the court's time. Koh, who was lead counsel, countered that their suit involved a class of people who did not exist when *Baker* was argued—namely, Haitians facing second interviews. There could be no overlap with *Baker*, he told the judge, as the policy at issue had not come into effect until after *Baker* was decided.

At one point in the proceedings one of the government attorneys asked for a delay in the trial. The solicitor general wanted to come to Brooklyn and argue the case himself, the lawyer explained to the judge, and would need an extra day to do so.

Lisa Daugaard remembers the Yale team's shock. Ken Starr? In the Federal District Court for the Eastern District of New York? She had the same reaction Ira Kurzban had had when Starr had showed up in Miami: it had to be an implied threat, an attempt to rattle the judge.

Everyone looked up at the bench. Judge Johnson was a heavy-set African American in his late fifties with a white beard. Of his legal background, the Yale team knew only that he was a former federal prosecutor who had been appointed by President Bush only a few months earlier. To everyone's surprise, Johnson got to his feet and pounded the bench with his hands. Thump! Thump! Thump!

"I am from *Bed-Stuy*," Johnson said, referring to Brooklyn's predominantly black neighbourhood. "And I will *not* be intimidated."

The members of Team Haiti could hardly contain their delight. The government's attempt to lay down the law had backfired. "It was *dead* silence," Daugaard recalls. "I have never seen a judge do anything like that . . . Until that moment they thought he was in their pocket. After that moment, they couldn't have had that expectation."

Judge Johnson made a second surprising remark. The administration's lawyers kept making elliptical references to "how it was for Marines on Guantánamo," without clarifying.

Finally Johnson looked down at the government attorneys. "Since you obviously know I served in the Marines at Guantánamo, it seems only fair that the plaintiffs know also."

It was a nasty shock for the Yale team. Would Johnson's experience at Guantánamo cause him to sympathize with the government, particularly its argument that admitting lawyers to the base would disrupt day-to-day operations? The government's lawyers certainly seemed to hope so. Koh had taken care to rebut this particular point, but on the trip back to Connecticut after the trial, the Yale team began to have doubts.

Unease turned to dread when the clinic members arrived back at the law school to find the fax machine spitting out court papers that had been filed by the government's lawyers. In restraining order hearings, it is normal for the person requesting the TRO to be asked to post a bond. What was abnormal, however, was the amount of the bond the government was now requesting: US$10 million, ten times larger than the biggest TRO bond in the history of the Brooklyn court district. To top it off, the government's lawyers were not only still asserting that the case was a repeat of *Baker*; they had filed a motion calling for Koh to be personally sanctioned for bringing forward such a "frivolous" lawsuit. If their motion succeeded, Koh could lose his house. This at least was one similarity with *Baker*: the government was not going to be gentle.

Ten anxious days later, Elizabeth Detweiler and a dozen other students were milling around in Yale's student-litigation office when Harold Koh came bursting into the room. The normally restrained law professor was yelling at the top of his lungs: "YOU GUYS! WE GOT IT! WE GOT THE TRO!"

Detweiler and the other students ran after Koh as he darted down the stairs to his small office on the floor below. With students crammed onto the couch and spilling out into the hall, Koh had Ratner recount via speakerphone the content of the highly favourable court order that was coming over his fax machine in New York. Ratner read aloud the document's golden prose, which characterized the government's policies as "arbitrary, capricious and perhaps even cruel."

Most TROs are a page long. This one was over five, and Koh excitedly remarked, "Michael, have you ever seen a TRO this long before?"

"I don't know," an equally excited Ratner recalled. "I've never gotten a TRO before!"

"That kind of summed it," Detweiler says of Koh and Ratner's giddy exchange. "[Ratner] filed for this stuff all the time, but to win something like that for these clients, it doesn't happen very much. As skilled a lawyer as Michael is, the kind of cases he chooses . . . he's fighting for the underdog all the time, and you're just not going to win those cases." This time, the TRO suggested, a case launched on behalf of the underdog might have a different outcome.

The legal team hoped to press their advantage at a second hearing five days later. In the interim, Judge Johnson had granted the lawyers access to the Guantánamo airport (but not the base itself) to hurriedly conduct depositions and prepare witnesses among the refugees. While one group of lawyers and students rushed to arrange flights on U.S. military planes, the only way to access the base, another group travelled to Washington to interview government officials, while a third contingent returned to the Budget Inn in Miami to gather more refugee testimony.

Tory Clawson was one of students on the second Miami trip; they arrived at the Budget Inn with less than twenty-four hours to find refugees and take affidavits. Clawson recalls the team being overcome with panic when they realized the motel was deserted. But when another student, Michelle Anderson, went across the street to the office of Catholic World Service, she saw it was full of refugees and quickly began conducting impromptu interviews. Anderson soon went running back to the Budget Inn to share with the others a major discovery: she had found a refugee who knew about a woman who had passed the credible-fear interview on Guantánamo, only to be returned to Haiti and killed. "It was a *huge* find," Clawson says. The death of a repatriated Haitian meant that irreversible harm was at issue in the interview process. "People were dying. It wasn't just a procedural glitch."

That night, students in Miami raced to send their discoveries back to Koh and the others. As Elizabeth Detweiler, who was also on the trip, says, "It was just crazy. There was a fax machine in the office of the Budget Inn and the hotel manager slept in the office. We woke him up two or three times that night to fax stuff to Harold. He must have thought we were crazy . . . [But] we got what the team needed, just in the nick of time."

The night before the second hearing, the student-lawyer teams that had fanned out to Washington, Miami and Guantánamo all returned to the Simpson Thacher office in New York, where Koh and Ratner were sifting through the stacks of evidence the discovery teams had gathered. Late that night, Tory Clawson and several other students sat down with Koh in a small conference room to brief him on what they had found in Miami. The name of the woman who had been returned was Marie Zette, Clawson explained, presenting Koh with a carefully annotated folder of evidence. According to an affidavit sworn out by another refugee, Zette had passed her credibility interview on Guantánamo, only to be mistakenly sent back to Haiti. The night after her return, she was killed.

"Wait a minute, tell me that again," Koh said. "She was *murdered?*"

Clawson looked up from her notes. Much to her surprise, tears were streaming down her professor's face.

During the hearing the next day, Koh again became emotional as he read aloud from the affidavit about Marie Zette, who had been mistakenly returned to Haiti only a day before she was scheduled to be released from Guantánamo and admitted to the United States. "She sang about hurting and that she regretted having to go back to Haiti . . . because she feared for her life," Koh told Judge Johnson's silent court. "She was sent back to Haiti. The next day, the guards called her name to be sent to Miami. It was too late." Koh's voice was unsteady as he reached the end of the document. "The military police came at night and killed her while she slept."

Like the other members of Team Haiti, Koh was exhausted from working twenty-hour days. His fraught emotions were partly a sign of the toll the case was taking, and also, perhaps, the realization of the scope of the responsibility that now rested with him. "I think if people didn't know, they would think he was deliberately being melodramatic," Clawson says, "but it was so emotionally disturbing."

In addition to the story of Marie Zette, Koh presented the court with other material students had obtained in Miami, documenting that twenty-seven other refugees who had not only been screened in but told they would be taken to the United States were instead sent back to Haiti. Koh also noted that when Haitians at Guantánamo committed minor "infractions" such as speaking too loudly or asking for a pair of sandals, they were sent to a punishment camp where they were forced to sleep on rocks. These and similar points of evidence were enough to win Team Haiti their second victory: Judge Johnson issued an injunction stopping repatriations until the case was heard in its entirety, which would not be until months later.

It was an incredible outcome. A ragtag band of human rights advocates had the United States government on the run, and the entire repatriation policy was suddenly hanging in the balance. Most incredible of all, the win was in large part due to the energy of a group of tirelessly devoted law students. Tory Clawson, Elizabeth Detweiler, Lisa Daugaard and the others had essentially put their law degrees on hold to work on behalf of Haitian refugees they had never met. Students contributed to law school legal clinics all the time, but the scope of their involvement in the Haitian refugee case was unprecedented.

Harold Koh would later write of the moment when he realized just how much the plight of Haitian refugees resonated with his students. In a law review article he described working in his office late at night, when the clinic was once again scrambling to complete a brief the night before it was due in court.

"Our litigation manager, a third-year law student, stuck his head in and asked if we would be cite-checking the brief before it was filed. I grunted that we could not do so without at least 10 cite-checkers. An hour later, I heard noises in the hallway and emerged to find 10 sleepy students waiting to cite-check sections of the brief. As I watched them disappear down the hall, I began to think that maybe we had a chance after all."

A chance of winning a case they believed in. It was perhaps the best education any idealistic young law student could hope for.

Things began to go to hell shortly after the second hearing. Refugees were still streaming out of Haiti, and the Bush administration was in crisis mode. Its lawyers launched a blizzard of appeals to try to overturn the injunction as quickly as possible. At one point Koh argued against a motion over the phone while standing at a maître d' stand in a New York hotel, while Ratner took part by cellphone from a New York Mets game. At first, Koh and Ratner swatted away the government's challenges. But then the administration's lawyers employed a rare legal manoeuvre known as an interlocutory appeal, according to which parties affected by an injunction can immediately seek a stay in the Supreme Court. Three weeks after Johnson's injunction was issued, the Supreme Court narrowly voted 5–4 to suspend it.

It was a temporary setback: the injunction could be reinstated depending on the outcome of another hearing that had already been scheduled. But *that* hearing was still weeks away. In the meantime, the government was free to resume sending people back to Haiti—which it quickly proceeded to do. A day after the Supreme Court decision came down, the Yale team received a secret phone call from a sympathetic source at Guantánamo. "If there is anything you can do for your clients," he said, "do it now; the government is beginning interviews and repatriations."

Koh and the others were still reeling from news of the resumed repatriations several days later when they received a second, even more devastating, call from Guantánamo. A group of eighty-nine Haitians were going to be forcibly repatriated that night. The base authorities had told the refugees they had no right to speak to a lawyer, so they might as well do their second interviews without one. The Haitians refused and demanded they be allowed to meet with a Team Haiti lawyer named Robert Rubin, who had briefly met with them at the Guantánamo airport in March. Under no circumstances, the refugees said, would they take part in another interview without an attorney. The Haitians, dubbed the "refuseniks" by their legal team, were promptly herded onto a Coast Guard cutter. As they walked on board the ship that would carry them back to Port-au-Prince, they held their palms in the air in a Haitian gesture of peace.

The legal team was crushed. Tory Clawson took it especially hard. The feeling of helplessness, she says, after having come so far, was too much to bear. "Up until then we had been winning and everything had been going our way," she says. "It felt amazing, as if nothing could stop us. I was a wide-eyed first-year law student who believed in justice and thought the court believed in justice too. But that was my first realization it doesn't always go your way. I thought it was the most incredible injustice I had ever seen."

Clawson was so upset that she announced a plan to light herself on fire in front of the Supreme Court. A classmate talked her out of it, as well as a subsequent plan to go on a hunger strike, by reminding her that neither action would make a difference for the refugees.

The larger legal team met that night in their office at Yale to determine a more pragmatic course of action. An emotionally drained Koh sat with his two-year-old son writhing on his knee, surrounded by exhausted and ashen-faced students. A sombre mood hung in the air as Koh went around the room asking each person what they thought they should do. Everyone present told Koh the same thing: whatever we do, we can't do nothing.

"It was a *very* intense meeting," says Lisa Daugaard. The argument about access to lawyers, she notes, was something of a pretext. It was enough to get a restraining order and an injunction, but access to lawyers was not ultimately what was at issue.

Yet because the legal team had framed the court challenge as being about a right to an attorney, their clients were now in effect taking them at their word.

"They were asserting the very right that we said was so important. And as a consequence they were being repatriated," says Daugaard. "And if we were really their lawyer then we had to do whatever we could do . . . I felt it was a *very* compelling moral obligation that we had at that point—because we had changed what they did by existing and asserting ourselves."

Whatever path Team Haiti decided upon, they would have to act fast: the boat was leaving that night. The group dispersed to comb through law books and research their options, reconvening several hours later, at midnight. Someone mentioned the possibility of a habeas corpus petition, which garnered murmurs of assent. Such a petition would allow the legal team to directly challenge the government's authority to hold the Haitians, without raising other, more contentious issues, such as whether or not the U.S. constitution applied at Guantánamo, an issue the opposing lawyers had debated before Judge Johnson.

Koh said he was worried about how long it would take to draft the necessary court papers. "We can't even do a habeas," he said. "There's no way we can have it ready before they get back to Haiti."

A voice spoke up from the back of the room. "Well, actually, I have one here."

Everyone turned to face a third-year student named Paul Sonn. He had disappeared several hours previously and had now reappeared with a completely drafted petition of precisely the kind Koh and the others were discussing. "It was a class-action habeas, which is possible but very unusual, and required a lot of drafting," recalls Lisa Daugaard. Like the others, she was inspired by Sonn's foresight. Yet they were still faced with the problem of where to file their petition. They could not file it with Judge Johnson: he was the one who would ultimately decide the fate of all the detained refugees, and Koh did not want to risk Johnson's displeasure by presenting him with a last-minute motion on behalf of a smaller group of clients, a motion that would only highlight the legal team's desperation. Students were still scrambling at 2 a.m. to find an outside lawyer who could file the habeas motion in a different court district when Koh finally told them to go home.

"There's nothing more we can do," he said. Even if they could find a lawyer to file the petition, "no judge would issue an order to stop a U.S. military vessel on the high seas and reverse its course."

Koh, Daugaard and the others later discovered that when the cutter pulled in to Port-au-Prince, members of the Haitian military were waiting for it on the dock. After the terrified Haitians refused to disembark, Coast Guard personnel forced them off the boat with firehoses.

Graduation day had come to Yale. First- and second-year law students had deserted the campus after finishing their exams. Third-years in academic gowns and mortarboards assembled in the law school courtyard to hear commencement speeches and say goodbye to old friends. For Michael Barr and the six other third-years who had first discussed the possibility of a lawsuit, commencement formally marked the end of their involvement in the Guantánamo case. The seven graduating Team Haiti students were posing for pictures with Professor Koh and members of their families as mementos of their extraordinary time together, when someone came running up to Koh.

"Did you hear Bush has issued an order?"

"What's the order?"

"Everyone who leaves Haiti is being sent back. Without an interview."

Yale's graduation coincided with the 1992 Memorial Day weekend, when President Bush was at his vacation home in

Kennebunkport, Maine. From his beachfront estate he issued an executive order stating that everyone leaving Haiti by boat was to be repatriated. Now there would not be even the pretense of an asylum interview. Desperate Haitians would be returned no matter what they were running from or where they were running to. Boats leaving Haiti for the United States, for the Bahamas, for Jamaica—boats leaving Haiti period—would be intercepted by the Coast Guard and their passengers taken back to the main pier in Port-au-Prince. If anyone on board could expect to meet a fate similar to that of Marie Zette upon return, that was of no concern. As the legal team would put it, the Bush administration had effectively created "a floating Berlin Wall."

Koh and the students huddled in the courtyard discussing what to do. Fighting an executive order by the president through the courts was a daunting challenge. On Team Haiti's side would be the fact that the United States had signed the Refugee Convention, which meant it was obliged not to return refugees to danger. In addition, the United States had incorporated the same principle in its own domestic law (back in 1980, right before the Mariel boat lift). But on the administration's side was the fact that the American system of government gives the president enormous latitude in the realm of foreign affairs, beyond the reach of any court. Koh and the others knew that the government's lawyers could simply argue that the Kennebunkport order was a foreign affairs matter. If a judge agreed, that would be that: no legal challenge could apply. Yet as so often before, the legal team felt they could not do nothing. The students took off their graduation robes and headed back into the library and the clinic office to research their options.

Later that day, Koh participated in an emergency conference call with refugee advocates from across the country. Everyone agreed that some major action had to be taken. The key question was exactly what and by whom.

"Let me try to get a restraining order," volunteered Ira Kurzban from Miami, where he had once squared off against Kenneth Starr.

Koh interjected: "Ira, they'll just appeal it. In *Baker* you were getting restraining orders in the morning and losing them on appeal in the afternoon. We already have a case ongoing. We're the best ones in a position to handle it."

The other attorneys and human rights advocates soon came around to Koh's point of view: his team could act the quickest and had already researched the relevant issues. Within days Koh was back in court. Only now, he and his students were arguing not one case, but two.

There was the original lawsuit involving 300 people, the HIV-positive refugees and their families. It was ongoing, the outcome uncertain. Alongside this challenge, christened "the Guantánamo case," Team Haiti was now obliged to fight and somehow win the new "non-return case," which affected the thousands of people who were trying to leave Haiti.

It was with a sinking feeling that Koh sat down at his computer and began typing up yet another restraining order request. It increasingly seemed that if he and the other members of Team Haiti were going to win, they would have to look outside the courts. But what else could they do?

THREE

A FLOATING BERLIN WALL

A MINUTE OF HER TIME. That's what they had asked the Clinton people for. Hillary Clinton was coming to Yale, and Harold Koh wanted to meet with her while she was on campus. By rights it was an impossible request. The 1992 election was four weeks away, and every second of Clinton's time during her visit was spoken for. But there was only one degree of separation between Koh and Hillary Clinton. Not only was Yale Law Clinton's alma mater but she was coming to campus to speak at the law school's alumni weekend. Koh knew some lawyers on the Clinton campaign team who said they would see what they could do. So it came to pass that, late on a windswept October afternoon, Koh and several of his students found themselves in a nondescript Yale meeting room, receiving Hillary Clinton and a young female aide as they came through the door.

Koh got straight to the point. The Bush administration's treatment of Haitian refugees raised serious human rights concerns. It was the view of Koh and the lawyers and students he was working with that the United States was in clear violation of its obligations under international law. Koh handed Clinton a briefing book that described the relevant legal issues with a concluding page of recommendations. It was designed, Koh says, "to impress on her the urgency of the situation."

As Koh rattled off his points, Clinton was responsive. According to Elizabeth Detweiler, one of the students present, "he knew the big points he wanted to hit, and as he started hitting them it was so clear that she had been briefed and she *got* it. She *had* this stuff. And you could just see Harold switch gears and go toward the more detailed analysis. . . . She was very receptive, so prepared and so bright. Naturally we were very heartened by that meeting."

Koh has a similarly positive memory of his meeting with Clinton, who told him, "I'm very proud of the work you're doing and I'm very proud of my school." Clinton said that she would take up the issue with her husband herself. After the meeting, Koh went to Yale's Battell Chapel to see Clinton deliver a speech. "My wife and I were sitting on the aisle, and she gave this tremendous speech," he says. "The whole place went wild. And afterwards she walked down the aisle. When she got to us she kind of winked at me. It was charming. I felt she was saying, 'I've got this under control.'"

It is not surprising that Koh would feel he was in good hands with Hillary Clinton. By the time of their October meeting, the Bush administration's treatment of Haitians, particularly its Kennebunkport order, as the legal team referred to the policy unveiled on Memorial Day, had become an issue in the presidential campaign. Immediately after Bush's announcement, Democratic candidate Bill Clinton spoke out against the repatriation policy. To this day, Harold Koh can quote by memory from Clinton's statement:

I am appalled by the decision of the Bush administration to pick up fleeing Haitians on the high seas and forcibly return them to Haiti before considering their claim to political asylum. It was bad enough when there were failures to offer them due process in making such a claim. Now they are offered no process at all before being returned.

This policy must not stand. It is a blow to the principle of first asylum and to America's moral authority in defending the rights of refugees around the world . . .

As I have said before, if I were President I would—in the absence of clear and compelling evidence that they weren't political refugees—give them temporary asylum until we restored the elected government of Haiti.

Candidate Clinton would make many similar remarks throughout the campaign. As a consequence, he had few more devoted supporters than Ratner, Koh and their students. If Clinton won and changed the policy, their litigation would become unnecessary. The Haitians would be released from Guantánamo and admitted to the United States, and the legal team could start getting back to a normal routine of teaching and attending classes again.

To hasten along that outcome, members of Team Haiti engaged in intense political lobbying. Michael Ratner remembers attending a fundraiser where he met with Bill Clinton face to face. "I was there because I had a family member who knew him," Ratner says. "I talked to him about Guantánamo for ten to twelve minutes. He took out a notepad and took down notes." Like his wife, Clinton had also gone to Yale Law School, and the Yale group had excellent contacts with Clinton's campaign team, whom they bombarded with information about Guantánamo to ensure that it remained a live issue in the presidential campaign. Ratner and other members of Team Haiti also reached out to lobby groups such as ACT UP and the National Coalition for Haitian Refugees, who came together to form a coalition of contrasts, whistle-blowing gay activists working alongside traditional Catholic Haitians to oppose Bush's refugee policy. After students sent out 100 press kits to the media labelled "The World's First HIV Detention Camp," television crews began to clamour to take their cameras to Guantánamo, which they were eventually allowed to visit.

While all the outside political agitation was going on, Team Haiti also lobbied sympathetic members of the Bush administration. Michael Ratner, in particular, developed a surprisingly amiable relationship with Paul Cappuccio, the associate deputy attorney general who handled the Guantánamo case for the Justice Department. Guantánamo was classified by the military as a "well base," meaning it had limited medical facilities, and this led to frequent negotiations between Ratner and Cappuccio regarding the release of sick or pregnant refugees. Although the two lawyers could hardly have been farther apart politically, Cappuccio's Reagan-era Republicanism in stark contrast to Ratner's sixties-style leftism, they developed a genuine regard for one another.

"Paul really was a warm person and particularly attuned to what was going on for human beings," Ratner says. "I think that's the area we connected on. So if I would describe to him somebody having a baby or getting a kid out of there, or somebody going through complications with AIDS, he was quite sympathetic. And he would be willing to work on trying to get each person out one by one."

In an essay he published after the case was over, Ratner wrote that there were no coherent medical criteria to dictate which refugees the government would admit into the United States. "There was no reason why eye infections were deemed worse than brain infections or liver infections." Perhaps more to the point, there were no clear political criteria. Negotiations between Cappuccio and Ratner resulted in a slow but steady trickle of Haitians allowed into the United States, eventually exceeding a hundred, or a third of the entire HIV group. They were attended to by organizations such as the AIDS Resource Foundation for Children, in New Jersey, an arrangement Yale students had made in order to gainsay any claims on the government's side that allowing the refugees into the country would be too expensive. (One of the major unanswered questions of the entire case is why the government would freely admit almost a third of the HIV-positive refugees but go to strenuous lengths to deny entry to the rest.)

Team Haiti eventually came to think of their efforts as having two components, a legal side and a political side. On the political side were the meetings with Bill and Hillary Clinton, the outreach work with Haitian and AIDS groups, days and nights spent finding a place for medically released refugees, and many other challenges. On the legal side were the two lawsuits themselves, and the many unanticipated and at times hair-raising dilemmas they gave rise to. But there was a third side, too. It was the one inhabited by the refugees themselves. And Guantánamo, it would turn out, would be the site of the most turbulent events of all.

A group of thirty Haitian children played in the corner of the enormous airplane hangar. Their parents sat quietly nearby in metal chairs. In front of the seated refugees, a Haitian man holding a clipboard tested a microphone. As Harold Koh, Michael Ratner, Lisa Daugaard and a half-dozen other members of the Yale team entered the hangar, they could see that the man with the clipboard was in his late twenties, wearing black pleated pants, a crisp white button-down shirt and sunglasses. While the lawyers and students found their seats among a row of chairs facing the refugees, the man, without taking off his glasses, introduced himself as Michel Vilsaint and explained that he had been elected camp president. At Vilsaint's signal, the refugees quietly stood and began chanting in unison a Creole slogan used by supporters of Jean-Bertrand Aristide: "Yon sèl nou fèb, ansanm nou fò, ansanm, ansanm nou se Lavalas." Alone we are weak, together we are strong, together, together we are Lavalas.

It was early October, less than a month before the 1992 presidential election, and mere days after Harold Koh's meeting with Hillary Clinton. The Yale attorneys had been representing the Haitians for seven gruelling months, but only now had they been granted access to the base beyond the Guantánamo airstrip. The official reason for their trip (the same one that would leave Harold Koh with nightmares) was to discuss with their clients an offer the government had made.

The government's newfound willingness to negotiate was in part a reaction to a grim episode that had concluded not long before. In May of 1992, a refugee, Sillieses Success, had given birth to a boy she named Ricardo. Shortly afterwards, there was an altercation between the refugees and their guards, during which several Haitians set fire to some of the camp's huts. In response, the military herded the refugees into open-air pavilions and kept them there for three days. This coincided with the Caribbean rainy season, and as a result of his exposure, Ricardo contracted pneumonia. In September he and his mother were evacuated to the United States to receive medical treatment, but it was too late, and Ricardo died two weeks after leaving Guantánamo. The government then proposed that his body be sent back to Guantánamo to be interred there rather than in American soil, but this aroused such fury on the part of both the legal team and Ricardo's mother that the idea was dropped, and Ricardo was buried in the United States.

A more conciliatory mood seemed to come over the government after that, at which point it raised the possibility of a settlement. For their part, Team Haiti had known all along that what they were fighting for—the right to talk to a lawyer—did not address the full needs of their clients, and so they were open to a negotiated outcome. The offer the negotiations eventually resulted in was the very thing the lawsuit was asking for: the HIV-positive group would be allowed to have lawyers present during their second interviews.

But there was a catch. Even if the Haitians passed their second interviews—even if they met the higher standard for demonstrating a fear of persecution—the administration would not guarantee that anyone would be taken to the United States. Discussions would continue about sick or pregnant people being admitted on a case-by-case basis, but the overall ban on entry to the country would remain in place. Team Haiti had been fighting for access to lawyers not primarily as a good in itself, but as a delaying tactic to prevent forced returns, and to keep pressure on the government overall. Now they were faced with an offer from the government that would technically grant what their lawsuit was asking for, and in so doing highlight the limits of the purely procedural legal challenge they had been able to launch. If Team Haiti kept fighting in court, by contrast, there was a strong chance Clinton, who was leading in the polls, would win the presidential election and release the Haitians.

The Yale team could not decide what was best for their clients without consulting them. So here they were in the airplane hangar, sweating in the tropical heat, finally able to meet the Haitians face to face. In addition to Ratner and Koh, the attorneys included Lisa Daugaard, who had left law school and was now working at the American Civil Liberties Union, where her duties included the Haitian refugee case. Accompanying the three attorneys were three students, Laura Ho, Tory Clawson and Veronique Sanchez, and three translators.

The hangar was surrounded by armed military personnel, and the strange situation put Harold Koh in mind of a science fiction film. "It was almost like a scene from a movie where the humans and the aliens meet in some special hangar for the first time," he says, "because we had heard about each other but without making any contact."

Initial contact would now take the form of a presentation by Koh, explaining to the Haitians where things stood with the lawsuit, and giving them an outline of the government's settlement offer. On the military flight from Virginia, Koh had devoted considerable thought to what he was going to say, but now, as he finally saw the faces of people who had risked the Windward Passage in flight from unimaginable violence, it suddenly came home to him that the lawyers and their clients inhabited completely different worlds.

"I was very struck by the huge visual difference between our [two] groups," Koh says. "Me, Asian, and this bunch of [Asian and] white students and lawyers. The women students were wearing these long batik skirts and sandals because it was so hot. And here were the refugees on the other side of the same hangar, wearing T-shirts and athletic shorts and flip-flops. And I thought, 'Gee, how can they relate to us?'"

As if the cultural barriers were not enough, Koh also knew that military personnel had been telling the Haitians that they were being detained because of the actions of the legal team—a falsehood, but one that the Yale group would have to put to rest if they were to gain their clients' trust.

Koh stood and addressed the expectant Haitians through a translator. "I know you're all wondering who is this Chinese or Japanese person and why is he here," Koh said before pausing for a moment. "The thing is, I'm actually Korean."

Laughter and murmurs of "*Kore, Kore*" came from the Haitians. Encouraged, Koh took out a photograph of his father and explained that he, too, had been a political refugee. "Like you, my father was born in another country. Like you, he wanted to live in a free country. Like you, he left his country and came to America. America took him in, and because of that I became a lawyer. It's because of my father that I fight for you."

Koh's father had sought asylum in the United States after a coup overthrew the South Korean government in 1960. The refugees nodded: this they could certainly understand. After Koh finished his remarks, Michel Vilsaint and other members of the camp leadership met with Koh to listen to what the law-yers had to say. It was as if, slowly and tentatively, the Haitians were dismantling the wall of mistrust that separated them from their would-be advocates: a wall that seemed as well fortified as the perimeter of land mines and razor wire around Guantánamo itself.

Within twenty-four hours the wall was back up. The legal team had divided into three groups, each made up of a lawyer, student and translator, to explain the details of the settlement offer to groups of two dozen refugees. As she headed into her meeting in a portable trailer, Lisa Daugaard was already feeling overwhelmed. In her view, the fundamental dynamics of the case had dramatically changed. No longer were the legal team's efforts primarily devoted to coming up with abstract legal arguments on behalf of a group of strangers who were themselves still some-thing of an abstraction. Now there were flesh-and-blood human beings involved, actual clients. But as Daugaard tried to initiate a normal attorney-client meeting, she began to wonder if it would work.

The refugees had organized their meeting so that they would rotate through a hot seat while Daugaard sat across the table and answered their questions through an interpreter.

Refugee one: How can we trust you? You're just in this for the money.

Daugaard: Oh no, no. We're not getting paid.

Refugee two: Well if that's the case, obviously we can't trust you, because you're such bad lawyers no one will pay you and you have to work for free.

Daugaard: Oh no, no. We're very good lawyers. There's this thing called pro bono . . .

Refugee three: Well if you're working for charity we can trust you even less, because there's nothing motivating you to do a good job!

On and on it went. Daugaard felt increasing despair at each answer. "The amount of scepticism was overwhelming," she says. On top of that, she was suffering from sleep deprivation because of all the hours she had been putting into the case. Now she had travelled over a thousand miles to this unnerving military environment, only to realize that the people on whose behalf she had been working considered her part of the problem. Tears began streaming down her face.

Daugaard stepped outside and tried to pull herself together. It was the second time she had cried on the trip: the first had occurred back at the hangar, when she had been overcome with emotion at meeting the Haitians for the first time. Now here she was, bawling again, on the trip that was supposed to be her big professional debut. What was I thinking? she asked herself. I'm the weak link in this chain. I'm the *woman*. I'm *young*. Very obviously *not* a lawyer. And on top of everything else, now I've *cried* like a baby . . .

Daugaard was sitting on the ground contemplating her failure when she felt a hand on her shoulder. She looked up to see the wrinkled face of a middle-aged Haitian woman.

"Come, come, come," she said softly in English, before leading Daugaard back inside to sit her down. The refugees had reorganized themselves into a huddle and looked at Daugaard expectantly.

"We're ready to talk about the case now," one of them said through the translator. "We're going to trust you because if you hadn't been sincere, then what we said wouldn't have hurt your feelings, and you wouldn't have cried."

Rather than a sign of failure, Daugaard realized, her tears had marked the possible beginning of a real relationship. (It was a realization, Daugaard says, "that has been very useful in subsequent professional life, every time I haven't behaved exactly like a standard lawyer.")

"Right," she began. "Let's talk about the case . . ."

Elsewhere on the base, other members of the team were also trying to break down the wall of mistrust. One of them was the Yale group's lead translator, a Haitian American named Ronald Aubourg. Aubourg worked for the National Coalition for Haitian Refugees, a New York organization that was formally a plaintiff in the lawsuit. Aubourg had been personally concerned about the Guantánamo situation ever since a refugee called his office and give a harrowing account of life at the base, describing rough treatment by the guards and worms in the Haitians' food. Upon arriving at Guantánamo, Aubourg saw that he actually knew several of the refugees: one was a cousin, while another had grown up in his old neighbourhood back in Haiti. Yet it was Aubourg whom the refugees singled out for constant needling. "You're working with *these* people?" the Haitians would say to him in Creole, referring to the legal team. "These people are a joke. They're not going to do a damn thing for us except turn around and leave."

Aubourg could understand the Haitians' wariness. In Haiti, the version of reality put forward by the military, politicians and most other authorities is usually a lie, a cynical distortion of events intended to prevent anyone in power from having to take responsibility for the country's corruption and injustice. The refugees were thus only exercising the same survival skill—suspicion—that had allowed them to successfully navigate Haiti's life-and-death political struggles. At the same time, however, Aubourg was frustrated by the refugees' attitude. Not only was it counterproductive, but he felt the sincerity of Ratner, Koh and the others was obvious to anyone who looked.

"I was hurt," Aubourg says. "When I met Harold and Michael . . . we clicked. I believed that these folks would get my people out of Guantánamo, and that had carried me throughout the whole case. So I told [the refugees], 'No, the lawyers are here to help you.'"

The Haitians refused to listen. Instead, their hectoring only grew more intense. After the lawyers had returned to the main hangar from their separate meetings, Aubourg found himself drawn into an argument with a group of younger refugees. If Aubourg was so committed to helping them, they challenged him, why didn't he come back to the camp and see for himself how bad it was? Why didn't he actually *do* something, instead of offer more empty talk? Aubourg knew that if he did so and was caught, the entire legal team could be kicked off the base. Yet he felt he had no choice but to accept the refugees' dare.

The Haitians had been brought to the hangar on a yellow school bus that ran back and forth from the camp. Aubourg put a towel on his head, as the refugees did to stave off the heat, and got on the bus beside a Haitian woman, making it appear as though he was her husband. Aubourg remembers looking in the rear-view mirror and exchanging stares with the female solider who was driving. To Aubourg's horror, he realized he had exchanged a few words with her before the hangar meeting. Yet rather than say anything, she simply continued driving. Aubourg believes it was because she was African American and privately objected to the way her government was treating other black people.

At the camp, Aubourg walked around and saw its foul conditions first hand. As he did so, a group of refugees became excited and began to run after him. Aubourg shooed them away to avoid attracting attention to himself, but not before noticing the smiles on their faces. A sign, he realized, that he had earned their respect.

After Aubourg made his way back to the hangar Koh and Ratner angrily told him he had jeopardized their access to the base. But to Aubourg's mind it had been worth it. "That move brought about some trust that the group was legitimate," he says. "It paid off [when] some of them came back and said, 'If one of you didn't do that, we probably would still be hostile.'"

Just how much it paid off may have become apparent the next day, when one of the most suspicious refugees stood up during another meeting to make a public statement. "My name is Harold Michel," he said. "Last night an angel came to me in a dream. That angel told me to trust the lawyers. I share my name with the two lawyers here, Harold and Michael. That is a sign I should trust the lawyers." After that it was as if a dam had burst. A deluge of stories issued forth from the Haitians: about what they had run from; relatives they feared had died; their constant thoughts of suicide.

Later, Lisa Daugaard speculated that Harold Michel's remark about an angel was actually a reference to Ronald Aubourg. In her view, what had inspired Michel was not some otherworldly messenger. It was the sight of a truly free Haitian, one whose spirit Guantánamo could not contain.

During their last night at Guantánamo the lawyers had a final meeting with Michel Vilsaint and several other camp leaders. It confirmed what they had been told throughout the group meetings: the Haitians would turn down the government's offer. The refugees were not interested in winning the right to have lawyers present at their second interviews. They were interested in being released from Guantánamo and in going anywhere other than back to Haiti. That would now be possible only if Bill Clinton won the election, and so Vilsaint and the others would hold out for a Democratic victory. But Vilsaint had a question. What would happen, he asked the lawyers, if Clinton lost?

Lisa Daugaard answered: "I want to promise you that we will try to develop an argument that will somehow lead to your release."

Koh quickly corrected her: "Strictly speaking, our case is about whether or not you can gain access to lawyers."

At best, Koh was telling both Daugaard and the refugees, the case was an indirect way of keeping the pressure on the government. But the refugees shouldn't expect—and the lawyers couldn't promise—anything more than that.

Daugaard was upset, and she and Koh got into an argument in front of their clients, which culminated in Koh curtly dismissing Daugaard ("Just stop *talking*," he snapped). To Daugaard's thinking, Koh was being high-handed in not taking her idea seriously. Moreover, the lawyers had a responsibility to follow the wishes of their clients. And the Haitians had been saying the same thing throughout their entire time at Guantánamo: get us out of here.

"Harold was very removed from the on-the-ground legal stuff that we had been doing that strongly suggested that we could win a case [involving release]," Daugaard says. "Instead, he was paying a tremendous amount of attention to the political dynamic. . . . His plan was that Clinton was going to get elected and we were going to control the Clinton administration's immigration agenda and so we wouldn't be litigating the issue."

For his part, Koh believed Daugaard was giving false hope to people who very much did not need their expectations dashed. It was not simply an accident, he felt, that the lawsuit had come to revolve around the issue of access to lawyers. There were solid legal reasons for that. What's more, Daugaard had risked the refugees' confidence in the legal team by publicly contradicting him when they needed to present a united front.

The lawyers and refugees had one last group meeting in the hangar. The Haitians sang songs and presented the Americans with a painting of the scales of justice attempting to break loose from Haiti's violent past. Afterwards, the legal team clambered into a van to be taken back to their military quarters. Koh and Daugaard, however, were both still angry. In Daugaard's words she "sulked" in the back of the van, saying nothing. Koh, for his part, revealed how upset he was when he stopped the van in front of the base McDonald's to get something to eat, and realized it had just closed.

"I can see seventeen Big Macs just sitting there," Koh yelled, kicking the glass. "I'm here under the authority of a federal judge! What do you think Judge Johnson's going to think when I call him!"

Daugaard felt her blood boil even more after Koh disappeared inside and re-emerged triumphantly holding several bags of Big Macs.

"They opened the door and gave him the damn food. I was so unhappy with him, it was just pathetic." Given her anger with him, any triumph by Koh was only cause for further irritation.

Daugaard and Koh reconciled later that night. But their argument highlighted the larger challenge of the team's sprawling project, namely that of keeping the various aspects of the case—the legal side, the political side and the human refugee side—held together in one unruly whole.

After returning to the United States, the legal team formally rejected the government's offer. Their clients had decided: it would be all or nothing.

A month later, students were gathered in the family room of Harold Koh's house in New Haven. After ordering pizza and eating a cake his wife had made, they settled in to watch the election returns. When the networks announced Clinton's victory, everyone let out a triumphant shout of joy. "We were *euphoric*," Elizabeth Detweiler says. "We thought this would mean we wouldn't have to file our court brief, we thought this would mean, more importantly, that the camp would be closed down . . . The need for the litigation had fundamentally changed, and a lot of it would become moot."

Koh and Ratner received congratulatory phone calls from human rights and refugee advocates around the country. The students got on the phone to Guantánamo, where the joy was even more intense. When Michel Vilsaint tried to speak with the students, his voice was drowned out by cheers in the background. "Clinton! Clinton! Miami! Miami!"

Right away, the Yale team stepped up their political lobbying. The number of contacts they now had among future Clinton administration officials was extraordinary. As Koh puts it, "One great thing about Yale Law School is this network of young movers and shakers, so there was almost no one in a position of power who we couldn't get to without one or two degrees of separation." Koh and Ratner knew the head of Clinton's Immigration transition team, and two of the outside lawyers working on the refugee case were on the team themselves. Various lawyers on Team Haiti knew members of Clinton's Health and Justice transition teams, the head of the Democratic National Committee, two lawyers who would serve as solicitors general under Clinton, Clinton's White House counsel, his personnel director and his attorney general. Before Clinton's inauguration, virtually his entire incoming administration was barraged with information about Guantánamo and interdiction and pleas to end Bush's policies.

In spite of the intense lobbying effort, Clinton was slow to act. After several weeks went by with nothing happening, two refugees tried to kill themselves. In mid-November, two Team Haiti lawyers, Joe Tringali and Lucas Guttentag, led a new legal team to the base. In Tringali's words, it was "a counselling visit," during which the lawyers would try to reassure the Haitians and keep their spirits up by explaining where things stood with the lawsuit. They would also choose Haitians who would make good witnesses, should things come to a trial.

Tringali, Guttentag and a half-dozen students and translators went to meet with the government lawyers at the same base McDonald's where Harold Koh had demanded his Big Macs. Upon arriving, Tringali was asked by one of the government attorneys to step outside. Tringali and Guttentag's trip marked the first time Team Haiti had gained access inside the Haitians' detention camp, and they were to go to the camp after the McDonald's meeting. Now, however, the government lawyer told Tringali that the administration had received threats against the legal team. If they entered the detention camp, the Haitians would take the lawyers hostage to secure their own release.

Tringali was shocked. He assumed the government was sincere in its belief that something might happen at the camp. But the idea of the Haitians taking him and the others hostage was barely credible. "The Haitians knew we were coming," Tringali says, "they were waiting for our visit, and for us not to go didn't make any sense."

In the event, the visit to the camp passed without incident, and Tringali's group was finally able to document its substandard conditions. Afterwards, he and the others on Team Haiti had a meeting in the mess hall with the Haitians in which Tringali and his colleagues stood on a makeshift podium and showed a videotaped message from Harold Koh. The tape was meant to establish continuity between the first group of lawyers who had come to Guantánamo and the new faces on this trip. In his video, Koh mentioned that last time they were there they had said that a Clinton victory would help the Haitians. At that point, several Haitians turned their chairs around so they had their backs to Tringali and to Koh's image on the screen.

The refugees were losing what little faith they had in their legal team. Once again, it fell to Ronald Aubourg to serve as bridge between two worlds. Aubourg notes that it was a constant point of contention among the Haitians as to whether or not they really were HIV positive. To their mind, the military's statements that they were infected was part of a larger disinformation campaign, a trick intended to confuse and demoralize them. Not only were the Haitians tired of constantly being told by their attorneys to be patient but Tringali and Guttentag's group had tried to raise the issue of HIV, which the Haitians did not want to entertain.

"There was some HIV expert on that trip," Aubourg says, "and I think the other aspect of it was that these people were coming to speak about HIV and not about [how they] were going to get out of here." Through much cajoling, however, Aubourg convinced the refugees not to give up hope just yet.

Yet the refugees' lack of faith in Clinton would soon prove prophetic. A week before he was to take office, Clinton announced that he was reversing the stance he had taken during the campaign, a promise he had repeated a week after his election victory. The Bush policy of forced repatriation without interviews would remain in place. The one concession was that the Clinton administration would attempt to increase the number of resettlements directly from Haiti.

Harold Koh was devastated. The day Clinton announced his reversal, he says, "was one of the most difficult days I've ever had." Some students had heard Clinton's announcement on the radio, and they once again gathered in Koh's basement to watch Clinton on the news. After the newscasts confirmed the worst, it was all Koh could do to keep his composure in front of his students.

"I was extremely cool while the students were there. But after they left, I broke down in tears. I said to my wife: I never thought that we would get screwed like this. And now we've got to fight this to the Supreme Court."

Michael Ratner also felt betrayed by Clinton's reversal. He describes Clinton as a reverse mirror image of Paul Cappuccio, the government lawyer Ratner befriended. Although Cappuccio never made a pretense of sharing Ratner's politics, he came through during negotiations to release 100 Haitians. Clinton was the opposite, issuing many promises that amounted to nothing. "One was a deeply warm human being and the other guy made you *feel* that at the initial meeting, but then went on and didn't do that," Ratner says. "Clinton screwed us completely over."

Yet if the lawyers were embittered by Clinton's change, it was nothing next to what the refugees felt. In February, several days before the Yale team was due to make another trip to Guantánamo, Michel Vilsaint called New Haven. He announced that the Haitians were going on a hunger strike. All the refugees, men, women and children alike, had moved to a field next to their huts, where they would refuse any food until they were released. If that resulted in their own deaths, Vilsaint told the lawyers, then so be it. Only freedom could stop them now.

Once again, there was agonizing debate among the legal team over what to do. Many members wanted to somehow persuade the refugees to abandon the strike. Tory Clawson and other students rushed to the phones to urge the Haitians to not go through with it. At the very least, they pleaded, don't involve the children. But other members of Team Haiti said that if this was what their clients wanted, then the lawyers should represent their wishes. In their view, the adage that "lawyers advise, clients instruct" should apply even in the case of a hunger strike.

In the end the legal team decided that they would respect the Haitians' desires, and duly sent out a press release noting what was going on. They would limit their entreaties to trying to plead with the refugees to drink liquids, stay in the shade, not exert themselves and at least allow the children and pregnant women to eat. And from now on, the lawyers would also bring Haitian doctors with them whenever they visited the camp.

When Team Haiti visited the camp several days into the strike, they saw the Haitians encamped in a field under the hot sun. The military personnel did not know how to deal with them. Many of the refugees were visibly thinner than when the legal team had last seen them. Yolande Jean, one of the camp leaders, who had gone without food for nearly a week, read the Americans a letter she was writing to her relatives back in Haiti.

"Don't count on me anymore, because I am lost in the struggle of life. . . . Hill and Jeff, you don't have a mother anymore. Realize that you do not have a bad mother, only that life took me away. . . . Good-bye my children. Good-bye my family. We will meet in another world."

As three Yale law students would note in an account they later wrote of the case, "ironically the refugees had regained control of their lives only by controlling the possibility of their own deaths."

From this point on, members of the legal team maintained a continuous presence at Camp Bulkeley, as the detention facility was called. For a few weeks it was simply because, with the non-return trial finally approaching, they needed to take depositions. But the reason for their presence evolved as the legal team sought to provide emotional and other forms of support. More than once they talked a refugee out of suicide, plans for self-destruction motivated by the belief that the death of a few Haitians might shame Clinton into admitting the others.

Causing members of Team Haiti to relocate to Guantánamo was not the only effect the hunger strike had. It also galvanized the attorneys and students to step up their political activities. At a pro-Aristide rally in New York City, they approached former

Democratic presidential candidate Jesse Jackson. He agreed to visit the camp, which he did on Valentine's Day, 1993. As Tory Clawson explains, "Part of our whole idea for having him down there was to urge them to go off the hunger strike, because we were worrying about their health." By this time, the lawyers were becoming concerned that some people might actually die. Accompanied by a retinue of media, a congresswoman and other black leaders, Jackson went into the camp and prayed with the refugees, holding in his arms one who broke down during the prayer. He then visited the thirty children in the camp, who had been waiting for him and chanting, "Guantánamo no good, Miami yes!" Then, to the astonishment of the people who had brought him there, Jackson looked into the TV cameras and made a surprise announcement. Rather than urge the Haitians to stop their hunger strike, he, too, would stop eating.

Clawson and her colleagues were dumbfounded. "I remember we were a little unpleasantly surprised." Clawson speculates that Jackson may have noticed, as the legal team had, that some of the refugees were in fact taking small amounts of food. If so, he may have decided that encouraging them to prolong their strike would not be dangerous.

Jackson's involvement immediately turned the case into a much larger issue. His personal hunger strike lasted for ten days. Jackson, together with the actor Susan Sarandon and the director Jonathan Demme, was also arrested at a rally in New York City. An emotional Sarandon read out Yolande Jean's letter to her children in front of gathered reporters. Several days later, Sarandon and the actor Tim Robbins appeared on stage at the Academy Awards. While presenting an Oscar, they drew attention to the red ribbons they were wearing, which they said they wore in support of the HIV-positive Haitians at Guantánamo, who were being imprisoned without having committed any crime. The famous actors were widely criticized and received waves of hate mail, some of which denounced them for helping "sick faggots." Nevertheless, they successfully raised the refugees' profile and kept their plight in the public eye.

Hollywood stars were not the Haitians' only supporters. A group of thirty Yale law students, most of them not members of Team Haiti, organized a rolling hunger strike across the United States. They built a replica detention camp, complete with barbed wire, which they occupied for a week as they went without food. From Yale, the strike spread to Harvard, Brown, Michigan, Columbia, Howard, Georgetown, Penn State and other universities. At the City University of New York Law School, the dean himself participated. Alongside the universities, many ministers organized hunger strikes among their congregations. By the time the non-return case was due to be heard in the Supreme Court, in March of 1993, Team Haiti had also obtained the support of three former attorneys general of the United States, Amnesty International, the United Nations High Commissioner for Refugees and a dozen other prominent human rights groups, all of which filed "friend of the court" briefs supporting Team Haiti's lawsuit. (The government, by contrast, received only one supporting brief, from the Federation for American Immigration Reform, an anti-immigration organization.)

In the end, however, it would come down to the argument before the Supreme Court. Harold Koh would argue the case for Team Haiti. The Supreme Court hearing was on a Tuesday. On the Friday before, Koh went to Washington to sit in on the court and observe the justices in action. (Before a case, he says, "you always want to go to the court and see how they're behaving.") Koh had all of his legal files FedExed from New Haven to D.C. and set up an office inside a hotel room near the courthouse, going over everything one last time.

Koh devoted special care to the closing words of his oral argument. In the Supreme Court of the United States, a white light goes off to indicate an attorney is nearing the end of his allotted time. A red light then tells the lawyer to stop, even if in mid-sentence. Koh reasoned that in between the white and red lights, he would need to budget forty seconds for a closing statement that would summarize the central issue in simple human terms. Throughout the entire case, the parties involved had been divided into Haitians versus Americans, us versus them. Koh's final goal before the court would be to attack this division at its root. As Koh says, he wanted to "put the court and crowd on side with the Haitians so that they were like us." Carefully timing his words, he settled on the following statement: "Ours is a nation of refugees. Most of our ancestors came here by boat. If they could do this to the Haitians, they could do this to any of us. For these reasons, this decision should be affirmed."

The night before the argument, Koh was joined by his wife and six-year-old daughter. They attended one last political demonstration with Jesse Jackson, with protestors holding up signs in the Washington twilight saying "Justice for Haitians." The next morning, Koh and his family, together with the student members of Team Haiti, gathered for breakfast in the Supreme Court cafeteria. Koh had once worked as a clerk for Supreme Court Justice Harry Blackmun, and he knew that Blackmun had breakfast with his clerks every morning at eight. Koh was thus unsurprised when he looked across the crowded dining hall and saw his former mentor. Koh wanted to avoid any hint of impropriety, and so he had taken great care not to come in contact with Blackmun before the case was decided. While his wife and daughter went over to say hello, Koh hung back and waved instead. Koh had been isolated for the past seventy-two hours—and, in a way, isolated for long before that—and he was nervous in the final hours before the 10 a.m. argument. But when Blackmun looked across at him and smiled, Koh felt his spirits rise.

"He gave a shy smile that was very confidence building," Koh says. "I could tell he was saying, 'I'm on your side.'"

Two hours later, Koh was sitting at the respondent's table, waiting for the argument to begin. As the final minutes before the arrival of the justices ticked away, Koh took one last look back at the visitors' gallery behind him. Everywhere he looked, he saw a sea of expectant black faces. Haitian Americans had come out in force to show their support for what he was doing. But then the justices in their gowns entered the room, and Koh felt a shiver of fear pass through him.

In every court case there are two different explanations of the events involved, ultimately two different versions of reality. For Harold Koh and the other members of the Yale team, the Haiti case was about the refugees themselves and their treatment by the United States government. But for Maureen Mahoney, the government lawyer who argued against Koh in the Supreme Court, the lawsuit was about the president of the United States. The president in question was not a flesh-and-blood person such as George Bush or Bill Clinton, but the entity of the presidency itself and the legitimate scope of its power. Like other lawyers who represented the Bush and Clinton administrations, Mahoney argued that the non-return lawsuit was a wrongful intrusion into the realm of foreign affairs, where the president, not the court system, is the final authority.

Mahoney brought this perspective to bear on the Refugee Convention, to which the United States had long been a signatory, and one of the central legal documents at issue in the non-return case. In particular, Mahoney devoted much attention to the following passage: "No Contracting State shall expel or return ('*refouler*') a refugee in any manner whatsoever to the frontiers of territories where his life or freedom would be threatened on account of his race, religion, nationality, membership of a particular social group or political opinion."

To the Yale team, the meaning of the passage was unambiguous: countries that signed the convention were committed to not returning refugees to places where their lives would be in danger. Mahoney, however, zeroed in on the word "expel" and the French phrase "*refouler*," a term of art in refugee law. According to the government's reading, expulsion referred to the formal process whereby a foreigner lawfully present in a country is legally removed. "*Refoulement*, by contrast," Mahoney and her colleagues argued in their brief, "connotes 'summary reconduction' (mere physical relocation) of an individual." On this reading the Refugee Convention referred to two different actions that can be performed only on a person actually present—either legally or physically—inside the United States. And if that was the case, then it meant that the convention had "limited territorial scope." As it is impossible to expel or *refoul* a refugee who is not inside the United States, and as the Haitians were interdicted hundreds of miles from U.S. shores on the high seas, it followed that the interdiction program was perfectly legal.

Mahoney had finished her argument and was about to sit down when one of the justices asked her to wait. It was Koh's old mentor, Justice Blackmun.

"Well, before you sit down, a couple of irrelevant questions. Have you ever been in Haiti?"

"No, Your Honor, I have not."

"Are you familiar with a book called *The Comedians* by Graham Greene?"

Blackmun would later be criticized for engaging in an off-topic line of questioning, but as Koh recalls the proceedings, Blackmun's closing exchange with Mahoney "was the most relevant thing said that day." *The Comedians* is set in Haiti and is filled with scenes of harrowing violence. According to Koh, "what he was basically saying was, 'You guys don't know what this situation on the ground is in Haiti, do you? You have no idea what you're sending these people back to.'"

At the time, however, Mahoney did not pause to ask what Blackmun might mean, and simply replied, "No, Your Honor, I'm sorry, I'm not."

Three months later, Michael Ratner and Harold Koh watched as a Hercules troop carrier rumbled down the runway toward them. They were standing on the tarmac of LaGuardia Airport in New York. As the camouflaged airplane opened its massive cargo doors, Koh yelled to Ratner above the roar of the engines, "Michael, we caused this plane to take off." A group of expectant Haitian faces was soon blinking out at them. Tears started to stream down the faces of the two veteran lawyers.

Because the case had split into two separate lawsuits, the question of whether the Guantánamo Haitians would be allowed to enter the United States was decided separately from the Supreme Court argument dealing with repatriation. Led by Joe Tringali, Team Haiti had argued for the release of the Guantánamo Haitians in front of Judge Sterling Johnson, the same Brooklyn judge who had issued their hard-won restraining order. Throughout the trial, a cool and unruffled Tringali methodically demolished each of the government's arguments. At one point a Coast Guard commander named Waldmann testified that a group of Haitians who were picked up at sea and taken to Guantánamo had "all stood up and started cheering and thanking the Coast Guard for saving them." Under cross-examination, Tringali calmly asked Commander Waldmann if the cheering refugees had been informed that they would be detained at Guantánamo for over a year. Waldmann admitted they had not. Tringali then asked about the eighty-nine refugees who had been forcibly returned to Haiti in April 1992 and forced off Waldmann's cutter with firehoses.

"When you left the Haitians on the dock in Port-au-Prince, do you recall whether they were clapping for you then?"

"No, sir," a defeated Waldmann replied.

When the decision came down, Team Haiti's victory was total. Judge Johnson had accepted every one of their arguments. "Each year many 'non-immigrants' enter the United States," he wrote, "and are not subject to HIV testing. To date, the Government has only enforced the ban against Haitians." Noting that admitting the Haitians was unlikely to affect the spread of AIDS, Judge Johnson concluded that continuing to imprison them "serves no purpose other than to punish them for being sick."

Now, on the tarmac, Ratner and Koh were seeing the human beings their lawsuit had benefited. For Ratner, it was the most emotional moment of the entire litigation.

"Winning the Guantánamo case, it was very important, but not in the same way. This was *human*. There were people we freed from Guantánamo. And they were coming off the plane."

The Haitians came tumbling out the back of the airplane and began filing toward a U.S. immigration station that had been set up to register their arrival. Each Haitian had a hospital bracelet bearing a bar code and his or her name, which would be checked against those listed on a court order Koh and Ratner had brought with them. Before they reached the immigration station, however, a Haitian man named Jean came running up to Koh.

"*Mon avocat*," he said in an agitated voice. He was waving a piece of paper and pointing to his name on his bracelet. "My name, my name," he said. Koh looked down and saw that it had been misspelled. Jean wanted him to fix it, and so Koh and the refugee began to walk toward the immigration table. After they took a few steps, however, Koh stopped.

"Suddenly I realized we couldn't do it," he remembers. "All of the rights he had in the U.S. came from the court order. And if we were actually to correct it, it might just confuse things and he could spend all of his time in the U.S. dealing with this and might be deported."

Koh pointed at the refugee's bracelet. "This is your name now," he said, tapping.

Jean paused. "What was your name when you came to America?"

"When we got to Ellis Island, they spelled it Koh."

"Well," Jean said, pointing to the paper with his misspelled name, "this is my name now."

Three months after Koh argued the non-return case, the Supreme Court released its decision. Leading up to the trial, members of the Yale team had mixed feelings about how well they would do. Michael Ratner thought they would probably lose. Koh, based on the unambiguous language of the Refugee Convention and other factors, thought that they might squeeze out a narrow win.

When the Supreme Court issued its decision, however, no one was prepared for it. Team Haiti lost 8–1. The only justice who sided with them was Blackmun. The rest of the justices had accepted a variation of the government's reading of the convention. The policy of returning Haitians to danger in Haiti, they ruled, was perfectly legal.

To members of Team Haiti, who had already been through so much, the court's decision was devastating. As Michael Barr puts it, "At bottom what we were saying was if refugee and asylum law means anything, either the refugee convention or U.S. immigration law, it means you can't do what you're doing. That's [the convention's] plain meaning, its *purpose*. . . . To get to the government's position, you have to have a really tortured reading of the words."

The Supreme Court case is now known as the *Sale* decision, so named after Clinton's acting commissioner of immigration, Chris Sale, a named party in the lawsuit. It remains the law of the United States. Since the decision was handed down, it has attracted a barrage of criticism. Normally staid law journals and many books have said that the judgment is based on "an arcane and highly dubious interpretation of what it is to *'refoule'* a refugee," and the reasoning by which the court arrived at its decision has been called "disingenuous." One law professor has gone as far as to label the *Sale* decision "the *Dred Scott* case of immigration law," referring to the 1857 U.S. Supreme Court decision that held that slaves had no legal rights.

One reason the *Sale* decision is unusually controversial is that it is based on a reading of the Refugee Convention that has few adherents outside the U.S. government. In a friend of the court brief submitted to support Yale's case, the Office of the United Nations High Commissioner for Refugees argued that the government had misinterpreted the plain meaning of the convention. "Under [the government's] reading, while the treaty purports to prohibit the return of refugees 'in any manner whatsoever' it actually excepts from this sweeping language all forms of return that do not entail removal of the refugee from the territory of the contracting State."

One of the most outspoken critics of the decision is Guy Goodwin-Gill, a scholar of international law affiliated with the University of Oxford, whose writings the Supreme Court justices quoted to justify their decision. In a scathing commentary published after the judgment came down, Goodwin-Gill repudiated any association with *Sale*. "The Supreme Court's citations are often adrift; it takes passages out of context, misquotes academic and other commentators . . . and ignores whatever might obstruct its policy decision to . . . *refoule* refugees."

Goodwin-Gill noted that the government's claim that the Refugee Convention applied only within U.S. borders was contradicted by numerous statements of American government officials going back over a decade. He cited a barrage of sources from all levels of the U.S. government, all expressing an "extraterritorial" understanding of the applicability of the Refugee Convention.

As Goodwin-Gill pointed out, such an understanding was written into the original Reagan-Duvalier agreement that had called the interdiction program into being. That was why the Coast Guard had begun screening people in the first place: there would have been no need to maintain the charade of on-deck interviews for ten years if the Refugee Convention had never applied to begin with. Goodwin-Gill concluded that the interpretation the government put before the court was a "newly minted" one, devised after the fact to justify its repatriation policy, and the Supreme Court had failed to see through it.

Finally, there is the plain meaning of the phrase "No Contracting State shall expel or return (*'refouler'*) a refugee in any manner whatsoever." On the government's interpretation, return and *refouler* both mean "expel." Not only does this fly in the face of how the French word is normally used but, as Koh pointed out in his Supreme Court brief, it creates an "absurdly redundant" sentence: no contracting state shall expel or expel a refugee. As a lower court judge had pointed out, the English word *return* "necessarily looks 'to' the place 'to' which a refugee is returned." The simplest and most straightforward reading of the Refugee Convention, therefore, takes it to rule out returning refugees to danger, regardless of where they are returned from. The United States government, alone among interpreters, reads the convention to say that a state can return refugees to danger if it catches them on the high seas.

In addition to the many legal arguments it made in the Supreme Court and elsewhere, the government offered a second rationale for its repatriation policy. This argument was not legal but political. It touches on what migration specialists refer to as pull factors, or the inducements that motivate people to leave home and head for a new country. Throughout the litigation, the government frequently argued that forced repatriation was the only way to prevent the United States from becoming a "magnet" for thousands of desperate Haitians. As the government put it in regard to the restraining orders that had temporarily prevented it from returning people to Haiti, "The bar to repatriations was exacerbating the crisis by providing an incentive for Haitians to take to the seas."

Call this the humanitarian incentive argument. Its force was brought home to Bill Clinton the week before his inauguration, when he and his advisers received members of the Central Intelligence Agency in his living room in Little Rock, Arkansas. The CIA officers presented President-elect Clinton with satellite photos taken in Haiti showing thousands of people cutting down trees to make boats. Word had spread in Haiti about his campaign promise, Clinton was told, and if he followed through on it he would be responsible for a hundred thousand people taking to the seas in all manner of craft, up to ten thousand of whom could be expected to die in the crossing. (After the CIA representatives left Clinton and his transition team pondering what to do, Vice-president-elect Al Gore reportedly cut the tension in the room by quipping, "Well, that's a worthy problem.")

One person present at the Little Rock meeting, Deputy National Security Advisor Sandy Berger, would later express doubt about the quality of the CIA's information. Clinton himself, however, was clearly swayed by it. After his presidency was over, it was the humanitarian incentive argument he would invoke as a defence for his actions. "Some of the criticism on the Haitian issue was justified, given the unqualified statements I had made during the campaign," Clinton wrote in his memoirs. But other considerations, he argued, needed to be taken into account:

I wanted to make it easier for Haitians to seek and obtain political asylum in the United States, but was concerned that large numbers of them would perish in trying to get here in rickety boats on the high seas, as about four hundred had done just a week earlier. So, on the advice of our security team, I said that, instead of taking in all the Haitians who could survive the voyage to America, we would beef up our official presence in Haiti and speed up asylum claims there. In the meantime, for safety reasons, we would continue to stop the boats and return the passengers.

It was in the Haitians' own interest, Clinton was saying, for the Coast Guard to pick them up. Despite the appearance otherwise, forcing them to return to Haiti was the most humane thing to do, as it gave people a powerful disincentive to take to the dangerous seas in the first place. According to Clinton, keeping people from leaving Haiti would be a temporary measure until he could restore Aristide to power. (He ultimately did so in the fall of 1994, when, after intense diplomatic efforts and repeated threats of military action, Haitian military leaders resigned just as U.S. forces were airborne en route to Port-au-Prince.)

Clinton's argument that refugee claims could be processed in Haiti was one George Bush had made before him. In neither case did it meet the concerns of critics, who labelled in-country processing "a complete sham." It was not just that Haiti became the only country on earth where in-country resettlement became a substitute for individuals being allowed to leave under their own power. In the program's first year under Bush, of 15,580 people who asked to leave Haiti, 136 were admitted to the United States, an acceptance rate of less than 1 percent. The acceptance rate under Clinton rose to almost 8 percent, but even then critics pointed out that the people most in need of protection would be unlikely to benefit from a process that involved passing roadblocks, presenting and identifying themselves to Haitian security forces before entering U.S. processing centres (in one case located across the street from the national Haitian police headquarters) and then repeating the entire process three times over an eight-month period to obtain all the necessary paperwork. According to Harold Koh, it would be "suicide" for many refugees to go through such a procedure.

There were other problems with the government's position. Throughout the Haitian refugee crisis, critics noted that similar measures were not employed with Cubans. When Cubans took to the sea in boats to escape their island, although they were interdicted by the Coast Guard, they were not returned to Cuba. Instead they were taken to the United States, where they have long received favourable treatment under immigration law. (Among other benefits, Cubans can file for permanent residency after living in the United States for only a year, whether they have been there legally or not.) In 1994 there was an increase in the number of Cuban arrivals. In response, Clinton reduced, but did not eliminate, the amount of favouritism shown to them. Under the so-called "wet foot, dry foot" policy, Cubans who make it to the United States are allowed to stay, whereas those stopped at sea are returned to Cuba. Cubans interdicted at sea, however, are allowed to make asylum claims. At the time of the Haitian refugee crisis, when favouritism toward Cubans was at its height, critics charged that U.S. policy toward Caribbean migrants and refugees exhibited a glaring double standard.

Joe Tringali, one of the lawyers who worked with Koh and Ratner, points out what may be the biggest problem with Clinton and Bush's rationale: it ran together the issues of stopping unseaworthy boats and forced repatriation. These are two separate questions. As Tringali puts it:

Many of these boats I'm sure were not capable of making it to Miami, so I have no doubt that taking them off those boats and bringing them onto the Coast Guard cutters was a humanitarian act. The issue isn't that. The issue is where do they *then* go? Do they go to Guantánamo or to the

United States for screening to see whether or not they are legitimate refugees? Or do they get summarily returned to Haiti? *That's* the real issue. . . . Once they are taken off those boats, should they be given some sort of hearing, or do you just summarily repatriate then and not even hear what [was] their basis for fleeing?

It was a strange form of humanitarianism, Tringali and others pointed out, that involved forcibly returning people to the clutches of a military dictatorship they had fled. More to the point, there were steps Bush and Clinton could have taken to deal with the refugee crisis other than admitting them all to the United States. One possibility was to set up a genuinely humanitarian camp at Guantánamo, run by the United Nations High Commissioner for Refugees or some other non-military organization, where refugees could be screened and the deserving cases resettled in the United States and elsewhere. "Our complaint was not with Guantánamo *per se*, but with the United States military's treatment of refugees there," Koh noted after the case was over. "With enough jawboning, the United States surely could have persuaded other nations in the region—such as Canada, Venezuela, and Mexico—to take their share of refugees while the political crisis in Haiti was being negotiated." In the 1950s, the United States had participated in just such an action on behalf of 180,000 Hungarians. Similarly, in the 1960s and 1970s, mass exoduses of boat people from Cuba had been dealt with without forced repatriations. But there was never any similar effort on behalf of Haitians.

In its brief before the Supreme Court, the UNHCR had predicted that a decision by the United States to return refugees to danger "may well influence, for years to come, the behaviour of other countries." These fears were soon borne out. In November of 1992, six months after George Bush issued his Kennebunkport order, the government of Thailand told the General Assembly of the United Nations that the U.S. policy of repatriating Haitian refugees demonstrated that the principle of first asylum was a "clever ploy" and a "Machiavellian device designed to satisfy and calm the conscience" of Western governments. Shortly after the *Sale* decision came down, Thailand engaged in mass expulsions of thousands of Burmese and Cambodian refugees.

An even more dramatic shift occurred in Tanzania. The East African country has traditionally been one of Africa's most generous refugee-receiving nations: in 1979 it had even extended citizenship to thirty-six thousand Rwandans in an act of mass welcome. But when roughly forty thousand refugees tried to enter Tanzania from Burundi in March of 1995, the Tanzanian government closed its border to prevent half of them from entering, and announced plans to expel all refugees already inside its borders. A key factor that prompted Tanzania to take such a severe step was the example set by the United States. Speaking at a refugee conference six months after the border closure, Tanzania's then foreign minister, Joseph Rwegasira, singled out the U.S. interdiction program as a precedent that had inspired his government. "Citing the example of the Haitian refugees," a conference organizer wrote in summarizing the minister's speech, "[Rwegasira] said that it was a double standard to expect weaker countries to live up to their humanitarian obligations when major powers did not do so whenever their own national rights and interests were at stake."

If incentives were the issue, the United States had provided one to any country looking for an excuse to turn refugees away.

Haitians sailing for the United States today continue to be turned away in large numbers. In the ten-year period between October 1999 and September 2009, the Coast Guard interdicted 17,254 Haitians, slightly less than the 18,230 Cubans stopped during the same period. Whereas Cubans are read a statement inviting them to express any fear of persecution, Haitians are given no such invitation. Instead, Coast Guard personnel decide whether to ask them about persecution according to a procedure known as the shout test. "Although the shout test purportedly allows a person to be interviewed for a credible fear who 'indicates' a fear," Bill Frelick of Amnesty International has written, "in practice the 'shout' nomenclature seems to be closer to the mark. Only those who wave their hands, jump up and down, and shout the loudest—and are recognized as having done such—are even afforded, in theory, a shipboard refugee pre-screening interview."

The result of this process has been similar to that of the 1980s version of interdiction. In 2005, when 1,850 Haitians were interdicted, nine people shouted loud enough to be deemed worthy of a credible-fear interview. Of these, one eventually passed a full interview at Guantánamo and was granted refugee status. Unlike during the 1980s, the tiny number of Haitians who are recognized as refugees today are not permitted to go to the United States, but are resettled in third countries (as are interdicted Cubans). Compared to the 1980s, in recent years there has been less pretense that the United States is not returning refugees to danger. As George W. Bush remarked in 2004, "I have made it abundantly clear to the Coast Guard that we will turn back any refugee that attempts to reach our shore."

Years after the Haitian refugee crisis, Guantánamo Bay would again feature in a major human rights controversy. During the so-called War on Terror that followed the September 11 attacks, suspected members of al-Qaeda and the Taliban were taken to the Cuban facility and classified as "enemy combatants." According to officials in the administration of George W. Bush, they were not subject to Geneva Convention protections regarding prisoners of war. The rationale for bringing War on Terror detainees to Guantánamo was made explicit by Mitt Romney, a 2008 candidate for the Republican presidential nomination, who stated, "I want them on Guantánamo, where they don't get the access to lawyers they get when they're on our soil." Michael Barr says the role Guantánamo played under George W. Bush was foreshadowed by the similar role it played during the Haiti crisis. "The legal and political antecedent of the idea of a law-free zone on Guantánamo today lies in the treatment of Haitian refugees fifteen years ago."

Both during the Haiti crisis and after, a key question about Guantánamo was the issue of its sovereignty. According to the 1903 lease of the base, Cuba retains "ultimate sovereignty" over the facility while the United States enjoys "complete jurisdiction and control." The reference to Cuban sovereignty was used by Clinton and both Bush administrations, father and son, to argue that the U.S. constitution and the rights it upholds do not have legal force at Guantánamo. Critics of this view, however, have noted that the wording of the lease is confusing: the term *sovereignty* is somehow detached from its common meaning, which is "jurisdiction and control." As one observer has put it, it is as if Cuba's sovereignty has somehow become purely "metaphysical."

The ambiguous nature of Guantánamo's sovereignty complicates Hannah Arendt's analysis of the relationship between sovereignty and human rights. Arendt, as we saw, argued that the special vulnerability of refugees was rooted in the division of the globe into sovereign states. Yet in the Haitian refugee crisis, asylum-seekers received better treatment on the U.S. mainland, where U.S. sovereignty is unambiguous, than they did at Guantánamo, where it is not. This possibility is not really allowed for under Arendt's view of sovereignty, which portrays sovereignty not only as something absolute and not given to degrees but also as more of a threat to the rights of refugees the starker and less ambiguous it is.

Arendt, however, was writing in the 1950s, long before Guantánamo ever became a "rights-free zone." An explanation of how the base came to perform this role can be gleaned from the writings of contemporary political scientists, who reject Arendt's monolithic view of sovereignty and prefer to distinguish between its different aspects. It has become common, for example, to distinguish between sovereignty understood as recognition by other states and sovereignty as effective control. The difference between these two aspects of sovereignty can be seen by contrasting Taiwan and Somalia. Because of pressure from China, which claims Taiwan for itself, many states today do not officially recognize Taiwan, which has no seat at the United Nations. The Taiwanese government nevertheless manages to govern its own territory. It thus enjoys sovereignty in the sense of control but not in the form of recognition. Somalia, by contrast, descended into anarchy and civil war in the early 1990s, to the point that many parts of the country came under the control of armed warlords. In 2000, a government in exile was formed, which has spent much of its time in Kenya, and which holds Somalia's seat at the UN. It is a regime that enjoys sovereignty in the form of recognition but not at the level of control.

What is unusual about Guantánamo's lease is that it formally separates sovereign recognition from sovereign control, granting recognition to Cuba and control to the United States. The result has been the creation of a territory where the U.S. government enjoys great power with little accountability; an arrangement that has proven disastrous from the point of view of human rights.

If Arendt's analysis cannot explain everything about the Haitian refugee crisis and its aftermath, much of what she said nevertheless remains prophetic. In one instance this was literal. "We became aware of a right to have rights," Arendt wrote of refugees in 1951, "only when millions of people emerged who had lost and could not regain these rights." Nizar Sassi, a French Guantánamo detainee, could not have made the parallel between Guantánamo prisoners and refugees more explicit when in 2002 he wrote a postcard to his family that contained the only political statement known to evade Guantánamo's mail censors: "If you want a definition of this place, you don't have the right to have rights."

On a broader level, the Haitian refugee crisis illustrates Arendt's claim that universal human rights will not necessarily be enforced by particular sovereign states. It is not just that throughout the case lawyers for the American government argued that the forced-return policy was undertaken "for the purposes of protecting the sovereignty" of the United States. In their decision, the Supreme Court justices who decided the non-return case gave the last word to a lower court judge whose sentiments they felt expressed their own: "This case presents a painfully common situation in which desperate people, convinced that they can no longer remain in their homeland, take desperate measures to escape. Although the human crisis is compelling, there is no solution to be found in a judicial remedy."

Writing about refugees forty years earlier, Arendt had stated that "their plight is not that they are not equal before the law, but that no law exists for them." It was as if the court deliberately set out to confirm Arendt's most bitter and pessimistic claim. Arendt had written that so far as Europe's liberal democracies were concerned, refugees were "the scum of the earth." So far as the law of the United States is concerned, refugees interdicted at sea have the same status. They are human insofar as they are members of our species, but less than human insofar as there is no law to protect them.

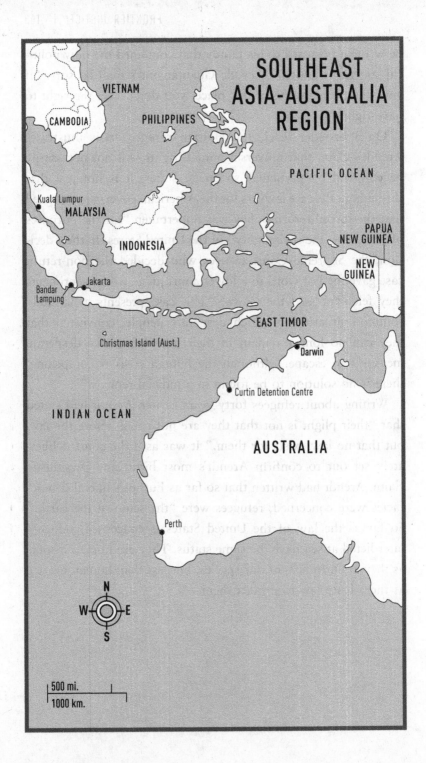

FOUR

THE FATAL SHORE

MOHAMMAD AL GHAZZI HAS SHORT black hair and a caramel complexion. Lines that run across his forehead and down his cheeks look as though they have been chiselled into his face, while a small, trim goatee tapers to a point beneath his lower lip, and bobs up and down as he speaks. In a past life, when Al Ghazzi was in his early twenties, he owned a furniture shop in Nasiriyah, Iraq. Nasiriyah is a city where political life has long been tumultuous. In 1991 it was home to a revolt against the government of Saddam Hussein that was violently repressed. Al Ghazzi, however, shied away from politics, devoting himself to the furniture business instead. Sales were usually brisk enough for him to keep four people on staff, to help out with woodworking and upholstery around the shop.

One night in 1994 Al Ghazzi was at home sleeping in the bedroom he shared with his raven-haired wife, Raghed. Their three-year old daughter, Reyam, was asleep in her own bedroom. At four o'clock in the morning the family was woken by the sound of their front door crashing in. The master bedroom was suddenly crowded with soldiers yelling "Stop!" at Mohammad and Raghed before they could move. Al Ghazzi was dragged outside, where there were more soldiers all along his street and on the roof of his one-storey house, acting under the command of an older man in civilian clothes. Al Ghazzi's hands and feet were bound and he was pushed into the back of a utility vehicle that contained two other shackled men. As he was driven away, a soldier placed his shoes on Al Ghazzi's head in a local gesture of contempt.

Al Ghazzi was taken to a prison, where he was interrogated for over a week. The interrogations were carried out by the same older man who had directed the arrest, who turned out to be a general in the security forces, and who kept Al Ghazzi blind-folded throughout the proceedings. The general's questions revolved around the Islamic Dawa Party, or Al-Dawa (The Call), a popular Islamic fundamentalist party that opposed the government; its armed wing had more than once tried to assassinate Saddam Hussein. Al Ghazzi had an older brother who belonged to Al-Dawa's militant wing. He had disappeared four months previously, almost certainly at the hands of the security forces. While Al Ghazzi himself worshipped at a mosque affiliated with Al-Dawa and sympathized with some of its goals, he was not involved with its militant wing. His captor, however, refused to believe him, and insisted he was involved in an impending Al-Dawa operation.

"Your brother came to your shop with his friend. We know you are Al-Dawa. What did you discuss?"

"Nothing."

"We know they came to see you."

"I let them into the shop, but they had tea while I worked. I didn't really talk to them."

"You were planning a suicide bombing. Where will it happen?"

"Please, I don't know . . . about Al-Dawa or any bombing."

The questioning continued for hours. To indicate his unhappiness with Al Ghazzi's answers, the general had his men beat him. When that did not elicit the right responses, electric shocks were applied to Al Ghazzi's tongue and penis. Al Ghazzi lost consciousness and was dragged back to his cell, left for an hour, then carried on a blanket back to the interrogation room. This time his blindfold was removed. After his eyes adjusted to the light he saw Raghed and Reyam sitting across from him. Raghed began crying when she saw his battered appearance.

The general made it known that if Al Ghazzi refused to confess, the next round of interrogation would be carried out on Raghed. Al Ghazzi told the general that if he let Raghed go, he would tell him what he wanted to know. Raghed was taken away, and half an hour later one of the soldiers dialled Al Ghazzi's number and thrust the receiver at him. After Raghed confirmed she had made it home all right, Al Ghazzi turned to his jailers.

"Bring me a blank piece of paper. I'll sign it, and you can fill in anything you want."

Every refugee journey has an unhappy beginning, but each beginning is unhappy in its own way. The events that set Al Ghazzi's flight in motion began even before his arrest, when the general fastened on to the belief that he was plotting against the government. In keeping with this belief, the general made Al Ghazzi write out the details of the bomb plot that had featured in his interrogation. Al Ghazzi was then taken to another prison, 370 kilometres to the northwest, in Baghdad, where he was housed in a crowded cell with twenty other men. What little food prisoners received was barely edible, and dysentery and other diseases were rife throughout the prison population. Al Ghazzi's situation was made worse by liver damage caused during his torture. His primary torment, however, was psychological: there was no way to let Raghed know where he was, or even that he was still alive. He slowly became disengaged from his surroundings, shuffling around his cell in a mute and lifeless manner when he bothered to move at all.

Two years after his arrest, Al Ghazzi was sitting in his crowded cell one day when the door swung open. The guards dragged him outside and took him to a processing area, as if they were going to release him. Al Ghazzi assumed it was a trick. But after he and several other prisoners were rushed out into the streets by guards yelling "Go, go, go!" he found himself blinking in the unfamiliar Baghdad sunlight, wondering if he might actually be a free man.

"Are you from the prison?"

A cab had stopped on the busy street. The door was open and the driver was addressing him. Confused, Al Ghazzi wondered how he knew where he had come from. Eventually he realized that his prison clothes, not to mention his dirty and unshaven appearance, made it obvious.

"Yeah, I was in prison."

"Then get in."

"Sorry, I don't have any money."

"Just get in!"

The driver had taken pity on him. Al Ghazzi directed him to the other side of the city, where one of his brothers lived. He would later discover that his release was due to the United Nations, which had imposed sanctions against Iraq. The sanctions were meant to force Saddam to abandon his chemical and nuclear weapons program, but a secondary goal was to pressure Iraq about its human rights record. In order to improve appearances on that score, the government decided to release 390 political prisoners who had been accused of belonging to Al-Dawa and another militant Islamic group, Hezbollah. To underscore their president's magnanimity, the government released Al Ghazzi and the rest on April 28, 1996, Saddam Hussein's birthday.

Al Ghazzi returned to Nasiriyah for a tearful reconciliation with Raghed. In prison he had felt a paralyzing numbness, as if he had been buried up to his neck in sand. Seeing Raghed and Reyam again, it was as though the sand began to drain away. Later, after he and Raghed had a second child, a boy named Ali, it felt as though normal life was on the verge of returning. But then the general who had arrested him appeared in the doorway of Al Ghazzi's shop. He announced that Al Ghazzi would need to start paying him if he wanted to keep the business. Al Ghazzi felt a bolt of dread at the thought of working for his torturer. But he reached his absolute breaking point when Raghed was taken in for questioning. She was interrogated about a brother who lived in Washington, D.C., which the general took as a sign she opposed the regime. After Raghed was released, shaken but unharmed, she and Al Ghazzi began planning their escape from Iraq.

Al Ghazzi's brother put them in touch with a people-smuggler. After taking a taxi to Baghdad, Mohammad, Raghed and the children had a late-night meeting with a Kurdish man who piled them all into his car and drove them to the northern, predominantly Kurdish part of Iraq. After a brief river crossing, they were able to slip into Syria and make their way to the outskirts of Damascus, where they rented a tiny apartment, living off savings and money sent to them by Raghed's brother in the United States.

Although Raghed had a sister in Syria, permanently relocating there was not a real option. Syria was controlled by the same Baath Party that ruled Iraq—"left and right of the same shoes," as Al Ghazzi puts it—and the Syrian government was notorious for returning refugees to Iraq. Refugees lived in constant fear of "the intimidating presence of all-powerful state security forces and an omnipresent intelligence network," as one refugee agency put it. Even if Al Ghazzi and his family avoided deportation, the

Syrian government did not grant Iraqis residency visas. Having no visa meant Mohammad and Raghed could not legally work and Reyam and Ali could not go to school. The Al Ghazzis thus lived with one eye constantly over their shoulder, petrified of attracting the attention of the authorities. When Raghed had an unplanned pregnancy and gave birth to their third child, Mohammad Jr., their situation became even more precarious. As Al Ghazzi recalls, living illegally in Syria in a state of permanent uncertainty felt like nothing so much as "waiting for death."

There was one possible way out. It was to travel to the West and make a refugee claim. This was a dangerous option involving many unknowns, but Al Ghazzi heard about other Iraqis who had managed to leave Syria that way. They sent word back about the people-smugglers they hired and the routes they had taken, and Al Ghazzi heard second-hand reports about Iraqis being accepted as refugees in Canada, Australia and Scandinavia. "I heard about Canada but it's too far, it costs too much," he says. The more he heard about Australia, though, the more it appealed to him. "They appreciate people, respect people . . . I heard something is special about Australia."

A willingness to admit refugees was not the only special thing about Australia. Al Ghazzi discovered that smugglers took people there via Malaysia. An officially Islamic state, Malaysia granted visitors from other Muslim countries short-term visas upon arrival. This made all the difference for someone in Al Ghazzi's position. If he tried to fly directly to the West he would be asked to present a visa at the boarding gate at Damascus airport, which he would be unable to produce. Getting on a flight to Malaysia, on the other hand, would require only a fake Iraqi passport. And those were not hard to find in the back streets of Damascus.

Late at night in their tiny living room, Mohammad and Raghed had an emotional conversation about what to do. Al Ghazzi thought that he should try to reach Australia on his own and then bring over her and the children. They had no idea what would happen, and he wanted to bear the risk of going first. Raghed hated the thought of their being apart, but the idea of staying in Syria equally filled her with terror. Their conversation ended with her weeping at their lack of positive options.

Reyam overheard her mother crying and came out to ask Mohammad what was going on. He tried to explain his plan in a way that would not alarm her, but all she understood was that he was going away.

"Does this mean we'll never live together again?"

"No, honey. We'll never be apart again, once I get to Australia."

With some effort he managed to convince Reyam not to worry. Raghed took longer, but eventually she agreed to his plan as well. He threw himself into making the necessary arrangements. He knew two other Iraqi men in similar predicaments, one from Nasiriyah, the other from the smaller city of Kut, and the three of them decided to make the journey together. When they arrived at the airport they saw another group of Iraqis in line for the same flight, and realized they would not be the only refugees on board. Al Ghazzi and his companions soon discovered that the other group had been given the same vague instructions that they had: look for smugglers at the airport in Malaysia, with whom they could make arrangements about getting to Australia.

Al Ghazzi was nervous from the moment the flight set down in Kuala Lumpur, Malaysia's sprawling capital. When he presented his passport at customs, the officer eyed it with suspicion and ordered Al Ghazzi out of the line. He was taken to a detention area, where he was soon joined by seven other Iraqis from the same flight. After two hours he was taken to an interview room and questioned by customs.

"Why are you in Malaysia?" the officer asked.

"Holiday."

"So you have money, then."

Al Ghazzi produced the wad of American dollars he was travelling with, money that had been given to him by his American brother-in-law. Eventually he managed to convince the officer that he was not planning to stay in Malaysia, and was free to go. Soon he was joined in the airport's vast arrivals hall by all but one of the Iraqis from his flight, who had been held back for using a fake passport. Looking out at the unfamiliar surroundings, Asian business travellers striding past advertisements for Samsung, the thought of finding a people-smuggler here seemed extremely unlikely. If he had managed to convince Raghed and Reyam that his plan made sense, he had never really convinced himself. Now he realized just how desperate it had been. As if there had ever been any chance of his reaching Australia when his real fate, he now realized, was to lose his mind inside an airport in Malaysia.

A Middle Eastern man stepped out of the crowd and strode toward them. "Australia?" he asked in Arabic. Al Ghazzi was overcome with relief and joy and an overwhelming sense of gratitude directed at no one in particular. He fell into negotiating prices and travel plans as if he were haggling over furniture back in Nasiriyah. Everyone negotiated their own price individually. In Al Ghazzi's case, the smuggler eventually agreed on US$2,000. As Al Ghazzi and the other arrivals from Damascus followed the man out to the parking lot, they passed knots of other Iraqi Arabs and Kurds outside the airport, making similar arrangements with other Middle Eastern travellers. Rather than a place of terror, the airport now struck him as a gateway to freedom, where people like him could start to live again.

Al Ghazzi's group was taken to an apartment maintained by half a dozen Iraqi smugglers. It was crowded with dozens of other Iraqis who were also trying to reach Australia. After Al

Ghazzi's group arrived, one of the smugglers collected their passports and left. When he returned a few hours later, each passport had somehow acquired a stamp that would allow the bearer to enter Indonesia. The next day, Al Ghazzi and his companions were on a flight to Jakarta. Acting on the smugglers' instructions, they each placed fifty American dollars in their passports before presenting them at Indonesian customs, which allowed them to pass through without incident. After clearing customs they were met by a Kurdish man named Omid, who took them first to a Jakarta hotel where they stayed for six nights, and then to a small port town on the Indonesian peninsula of Sumatra.

Omid was friendly and talkative. "We're going to get a big boat for you," he would often say. When asked when they might leave, "tomorrow, tomorrow" was always his answer. But when tomorrow would come, nothing would happen. Every five or six days the smugglers would move Al Ghazzi and the other Iraqis to a new apartment, a step they said was necessary to avoid detection. Al Ghazzi and the others were strongly discouraged from going outside, and with nothing to do they grew increasingly irritated and argued with each other. Finally, after a month of waiting, Al Ghazzi's group was woken before dawn and driven to a harbour where carloads of Iraqis were being assembling into a group of 180 people. There Al Ghazzi saw the "big boat" they had been promised: a broken-down fishing vessel that was barely seaworthy. People rushed on board, jamming themselves into the cabin and filling the deck before still more passengers climbed onto the crowded roof. As they cast off and slowly began chugging out of the harbour, they were accompanied by an Indonesian navy vessel, one of several signs to Al Ghazzi that, despite the smugglers' claims to the contrary, they were working hand in hand with the Indonesian authorities.

After half an hour the navy ship turned back, leaving the fishing vessel's small Indonesian crew to guide the boat out to open sea. Their destination now was Christmas Island, an Australian Indian Ocean Territory located 1,500 kilometres northwest of continental Australia. According to Michelle Dimasi, a Swinburne University PhD student who does fieldwork there, Christmas Island's unusual status has long been a pull factor for its Australian residents. "People will come to maybe escape a bad marriage or something that's happened to them. It's a good change because it's still part of Australia, but it's not."

In the early 1990s Christmas Island began to exert a similar pull on asylum-seekers. Between 1992 and 1998 an average of 115 people arrived there every year in treacherous boat crossings similar to Al Ghazzi's. At first they came from Vietnam, Cambodia and other parts of East Asia. But in 1997, following the rise of an "Iran for Iranians" movement, Iran clamped down on its large refugee population. As a result the boats increasingly began to carry people like Al Ghazzi, Muslim refugees from Iraq and Afghanistan whose only avenue of escape was via Malaysia. The number of boats also increased, so that in 1999 the number of people arriving at Christmas Island rose to 906, its highest number to that date. The smugglers who organized the crossings scrambled to meet the rise in demand. Al Ghazzi overheard someone say that Indonesian fishermen were offered as much as US$1,000 to work as crew. That was enough to make the journey worthwhile to them even when they were caught, which they usually were, and ensured there was no shortage of boats.

During Al Ghazzi's crossing the ocean was rough. Many passengers vomited with seasickness, and as the journey progressed the ship took on dangerous amounts of water. Al Ghazzi was packed so tight with other people that he could neither move nor fall asleep, and children screamed every time the boat was rocked by a wave. At night the swells grew so great that the boat nearly capsized, and Al Ghazzi feared for his life more than once, wondering why he had ever embarked on such a dangerous voyage. "Honestly, when I think about it, [boarding] was like someone commit suicide, but in different way."

The next day the sea was calm. Early in the afternoon, thirty-six hours after departure, the crew brought the boat to a halt. They told the passengers it was too rocky to go all the way to Christmas Island. Instead, they would remain offshore and attract the attention of the Australian military, which patrolled the area. The passengers began waving their arms and yelling, "Help, refugees!" Within half an hour they had boarded an Australian navy vessel that took them to Christmas Island. Al Ghazzi and the others were taken to a sports centre where a hot meal and a cot were waiting for each of them. Al Ghazzi marvelled at how the Australians seemed to know in advance exactly how many meals and beds to provide, until someone told him that their boat had been tracked by satellite. When he drifted off to sleep, it was with a feeling of exhaustion and relief. He had taken the biggest risk of his life and survived. Raghed and the children were not with him but they would be in time. His crossing was the low point. Everything from here was up.

Al Ghazzi spent several days on Christmas Island. He knew something was not quite right when he was not allowed to contact his family. Then he and the other arrivals were herded onto a plane and flown to the mainland. As it prepared for descent, Al Ghazzi could see that they were landing at a remote location. They were transferred onto buses and driven through the desert until they came to a ramshackle collection of trailers surrounded on all sides by barbed wire and a vast expanse of red earth. Curtin Detention Centre, as it was called, was a converted air force base. Al Ghazzi and the other residents soon discovered that many of its basic facilities were broken: the fencing did not keep out snakes and the toilets and showers leaked, creating flows of open sewage. The camp was also located in one of the hottest parts of Australia, and lining up for food and other outdoor activities required standing for hours in the relentless sun.

When Al Ghazzi arrived the atmosphere in the camp was tense. Curtin was run by Australasian Correctional Management, or ACM, a U.S.-owned firm that operated half a dozen immigration detention facilities in remote parts of Australia. ACM camps had many features of a prison, including that of detainees being referred to by number rather than by name. Detainees were also frequently searched during the day or woken up at night, when flashlights were shone in their eyes during head counts. Most troubling to Al Ghazzi was that detainees were not allowed to make contact with the outside world, even to let their families know they had survived the journey from Indonesia.

Curtin had come into being three months before Al Ghazzi's arrival. Its rationale was to deter "unauthorized arrivals," those who tried to enter Australia without visas. Ninety percent of its occupants were Iraqi, the rest predominantly Afghan. Most of them had been seeking refuge in a country that would not return them to persecution. Curtin, however, was no one's idea of a refuge. Unlike convicted criminals, who know the length of their sentences, the inmates at Curtin were not told how long they would be detained. This created an environment of powerlessness, which manifested itself in various ways. Parents in the camp were unable to provide for the needs of their children, and would succumb to depression. After seeing their parents lose interest in their surroundings or release their stress through violence, child detainees lost their ability to concentrate or to trust adults. As one Australian psychiatrist later put it, "You couldn't really design an environment more destructive to child development than immigration detention."

The stress and uncertainty of indefinite detention were exacerbated by ACM staff. Although detainees were interviewed upon arrival to determine whether they were eligible to make refugee claims, ACM employees would routinely not tell new arrivals that they had been found eligible. In other cases they would withhold crucial information, such as the fact that a detainee had a right to legal assistance. Many new arrivals were able to glean such information only after speaking to camp residents who had already filed their own claims. Even when detainees were able to lodge a claim, they were often not told what was happening with their file. Questions would be met with insults and criticisms of their religious beliefs. Those who pressed for information were threatened with being returned to Iraq or Afghanistan, a terrifying prospect for those like Al Ghazzi who were fleeing persecution.

Curtin was set in an extreme landscape where wind and erosion had long ago removed most of the soil and vegetation. Over time, something similar happened to the sanity of the people made to live there. Gradually, it too was stripped away. The longer people were incarcerated, the more unwell they became. Eria Clapton, an Anglican minister who worked with detainees, observed that large numbers of them needed to be medicated in order to perform daily tasks. "By the time they have been in detention for six months they are probably taking sleeping pills and tranquillizers," Clapton noted. "Longer than 12 months and they are seriously at risk; they may be suicidal and suffering extreme anxiety symptoms . . . because they are in such a state of mental and physical anxiety about being sent back."

Three months after Al Ghazzi arrived, a group of Iraqi detainees decided they could not put up with camp conditions anymore. They organized a hunger strike that quickly grew to include about three hundred people. Participants sat in the yard under a large banner they had created depicting Saddam Hussein. He was shown thanking Australia's Immigration Department for jailing his critics. Occasionally a member of the group would rise and begin a chant: "Where are human rights? Where is freedom? We want freedom!" The most committed participants, a group of twelve to twenty men, jabbed sewing needles through their lips and sewed them shut to symbolize their helplessness.

To defuse the crisis, the government brought in a prominent member of Australia's Muslim community, Dr. Mohammed Taha Alsalami. After travelling nine hours from Sydney, Alsalami was shocked to see Curtin's "subhuman" conditions. As he walked around, the camp residents besieged him with over four hundred messages to pass on to their families. He tore pages out of his diary for people to write phone numbers on, while others passed him addresses scrawled on pieces of discarded cardboard. Alsalami would later contact the Sydney-based family of a Kuwaiti detainee, who collectively broke down in tears. After not hearing from their relative for months, they had assumed that he had died during the crossing from Indonesia, and had held his funeral ten months earlier.

Conditions improved after the hunger strike. Al Ghazzi and other detainees were allowed to fax a form letter to their families informing them they were alive. Detainees were also granted local telephone access, the toilets and showers were fixed, and children were allowed to leave the camp for volleyball outings. New arrivals, however, continued to be denied information that would allow them to file a successful refugee claim, and stress among detainees remained high. Camp residents swallowed bleach or tried to hang themselves in four separate suicide attempts.

Eleven months after he arrived, Al Ghazzi was sitting in his trailer when he was called outside. The camp manager told him he had been granted a temporary protection visa and would be allowed to leave. Al Ghazzi felt no relief or excitement at the news. In Iraq, at least, he never placed any hope in the government. In Australia he had allowed himself to hope for better, only to have his expectations dashed. "[Curtin] destroyed us from the beginning," he says. "Honestly, I feel dead. I'm not active anymore, not existing in this life."

Al Ghazzi moved to Perth, the largest city in Western Australia. During his first phone call to Raghed she broke down at the sound of his voice. Then Reyam came on the line. Al Ghazzi had hoped his call would have a reassuring effect on her, but she sounded withdrawn. He asked what was wrong. "You lied to me," she said.

Al Ghazzi was stunned. What had he possibly lied about?

"You said that when you got to Australia we'd be together. We'd have a normal life."

Al Ghazzi tried to convince her that it wouldn't be long now. But inwardly, he was crushed. No matter how bad things had got in Iraq and Syria, his daughter had never lost faith in him. If Curtin took that away, it would break him in a way even the general had not. It was if he was sinking into the sand again, and could feel it rising above his head.

Perth is a quiet city of sprawling suburbs. After settling there Al Ghazzi resolved not to succumb to despair. "I said look, this is good reason to live again. Is good point to start again." He got a job as a farm labourer and then as a kitchen hand. His overwhelming preoccupation was Raghed and the children. During long-distance calls to Syria, he and Raghed would discuss how the family could reunite. She insisted that she and the children had to make their own boat crossing. Al Ghazzi was shocked to hear her suggest it. He had barely made it travelling by himself. The thought of Raghed doing it with the children filled him with fear. "Are you crazy?" he snapped at her. "It's *dangerous*."

But Raghed would not be swayed. "You know what Syria is like," she would say during their many conversations. She told him that the situation in Damascus had deteriorated. The security forces had finally caught up with her family. Policemen had

come around to the apartment and told her they knew her husband was gone, and threatened her with extortion. As a result,
she and her sister were now planning to spend their life savings
on a collective voyage to Australia.

Mohammad begged her to reconsider. "Please. Think of the
children. You could all be killed."

"If it's a choice between living this way and dying, then I
would rather die."

Al Ghazzi was torn, but eventually stopped trying to talk her
out of it. "Part of me accept it, and part of me refuse it, but I
have no way to stop it." When Raghed asked him to borrow
money to help finance their trip, he reluctantly agreed.

Raghed did not know it at the time, but the Indian Ocean
was not the only thing standing between her and Australia. In
August of 2001, a Norwegian cargo ship, MV *Tampa*, responded
to a telex from Australian coastal officials. The telex directed
the *Tampa* to rescue 438 asylum-seekers from a floundering
Indonesian vessel near Christmas Island. After the last member
of the predominantly Afghan group was hoisted onto the
Tampa's deck, the ship's captain, Arne Rinnan, made course for
Indonesia. This immediately caused a protest from his passengers, some of whom threatened to throw themselves overboard
if he continued. They had seen Indonesia, they said, and knew
they could not survive there. In response, Rinnan set a new
course for Christmas Island. He soon received a call from
Australian Immigration officials, who told him he would be
prosecuted for people-smuggling if he did not turn around and
resume course for Indonesia. When Rinnan stopped the ship just
outside Christmas Island's twelve-mile exclusion zone, it triggered the exchange of many angry words between Australia,
Indonesia, Norway and the *Tampa*'s bridge. Finally, three days
after picking up the asylum-seekers, with food and medical supplies running low, Rinnan entered Australian waters. His ship

was soon boarded by Special Air Service commandos who brought it under Australian control.

Australia's prime minister at the time was John Howard. In justifying his government's actions, Howard said he wanted to send a message to people thinking of coming to Australia. "We simply cannot allow a situation to develop where Australia is seen around the world as a country of easy destination." Two weeks later, Howard stepped up his efforts. He announced that Christmas Island and other remote territories would be "excised" from Australia's migration zone. People who arrived on Christmas Island or other excised places would not be permitted to apply for any type of Australian visa. If they filed a refugee claim, they would be sent to places such as Papua New Guinea and Nauru, a desolate Pacific micro-state, where their claims would be processed and those deemed refugees resettled in third countries. If such a claim were rejected, unlike those filed within Australia, there would be no way to appeal it.

Howard's new policy was called the Pacific Solution. By the time it was announced in September of 2001, Raghed and her siblings had already bought tickets to Malaysia. Even if they had wanted to turn back, it was too late. Raghed thus left for Malaysia as she had planned. Travelling with her was her sister as well as her brother and her brother-in-law, who had recently made their own flight to Syria from Iraq. Between them the four adults had ten children in tow. Mohammad coached them on what to expect in Malaysia and Indonesia, and kept them in his thoughts as they landed in Kuala Lumpur. From there, unlike Al Ghazzi, they had to reach Indonesia by boat. Al Ghazzi was in constant touch with Raghed on her cellphone as she and her family made the dangerous crossing to Indonesia and waited for a second boat in the port city of Bandar Lampung. Finally, the night before they were scheduled to sail for Christmas Island, Al Ghazzi had a nightmare in which he saw the children drowning at sea. He awoke with a start and called Raghed in a panic. This time, he was the one in tears who needed reassurance. "It's okay, it's okay," she said, "we're still here. Don't worry, we'll be together soon."

When Raghed and her relatives finally made their way to the beach where they were to depart, they saw that the boat the smugglers were using was a rotting old fishing vessel. It was in even worse condition than the one Mohammad had described. It was also going to be even more crowded. The smugglers had promised two boats but delivered only one, onto which they were now herding two boatloads of people, more than four hundred passengers from Iraq, Afghanistan and Iran. After seeing the ship's cracked and decaying condition, some of them tried to get their money back. Their protests resulted in Indonesian police pointing guns at them. Working under the smugglers' command, they ordered the protestors aboard the barely seaworthy vessel.

When the boat departed, it was so low in the water that the crew had trouble drawing anchor. The boat smelled of fresh paint, which made some of the passengers sick. Everyone had been promised life jackets, but there were only enough for sixty people. Several hours out of port, a group of two dozen passengers flagged down a passing fishing vessel. They were so convinced that the boat was going to sink that they paid the fishing boat captain US$100 to take them back to Indonesia. As the remaining passengers watched the fishing boat pull away, more than one prayed to Allah for reassurance that they were not making a terrible mistake.

As the ship cleared the Sundra Strait and reached the ocean, the waves grew rough, and it started to rain. Then, thirty hours from port, the engine broke down. The water pumps it had been powering were now dead. The crew told the passengers to throw their luggage overboard. People began frantically bailing water using their hands, dishes, anything. The boat was pounded by waves and lashed by hard sluices of rain. Then there was a roar as the ship flipped and broke apart. People were clutching each other, praying and screaming. Some managed to jump clear of the wreckage, but hundreds of others were trapped inside the hull. Among them were three pregnant women, one of whom went into stress-induced labour as the ship went down.

A hundred people survived the breakup of the ship. But as day turned to night, most of them gradually succumbed to exhaustion and were pulled beneath the waves. Those who could find pieces of wood or bodies to clutch onto spent hours treading water. One survivor later said it was as if the gate to hell had opened beneath them. Bodies bobbed to the surface after being bitten by fish. A shark came into view, only to swim away. The body of a baby floated among the wreckage, still attached to its mother by the umbilical cord.

Twenty-two hours after the sinking, an Indonesian fishing boat came across the passengers' luggage. Its crew realized there had to be a sinking nearby, and spent hours looking for survivors. But as the fishermen came across bodies floating in the water, most of them turned out to be dead. In the end, only forty-five survivors were recovered. Al Ghazzi's family was not among them.

When he heard the news, Al Ghazzi had a nervous breakdown. He can recall being hospitalized, but not what happened after that. "I didn't see for seven days, eight days. It's like a big hammer on my head. I don't see anything. I feel everything is dark; everything is gone."

In the aftermath of the sinking, Al Ghazzi asked Immigration officials if he could go to Indonesia. Like many people who lose relatives in large-scale disasters, he wanted to speak to the remaining survivors to find out exactly how his family died. Eyewitness accounts are known to make survivors feel closer to their loved ones and to help the grieving process begin. Four unidentified bodies had also been recovered from the wreckage. If they were members of his family, Al Ghazzi would be able to identify them and arrange a Muslim burial.

Al Ghazzi's temporary visa did not permit return travel outside Australia, but he hoped the government might make an exception given his circumstances. His request was denied. If he left Australia, he was told, he would not be allowed to return. Al Ghazzi was thus left to try to stave off despair as best he could on his own. Among other tasks he set for himself was to stay busy with work and to try to learn English.

Through these and other projects, a new social network began to form around Al Ghazzi. An important early member of it was Sue Hoffman. Hoffman, who wears glasses and has a frizzy mane of dark brown hair, is a former investigator for the Western Australian tax office. In 2001 she grew "bored and fed up with accounting," as she puts it, and started doing community work with refugees, which she found she enjoyed. Al Ghazzi was just another one of the refugees she had met until she helped arrange an interview he gave to a newspaper reporter. The day of the interview saw Hoffman sitting beside Al Ghazzi on a café patio as he spoke to the reporter through an interpreter.

As she heard Al Ghazzi talk about his tragedy for the first time, Hoffman was struck by its scope. His family had died fifteen months previously, and Al Ghazzi was clearly still in mourning. "This overwhelming grief was palpable, and you just wanted to take it off him," Hoffman recalls. Yet she was equally struck by the polite and respectful way he dealt with people. If anyone had an excuse to become self-absorbed or bitter, Al Ghazzi did. Yet he had refused to allow that to happen.

Hoffman and Al Ghazzi eventually struck up a friendship. After one of the smugglers who ran the syndicate responsible for Raghed's voyage was arrested in Sweden and brought to Australia to face charges, Hoffman raised enough money for her, Al Ghazzi and two other Iraqi men whose families had drowned to fly to Brisbane to watch the trial. The trial resulted in a conviction, which Al Ghazzi welcomed, but it did not bring a sense of closure. "They don't do it for us. They do it for themselves," he recalls. "They talking about law: 'They break law, they break law.' . . . They don't say anything about us."

If the smuggler's trial was mainly concerned with the issue of border enforcement, this was reflective of the wider debate over refugee issues in Australia. People like Al Ghazzi who made desperate sea crossings invariably arrived without visas. They were thus often labelled "queue-jumpers" in the press. The label was inaccurate, as it was not actually illegal for a genuine refugee, as opposed to an economic migrant, to arrive without travel papers. Al Ghazzi and other refugees, however, were often criticized by people who did not seem to understand their situation. Six weeks after Al Ghazzi arrived, a Western Australian senator sent out a press release describing asylum-seekers as "criminals" and "law-breakers." The release went on to summarize the view of the senator's constituents. "Several of our callers have questioned the morality of the male refugees for abandoning their wives and children in their poverty stricken war-torn countries and for using their families' life savings to escape to a life of comparative comfort."

Sue Hoffman hated the "queue-jumper" label. If Australians got to know people like Al Ghazzi, she felt, they would see just how misguided and misinformed it was. But as it stood, Hoffman knew that the fact that fourteen members of Al Ghazzi's family had died en route to Australia would not generate any sympathy for him from Immigration officials. For this reason, when Al Ghazzi had an interview to determine whether he would be granted permanent residency, Hoffman offered to provide moral and practical support by accompanying him as a transcriber. On the day of the interview things proceeded normally, until Al Ghazzi mentioned the death of Raghed and the children.

The Immigration officer replied offhandedly, "Many people have claimed they had relatives on that boat, more than it could carry."

Hoffman was taken aback by the insensitivity. "The room just went quiet. We were all shocked," she recalls. Al Ghazzi, for his part, felt wounded. "That hurt me so much," he says. "I don't think, if you haven't lost your family, you will say you lost your family. There is no point."

When the decision came back, it was negative. The official who had interviewed Al Ghazzi had based his decision on what he saw as Al Ghazzi's lack of credibility. In his report, he wrote that although Al Ghazzi claimed to have lost his family at sea, there was no record of his mentioning their deaths to the Department of Immigration.

Al Ghazzi and Hoffman were dumbfounded. Al Ghazzi had been in contact with Immigration many times about his family's deaths. This had been the case ever since he had asked to go to Indonesia, a request he made through Immigration. During the height of his grief, Al Ghazzi had also come across a newspaper story about animal rights and stormed into an Immigration office shouting about it. "I went to Immigration, I put it in the table, I said, 'Look, you're looking for animal rights, and you kill people! That's too pathetic!'" Immigration officials responded by seeking assurances he was not going to kill himself or set off a bomb. "I said, 'What bomb? I want my right.'" Yet now it was if the entire episode had never happened.

Al Ghazzi's lawyer filed a freedom of information request to obtain Al Ghazzi's immigration file. When it came back it indicated that Al Ghazzi had informed Immigration of his family's deaths on seven separate occasions. Hoffman says, "The person asking the questions had suggested that Mohammad may have been lying because there was nothing on his file, but there was lots of evidence on his file." The most charitable explanation was that the deciding officer had made a terrible mistake in reviewing Al Ghazzi's paperwork. Regardless, Al Ghazzi was now a failed refugee claimant in the eyes of the law.

The only possible option was to file an appeal. If it failed, it would be the end of Al Ghazzi's Australian journey. By this time, as part of his vow to begin life again, Al Ghazzi had begun seeing a woman named Cherie whom he had met at a garage sale, and she accompanied him to his hearing. It took place in an office in downtown Perth, where Al Ghazzi would be interviewed over a video hookup to Melbourne.

Cherie was nervous and squeezed his hand. Al Ghazzi, for his part, was stoic. For a long time, he had had to fight. To make it to Australia; to be released from detention; to have his family's death acknowledged. He didn't know if he had the energy to keep fighting anymore. "I feel dead. I'm not active anymore and I feel I'm not existing in this life. I'm just waiting for a time to go."

There was movement on the video screen. A member of the Refugee Review Tribunal was looking at them from Melbourne. She began the proceedings by addressing Al Ghazzi.

"Mr. Al Ghazzi, I'm sorry for your loss."

Al Ghazzi was struck by the greeting. Up until now, Australia had refused to accept the reality of his family's death. But here was a representative of the government acknowledging what he had been through. Eventually the tribunal would rule that Al Ghazzi should be recognized as a refugee, which was not a small event in his life. Yet what Al Ghazzi remembers even more than the decision was the way the member first spoke to him.

"When she said that, honestly, I just feel all the Australian people [are] around me and catch me and give me big hug. And I feel my tears go down by themselves."

Mohammad Al Ghazzi arrived in Australia when it had the most severe asylum system in the Western world. In Australia at the turn of the century, asylum was seen primarily as a border-enforcement issue. The government's overriding goal was to reduce the number of people arriving by boat. The most controversial measure in that regard, mandatory detention, was introduced by the left-wing Labour Party in 1992. John Howard's right-wing Liberal Party then added other elements in the late 1990s, such as temporary protection visas for refugees and contracting out the management of detention camps to ACM. In 2002 the government achieved its goal when the number of boat arrivals sank to zero. The same year saw Curtin close following a riot and further instances of self-harm. Three years later many of the most extreme policies were revised. Among other changes, after 2005 families with children were detained in the community, and people incarcerated for more than two years had their cases investigated. These and other modifications were a result of a revolt by backbench members of the governing Liberal Party. One of the MPs involved said he was motivated by the realization that if Australia's refugee system had been in place during the 1940s, it would have turned away Jews fleeing Hitler's Germany. Five years later, in 2010, the Pacific Solution was called into question when the High Court of Australia ruled that asylum-seekers on Christmas Island were entitled to the same protections as those on the mainland.

Between 1992 and 2005, refugees in Australia were known to be incarcerated longer than serious criminals. The difference between the two groups was underscored by an unidentified refugee who addressed an inquiry into mandatory detention, which he had experienced for five years: "I have been in detention. I got a paper and there was a big article about the dangerous man who was a rapist in Adelaide. He had raped three women, but he was jailed about four years with parole after three years. This is your law—this man is a criminal, he is a serious offence against women, but he has only been jailed for four years. For me I don't know what I have done after five years. I am still waiting and waiting."

This refugee was not the first person to observe the lower status that refugees occupied relative to criminals. Hannah Arendt had made a similar observation fifty years before, when she noted that a refugee was the one type of person who would not lose, but actually *gain*, legal rights by committing a crime. As Arendt put it, "Even if he is penniless he can now get a lawyer, complain about his jailers, and he will be listened to respectfully. He is no longer the scum of the earth, but important enough to be informed of all the details of the law under which he will be tried." Twenty-first-century Australia was one of the world's most advanced democratic states. But even there, refugees could slip back into the condition Arendt diagnosed in an earlier age.

The world's eyes were on Australia when it incarcerated refugees such as Al Ghazzi. While the country's policies were criticized by the United Nations and international human rights organizations, they were also held up as a model by politicians in other countries. In 2005 the British Conservative Party campaigned on an "Australian-style annual limit" on the number of people who came to Britain, with a special emphasis on reducing the number of asylum-seekers. Commentators on refugee issues in North America similarly argued that "Canada and the United States need only look at Australia . . . to prevent the flood of undesirables through the refugee loophole." Australian officials travelled overseas to make presentations before the United Nations and other organizations, offering arguments that were widely publicized around the world. In these and other ways, the debate over refugee issues in Australia took on a significance that extended far beyond Australia's shores.

One of the most vigorous defenders of Australia's policies was cabinet minister Philip Ruddock. In the 1980s and early 1990s Ruddock was a high-profile supporter of Amnesty International who wore the group's badge on his lapel while giving speeches in Parliament. In 1988, when his party's leader ignited a controversy by saying Asian immigration was too high, Ruddock crossed the floor to vote in support of a bill affirming non-discrimination as a bedrock principle of immigration policy. But after Ruddock became minister of immigration, he oversaw the introduction of harsh policies regarding asylum-seekers. Many observers commented on the disjunction between Ruddock the former defender of human rights and Ruddock the minister in charge of mandatory detention. Ruddock, however, paid little attention to his critics. After he left cabinet, he was asked what he thought of the refugee advocates who dogged him during his years in power. He dismissed them as do-gooders with too much time on their hands. "I mean, it's called the doctors' wives syndrome."

While in government Ruddock never lost a chance to speak out in defence of Australia's approach. The zeal with which he did so was on display in a 2001 interview he gave to Australian journalist Peter Mares. As Mares described it in his 2002 book *Borderline*, he and Ruddock had a patient back-and-forth about Australian asylum policy and the situation of the world's 21 million refugees. Then Mares began to challenge Ruddock's arguments. At that point, Mares writes, "the minister swivelled around in his beige leather chair to face me. The tables were turned as he became the interviewer, I the subject."

RUDDOCK: Why not take 21 million?
MARES: 21 million people aren't arriving on our shores . . .
RUDDOCK: No, no, no. Let's deal with the issue of principle first. Why not 21 million? The issue of principle is

that there are people who have refugee requirements,
and here is Australia. Why not 21 million? You tell me.
Why not 21 million?

MARES: The reasons are probably fairly obvious.

RUDDOCK: Well? What are they? Just give me the reasons.

MARES: The capacity administratively to deal with it?

RUDDOCK: Cost is it? Cost? Do you think it's cost?

MARES: Partly. Political acceptability. All sorts of reasons.

RUDDOCK: Oh, all sorts of reasons! Well look, you know,
once you start . . . I mean, I don't know whether I want
this in your book. I think now that we've established the
price, we know what you are.

Ruddock laughed after the final remark. He was asking Mares
to face up to the reality that any immigration system will of
necessity include measures consciously designed to keep people
out. Or, as Mares put it, "He has found out the weak point in
my position. . . . Where would I, a heart-on-sleeve liberal, draw
the line on people seeking asylum in Australia?" Mares gave the
example of airport liaison officers who are posted overseas to
help airline staff detect fake passports. They inevitably prevent
some refugees from reaching Australia. Yet very few people
believe all such border-control measures should be dismantled.
Hence the message in the minister's laughter: any realistic alternative to Ruddockism will contain its own stiff dose of exclusionary measures, whether human rights advocates like to admit
it or not.

Ruddock offered an additional rationale for his government's
policies. It was to counter the "incentive pull factors" that drew
people to Australia. In Ruddock's view, most of the people
coming by boat were not genuine refugees. Rather, they were
economic migrants who risked their lives to reach Australia in
order to improve their standard of living. As Ruddock put it in

a 2001 speech in Geneva, "People are forsaking opportunities for protection in neighbouring countries and are using people-smugglers and the asylum system to seek access to Western countries and some are tragically dying in the attempt." There was thus a humanitarian justification for policies such as mandatory detention. When they were in effect, word would get back to the Middle East and other refugee-producing regions, causing fewer people to take voyages like the one that killed Mohammad Al Ghazzi's family.

How sound is the case for Ruddockism? It is undeniable that we live in a world of border control and that there is no sign of that changing any time soon. But as a justification for mandatory detention, the need to control Australia's border was a red herring. Many countries receive asylum claimants, often in greater numbers than Australia, yet it alone responded to their arrival by incarcerating them en masse. As the United Nations noted in 2002, "a system combining mandatory, automatic, indiscriminate and indefinite detention without real access to court challenge is not practiced by any other country in the world." Australia's emphasis on keeping people out reached such an extreme that between 1999 and 2005, there were fifteen instances in which rejected asylum-seekers were killed after being deported from Australia. Ruddock's government could have avoided these and other preventable outcomes while still maintaining border control.

This brings us to Ruddock's second argument. It drew attention to the route Iraqis, Afghans and asylum-seekers coming by boat took to Australia, one that saw them travel through other countries. At first glance this may seem a strike against people like the asylum-seekers on board the *Tampa*, who insisted that the captain take them to Australia. Should asylum-seekers really be allowed to pick and choose their destination in this way?

This question overlooks a key point: Middle Eastern and

Asian refugees could not actually receive protection in the countries they travelled through. Mohammad Al Ghazzi was typical in this regard. Syria, the first country to which he fled, was not really a safe haven. This was evident not only in the difficulty he and his family experienced there but also in the fact that Syria has not signed the Refugee Convention. That means it does not even pretend to respect the minimal right of *non-refoulement*, or the right of a refugee not to be returned to a place of persecution (one reason why Raghed was vulnerable to extortion).

As for Malaysia, which Al Ghazzi also passed through, it has not signed the Refugee Convention either. And although it may be willing to admit foreign Muslims as visitors, letting them settle in Malaysia is quite a different matter. Sue Hoffman, who has interviewed dozens of refugees as part of an academic research project, notes that Malaysia admits Muslims on the condition that they stay only for two or three weeks and do not seek work: "When you start to see how the Malays treated refugees from within that part of Asia, countries neighbouring Malaysia, they were horrendously treated. Malaysia had no system at that time of recognizing asylum-seekers. Once your visa ran out you were illegal, full stop. And you were subject, if you were caught, to any or all four of being lashed, detained, fined and deported. That was the standard procedure."

The situation in Indonesia was no better. It too has yet to sign the Refugee Convention. A UNHCR office in Jakarta does try to resettle refugees abroad, but of the 476 cases it approved between August 1999 and August 2001, it could find governments willing to take only 18. As for seeking refuge in Indonesia itself, it is legally impossible. "Indonesia unequivocally refuses to grant any legal status that would facilitate the local integration of refugees," Human Rights Watch noted in a 2002 report, which described asylum-seekers being attacked by Indonesia mobs, among other terrors. For refugees, stopping in Indonesia or Malaysia would have prolonged their persecution rather than ended it.

This situation highlights the central paradox of mandatory detention. In time, over 90 percent of the people who experienced it were recognized by Ruddock's own government as refugees. Almost twelve thousand people arrived by boat between 1999, when the harshest measures were introduced, and 2002, when boat arrivals fell to zero. Of this group over eleven thousand were eventually recognized as refugees. This meant that the primary burden of detention was placed on people who had already experienced persecution by their own governments. This was the opposite of what Australia had pledged to do when it signed the Refugee Convention. "Often refugees have come from situations in which they've been arbitrarily detained," notes refugee scholar Matthew Gibney. "If the first thing that they encounter is that [they are detained], not on the basis of some individual action but as a group . . . that is a very scary, a very horrific situation for them to face. It sends out a very bad message for the respect of human rights in the country in which they've arrived."

Philip Ruddock had something in common with Bill Clinton and other defenders of the Haitian interdiction program. Like them, he appealed to "incentive pull factors" to justify his government's actions. The frequency with which this argument is made by politicians in the United States, Australia and many other countries today captures something about the political universe we inhabit. It has been said that economics is the study of incentives. By that standard, asylum policy is one of many areas governments increasingly understand in economic terms. Not in the sense that it is a money-maker, but in the sense that policies are designed with an eye to what their long-term incentives will be. In the case of Australia, refugees who arrived there were dealt with harshly to send a message to future refugees not to come.

Many human rights advocates object to an incentives-based approach to asylum. Julian Burnside, a prominent Australian lawyer, expressed this view when he said that mandatory detention was objectionable on the grounds that it "involves instrumentalising innocent people in order to achieve another objective." Burnside's remark crisply captures the dubious moral foundation of Ruddockism. The incentive message that would be sent to future refugees was the only consideration that mattered. Creating that incentive justified treating refugees as nothing but means.

It would be a mistake, however, to conclude that incentives and moral considerations must inevitably be in conflict. Adam Smith once said that economics is properly understood as a branch of moral philosophy. By that standard, the problem with Australia's approach was not that it gave too much weight to incentives, but that it did not recognize all the incentives in play.

In addition to pull factors, migration patterns are also influenced by push factors, or considerations that drive people out of a particular country or region. Sue Hoffman and others who work with refugees often point to the clampdown on Iran when explaining why the number of refugees travelling to Australia increased in 1999. Such policies were a powerful incentive for Mohammad Al Ghazzi and other refugees to run for their lives. For all Ruddock and other Australian officials spoke of incentives, their approach was based on overlooking incentives to flee created by other governments. It was as if the only reason anyone ever came to Australia was because it was seen as a soft touch.

Ruddock's approach also ignored what Matthew Gibney calls the problem of the ethical state. When Australia and other countries introduce severe policies, some refugees choose instead to go to countries with more reasonable asylum systems. Given the tendency of many politicians to interpret every uptick in the number of arrivals as a sign that their own system is too open, the result is a race to the bottom, in which governments create incentives for each other to make their systems ever more unwelcoming.

Ruddock and other politicians can be faulted for conveniently selecting which incentives to highlight. But there was a deeper problem. Ruddock's government said its policies were meant to serve a humanitarian goal by reducing boat arrivals. Yet the same government put in place two incentive structures that worked against humanitarian outcomes, and could have been foreseen to do so.

The first of these concerned the visas Ruddock's government issued to refugees. Temporary protection visas, as they were called, were a key element of Australia's deterrence program. After they were introduced in 1999, temporary protection visas were issued overwhelmingly to men, including Mohammad Al Ghazzi. A condition of receiving the visa, which was good for three years, was that a holder could not bring his family to Australia, a policy that set Australia apart from several other refugee-receiving countries. Had Al Ghazzi, for example, reached Canada from Syria and filed a successful refugee claim, he would have been able to sponsor Raghed and his children to join him. By denying people like Al Ghazzi this option for three or more years, Australia's asylum policy did precisely what Ruddock claimed it was designed not to do: it created an incentive for people to make dangerous sea crossings. The only way for people like Raghed to be with their husbands was to risk their own smugglers' passage.

Sue Hoffman has documented the effect temporary visas had on Australia's intake of asylum-seekers. She draws a comparison before and after October 1999, when temporary visas were introduced. In the first ten months of 1999, 111 children attempted to reach Australia by boat. In the two months after the new visas were introduced, the number of children shot up to 313. And it kept increasing, to the point that 1,563 children attempted sea crossings in 2001. The information that is available suggests the ratio of women also increased considerably. This upsurge might well have been avoided had different conditions been imposed on refugee visas.

As Hoffman puts it in regard to Raghed's boat: "There's no question that the government was culpable in terms of the fact that there were so many women and children there. And that the policy increased the number who came by boat. I mean, we'll never know what would have happened if that policy, if these restrictions on the men's visas, hadn't been introduced . . . but it does seem as though huge numbers [were involved], because suddenly instead of single men you had whole family groups."

This is what Al Ghazzi had been so angry about when he stormed into the Immigration Department and accused its staff of killing people. His visa had left his family with little choice. "Why you just decide for temporary visa?" he asks. "That's a huge thing. If we came here by permanent visa, it didn't happen."

The second negative incentive involved the issue of humanitarian rescues. The sea voyage from Indonesia to Australia is dangerous because, among other reasons, ships such as that carrying Al Ghazzi's family frequently break down. In such situations, passing cargo ships are expected to respond to distress calls, just as the *Tampa* did. This is the case even though modern ship captains now sail a "free-market sea," as the author William Langewiesche has put it, "where profit margins are slim, [and] delays of even a few hours can seem unacceptably costly." By involving the *Tampa* in a standoff after it responded to a distress call, the Australian government created an incentive for commercial ships not to perform ocean rescues near Australia. Captains who simply let people drown would avoid the possibility of being involved in a potentially costly episode of the kind that engulfed the *Tampa*.

The idea that any captain could sail past people drowning at sea may seem far-fetched, yet it has been known to happen. Tragically, one such case involved the ship carrying Al Ghazzi's family. Many survivors of the sinking have described two ships coming upon them in the water at night. One eighteen-year-old Iraqi survivor summarized the view from the wreckage: "The people on the top deck of the boat as it was rocking before cap-sizing saw 2 large ships. They thought that they would be res-cued. None of them came to the rescue. When night came the two ships turned flood lights and projectors on the people. One felt as if the light was so close that it was next to him. [When the night came] we were very close to Australian waters."

People in the water blew whistles and shouted to attract the ships' attention. But after shining their lights on them and cir-cling several times, the two boats glided silently away.

An enduring mystery of the sinking concerns the identity of the passing ships. "What kind of situation would it be where you get two big ships together?" Sue Hoffman asks. A possible answer was suggested during Hoffman's research project in which she interviewed refugees. One of Hoffman's interviews was with an asylum seeker who made a failed attempt to reach Australia in a small boat that stalled along the way. After the boat stalled it encountered two fishing vessels working together. "I might get the nationalities wrong, but it was like a Filipino and a Korean ship working in tandem. One was a fishing vessel and the other one was a refrigeration vessel. So there were these two big ships working in tandem, and [perhaps] it was something like that."

Some observers have suggested that the two passing ships may have been commercial vessels which were disinclined to pick people up between Indonesia and Christmas Island, as they would not have been able to let them off in Australia. But as Sue Hoffman points out, the identity of the ships remains unknown. "It's all speculation. Nobody really knows."

The passing ships should cause us to ask what the predictable incentive effects will be of *Tampa*-style standoffs. To be sure, there is no evidence of a direct causal link between the *Tampa* episode and the death of Mohammad Al Ghazzi's family. Yet turning away a commercial vessel after it rescued people at sea was likely to reduce, rather than increase, the incentives for commercial vessels to perform humanitarian rescues. But the Australian government turned away the *Tampa* regardless. It then asked the world to take seriously the notion that it was acting with humanitarian considerations uppermost in mind. As we will see in the next chapter, this typifies the situation of refugees who sail for Western shores. Whether they come via the Windward Passage, the Sundra Strait or points in between, a phony and corrupt humanitarianism is the only humanitarianism many will ever experience.

Postscript: In 2010, Australia reintroduced a version of mandatory detention. It saw children and family groups released into the community after only a brief period in detention. Single men were again subject to extended incarceration. Eight years after it had closed, Curtin Detention Centre was reopened.

FIVE

RAISING THE CASTLE

IT WAS THE LARGEST DEMONSTRATION in the history of Bonn. Rocks and bottles thrown by youths in ski masks and leather jackets fell like hailstones on the shields of riot police who had barricaded the German Parliament. Behind the rock throwers, thousands of demonstrators chanted "Deportation is murder" and "We are one people." They filled the streets in such numbers that traffic throughout the government quarter was brought to a standstill. Politicians who had been unable to get through the crush of bodies were being taken to the Parliament by helicopters and police launches that normally patrolled the Rhine. A member of the ruling Christian Democrats who was hit by a protestor's balloon entered the plenary chamber splattered in paint, triggering angry shouts of "Anarchists!" from the government benches.

The government was proposing to change Germany's asylum law. Inside the Parliament, the proposal was the subject of what would become an epic thirteen-hour debate, during which the besieged lawmakers denounced not merely the protestors but also each other in historically charged terms. When a Far Right politician rose to speak, other politicians stormed out while shouting, "Neo-Nazi out of Parliament!" Members of the Party of Democratic Socialism gave several inflammatory speeches suggesting that the government's proposal amounted to rebuilding the Berlin Wall. One PDS representative said, "You will see: whoever votes today to essentially eliminate the right to asylum must know that he is partially responsible for future shootings of refugees at the border." In response, a member of the Green Party reminded the assembled lawmakers that the PDS was the successor to the East German Communist Party, "the party that built the wall and that in East Germany did everything that was contrary to granting asylum." As he spoke, waves of applause emanated from the benches of all the major parties.

Germany's asylum debate occurred in the spring of 1993. It eventually resulted in radical changes to the country's refugee laws. Before then, Germany had one of the most strongly worded asylum laws in the world. Afterwards, the legal protection it offered people seeking refuge shrank dramatically. Germany's transformation in this regard illustrates three international trends that have long since come to define the treatment of refugees, particularly in Europe. Germany is an influential member of the European Union, and its experience with refugee issues in the 1990s reflects a darker mood regarding asylum that was settling across Europe during the same period. Germany has also not traditionally seen itself as a country of immigration, and the collapse of the protections it had extended to refugees is in part a reflection of the difficulty of guaranteeing the rights of refugees in societies with descent-based models of belonging.

The most important reason to take note of what happened in Germany, however, is that until 1993, the concept of human rights was at the core of the country's approach to asylum. In particular, Germany had enshrined a right to asylum in its constitution. This is a plausible way of responding to the needs of refugees, and more than one country has affirmed a constitutional right to asylum. So far, however, a constitutional right to asylum has not proved a durable long-term solution, in Germany or anywhere else. Understanding why this is the case is a necessary condition of making progress on the refugee predicament Hannah Arendt left us with. Assuming, that is, that the rise and fall of a right to German asylum does not cast the very idea of refugee rights into radical doubt.

Nineteen ninety-three was not the first time Bonn was home to a tumultuous constitutional debate. In 1948 the founders of what would soon become the new state of West Germany gathered there in a natural history museum—one of the few large buildings still standing after the war—to begin the arduous task of rebuilding their country's political institutions. The meeting's location was not its only aspect influenced by the Nazi years. The Bonn politicians also decided on a new constitution, one that was shaped by their memories of Germany's descent into fascism.

The Basic Law, as the German constitution is known, is one of the most powerful legal documents ever created. It has been characterized as containing "a more rigid general version of the rule of law than any other constitution in the world." The constitution gives German courts far broader powers than courts possess in other countries. Over the years German judges have addressed whether nuclear missiles can be located on German soil, how big the public debt should be and other questions that are normally regarded as the purview of politicians. The Basic Law is also extremely difficult to change, requiring two-thirds majorities in both houses of the German Parliament.

Both of these aspects reflected the 1948 lawmakers' memory of the democratic Weimar Republic that existed in Germany from 1919 to 1933. Weimar's constitution contained clauses concerning emergency powers and other loopholes that were widely seen as having enabling Hitler's ascent. The "anti-Weimar Constitution," as the Basic Law has been called, was thus deliberately designed to prevent an extremist movement from ever wielding power again, by limiting the authority that would be given to politicians. Political leaders would instead be made to operate within the strict parameters set down by the Basic Law as interpreted by judges.

It was in this context that West Germany's founders included the following sentence in the Basic Law: "Persons persecuted on political grounds shall enjoy the right to asylum." The lawmakers were conscious of Germany's responsibility for not only creating but also mistreating large numbers of refugees during the Nazi years. They recalled episodes at the Swiss border during which fleeing Jews were denied entry to Switzerland and instead handed over to German authorities. "If we include limitations [on the right of asylum], the police at the border can do as they will," one of the Bonn politicians argued during the constitutional deliberations. "This makes the right to asylum absolutely ineffective. We have our experiences from the last war, namely with Switzerland. We can only preserve the right to asylum with a clear and simple rule."

The clear and simple rule the founders of West Germany eventually settled on applied the logic of the Basic Law to an issue, asylum, that was normally left up to politicians. By limiting political officials' ability to turn away refugees, the drafters of the constitution sought to ensure that no genuine refugee would ever again be mistreated on German soil. West Germany would thus make a dramatic break from its past. Where Germany had once been a major producer of refugees, now it would be a moral exemplar among nations when it came to the rule of law in general and the treatment of refugees in particular.

In the late 1940s West Germany witnessed a massive influx of people. More than 12 million arrived from Eastern and Central Europe between 1945 and 1949 alone. The new arrivals, however, were the descendants of people who had lived in Germany before 1937 or were for some other reason legally classified as being of German descent. For this reason, the West German government did not regard them as foreigners and they did not need to make asylum claims. The same was true of the 3.8 million people who moved from East to West Germany between 1945 and the construction of the Berlin Wall in 1961. They were seen as members of the German people who happened to have been caught on the wrong side of the Iron Curtain, and were automatically entitled to West German citizenship.

Postwar Germany's understanding of national identity was very different from that found in the contemporary United States, Australia and other countries of immigration. It has been well described by migration scholar William Brubaker: "Because national feeling developed before the nation-state, the German idea of the nation was not, originally, a political one, nor was it linked with the abstract idea of citizenship. The pre-political German nation, this nation in search of a state, was conceived not as the bearer of universal political values, but as an organic, cultural, linguistic or racial community—as an irreducibly particular *Volksgemeinschaft* [people's community]. On this understanding, nationhood is constituted by ethnocultural unity and expressed in political unity."

In countries of immigration it is customary for membership to be defined according to the principle of *jus soli*, which grants citizenship to anyone born on domestic soil. West Germany citizenship, by contrast, was granted according to the principle of *jus sanguinis*, literally, as a "right of blood." Germany's economy was so booming during the 1950s and '60s that not only could it absorb millions of ethnic Germans, it also began seeking out "guest workers" from Italy, Greece, Turkey and other Mediterranean countries. They were classified as guest workers because the German conception of belonging did not extend to foreigners gaining permanent admission (even if, in the end, many would in fact become permanent and prove the guest worker label something of a fiction).

By contrast, the number of people who tried to exercise a right to asylum during the postwar years was small. During the 1950s and '60s, roughly five thousand people a year made asylum claims. Most of these were defectors from the Eastern bloc, and so were eagerly welcomed. Not only did such a reception demonstrate the West's superiority over the illiberal East, but the roaring German economy created a steady demand for their labour. Insofar as anyone thought about asylum as a political issue, therefore, it was seen not as a source of crisis, but as a point of pride: proof that West Germany had succeeded in making a decisive break from authoritarianism, a variation of which still existed just over the Berlin Wall.

Flash forward to 1980, when a coup in Turkey resulted in ninety-two thousand Turks claiming asylum in West Germany. Neither ethnic Germans nor refugees from communism, they received a much cooler reception. The government introduced a variety of measures designed to make West Germany a less attractive destination. Appeals were restricted and welfare payments were slashed. These and other measures succeeded in reducing the number of claims through the mid-1980s, but in the final years of the decade a global rise in the number of refugees saw asylum applications rise again. In 1987 the government redoubled its border-control efforts: airlines were made to pay "carrier sanctions" when they transported passengers who filed asylum claims without identity documents, and people requesting asylum were denied the right to work for five years. Despite these efforts, in 1988 West Germany received 103,000 asylum claims from Sri Lanka, Lebanon and other war-torn regions, the highest number in its history.

Then the Berlin Wall came down. Millions of Eastern Europeans yearned to start a new life in the West. Germany was an obvious place to do so, but its citizenship laws made it a difficult place to emigrate to for anyone who was not an ethnic German. The constitutional asylum clause, however, which now applied to a reunified Germany, presented an alternative means of entry. Anyone who made a successful claim would be able to permanently live in Germany. But even someone with a weak claim had an incentive to make an application. The asylum clause meant that everyone who sought asylum had to have their claim processed within Germany, a process that could take years. During that time applicants could easily work under the table and earn an income for themselves.

Germany in the early 1990s continued to receive genuine refugees, both because of the crisis in the former Yugoslavia and because Denmark and Sweden made their own asylum systems more restrictive. Yet refugees fleeing persecution were quickly crowded out by applicants from places such as Bulgaria and Romania. They were overwhelmingly economic migrants seeking a better standard of living, and so did not meet the international definition of a refugee. Yet now they accounted for up to 70 percent of the refugee claims Germany was receiving each year.

A vicious circle quickly developed. The more people who filed refugee claims, the longer it took for each one to be decided, leading to a further rise in the number of weak claims. Eventually the average processing time grew to three years, long enough for failed applicants to put down strong roots in Germany. "While the number of applicants who actually attained refugee status could probably have been integrated into Germany with relative ease, pressure built up because most unsuccessful applicants failed to leave or were not deported," Matthew Gibney has noted. "[The] extended time period allowed asylum seekers to become firmly settled in the country, making deportation politically and ethically controversial."

The number of applications kept rising and rising until in 1992 it peaked at 438,000. To put this number in perspective, Germany's post-1989 asylum boom meant that it received two-thirds of all asylum claims lodged in Europe during the 1980s and 1990s combined. As the numbers steadily ticked upwards, breaking record after record, the government went into crisis mode. It introduced still more restrictive measures, including housing asylum-seekers in "collection camps." But by the time military bases began to be converted for this purpose, too many people were arriving for all but a small portion to be housed this way.

German politicians were not the only people to step up their efforts as the crisis deepened. So too did political extremists. In 1990 the Far Right engaged in three hundred acts of violence. Two years later the number exceeded two thousand. The violence was particularly prevalent in the former East Germany, which was struggling economically in the wake of reunification. According to Free Berlin University historian Wolfgang Wippermann, East Germans were manifesting the strong form of German nationalism that had been preserved behind the Iron Curtain. "Their tradition of nationalism was unbroken. They were isolated . . . and criticized now by West Germans for being less capable and less productive, they say, 'This may be so . . . but we are Germans!'" West Germany saw less violence but a sharper rise in support for the Far Right Republican Party, which reached 6 percent in the polls. Its platform was summed up in flyers proclaiming, "Don't stone foreigners if you disagree with asylum. Use your vote!"

Attacks on "foreigners" became increasingly indiscriminate. They eventually claimed seventeen lives, culminating with the firebombing of the home of a Turkish-German family in the town of Mölln, near Hamburg. After the family's apartment building was set on fire and a ten-year-old girl and two members of her extended family burned to death, someone called the police to take credit for the attack and ended the call with "Heil Hitler!" The attack galvanized mainstream society, and hundreds of thousands of people marched in Hamburg, Munich and elsewhere to condemn the violence. This and other attacks nonetheless contributed to the atmosphere of crisis, in which curtailing the asylum problem was seen as the only way to halt the spread of extremism.

The crisis posed a special challenge for Germany's Social Democrats (SDP). The leading left-wing party, it had been out of power for over a decade. Under leader Björn Engholm, the Social Democrats were in the process of moving to the centre and making themselves more electable, in the mould of the U.K.'s Labour Party under Tony Blair or the U.S. Democrats under Bill Clinton. The asylum crisis, however, was a major obstacle in the way of this goal. The ruling Christian Democrats (CDU) and their wily leader, Helmut Kohl, never missed an opportunity to blame the influx of foreigners on the Social Democrats. Kohl and the CDU had long argued that the only solution to the crisis was to change the constitution, which would require the Social Democrats' support. SDP stalwarts, however, viewed the asylum clause as a fundamental pillar of justice. But now, with a thousand people entering Germany every day, the government was pounding home the message that every new asylum-seeker could be blamed on the SDP.

At an emergency meeting in Bonn, Engholm told assembled SDP delegates that the party had to act or risk fostering xenophobia. "Let's not wait until the immigration problem creates new political majorities that we can no longer influence." His position was echoed by the convention's only guest speaker,

Jewish leader Ignatz Bubis. "We have the freest constitution ever on German soil and never has a democracy lasted so long as the one we have now," Bubis said from the dais. "But if all democratic parties do not stand together now against neo-Nazism, Weimar cannot be ruled out." In 1948 the asylum clause had been a means of breaking from Germany's past. Now the same goal required its abolition. Bubis's parallel drew applause from the floor, and a majority of the fractured party voted to support changing the constitution. Six months later, Bonn witnessed its historic demonstration and vote. The constitutional amendment won 521–132 and went into effect shortly thereafter.

The compromise the SDP reached with the government included two measures not directly related to asylum. The commitment to blood-based citizenship was loosened, making it easier for long-time foreign residents and their German-born children to acquire citizenship. A cap was also placed on the number of ethnic Germans that could immigrate to Germany. The centrepiece of the asylum compromise, however, involved amending the constitution to permit two measures that made Germany's asylum system much more difficult to access. The first was a streamlined procedure that permitted the government to automatically reject asylum claims by applicants from countries with acceptable human rights records. The second was a series of so-called "safe third country" agreements. Such agreements stated that any asylum applicant who had passed through any country neighbouring Germany could be returned to that state and have his or her asylum claim determined there.

These procedures had a dramatic effect on the number of asylum claims. They dropped to 122,210 in 1994 and kept falling throughout the 1990s. In that sense the asylum compromise solved the crisis. The new arrangement, however, has been decried by refugee advocates. The revised laws permit the automatic rejection of claims by nationals of countries with human rights records that are of debatable acceptability, including the Czech Republic, Romania, Poland, Ghana and Senegal. The network of safe third country agreements also makes it extraordinarily difficult to enter Germany and legally file an asylum claim. One estimate has suggested that 98 percent of pre-1993 cases would have been ineligible under the new rules.

The end of an era had been reached. "Granting asylum is always a question of generosity, and if one wants to be generous, one has to risk helping the wrong people." So argued German statesman Carlo Schmid in 1948 when the asylum clause was introduced. "This is the other side of the coin, and this at the same time probably constitutes the dignity of such an act." After 1993, this sentiment no longer informed Germany's asylum law. It was replaced by a new arrangement, the spirit of which has perhaps best been captured by Matthew Gibney: "While applying for asylum in Germany is not illegal, it is virtually impossible now to gain protection without violating immigration laws."

Germany's asylum crisis had numerous causes that sprang out of the country's unique historical situation. The most obvious one was the fall of the Berlin Wall and the unprecedented influx it triggered. Germany's struggle to economically integrate East and West after reunification also influenced the course of events, most clearly in the rise of violence in the former East Germany. An awareness of Germany's authoritarian past, finally, also permeated the debate leading up to the constitutional amendment. Invocations of Weimar during this time reflected not the possibility that Germany might actually become a fascist state—the drafters of the Basic Law succeeded in creating enduring liberal institutions— but rather a common field of meaning. Calls to avoid the route of Weimar were a means of disassociating asylum reform from xenophobia and of mobilizing public opinion, successfully as it turned out, in favour of changing the constitution.

Yet Germany's crisis also reflected trends that are thoroughly international. Germany's status as a bellwether state was noted during the crisis by the writer Günter Grass, who resigned from the Social Democrats when they voted to support the asylum compromise. "I was disappointed because this is the first step to building a castle of Western Europe, beginning in Germany," Grass said in explaining his decision. Grass's image of a castle of exclusion is an apt one. From its high towers it is possible to identify three international trends regarding asylum, occurring not only in Europe but far beyond, of which Germany's experience forms merely one part of a larger, disquieting whole.

The first trend concerns the situation across Europe. Germany is one of the most prominent members of the European Union, and the sharp contraction of the legal safeguards it extends to refugees is part of a continental trend against admitting asylum-seekers. Consider the following snapshots from the history of European asylum, both during and after the fall of refugee rights in Germany.

- In 1990 three Tamils were "kidnapped" by British Airways staff at Heathrow Airport. After being held against their will they were deported to Sri Lanka without the knowledge of the British government. The incident occurred after the British government introduced fines for airlines that transported inadmissible passengers, making airlines "increasingly reluctant to carry passengers whenever there is the slightest doubt about their admissibility," as one report put it.

- In 1992, also in Britain, the government introduced visa requirements for Bosnian refugees. The fact that Great Britain had no embassies or consulates in Bosnia at the time made it extraordinarily difficult for people fleeing the civil war in the former Yugoslavia to find asylum in the U.K. The next year the British government introduced a restrictive new asylum bill, the first of six it would introduce over the following thirteen years, each making it more difficult for refugees to obtain asylum. During this period a refugee protection charity released a report documenting that "many asylum-seekers are refused asylum because evidence and proof of their persecution is demanded of them to a standard which is not only impossible to obtain in circumstances of flight, but contrary to international law."

- In 1998 Belgian policemen smothered to death Semira Adamu, a failed asylum-seeker, during her forced deportation to Nigeria. In a 2003 report triggered by the case, Amnesty International found that although Belgium had abolished use of the "cushion technique" that had been used to restrain Adamu and had resulted in her death, many irregularities still remained in Belgium's treatment of asylum-seekers. "Several asylum-seekers have been 'released' from formal detention but immediately transferred to the transit zone of the national airport by police officers and subjected to cruel, inhuman and degrading treatment—unable to leave the transit zone but without the basic means of survival such as money, food, drink, hygiene products, or access to beds and forced to rely on the charity of strangers."

- In 1999 a forty-year-old Algerian woman, Naimah Hadjar, arrived at the Frankfurt airport where she hoped to obtain asylum, telling authorities she had been repeatedly raped by Algerian police. Her claim was rejected and, because she lacked identity documents, she spent over seven months being detained at the airport, with occasional trips to a prison and a hospital. After having a nervous breakdown, she hanged herself in a shower room in the airport's transit zone. At the time of her death, ten other people had been held in the airport's detention facility for more than a hundred days.

- In 2003 a Human Rights Watch report on asylum policy in the Netherlands found that the government was using an accelerated application procedure, originally designed to weed out "manifestly unfounded" claims, in the majority of its asylum applications. "Certain key aspects of Dutch asylum policy and practice violate international and regional human rights norms," the report said. "At present the procedure is being used for applicants from war-torn and repressive countries, for those with claims involving complex legal and factual issues, and for those who demonstrate signs of trauma, illness, or difficulties presenting their claims. The process is swift and affords applicants little opportunity to benefit from the assistance of lawyers assigned to them."

- In a case reminiscent of Naimah Hadjar, Ibrahim Zijad, a thirty-one-year-old Palestinian refugee, spent seven months living in the transit zone of the Prague airport. Zijad arrived in the Czech Republic in August of 2003 and tried to make an asylum claim. Citing the fact that he had no passport or other identity documents, Czech officials rejected his application and put him on a plane to Istanbul, from where he had departed, only for Turkish authorities to send him back to Prague. Denied entry to the Czech Republic, Zijad lived off of meal tickets provided by a Czech airline company and washed himself in public toilets until Czech authorities finally granted him asylum. A few days after the government's decision, Zijad fled to Germany and obtained asylum there.

- In 2006 Switzerland made a "dramatic retreat" from international legal standards when it introduced sweeping changes to its asylum law. Among other punitive changes, applicants who did not produce travel documents or identity papers within forty-eight hours of filing would have their application automatically rejected, unless they could demonstrate some compelling reason for their lack of identification. Birth certificates and driver's licences were deemed unacceptable for this purpose. A report into Switzerland's policy characterized it as "contrary to the Universal Declaration of Human Rights, which upholds as fundamental the right of everyone to seek and enjoy asylum from persecution."

- In 2008 Slovenia introduced an asylum law that saw accelerated procedures replace full hearings for all asylum applications *except* those the government considered "manifestly well-founded," or those lodged by children or adults with special needs. The new law also allowed the government to expel persons appealing negative decisions before the appeal had been decided.

- A 2008 survey documenting the world's worst places for refugees included the European Union because of its excessive no-entry policies. "European countries have crafted policies that essentially deny access by making it as difficult as possible to enter their territory. Countries on the periphery of Europe had the harshest policies, protecting their wealthy neighbors to the north and west, often for money," the report noted. "The European Union required asylum seekers to file their claims in the first European country they entered, meaning that most had to file claims in countries like Greece, Ukraine, Poland, and Slovenia, which denied asylum at rates far greater than other European countries."

- In 2009 Greece rejected 99.95 percent of asylum claims at the first interview and formally abolished its appeal process. Human rights observers interviewed people who had tried to make asylum claims only to be imprisoned and forcibly transferred to Turkey, where they were beaten by Turkish police and returned to violent countries such as Afghanistan or Iraq. According to Human Rights Watch, "Greece effectively has no asylum system."

These images paint a bleak picture of contemporary European asylum. Consider the situation that now awaits asylum-seekers who arrive in Europe by air. Across Europe, they must negotiate their way through so-called international or transit zones. These are portions of the airport in which they are effectively deemed not to have set foot on the soil of the country in question for the purposes of refugee law, and so they are unable to access its court system to enforce their rights. In this way Europe's airports have become examples of what legal analysts sometimes refer to as "anomalous zones," or special areas where fundamental legal rules are suspended.

The concept of an anomalous zone was first used to characterize Guantánamo Bay and the limited legal rights Haitian asylum-seekers were able to exercise there. Since that time, human rights advocates in Australia have suggested that their country has its own anomalous zones. "People have said we have our own Guantánamo," says Linda Briskman, chair of Human Rights Education at Australia's Curtin University. "You know how certain parts of Australia were excised from the migration zone? That blocked access to Australian courts . . . people going to Christmas Island [didn't] have that full access that they would on the mainland." In Europe, airports now perform the same grim function as Guantánamo and Christmas Island. A place that for business travellers and tourists conjures up images of layover boredom and holiday anticipation is for refugees a legal and moral limbo.

The problem, however, does not stop at the airport. In recent years EU states may have eased travel restrictions for citizens of other EU states, but when it comes to non-Europeans seeking asylum, the overall trend has been in the opposite direction, in favour of increased restrictions of every kind, whether they concern employment, welfare or rights to appeals. Such measures are justified in the name of border control, by preventing unwanted economic migrants from making false asylum claims. Yet however reasonable such a goal may be in principle, to date there has been little sign that only economic migrants are affected by no-entry policies. Were no-entry policies effective at weeding out false claims, then logic holds that acceptance rates would increase after they are introduced. But European acceptance rates have rarely increased in the wake of tougher entry policies. Instead, both economic migrants and genuine refugees have been made to bear the brunt of Europe's measures, the effect of which has been to make it more difficult for anyone to obtain asylum, no matter how well founded their claim of persecution.

The overall impact of Europe's exclusionist turn is difficult to measure, as many people are discouraged from even attempting to obtain asylum there. One outcome that has been noted, however, is a race to the bottom, as European countries compete to appear even more unwelcoming than their neighbours. In Germany's case, for example, a secondary contributing factor to its refugee influx was Sweden and Denmark making their own systems more restrictive. After Germany changed its system, increased pressure was put on the Netherlands, the United Kingdom and other countries, which in turn introduced more restrictive measures of their own.

Refugee advocates now speak of Fortress Europe. The fortress is not impenetrable: between 1995 and 2004, an annual average of 150,000 refugee applicants received permanent or temporary protection in European countries. But while the lucky ones were being accepted, an unknown number were either turned away or discouraged from even attempting to seek asylum by the many different no-entry policies now in place across the continent. If human rights were born in Europe, they now occupy an autumnal twilight there in regard to asylum.

Germany's asylum crisis culminated in its loosening, but not abolishing, its descent-based model of citizenship. It is worth noting how this conception of belonging influenced the country's treatment of refugees, both before and during the crisis. On the one hand, Germany's understanding of what it was to be German had an inclusive aspect. This was evident not only in the fact that between 1990 and 1994 over 1.5 million ethnic Germans from Eastern Europe and elsewhere were granted citizenship, but also in West Germany's ability to absorb over 12 million people before the Berlin Wall went up. During both periods, Germany's right-of-blood approach to citizenship made a considerable difference for ethnic Germans seeking a new start inside Germany.

The flip side of the inclusiveness toward ethnic Germans, however, was a less welcoming attitude toward non-Germans. This was the case even though the dividing line between these groups was a shadowy one. Many of the ethnic Germans granted citizenship in the early 1990s came from families that had lived for decades outside of Germany and did not speak German. They would have appeared no more obviously German than the Bulgarian and Romanian economic migrants whose refugee claims were rejected. In spite of the ambiguity concerning who was an ethnic German, however, Germany's ethnic approach to belonging still exerted a strong influence on its asylum program. In the lead-up to the constitutional amendment, the atmosphere of crisis was exacerbated by the classification of people making asylum claims as cultural foreigners who did not belong inside the imagined community of the German nation. Moreover, even when the old asylum clause was in place, Germany had a lower acceptance rate than countries of immigration such as the United States and Australia. As we have seen, these countries have their own problems when it comes to admitting refugees. But they have historically accepted a higher percentage of claims than Germany, whose average annual recognition rate between 1980 and 1989 was only 14 percent.

Germany's restricted conception of citizenship meant that even when the asylum clause was in place, its effectiveness was limited by the country's view of who did and did not belong in Germany. Arendt referred to such an arrangement, in which membership in a national ethnicity determined membership in a civic community, as "the perversion of the state into an instrument of the nation." In her view, this was the defining feature of all Western states except the United States, which took a more welcoming view of immigrants. This phenomenon was of course far more extreme in Arendt's time than ours, and large numbers of immigrants today routinely relocate not merely to Australasia and North America but also to Western Europe.

Nevertheless, it is still the case that national conceptions of belonging influence how welcoming a society is to refugees. Western European states such as France, Great Britain and Belgium have been termed reluctant countries of immigration. The phrase highlights the fact that, although such countries have historically admitted immigrants in significant numbers (in the case of France, there have been decades in which it has admitted more immigrants on a per capita level than the United States), the attitude toward immigration is nonetheless less enthusiastic than in former settler societies such as Australia and the United States, where immigration is part of the national mythology.

Germany is very much a reluctant country of immigration in this sense. And in this way it is indicative of a second larger trend— namely, the difficulty of enforcing the rights of asylum-seekers in countries with descent-based conceptions of belonging. Indeed, when viewed alongside some other descent-based societies, Germany's reluctance to admit foreigners is comparatively mild.

Consider Israel. Like West Germany, its birth in the late 1940s was strongly influenced by events during the Nazi period. Even more so than the founders of the Federal Republic, the founders of the Jewish state were acutely conscious of the treatment of

Jewish refugees. The founders of Israel never drew up a national constitution (because of an inability to agree on the relationship between synagogue and state), but in other ways the state they created would become similar to West Germany. The society that developed in Israel was one that embodied a descent-based model of belonging. But much like West Germany and its guest workers, Israel's makeup is not homogeneous: 20 percent of its citizens today are Arabs. Nevertheless, when it comes to Israel's immigration laws, the right-of-blood principle prevails. Under Israel's famous law of return, Jews who migrate to Israel are automatically eligible for citizenship.

As in Germany, this conception of belonging has at times functioned as a force of inclusion. In 1992, for example, Israel was able to absorb 200,000 Soviet Jews, a remarkable feat for a country of its size. But also like Germany, Israel's inclusive attitude toward members of its designated in-group has an exclusionary flip side regarding non-members. In Israel's case, this is most evident in regard to the Palestinians, who enjoy no equivalent to the law of return, and instead comprise a population of more than 1.3 million people living in refugee camps that in some cases are now sixty years old. Unlike any other refugee group in the world, Palestinian families have been displaced long enough to pass refugee status on to their grandchildren.

The Israeli-Palestinian conflict is a familiar one. But what is less well known is that Israel has a second refugee problem. It has long taken an unwelcoming attitude toward asylum-seekers. Although Israel signed the Refugee Convention in 1951, it took the first hesitant and tentative steps toward entrenching the convention in its domestic laws only in 2002. A 2003 Tel Aviv University report suggested that the unwillingness of Israeli politicians to enforce the refugee convention was likely due to the Israeli-Palestinian conflict: "Possibly, one of the reasons why the implementation of the Convention was delayed until now was the fear felt by the

State of Israel that applying the Convention would open the door to the return of Palestinian refugees to its territory."

Whatever the cause, Israel today places a daunting set of obstacles in the way of anyone who attempts to claim asylum. One major hurdle is the Israeli border itself. Highly militarized, it separates Israel from countries with which it is still legally at war. The border remains governed by a law from the 1950s that classifies anyone who might try to enter Israel by land without an entry permit as an "infiltrator." As the Tel Aviv report summarizes the law, infiltrator status applies to "any person who has entered Israel knowingly and unlawfully and who is a national or citizen of Lebanon, Egypt, Syria, Saudi-Arabia, Trans-Jordan, Iraq or Yemen, or is a resident or visitor in one of those countries." The law's wide scope meant that during the 1990s, when the total number of asylum-seekers Israel received from Sudan, Iraq and other nearby oppressive states amounted to sixty people, applicants were automatically classified as infiltrators and imprisoned rather than allowed to file asylum claims. In recent years Israel has witnessed a dramatic increase in the number of people seeking asylum. According to UNHCR, over 26,000 asylum-seekers from Eritrea, Sudan and other African countries entered the Jewish state between 2004 and 2009. The treatment they received was little better than in previous years, however, and Israel was known to engage in instances of "hot return," forcibly returning Eritrean asylum-seekers to Egypt, from where they have been sent back to Eritrea, the worst possible outcome for any refugee.

Even when refugees do manage to enter Israel, their problems do not end. Israel's asylum system is highly secretive and bureaucratic, and the government does not publicize the fact that it is legal to seek asylum. People who manage to lodge a claim cannot legally work or receive public medical services, which obliges them to either work illegally or spend long periods in destitution. Should they seek a work permit they face the Catch-22 of having to first pay a fine, often thousands of shekels, to cover the period during which they had no legal status in Israel. Israel's asylum system is so unwelcoming that UNHCR says it amounts to a form of "constructive *refoulement*," one that provides strong incentives for refugees to return to or remain in the same countries where their lives are in danger.

Israel's asylum problem may be extreme but it is not unique. A similar situation prevails in Japan, which has its own debt to Germany. During the second half of the nineteenth century, Japan looked to Germany as a cultural and political model to emulate. This was evident in everything from the Prussian military uniforms the Meiji emperor would parade in to the Prussian-inspired constitution Japan introduced in 1890. A strange quirk of Japan's Germanophilia is that the East Asian nation is today a more direct descendant of nineteenth-century Germany than is Germany itself. As writer Ian Buruma has put it, "Much of what attracted Japanese to Germany before the war—Prussian authoritarianism, romantic nationalism, pseudo-scientific racialism—has lingered in Japan while becoming distinctly unfashionable in Germany."

Contemporary Japan's essentially nineteenth-century conception of belonging manifests itself in a variety of ways, including a suspicious view of foreigners. The influence of this attitude on Japan's asylum system has been vividly documented by former Amnesty International caseworker Saul Takahashi, who worked in Japan in the 1990s, during which time he encountered an asylum system deliberately designed to turn people away. The experience of a Somali man named Ahmed whom Takahashi tried to help was typical: "He saw the people in the refugee division and told them that he needed asylum, that he couldn't go back to his country. He asked them for help. They just kicked him out. No explanation, nothing. They didn't even give him the form to apply. He is confused and angry. I am not. It happens all the time."

Takahashi and other chroniclers of Japan's asylum system depict something out of Kafka. Legal aid is "hopelessly inadequate," so lawyers representing refugees must often do so pro bono. Even if a lawyer does decide to work for free, it is up to the interviewing officer whether the attorney will be allowed to attend the hearing or not. During the hearing, the applicant is expected to meet an "unusually high standard of proof," as the UNHCR puts it, and is asked to present arrest records and other documents few refugees can provide. Once the hearing is over, the deciding officer can issue a negative decision without providing any reasons. Needless to say, not knowing what a decision is based on makes it difficult to appeal.

Japanese officials are quick to point to Japan's record on helping refugees outside of Japan. In recent years Japan has been one of the top three donors to UNHCR, giving between US$75 and $110 million every year (only the United States and the European Union give more). Many countries fail to help refugees of any kind, whether abroad or at their borders, so Japan's record of generosity to the UN is to be commended. Yet when Japan's UN donations are measured in per capita rather than absolute terms, Japan's ranking drops to seventeenth or twentieth place depending on the year. More importantly, the argument that Japan's aid to refugees abroad allows it to ignore asylum-seekers at home is a bit like a hospital saying it is going to let leukemia patients die while it focuses on cancer patients. The two groups represent people in distress who need different forms of help, one through international aid, the other through migration law. Yet Japan is so uncomfortable offering the second form of aid that, as Takahashi puts it, "it is practically impossible to get asylum in Japan."

Takahashi's pessimism is born out by the minuscule number of people who are able to obtain Japanese asylum. In 2005, for example, when the United States recognized 18,766 asylum claims, Japan recognized 145—and that year's level was unusually high. Between 1993 and 2002 Japan recognized an average of 27 asylum claims per year; between 1994 and 1997 it accepted exactly one asylum application a year. These statistics are the result of an asylum system designed not to protect refugees from danger, but to protect Japanese people from refugees.

Much like Israel, Japan represents German-style restrictiveness taken to an extreme. But in the degree of explicitness each country has been willing to write human rights into its constitution, Japan and Germany are opposites. Whereas Germany's asylum clause was a ringing declaration of the right to asylum, albeit one that was undermined by Germany's narrow conception of belonging, Japan's commitment to human rights was artful and ambiguous from the start. The English version of Japan's constitution prohibits discrimination by nationality or race and states that "all of the people are equal under the law." The Japanese text, in contrast, replaces the unrestricted term "people" with *kokumin*, or "citizen of the country," which of course excludes non-citizens. When read against the backdrop of Japan's treatment of refugees, the difference in meaning between the two documents all too vividly illustrates the gap Arendt identified between the rights of citizens and those of human beings.

The asylum systems of Israel and Japan are among the most extreme of any democratic state. They highlight the inverse relationship that exists between the narrowness of a country's conception of belonging and its ability to uphold human rights. In theory a descent-based society could respect the rights of out-group asylum-seekers by subjecting their claims to fair hearings and resettling those determined to be refugees in other countries. In practice, the ethnic favouritism that defines the migration law of descent-based societies makes it very difficult if not impossible for refugees to find asylum there.

The plight of refugees who seek asylum in countries that uphold a tight model of citizenship calls into question two arguments that are commonly made in refugee debates. The first is what we might call the geographic theory of refugee migration. This view was well expressed by Mark Krikorian of the Center for Immigration Studies, a Washington, D.C., think tank that advocates reduced immigration. "Asylum is analogous to offering a drowning man a berth in your lifeboat," Krikorian has said, "and a genuinely desperate man grabs at the first lifeboat that comes his way. A person who seeks to pick and choose among lifeboats is, by definition, not seeking immediate protection." This argument is often made by critics who say that the United States and other countries take in too many "bogus" refugees. A real refugee, they say, will run immediately to the nearest democratic state and seek asylum there. In Krikorian's view, if someone bypasses one democratic country and files a claim in another one farther away, then that is a sign the person is not a true refugee.

If this view of asylum were true, then Israel and Japan would receive more refugee claims than the United States or Australia. After all, both are democracies located near African, Middle Eastern or Asian crisis zones. Despite their frontline status, however, both countries have witnessed periods in which they received only tiny numbers of refugee applications. Between 1993 and 2002, for example, Japan received an average of only 174 applications per year, while during the same period Israel averaged 150. (This period includes six years during which Israel received no applications at all.) In both cases, the brutally unwelcoming asylum program functioned as a powerful disincentive against refugee arrivals. Just as Mohammad Al Ghazzi asked around about Canada, Sweden and Australia while he was in Syria, it is common for refugees to put some forethought into where they will run. Historically, anyone who looked into the possibility of seeking asylum in Israel or Japan quickly discovered that it was a lost cause and redirected their energies elsewhere.

This shows the problem with the geographic theory. Geography obviously plays some role in determining where refugees will flee, but it is not the only consideration. Refugees' decisions about where to escape to are also influenced by whether or not the country they run to is likely to accept them. To borrow Krikorian's metaphor, they care whether or not the country they will place their faith in really is a lifeboat. This practice is sometimes dismissively referred to as "asylum shopping." In reality it is a reasonable and necessary precaution to take regarding a decision that is potentially a matter of life and death.

The case of Japan highlights a second problem, namely, the concept of a safe third country. Many countries today now have signed safe third country agreements. As in the case of Germany, such agreements allow a country to turn away refugee applicants who have passed through another nation that has signed the Refugee Convention and have the applicants file their claim in the first such country they entered. That Japan and Israel have signed the Convention shows it is not much of a safeguard.

Moreover, for a tourist or Japanese person, Japan is one of the safest places on earth, as reflected in its low rates of crime and violence. The language of "safe" third countries, however, misleadingly suggests that the standard to employ when deciding if refugees should be returned to a particular country is whether that country is safe from a tourist's or citizen's point of view. It would be better to speak instead of "fair" third countries. That would focus attention on whether the country in question used proper procedures in determining refugee claims. When judged by that standard, many existing third country agreements fail to meet minimum standards of justice.

Here then are the first two vistas viewable from Germany's castle of exclusion. We see an entire continent increasingly unwelcoming to people running for their lives. And we see the influence that a country's conception of belonging plays in determining how it treats refugees. There is also a third vista, one that may be even more demoralizing than the first two. Looking out over it, we are forced to confront the historic failure of enforcing a right to asylum at a constitutional level. To see the larger trend here, we need to briefly look at two final countries that have inserted ringing language about asylum in their constitutions, France and Italy.

Like Germany, France introduced a new constitution in the aftermath of World War II, one that also touched on the issue of asylum. In the words of the Preamble of the 1946 Constitution, "Anyone persecuted in virtue of his actions in favour of liberty may claim the right of asylum upon the territories of the Republic." Even more so than in the case of Germany, France's asylum clause reflected the history and preoccupations of its drafters. The reference to "actions in favour of liberty" echoed a similar clause in the French constitution of 1793, which had been inspired by the Declaration of the Rights of Man and of the Citizen, but which had legal force only for two years. The phrase's reappearance in 1946 occurred at a time when memories of French collaboration with fascism under the Vichy government were fresh in mind. As in Germany, the ringing affirmation of the right to asylum was a way of breaking sharply from an authoritarian national past. Unlike in Germany, however, the right in question was not one that any refugee could in principle exercise. Someone like Hannah Arendt, who was persecuted because of her membership in an ethnic group, would not be eligible for France's versions of constitutional asylum. It was, rather, reserved for someone who belonged to his country's equivalent of the French Resistance.

When France brought in another constitution, in 1958, it retained the sentence about asylum. Yet even though the right to asylum was affirmed by both postwar constitutions, it had little influence on France's asylum system. One reason was because it was redundant. The constitutional clause mentioned only a narrow class of exiles. To deal with refugees as such, France took the same steps as other countries, signing the 1951 Refugee Convention and setting up a domestic asylum system that employed the convention's definition of refugee as someone who feared persecution "for reasons of race, religion, nationality, membership of a particular social group or political opinion." That definition meant that were a real freedom fighter to wash up in France, he or she could simply file a normal refugee claim, of the same kind someone fleeing racial or religious persecution might, without any special rights based on the constitution becoming involved.

As a result of its irrelevance, France's asylum clause functioned more as a legal decoration than a meaningful law. It was not until 1993 that a French court recognized asylum as an enforceable constitutional right. By that time, however, France had begun efforts to harmonize its asylum system with those of its neighbours, so that people seeking asylum could be made to file their claim in the first European country in which they touched down. The French government promptly amended the constitution (something that is comparatively easy to do in France) to make it legal to transfer refugees to other European states. As a result, many refugee claimants arriving in France became ineligible for constitutional protection. Today, while "constitutional asylum" still exists on the books as a legal category, it remains as irrelevant as ever and is almost never used. As a study by a group of European law professors put it, "In reality, constitutional asylum was never taken seriously . . . [and] has remained largely without jurisprudential content." The irrelevance of the asylum clause is one reason why France today operates an asylum system that has been widely criticized for failing to uphold human rights. The UN Committee against Torture, Amnesty International and other groups have documented shortcomings ranging from asylum cases being decided without hearings to individuals being deported to face torture.

Italy drew up a postwar constitution of its own in 1948. The drafters included politicians and intellectuals who had been exiled under Mussolini, and this experience caused them to affirm Italy's variation of a right to asylum: "An alien who is denied the effective exercise of the democratic liberties guaranteed by the Italian Constitution in his or her own country has the right of asylum in the territory of the Italian Republic." However, no law has ever incorporated the constitutional right to asylum into Italy's domestic laws. As a result, it was left to the discretion of judges whether to refer to it in deciding asylum cases. Overwhelmingly, they have chosen to ignore it.

Italy's asylum clause has microscopic influence: the country accepts a few thousand refugees every year, and in 2006 was home to a total refugee population of 26,875 people. Almost none of these cases involved the constitutional right to asylum. Precise statistics do not exist, partly because the power to grant constitutional asylum is exercised by local courts, whose decisions are rarely reported. One 2008 estimate speculated that in the sixty years since it was introduced, the asylum clause has been employed in sixty cases. As in the case of France, the legal right enshrined in the constitution is irrelevant to the day-to-day workings of Italy's asylum system. It instead lingers, as a 2008 report put it, "in the world of betrayed constitutional provisions, only occasionally being brought to ephemeral life by random enlightened judges across the country."

Just how ephemeral the right to asylum is in Italy today can be seen by noting the country's response to asylum-seekers entering from its former colony Libya. During the 1990s Libya had been a pariah state, subject to an arms and air embargo for supporting international terrorism. Libyan leader Moammar Qadhafi grew disappointed during this time by what he saw as a lack of support from fellow Arab leaders, and sought to improve his international standing by repositioning himself as an African leader. "As part of his new pan-African policy," migration scholar Hein de Haas has noted, "Qadhafi started to welcome sub-Saharan Africans to work in Libya in the spirit of pan-African solidarity."

The influx of newcomers to Libya eventually resulted in an anti-immigrant backlash. As a result, migrants who would have otherwise stayed in Libya now continued travelling northward. Beginning in 2001, thousands of migrants began to hire smugglers to take them to the island of Lampedusa, a popular Italian holiday destination. Italy's equivalent of Christmas Island, Lampedusa is located only 113 kilometres from Africa, of which it is geologically a part. Some observers have suggested that Qadhafi was pleased by and encouraged the influx of black Africans into Lampedusa, as it provided him with a means by which to extract concession from Italy. If so, his strategy worked. In 2004, Italy signed the first of a series of treaties with Libya that permitted Italy to return migrants to Libya and that would see the two countries conduct joint naval patrols. Two months after agreeing to accept returnees—by which time Libya had also paid compensation to victims of terrorism—the European Union lifted its embargo. The EU move followed strong lobbying by Italy, which had argued that Libya needed to import military equipment in order to better patrol its borders.

Italy's interdiction program followed a similar trajectory to that employed by the United States against Haitians. At first, efforts were made to screen out refugees to ensure that they were not returned to Libya. In 2009, however, screening efforts were suspended and Italy returned over 600 people to Libya without determining whether they were refugees. Yet Italy's own screening program indicates that the Lampedusa arrivals contained genuine refugees seeking to escape persecution. During the first eight months of 2008, for example, Italy's Trapani district, which includes Lampedusa, had a 78 percent asylum acceptance rate. Italy in 2009 was thus likely handing over refugees to Libyan authorities, even though the North African dictatorship had no asylum system of any kind, and even though Libya regularly returned people to Egypt, Eritrea, Syria and other persecution regimes. As Human Rights Watch summed up Italy's regressive move, "For the first time in the post-World War II era, a European state ordered its coast guard and naval vessels to interdict and forcibly return boat migrants on the high seas without doing any screening whatsoever." Viewed against this backdrop, Italy's constitutional commitment to asylum is a cruel mockery of the human rights it purports to uphold.

The asylum clauses of Germany, France and Italy all reflected a common desire on the part of their drafters. It was to make a strong break from a historical romance with fascism, whether under Hitler, Pétain or Mussolini. In each case, the asylum clause failed to function as an effective and adequate response to the needs of refugees seeking asylum. This is least true of Germany, where the clause did have the force of law. But as we have seen, even when the asylum clause was in place, Germany's commitment to asylum was compromised by its narrow conception of belonging. Eventually the clause's most powerful effect proved to be negative, when it created an incentive for economic migrants to file unfounded asylum claims. In the end, the law's very power led to a crisis in which the only solution was to severely reduce Germany's already limited commitment to asylum. Refugees arriving in Germany today can no more take asylum for granted than can those who seek protection in France or Italy. On the whole, the European experiment with a constitutional right to asylum must be judged a failure.

What are we to make of the world we now inhabit? The current international situation confirms Arendt's analysis of the condition of refugees and her emphasis on the power of states. "We don't have an internationally agreed system," says Howard Adelman, a former director of the Centre for Refugee Studies at Canada's York University. "We don't have a system where refugees can go internationally and make a claim under a common set of rules. Instead, the very system forces them to shop around and reinforces the Hannah Arendt principle, that in fact it's predominated by a state-run system, and rather than being a system of rights it's a system of state power. One that never resolves the central problem of giving political membership to these people who don't have that membership."

For Arendt, the central dilemma for refugees was the incompatibility of national sovereignty and human rights. All the evidence to date suggests that despite the genuine improvements since Arendt's time, we have not yet fully reconciled these two central aspects of modern politics. Most of the time it makes sense to think of rights not merely being compatible with sovereignty, but presupposing it. The absence of functioning governments in Somalia and elsewhere hardly represents a breakthrough for the enforcement of civic rights. And while liberal democratic states are hardly perfect, they do often uphold the rights of their own citizens.

With refugees, the situation is different for a reason Adelman highlights: membership. Democratic states respect the rights of their own citizens partly because members of a democratic society have the power to change their government. This creates an incentive for political leaders to be at least minimally responsive to the needs of the electorate. With asylum issues, however, the people most adversely affected by negative decisions, the refugees themselves, are not able to directly influence the law. It is also a sad fact that restrictive measures regarding asylum are popular enough with voters to attract bipartisan support. This is evident in the United States, Australia and Germany, where both right-wing and left-wing parties implemented or supported no-entry policies. The result is that it is all too easy for liberal democratic states to fail to take the rights of refugees seriously.

This paradoxical relationship, the same institution that makes possible the enforcement of our own rights routinely violating the rights of desperate outsiders, recalls something Carl Jung once said about the human psyche. Jung believed that each of us has what he called a shadow side, a negative aspect of our personality that we prefer not to think about. Refugees seeking asylum in the West illustrate the shadow side of democracy. The same democratic governments we rightly value as superior to any undemocratic alternative routinely fail to respond to the needs of refugees in a rights-respecting way, and instead contribute to their oppression by closing the doors of escape.

Is there a solution to this problem? In other areas involving rights, the solution to democratic injustices has been to protect them at the constitutional level. This is what separates liberal from pure democracy. The tyrannical potential of the majority is limited by a constitution, which says some rights are fundamental and cannot be overridden by a simple majority vote in Congress or Parliament. Given the effectiveness of this approach in other areas, it is no surprise that European lawmakers of the 1940s would see a constitutional right to asylum as the means by which the horrors of the past would be avoided. In seeking a constitutional solution, they were turning to a plausible and potentially powerful rights-enforcement mechanism. The failure of a constitutional asylum in this regard is therefore not a small failure. One of the most powerful tools of rights-enforcement our civilization is capable of, constitutional law, has to date been unable to guarantee refugees asylum.

One possible response to this state of affairs is to continue to affirm the value of a constitutional right to asylum. We should not dismiss such a right based on the experience of only three countries. After all, Germany was dealing with unique historical circumstances in the early 1990s, and France and Italy never enforced the right to asylum in a meaningful way. What if that right were taken seriously and implemented under different circumstances? Surely then it could function as an effective solution.

This is an understandable response to the rise and fall of a right to asylum. What it overlooks, however, is that any asylum system based on a constitutional right to asylum will suffer from three limitations. The first is that such a right is all too easily rendered ineffective by a government's ability to determine who is and is not a genuine refugee. Germany's constitution before 1993 may have formally denied politicians the ability to turn away refugees, but they always retained the power to classify any individual case as illegitimate. A right to asylum focuses on an outcome, that of obtaining refuge, but says nothing about the methods that are used to determine who is entitled to that refuge. For this reason, it is easily subverted. Any state determined to clamp down on its borders can still do so by refusing to recognize the overwhelming majority of claims.

The second problem with a constitutional right to asylum is that even if a government takes it seriously, its implementation can be undermined by the actions of neighbouring states. Part of Germany's problem was that none of its neighbours had equally strong asylum clauses. Rather it was an island of constitutional refuge in a sea of comparatively unwelcoming states. This arrangement punished Germany for its commitment to asylum and rewarded nearby states with more punitive systems by seeing Germany's inflow of claims dramatically increase as those of its neighbours held steady. This was one of the factors that made the constitutional amendment possible, in that there emerged a widespread view among Germans that it was unfair for them to have to process so many more claims than other EU states. Given how many states today continue to approach asylum in a spirit of deterrence, it is a real possibility that, were any future state to adopt a constitutional right to asylum, it could again see a huge spike in claims due to the comparative unattractiveness of its neighbours' refugee systems. This makes it less likely that any state will ever again introduce a right to asylum. It also means that even if a serious right to asylum does reappear, it could all to easily have the same outcome as occurred in Germany.

Finally, there is the third problem. It is that a right to asylum may not actually be the best right to enforce on refugees' behalf. The foundational right of refugee law is the right of *non-refoulement*, or the right not to be returned to a place of persecution. The right to asylum affirmed in the Basic Law was slightly different. Suppose a genuine refugee arrived in Germany and was relocated to another country where they were in no danger of persecution. That would violate a right to asylum within Germany itself but still respect the refugee's right not to be returned to danger.

Once we recognize that a right to asylum within an individual state is conceptually distinct from *non-refoulement*, we are obliged to ask where refugees should be able to exercise such a right. That is, in which state in particular should refugees enjoy a right to asylum? In 2008 the global population of refugees was nine million, not counting internally displaced persons. There are many countries with much smaller populations. Iceland's, for example, is 317,000. If we concede that not all nine million refugees have a right to move to Iceland, which would result in Iceland's culture and institutions being overwhelmed, then we recognize a competing good that can in principle trump a right to asylum. The right to *non-refoulement*, by contrast, can be respected without obliging any particular state to admit refugees in numbers that would overwhelm local institutions. The claims of refugees and host societies can be simultaneously respected by transferring refugees from one state to another so long as the receiving state respects their rights. *Non-refoulement* is thus a more ultimate principle, in the sense that its exercise and enforcement is less conditional upon the circumstances of the society and state that first recognizes such a right.

These considerations suggest that a right to asylum is not the most effective means by which to help refugees. It does not follow, however, that we should reject the idea of constitutional rights for refugees. Taking some decisions out of the hands of elected officials is a time-honoured and effective way of increasing the likelihood that rights claims will be respected. What the evidence to date suggests, though, is that what refugees need most is not the right to asylum in any particular state, but the constitutional right to have proper procedures used when their claims are being decided. Procedures, that is, that would decrease the likelihood of well-founded claims failing to be recognized. That would in turn reduce the possibility of refugees being returned to danger.

Such at least is the basis of the framework of refugee rights I will shortly defend. Not everyone, however, would agree that what refugees seeking asylum need is another set of constitutional rights. Before putting forward my proposal, therefore, it is necessary to see how other observers have responded to the Arendtian refugee dilemma. As we are about to see, those responses include the suggestion that there is no solution at all.

SIX

AN ASYLUM MADE OF THOUGHTS

IT WAS DURING A VISIT to hell that Samantha Power heard the voice of Hannah Arendt. It was the summer of 2004, and Power was a Harvard University professor and author of a Pulitzer Prize–winning book about the United States' failure to respond to genocides during the twentieth century. Now Power had come to northern Chad, near the African nation's border with Sudan, to document the first mass slaughter of the new millennium. According to conservative estimates, fifty thousand people had by then been killed in Darfur, Sudan's western region, a figure that would rise after Power's visit. More than two million people had also been ethnically cleansed from their homes, creating a mass exodus of Darfuris into makeshift camps in Chad. As Power went about interviewing refugees living in mud huts, listening to why they had come to such a desolate and forsaken place, she began to hear, she says, "Arendt's voice inside my head, either whispering or bellowing loudly."

Power's study of genocide begins with the Armenians, whom

Turkish authorities targeted for mass murder during World War I. A key element of the Armenian genocide was the forced deportation of entire villages, conducted by Turkish soldiers on horseback. In Darfur, it was as if the killers were trying to emulate this legacy. The killings were conducted not by uniformed Sudanese soldiers but by a government-supported militia known as the Janjaweed, an Arabic word that loosely means "evil horseman." Like the Turks before them, the perpetrators in Sudan singled out their female victims for systematic sexual abuse, raping thousands, even hundreds of thousands, of women. But the Janjaweed did not stop there. They took the trouble to brand their victims. In Sudan's traditional Muslim society, which emphasizes a woman's sexual purity, branding the survivors stigmatized them as sexually defiled, and so ensured their status as permanent outcasts.

As one Darfuri woman after another pointed to the scar on her leg, explaining how she came to have it and what it meant, Power reeled at what she was hearing. *This can't be*, she thought. *Persecution on this scale can't exist*. It was a perfectly natural reaction. But Power knew from reading Arendt that this normal response to atrocity was actually part of the problem. Such events so defy comprehension that they can cause outside observers to hesitate to respond, until it is too late.

"That's one major lesson I take with me from Arendt's writing," Power says. "When [traumatized] refugees tell you stories about what they've gone through, they may get a detail wrong here and there, but when they tell you these horrific tales, do not think just because it sounds too awful to be true that it is. The 'evildoers,' or aggressors, will forever come up with new ways to surprise, new ways to exceed the powers of our imaginations."

Power's experience in Chad testifies to the enduring relevance of Arendt's work. Many writers who grapple with refugee and human rights issues still hear Hannah Arendt's voice "whispering or bellowing loudly" inside their heads, and seek to respond to that at times disturbing voice. Thinkers who fall into this category are hard to pigeonhole for several reasons, not least because they occupy more than one point on the Left–Right political spectrum. Nevertheless, it is possible to divide contemporary writers who respond to Arendt's critique of human rights into two broad groups.

The first are those, like Power, whom we might think of as pragmatists. Pragmatists tend to eschew grand investigations into the nature of sovereignty or rights, and focus instead on concrete steps we can take to improve the plight of refugees, whose situation Arendt took to illustrate the impossibility of human rights. In contrast to this group are writers who respond to Arendt at a more abstract level, whom we can call the philosophers. Philosophers point out that Arendt took the plight of refugees to show the impossibility of reconciling human rights with national sovereignty, and they go on to rethink either rights or sovereignty in order to overcome the dilemma. Their responses to Arendt therefore tend to be more high-flown and conceptual than those put forward by pragmatists.

If we want to find out whether enforceable rights can be rooted in humanity rather than citizenship, we will gain much by noting what pragmatists and philosophers have said in reply to Arendt. A solution may have been found to the problem Arendt left us with regarding human rights, and what we may need to do is act on a proposal already in circulation. Alternatively, no solution may have in fact been found, and seeing why this is the case will help us recognize what a real solution might look like. Either way, familiarity with the ongoing debate around Arendt's critique of human rights will be of benefit in making those rights more meaningful.

As we are about to see, however, there is a third option in play in the debate around Arendt. That is to give up on human rights as a desirable or even coherent concept. And so our examination starts with a philosopher who recommends that we abandon one of the central moral notions of our time and go "beyond human rights."

Giorgio Agamben is an Italian academic who splits his time between universities in Paris and Venice. Born in 1942, Agamben spent the early part of his career writing on issues related to language and literature before gradually turning to politics. In recent years he has gained a wide audience in North America, where he has often taught, but interest in his work is even stronger in Europe, where his public lectures fill theatres and articles by or about him appear frequently in the press. "With his collarless shirts and dark suits, he comes across like something of a cleric," a German newspaper writer once remarked of Agamben, and the image of him as a kind of prophet is a fitting one. Like all true prophets, Agamben has an otherworldly vision that seeks to transcend the fallen world around him. Nowhere is this more evident than in his scathing view of the modern state, which he considers fundamentally incapable of respecting the moral worth of human beings.

To appreciate Agamben's skeptical view of government, we should recall events in his native Italy in the 1960s and '70s, when the country was racked by extremist violence carried out by both the Right and the Left. The most well-known incident occurred in Rome in 1978, where the car of former Italian prime minister Aldo Moro was stopped by a dozen men wearing Alitalia airline uniforms. They turned out to be members of the Red Brigades, an ultra-leftist cell. After shooting five of Moro's bodyguards, the Brigades abducted Moro himself and kept him in captivity for two months. Eventually Moro was assassinated and his body found in an abandoned car.

In response to this and similar events, Italian politicians became consumed with combating terrorism. While few observers objected to such a goal, the measures the authorities employed were extreme. They included mass arrests, detention without trial and, more than once, firing into crowds of unarmed demonstrators. As one Italian politician later put it, "The battle [against terrorism] completely absorbed us, so we did not see all the rest with the necessary clarity." Historians have long debated why the Italian government acted with such ferocity during Italy's so-called Years of Lead. One factor that is often cited is the popularity of the Italian Communist Party, which was on the verge of joining a government coalition and so went to great lengths to establish its anti-extremist credentials. As historian Paul Ginsborg puts it, the influential party, "instead of championing civil-rights issues, rapidly became a most zealous defender of traditional law and order measures."

Against this backdrop, it is not hard to see how an Italian of Agamben's generation could wind up with a pessimistic view of government. However, the main reason to recall Italy's years of upheaval is because they provide an example of a Western state committing major human rights infractions. This is a subject Agamben's writings frequently seek to explain. How is it that representatives of liberal-democratic states come to detain thousands of people without trial, or open fire on crowds of civilians? In Agamben's view, Ginsborg and other historians who explain such events by focusing on the decisions of particular actors, whether they be political parties, terrorist groups or individual politicians, are making a fundamental mistake. For the real cause of state crimes is the nature of sovereignty itself.

Agamben often quotes a remark by a previous philosopher that summarizes his own view of government: the sovereign is he who decides on the state of exception. In other words, a key function of political power is not only deciding what the rules will be but to whom they will apply. Agamben's writings illustrate this idea with many learned historical examples, stretching as far back as ancient Rome, of political authorities suspending the law's normal operation. A modern case Agamben often refers to is that of 1930s Germany. When the Nazis came to power they declared a state of emergency that suspended the German constitution. "The decree was never repealed," Agamben notes, "so that from a [legal] standpoint, the entire Third Reich can be considered a state of exception that lasted twelve years." Other nations may not commit atrocities on the scale of the Nazis, but they have also exercised their capacity to declare states of exception in disturbing ways. Between World War I and the Depression, Agamben points out, France, Belgium and other Western states engaged in acts of mass "denationalization," stripping thousands of people of their citizenship on the grounds that they were of "enemy" origins or "unworthy of Italian citizenship," as Mussolini's regime put it.

Agamben uses a Latin phrase to identify people who are placed beyond the law's reach this way: *homo sacer*. This idiosyncratic term of art (which is pronounced "homo soccer" and means "sacred man" or "cursed man") refers to an obscure figure of Roman law, one whose significance has long been debated. According to sources Agamben draws on, *homo sacer* was a legal category during Rome's early period, when secular and sacred law overlapped, and certain crimes were punishable by sacrificing the perpetrator to the relevant god. (Someone who struck his father, for example, would be offered up to the gods of parents.) A cursed man was similar to this category of criminal, in that he too had been condemned for committing a crime. The difference was that a cursed man could not be officially sacrificed. Instead, anyone who took it upon himself to kill an accursed person would not be deemed to have committed murder. There was thus something paradoxical about the position of the cursed. The authorities would not execute them, yet at the same time, they could be killed with impunity. They were excluded from human jurisdiction, but did not receive any protection from the gods to whom they belonged. As Agamben sums it up, they were "truly *sacred*, in the sense that this term had in archaic Roman law: destined to die."

For Agamben, the story of modern politics is the story of increasing numbers of individuals reduced to such a disposable state, people whom the authorities can be bothered neither to execute nor to protect. The group Agamben most often uses as an example of this phenomenon is refugees: Arendt and other Germans rounded up in the Velodrome in 1930s France; thousands of Albanians in Italy herded into a stadium in 1991 where they lived on bread and water; individual asylum claimants trapped in the international zones of European airports, where they can be held for days without access to a lawyer and potentially returned to danger. All of these cases, Agamben writes, create modern equivalents of *homo sacer*. All involve situations "in which the normal order is de facto suspended and in which whether or not atrocities are committed depends not on law but on the civility and ethical sense of the police who temporarily act as sovereign."

We can easily imagine someone responding to the scenarios Agamben describes by saying that we need to do a better job protecting the rights of the refugees involved. What makes Agamben a unique voice, however, is that in his view this common-sense reaction is itself part of the problem. This side of his thinking is evident in his attitude toward human rights, which is just as skeptical as his attitude toward governments. Agamben's thinking is strongly influenced by Arendt, and he agrees with her that refugees point up a deep tension in the concept of human rights. As he puts it, "The paradox from which Arendt departs is that the very figure who should have embodied the rights of man par excellence—the refugee—signals instead the concept's radical crisis." Unlike Arendt, however, Agamben does not depict human rights as merely an ineffective concept. He sees it as a counterproductive, even sinister notion.

Agamben argues that the chief effect of human rights has been a dangerous expansion of state power. He points to milestones in the rise of rights, such as the French Revolution's Declaration of the Rights of Man and the Citizen. Before that time, the kings who ruled France made no pretense of upholding the rights of their subjects. If people lived in grinding poverty or died during childbirth, that was a matter of royal indifference. At first glance, few arrangements may sound less appealing. But precisely because the state took so little interest in the welfare of its people, questions of who was French and who was not had no significance at the state level. So long as foreigners respected the authority of the king, little notice was taken of their activities. With the rise of the idea of rights, however, states have been invested with the responsibility of guaranteeing the rights of their people. A consequence of this shift is that governments have become increasingly concerned with questions such as "Who is French?" or "Who is Italian?" By answering such questions in narrow or exclusionary terms, states can recognize the rights not of universal humanity, but merely those of their own citizens.

For Agamben, the expansion of government authority to meet the needs of our biology—our rights to food, shelter, health—has been a historical disaster. Just how disastrous can be seen in one of the many eyebrow-raising passages in which he draws a connection between the doctrine of human rights and the ideology of the Third Reich. "Fascism and Nazism," Agamben writes, "are, above all, redefinitions of the relations between man and citizen, and become fully intelligible only when situated—no matter how paradoxical it may seem—in the biopolitical context inaugurated by national sovereignty and declarations of rights." In Agamben's view, a dark thread connects the rise of governments founded on rights in the eighteenth century to the Nazis.

In both cases national identity is a political question, and the state is preoccupied with determining who belongs to the community. That one regime gives a far more extreme answer than the others is a difference of degree, not of kind.

Agamben's suspicion of government was on display in 2004, when he made headlines after cancelling a visiting professorship at New York University. Agamben cancelled his stay to protest a new U.S. policy of fingerprinting international travellers. "By applying these techniques and these devices invented for the dangerous classes to a citizen," the *New York Times* quoted him as saying, "[governments] have made the person the ideal suspect, to the point that it's humanity itself that has become the dangerous class." Whatever the drawbacks of political life before the French Revolution, there was no all-powerful state that could track and record our every movement. For Agamben, surrendering biometric information to such states today crosses a dangerous threshold in the loss of our freedom.

In Agamben's view, one of the most disturbing aspects of the trend of diminished freedom is that it is being cheered along by groups that act in the name of human rights. Rather than challenge the scope of state power, they actively welcome its intrusion in matters of life and death by proclaiming the state the enforcer of rights. Human rights organizations fail to realize that making the state responsible for matters of survival gives it an enormous amount of power in determining who will live and who will die. Or as Agamben puts it in one of his most widely quoted passages, "Humanitarian organizations . . . maintain a secret solidarity with the very powers they ought to fight."

In North America, the argument that a government intrusive enough to satisfy every need of its people will face a totalitarian temptation has usually come from the Right. Such was the theme of the famous 1944 book *The Road to Serfdom*, by the distinguished critic of socialism Friedrich Hayek. Agamben's work, by contrast, has been described as exuding "the perfume of the radical." No doubt this is partly because Agamben, unlike Hayek, is just as scathing on markets as he is on governments. But another reason Agamben has become an icon of the Left rather than the Right would appear to be the way his work can explain the recent history of the United States.

It is often noted of political magazines that they thrive in opposition. The conservative monthly *The American Spectator*, for example, saw its biggest readership during the Clinton administration, while the Iraq War resulted in a sharp circulation increase for *The Nation*, a left-wing weekly. Something similar seems to happen with political theorists. In Agamben's case, his rise to prominence occurred during the War on Terror. Many academic critics of the U.S. government's response to September 11 used Agamben's concept of *homo sacer* to explain the legal limbo in which so-called enemy combatants were detained at Guantánamo. Similarly, Agamben himself has characterized the 2001 Patriot Act, and the sweeping emergency powers it granted the U.S. government in the name of counterterrorism, as yet another state of exception instituted by a sovereign.

It is not hard to see why many people would invoke Agamben's ideas to understand the actions of the U.S. government in the aftermath of September 11. Few administrations have so clearly exemplified "the strange relationship of law and lawlessness" that Agamben is uniquely concerned with. It would be shortsighted, however, to regard Agamben as merely an especially severe critic of George W. Bush. His theory applies just as much to Italian Communist politicians of the 1970s as it does to U.S. Republicans thirty years later. This is because Agamben is a critic not of a particular party or state, but of the modern state as such, and of its ability to consign refugees, Guantánamo Bay detainees and many other groups to an enduring state of exception. Advocates who invoke human rights in response only hasten along the state's invasive and limitless scope. Such advocates fail to realize that the sovereign state represents not the solution to any human rights crisis, but the cause. "This is what, in our culture, the hypocritical dogma of the sacredness of human rights and the vacuous declarations of human rights are meant to hide."

Agamben's arguments provoke strong reactions. A book he wrote on the Holocaust was once branded "pornographic" in the normally calm pages of an academic journal. Another critic has denounced his political writings for exhibiting an "ontological loathing for government." It is easy to imagine Agamben's debunking view of human rights also garnering a hostile reaction. It is important to note, however, that Agamben's criticism of human rights places him in distinguished company.

Ever since the rights of man were widely promulgated in the eighteenth century, there have been thinkers who offer principled reason for rejecting those rights. Hannah Arendt, who also belongs to this skeptical tradition, gives a sense of its lineage when she invokes the father of modern conservatism, Edmund Burke, in her analysis of the situation of refugees. "These facts and reflections," Arendt writes, "offer what seem an ironical, bitter and belated confirmation of the famous arguments with which Edmund Burke opposed the French Revolution's Declaration of the Rights of Man. They appear to buttress his assertion that human rights were an 'abstraction,' that it was much wiser to rely on an 'entitled inheritance' of rights which one transmits to one's children like life itself, and to claim one's rights to the 'rights of an Englishman' rather that the inalienable rights of man."

Burke criticized the rights of man as part of a rejection of the French Revolution and an affirmation of a more conservative approach to politics. Yet before the twentieth century, it was not just conservatives who rejected human rights. Many thinkers who otherwise disagreed profoundly with Burke also took a dim view of the rights of man. Karl Marx, for example, ridiculed "so-called human rights," which he felt did little more than reinforce capitalism and the right to private property. Similarly, nineteenth-century liberal Jeremy Bentham famously denounced the rights referred to in the Declaration of the Rights of Man as nonsense upon stilts.

Agamben's philosophy contains many original insights, and his references to Guantánamo Bay and the international zones of European airports could not be more contemporary. But the most significant aspect of his work may be that it has kept alive the skeptical tradition regarding human rights. Agamben himself suggests such an affinity when, like Arendt, he singles out Burke's critique for praise. According to Agamben, the Old Whig's remark that "he preferred his 'Rights of an Englishman' to the inalienable rights of man [contains] an unsuspected profundity." In the matter of human rights, we thus appear to have come full circle. A thinker of the twenty-first century Left urges upon us the wisdom of the eighteenth-century Right.

What are we to make of Giorgio Agamben and the larger tradition of human rights skepticism he represents? Some rights advocates feel the justification of human rights is too obvious to be worth debating, and so dismiss Agamben's criticisms. This response is short-sighted. Agamben's books and articles speak to a large audience, and his ideas are given a respectful hearing in classrooms, conference sessions and editorial offices around the world. Many people believe Agamben is on to something, however much excess his position may contain. Nothing could be more detrimental to the future of human rights than to turn it into a dogma that never responds to probing critiques such as his. We should, therefore, take Agamben's criticisms seriously.

But should we agree with them? In Agamben's view, governments became dangerously intrusive only in the eighteenth century, with the rise of rights. But is this really true? Agamben ignores the many ways governments intervened at a "biopolitical" level prior to the age of rights, as when they classified some people as slaves from the time of birth, and devoted a vast legal apparatus to making sure they stayed slaves throughout their lives. As for the suggestion that there is a hidden affinity between human rights and Nazi ideology, it is even harder to take. It is true that when viewed from a high level of abstraction, both doctrines can be said to grant the state a large role in matters relating to the basic biological needs of its subjects. But that is *all* they have in common. Agamben's suggestion of a family resemblance passes silently over the role that hatred, racism and anti-Semitism played in Nazi ideology, as if these were minor elements, not worth distinguishing from the inclusiveness and impartiality of human rights.

Make no mistake, Agamben's analysis contains genuine insights. His emphasis on the power of political authorities to declare states of exception and suspend the normal operation of law captures a disturbing feature of how governments actually operate, especially during times of crisis. Similarly, his philosophy would seem well suited to explain how politicians from the United States to Australia justify harsh non-arrival measures for refugees under the guise of humanitarianism: policies that put refugees' lives at risk are justified by rhetorical appeals to concerns about the same refugees' welfare. But for every thought-provoking insight that Agamben throws out, there are one or more key questions he leaves unaddressed. And nowhere is this truer than in regard to his argument against human rights.

When someone asks us to let go of our commitment to human rights, what exactly are we being asked to give up? Human rights, after all, is an idea with several distinct parts. One component, for example, involves a commitment to moral universalism. All human beings occupy a position of moral worth, and we cannot just write off this or that group because they are the wrong ethnicity, the wrong religion or the wrong nationality. A second aspect of human rights is a commitment to some basic minimum standard of treatment. Human rights advocates may disagree whether any particular entitlement is a right or not, but they all share the view that there is some minimum threshold of fundamental rights that no human being should be deprived of. A third aspect of human rights involves idealism: rights advocates believe rights are worth insisting on even, or especially, in situations in which someone's rights are not being respected (an aspect of human rights, as we saw, that Arendt failed to recognize). Finally, a commitment to human rights is also a commitment to realism, as human rights advocates recognize that rights will not be upheld spontaneously, but must rather be written into law. Rights need to be enforced.

Universalism. Minimalism. Idealism. Realism. Critics and supporters of human rights could potentially have different items on this list in mind when they are debating whether or not to abandon human rights. Agamben does not seem to object to universalism or minimalism. This is perhaps unsurprising. The episodes he highlights of refugees being mistreated, in internment camps during World War II or in airports today, derive their force from the fact that they involve human beings being denied dignity and respect. (If Agamben were urging us not to care how human beings are treated, such stories of injustice would have no point.) Agamben also does not seem to object to the fact that human rights is an idealistic doctrine, one that is invoked in situations in which human rights are violated. Rather, his objection seems to centre primarily on the realist aspect of human rights, as something subject to enforcement by government.

No human rights advocates can be complacent about the role governments play as upholders of rights. As Samantha Power has written, the reason rights were needed historically was that states could not be trusted to automatically respect the moral worth of the human beings under their control. "Yet the evolving human rights system left those same untrustworthy states in charge of enforcing these allegedly inalienable rights." There is thus a paradox involved in the implementation of rights: the same institution that commits the grossest human rights abuses, the state, is simultaneously tasked with ensuring such abuses do not occur. And states, there is no denying, often fail to live up to this crucial responsibility.

But if the authority that human rights invest in the state is the core of Agamben's objection, then a key question his argument raises is, what is the alternative? Is there some better arrangement that would allow us to hang on to the universalism, minimalism and idealism of human rights without granting such a central role to governments? A major shortcoming of Agamben's work is that it never addresses this question. The only concrete political proposal I am aware of in his writings occurs when Agamben endorses a suggestion to make Jerusalem the capital of two states, one Israeli and the other Palestinian (although it is not clear why Agamben would want Palestinians, Israelis or anyone else to have a state of their own, given the low regard in which he holds all governments). More common is for him to discuss problems associated with states and to speculate about "the possibility of a nonstatist politics" without suggesting how the problems of the state can be avoided or saying anything about what a nonstatist politics might look like.

Agamben's bleak view of the state, combined with his enduring silence in regard to alternatives, has led some commentators to take him for an anarchist. Perhaps Agamben does not mean to go quite that far. But insofar as his philosophy even flirts with anarchism, it shows that the problem he is grappling with is not a problem unique to human rights. It is a problem that will occur when any moral concept is written into law, whether the concept at hand is human rights, citizen rights or some pre-modern alternatives to rights such as virtues or manners or divine commands. Agamben's real problem, in other words, is not with human rights as a moral concept. His problem is with any political institution powerful enough to enforce moral claims—with political authority as such.

Once we see this, it becomes clear why another Italian philosopher would call Agamben "a thinker of great value but also, in my opinion, a thinker with no political vocation." Agamben's lack of a political vocation is evident in his lack of realism. He is not concerned to point to any solutions, propose any new arrangements or endorse any existing political institution on the face of the earth. He is here to bring home to us, relentlessly and unblinkingly if he must, the many negative aspects of the system of sovereign states that dominates the globe. But the more the state itself is taken as the real problem, the less it matters that different governments employ vastly different measures when it comes to refugees and human rights. Agamben's analysis shifts our attention away from any individual government to focus exclusively on the institution of government itself. Policy-makers who implement the worst measures are thus given an alibi for their actions: the state did it, not us.

Making progress on refugee issues requires distinguishing between better and worse states. We also need to conceptually distinguish politicians who administer severe policies such as interdiction and mandatory detention from the human rights groups who speak out against the same measures. And if we are to make any progress in the world we inhabit, we need to see states themselves as worthy receptacles of our hopes. These are all impulses Agamben's philosophy would wrongly have us overcome. As sometimes happens with hyper-radicalism, his political stance is ultimately one of arch-conservatism. The radicalism occurs at the level of expression. But at the level of consequences, absolutely everything is left in place.

By keeping alive the anti–human rights tradition, Agamben performs the valuable service of reminding us how contingent was the rise of human rights to a position of prominence today. Before the modern era, people used many concepts other than rights to organize and express their moral and political commitments, and regarded institutions other than the state, such as the family and the church, as morality's rightful custodians and enforcers. That we now live in a world in which international treaties and organizations use human rights as their justification, and the Universal Declaration of Human Rights is one of the most translated documents on earth, is a contingent rather than necessary truth. It is good to be reminded of this, and that history could have gone a different way. But by offering nothing to replace human rights, Agamben would have us risk those gains that human rights have allowed us to achieve for the sake of an unknown and untested alternative. An alternative, moreover, that could all too easily exhibit the same problems Agamben associates with human rights.

When historians look back at Agamben's rise during the early years of the twenty-first century, they may take it as a sad commentary on just how poorly the United States and other governments upheld human rights during the same period. But that would at least explain how a thinker as unworldly and unrealistic as Giorgio Agamben became a prominent interpreter of such a worldly and realistic doctrine as human rights.

In the early 1990s Algeria descended into a civil war that saw writers and journalists targeted for arrest, imprisonment and assassination. Events in Algeria inspired Salman Rushdie, Václav Havel, Susan Sontag and roughly three hundred other authors to establish the International Parliament of Writers. A founding belief of the IPW was that traditional forms of literary protest were worn out and inadequate. In the words of IPW member

Pierre Bourdieu, "writers and intellectuals can no longer content themselves with petitions and protests. Their first priority today is to reply to censorship with the creation of new spaces of freedom." In keeping with this philosophy, the IPW held a congress in Strasbourg, France, in 1996, at which a distinguished group of mayors, European Union dignitaries and intellectuals gathered to hear French philosopher Jacques Derrida issue a call for "a genuine innovation in the history of the right to asylum."

Derrida is our second philosophical responder to Arendt. At the time of his IPW speech he was sixty-five years old. Born and raised in Algeria, he had gained prominence in France in the 1960s as the founder of the philosophy known as deconstruction. Deconstruction is notoriously difficult to sum up, but one undaunted reference work describes it as a way of reading literary and philosophical texts that "casts doubt upon the possibility of finding in them a definitive meaning and traces instead the multiplication . . . of possible meanings." This manner of reading is controversial because, in the view of some critics, deconstruction presses its case too far and winds up abolishing truth and meaning altogether. (Derrida also has an idiosyncratic and difficult writing style, and this has given rise to the additional charge that deconstruction is a form of obscurantism.)

Derrida gained an unusual degree of prominence over the course of his career. A 2002 documentary depicts him speaking to large and enthusiastic audiences from New York to South Africa, generating a level of fascination we tend to associate more with rock stars than university professors. A consequence of Derrida's fame was that he was frequently asked to lend his name to political causes. As a friend of the Derrida family remarked after his death in 2004, "Toward the end of his life, [Derrida] enjoyed the same status as Aristotle among the ancients, and every perception of injustice was routed to his desk." In response to these requests, Derrida produced a steady stream of speeches, letters and articles that are quite unlike his academic writings. Written in a straightforward prose style, they address concrete issues such as the death penalty or the European Union. As these political writings do not involve deconstruction, even Derrida's most severe academic critics could in principle agree with them.

Derrida's speech to the International Parliament of Writers is of this type. It addresses two developments involving immigrants and refugees that had recently occurred in France. The first was an immigration reform known as the Pasqua law. Named after Charles Pasqua, France's interior minister at the time of its introduction, the 1993 Pasqua law gave French police the power to stop and check the papers of anyone who might be a foreigner. The law also ended the practice of automatically granting citizenship to the children of foreigners who were born on French soil once they turned eighteen. Such children would now have to apply for French citizenship in young adulthood, an application that could potentially be rejected. Shortly after Derrida's speech, France's centre-right government would introduce draft legislation that went even further. It would have required any French citizen who hosted a guest from outside the European Union to notify the authorities of the foreigner's arrival and departure. Derrida's speech, delivered at a time when such measures enjoyed a broad plurality of support in public opinion, is a sustained protest against the "mean-minded" attitude he takes them to express.

The second and more immediate development addressed in Derrida's speech was the creation of a network of "cities of asylum." This IPW initiative, which began in 1994, saw the writers' group take it upon itself to place refugee authors with host municipalities. Each exiled writer received a place to work, stipends of up to US$50,000, assistance with immigration and publishing and, where necessary, physical protection. A conscious goal of the project was to seek out the co-operation of cities rather than states. As IPW executive director Christian Salmon summarized the organizations' thinking, "Since the Middle Ages, cities, being more liberal in this regard than states, have very often welcomed people who had been banished, and protected those who were threatened." Within five years of its founding, the asylum network came to include thirty municipalities, including Barcelona, Frankfurt, Salzburg and Venice, and had spread as far as Brazil, Mexico, Senegal and Nigeria.

Derrida's speech is a meditation on the cities of asylum project and how it might serve as an inspiration for a new model of protection, one that would be extended not merely to exiled writers, but to asylum-seekers in general. Derrida points to a crisis of asylum in France, and argues that the traditional state-level system is no longer effective. The underlying cause of this breakdown, he argues, is the tension between human rights and national sovereignty highlighted by Arendt. As he puts it, "Arendt was writing of something which still remains true today."

Derrida's use of Arendt's ideas to explain contemporary European trends is confident and clear. When it comes to offering solutions to the asylum problem, however, he grows tentative and hesitant. He argues that experimentation with different forms of protection is necessary, and that the cities of asylum project should serve as a model for what one new form of asylum might look like. When it comes to specifics, however, Derrida seems reluctant to put forward his own blueprint for reform. Instead, he seems to want his remarks to inspire the imagination of his audience, who will conceive their own solutions to the problem. (This position is one Derrida also adopts in his philosophical works, perhaps out of distaste for the idea of a philosopher serving as an authoritative guru.) If that is the case, it is worth noting that Derrida's remarks can be taken to suggest two different understandings of what a "city of asylum" might mean.

Sometimes Derrida seems to be concerned with cities of asylum in a more or less literal sense, as when he speaks of a new role for cities, "equipped with new rights and greater sovereignty." Here and elsewhere, he seem to suggest that the city is the last, best hope for human rights. The state is exhausted, and the history of the European Union to date has not revealed continental entities to be any better. As Derrida puts it, "At a time when we claim to be lifting internal borders, we proceed to bolt the external borders of the European Union tightly." But what if we have been looking in the wrong place? What if instead of looking above states, we should instead be looking below them? In regard to the city, Derrida asks, "could it, when dealing with the related questions of hospitality and refuge, elevate itself above nation-states, or at least free itself from them, in order to become . . . a *free city*?"

This proposal may sound unrealistic. As if to allay this fear, Derrida points out that his speech is taking place in Strasbourg. Located on France's border with Germany, the Alsace capital embodies sovereignty's changing history. Before its annexation by France in the 1600s, Strasbourg was part of the Roman Empire, a disputed territory fought over by religious and civic authorities, and a Free Imperial City with special status under jurisdiction of the Holy Roman Emperor. Between the 1870s and 1940s, France and Germany exchanged control of Strasbourg four times. After World War II it became home to pan-European institutions such as the Council of Europe and the European Court of Human Rights, and it has since come to symbolize a united Europe. In keeping with this unique status, in 2005 Strasbourg was designated one of the EU's first Eurodistricts, a new administrative entity that integrates urban areas that straddle national borders.

When Derrida gave his speech, Strasbourg, the Council of Europe and the European Parliament all had representatives in the audience, and they would have been familiar with the city's history. Derrida would thus appear to be drawing attention to the uncharted possibilities Strasbourg represents when he refers to it as "this generous border city, this eminently European city, the capital city of Europe, and the first of our refuge cities." At a time when European institutions were rapidly evolving, Derrida was saying, Europeans should take seriously the idea that that evolution be directed in such a way as to give greater autonomy to cities, so that they might function as islands of asylum in an ocean of unwelcoming states.

This, then, is the first understanding of a city of asylum Derrida's remarks suggest: give actual cities more sovereignty. The second interpretation, by contrast, takes a more metaphoric form. It is hinted at by the many religious references scattered throughout Derrida's remarks. At one point, for example, he argues that the asylum cities project evokes the notion of a city of refuge as described in the Book of Numbers. As Derrida summarizes the relevant biblical passage, "God orders Moses to institute cities which would be, according to the very letter of the bible itself, 'cities of refuge,' or 'asylum,' and to begin with there would be six cities of refuge, in particular for the 'resident alien,' or 'temporary settler.'" In a similar spirit, Derrida urges his audience to study the medieval practice of sanctuary, which saw European churches offer refuge to criminals and other individuals wanted by political authorities. Finally, he evokes the concept of hospitality, a term with special meaning in his philosophy, one that functions as a broad synonym for ethics. This occurs when Derrida refers to an "unconditional Law of hospitality," a phrase that is meant to suggest the notion of a moral law that is conditioned by human-made laws but is not reducible to any one of them.

A moral law above the law. Biblical cities of refugee. The medieval practice of sanctuary. These ideas all have something in common. Each has traditionally been used to justify the so-called sanctuary movement. This term became prominent in the United States in the 1980s, and has since come to refer to churches that proclaim themselves "sanctuaries" for non-citizens who have run afoul of immigration laws, particularly people whose refugee claims have been rejected. These types of sanctuary cases, which usually see church officials arguing that their government has failed to recognize a genuine refugee, are now a fact of life everywhere from North America and Europe to Australia and South Africa. Such cases can see a failed refugee claimant and his or her family living inside a church for months or even years. Governments are often slow to take action in response, no doubt because of the bad publicity that raids on churches can generate.

Derrida's references to what he calls our "secularized theological heritage" suggests an affinity between church-based sanctuary and the form of protection offered by the International Parliament of Writers. In both cases, offering protection to refugees is not something left to governments. It is rather a social good that private groups take it upon themselves to provide, the difference being that one group is literary while the others are religious. Such a parallel is further suggested by Derrida's remarks about hospitality, which he sees as an ethical idea that can be embodied on a public or a private level. The parallel to religious sanctuary is also in keeping with the positive attitude Derrida exhibits toward people in France who were willing to break the law in the name of welcoming foreigners, in defiance of the measures French politicians were then proposing. Referring to the government's plan to criminalize certain forms of hospitality extended toward foreigners, Derrida remarks, "We have doubtless chosen the term 'cities of refuge' because, for quite specific historical reasons, it commands our respect, and also out of respect for those who cultivate an 'ethic of hospitality.'"

What to make of Derrida's unusual speech? Many of the restrictive immigration measures he criticized would later attract widespread opposition. In 1997, 100,000 people marched in Paris to defend their right to have non-Europeans in their homes without informing the authorities, causing the government to abandon its planned legislation. Similarly, the Pasqua law was eventually revised. It is to Derrida's credit that he spoke out against such policies when they still enjoyed significant support in public opinion. He is also right to stress the relevance of Arendt's ideas for contemporary European debates, and he displays an admirable independence of mind by treating sovereignty not as a brute and unchanging fact of nature, but as an institution within the realm of rational scrutiny and revision. In short, there is much to admire in Derrida's position.

But when it comes to human rights, the question is whether Derrida points us toward a solution to the problem Arendt identified. Does either interpretation of his notion of a city of asylum grant meaningful rights to refugees?

In regard to cities of asylum taken in a literal sense, it is worth noting that there once was something like such a city. This was Shanghai, which on the eve of World War II became an unlikely haven for refugees. In the late 1930s the Far Eastern metropolis was populated by over four million Chinese people and roughly 100,000 foreigners. It was, in the words of historian Michael Marrus, "the fifth largest port in the world—crowded, dirty, cosmopolitan, with a reputation for crime, violence, and intrigue." In 1938 and 1939 Shanghai, unlike every other jurisdiction on earth, required no visas or travel papers for entry. This meant it would not turn away Jews, who began sailing for Shanghai in large numbers after Germany annexed Austria. So many refugees arrived that, by the summer of 1939, several Shanghai neighbourhoods had a Germanic feel, having become home to German-language newspapers, concert halls and coffeehouses. In its status as the "port of last resort," Shanghai eventually allowed between fifteen thousand and seventeen thousand Jews to escape the gas chambers.

At first glance Shanghai might appear to lend support to Derrida's proposal, in that its openness to refugees was a result of an unusual form of government. Since 1854 Shanghai had been home to two foreign-controlled districts, known as the French Concession and the International Settlement, both of which were administered by municipal councils made up primarily of Westerners. After Japan invaded in 1937 and took over all Chinese-administered parts of the city, power was split between three entities, none of which was authorized to control immigration (hence the openness to foreigners). However, in August of 1939, Japan, which controlled Shanghai's harbour, imposed entry requirements that eventually brought Jewish immigration to a halt. The governments of France, the United States and the United Kingdom also worked to close Shanghai's doors. The resulting effort, according to historian David Kranzler, "took on the character of a universal conspiracy to prevent further emigration from Germany of those thousands of potential refugees whose only haven was Shanghai."

National governments played a key role in ending Shanghai's status as a city of refuge. But it is also important to note the actions of the Shanghai Municipal Council, the democratically elected body that oversaw the International Settlement (the French council took similar steps, but reported to an unelected French official). Rather than protest the actions of the Japanese authorities, the council acted as quickly as it could to put in place a similar policy for the International Settlement. As historian Marcia Ristaino has noted, anti-refugee attitudes were widespread among Shanghai's English-speaking community. "Both American and British residents displayed the garden variety of country-club anti-Semitism by wanting to exclude these poor and 'foreign' persons from their neighborhoods. It was common to see advertisements in the prestigious *North China Daily News* that blatantly refused rentals to refugees."

The fact that a democratically elected municipal body such as the Shanghai Municipal Council could close the door to deserving refugees highlights a problem with Derrida's suggestion that cities be granted "new rights and greater sovereignty." The problem is not that any contemporary city with greater sovereignty will necessarily share the prejudices of 1930s Shanghailanders. The problem is that shifting sovereignty to an entity other than a state is no guarantee that the entity in question will uphold the rights of refugees. Just as a larger sovereign entity above states is not more likely to enforce the rights of asylum-seekers simply because it is larger (as European Union asylum policy would appear to attest), a sub-state entity such as a city is no more likely to uphold the rights of asylum-seekers simply because it is smaller.

Indeed, if anything, sovereign cities might well be *less* welcoming to refugees than are states. As it is now, when refugees arrive in Western countries they are often portrayed as overwhelming the host society's capacity to absorb them, even when the refugees in question represent a minuscule proportion of the receiving society's population. Given that the average city has a smaller population than the average state, this anxiety-driven response to refugees could easily become even more pronounced if cities became the primary receiving entities. (If a city were small enough and received a large enough influx, the concern might actually be true for once.) Derrida's proposal requires a greater level of detail outlining how civic sovereignty could be designed so as to avoid this problem. It also needs to be explained why, assuming some such model of sovereignty exists, it cannot be implemented on a national level.

This brings us to the second version of the city of refuge suggested by Derrida's remarks, the one that implicitly likens the

Parliament of Writers project to a church sanctuary. It is not clear how far Derrida wants to push the parallel: he may be suggesting the writers' group go so far as to break the law, the same way churches do when they shelter refugee claimants. Alternatively, he may merely be suggesting that as a private group, the IPW should do what it can to ensure asylum to individual refugees and their families. But insofar as Derrida's proposal even hints at illegal activity, our assessment of it will be influenced by where we stand on church-based sanctuary, a question that requires a brief detour into the debate over this controversial practice.

Church-based sanctuary has been called everything from an "obsolete privilege" to an institution that "facilitates lawlessness." Critics are right to stress the importance of obeying the law, but wrong to think that this represents a knock-down argument against sanctuary. Leaving aside religious defences of the practice, which are usually aimed at a particular religious community, sanctuary for genuine refugees can be justified on inclusive grounds as a form of civil disobedience.

People who engage in certain forms of law-breaking can be separated from common criminals if they meet five conditions. The first is that they break the law in a non-violent way. Second, they must do so publicly, and not try to mask their identities or hide from the police. Third, they must be willing to go to jail if the authorities choose to press charges. Fourth, their disobedience needs to be plausibly construed as correcting an injustice, rather than advancing their own gain (law-breaking aimed at maximizing profits or changing a zoning bylaw to build a mansion could never count as civil disobedience). Finally, the illegal activity must be undertaken as a last resort, either after all avenues of democratic change have been exhausted, or to avert some serious and immanent wrong that the authorities cannot or will not prevent.

When church sanctuary meets all of these conditions, it should cause us to reject "the mindless view that conscientious disobedience is the same as lawlessness," as the legal theorist Ronald Dworkin once put it. From this point of view, everything hangs on the circumstances of the individual asylum-seeker involved, and how much evidence there is that the government has made a mistake with his or her file. Given the fallibility of human judgment, it seems reasonable to expect that governments will sometimes make mistakes and fail to recognize a genuine refugee. By the same token, however, churches may also sometimes go astray and offer sanctuary to individuals who do not really warrant it. This means that there can be no across-the-board justification or rejection of sanctuary, only judgments about individual cases.

Is it possible to determine how many sanctuary cases to date have involved genuine refugees? There is no uncontroversial way to answer this question. It is worth noting, however, that governments have acknowledged that deportation decisions are sometimes mistaken. A study of church sanctuary in Canada, where the practice is comparatively common, found that there were thirty-six sanctuary cases between 1983 and 2003, involving 261 people made up of asylum claimants and their family members. Eventually 70 percent of the people being sheltered this way obtained legal status.

What does Canada's experience show? Suppose for the sake of argument that the Canadian government was far too lenient in the majority of its reversals, and only 20 percent of those 261 individuals really deserved to avoid deportation. Even if that were the case, it would suggest that twenty years of sanctuary had the overall effect of not making a difference in a third of instances; allowed seventy-odd people to circumvent normal immigration procedures to remain in Canada; and prevented the deportation of fifty-two deserving people, made up of refugees and their family members. Given that someone who obtained citizenship this way would be committing a victimless crime, while a deported refugee family is at risk of seeing at least one of its members killed, the record of Canadian sanctuary to date would appear on balance to be more good than bad.

The upshot of this excursion into the sanctuary debate? Derrida is not crazy to find inspiration in church-based refugee sanctuary. Indeed, if he were encouraging the writers' parliament to commit civil disobedience, it would only strengthen his proposal. If the IPW were to get into the asylum business, it would do the most good if it devoted its energies to helping genuine refugees who had been mistakenly rejected by governments. Yet even so, there is still a problem with Derrida's finding inspiration in church-based sanctuary. It is that sanctuary can at best be an occasional corrective to a government-run asylum system, rather than a replacement.

The largest sanctuary initiative of all time was probably the one that developed in the United States in the 1980s. At the time, critics charged that U.S. Immigration authorities were deliberately rejecting asylum claims by people from Central American countries that were U.S. client-states. In response, a group of priests, nuns and lay church members based in Arizona began to help Hondurans and Salvadorans, either picking them up just after they crawled through holes in the international fence or hiding them in the backs of station wagons and driving them over the border. Between 1981 and 1986, the Arizona sanctuary movement built up a network of churches (and a few synagogues) that eventually stretched as far north as Chicago. Yet even though the Arizona activists managed to develop a national network of sanctuaries, and went so far as to engage in people-smuggling, the total number of people they helped is estimated at two to three thousand. That is a tiny proportion of the tens of thousands of asylum cases that the United States accepted during the same six-year period.

This discrepancy should remind us that when it comes to asylum there is no comparing the power of churches to that of a state. The vast power imbalance between the two institutions was vividly brought home when the U.S. government eventually sent eight members of the Arizona network to prison for people-smuggling. Since that time, authorities in other countries have also demonstrated a willingness to bring the law to bear against sanctuary providers. In 2004, for example, Canadian police launched their first raid on a sanctuary church, St.-Pierre United in Quebec City, and deported an Algerian refugee claimant who was staying there. A similar raid occurred on an even larger scale in Derrida's own city in 1996, when fifteen hundred police used tear gas, clubs and axes to storm Paris's St. Bernard Church and evict three hundred African migrants who had been living inside (a raid carried out with such force that when it was broadcast on the news it triggered national protests). Derrida's private sanctuaries would ultimately seem no match for a government determined to deny hospitality to an individual.

In 2004 the International Parliament of Writers dissolved and was replaced by two separate organizations in North America and Europe. The website of the International Cities of Refuge Network, or ICORN, as the European successor group is called, features the following disclaimer: "Neither the network nor its individual cities have authority over the laws and regulations of any country. Therefore [it] strongly discourages all applicants and candidates from relying on ICORN as their only option for refuge." Private organizations that offer help to refugees perform an important and necessary task, and the lengths to which many religious individuals have gone is nothing short of heroic. But the limitation noted by ICORN will apply to any private asylum initiative, whatever its form. For this reason, it does not represent an adequate response to the problem Hannah Arendt identified.

Agamben and Derrida represent two different philosophical responses to Arendt. Agamben seeks to disabuse us of our commitment to human rights and what he sees as its negative dependence on the state. Derrida, by contrast, focuses on sovereignty and urges us to think outside its current bounds. Derrida employs the language of hospitality rather than rights, but he is much more comfortable than Agamben is with the commonsense idea, shared by human rights advocates, that we need political institutions to enforce, through law, our moral commitments. Yet both Derrida and Agamben take it for granted that the appropriate response to Arendt involves a fundamental rethinking of one of the basic political categories she pointed to. But not everyone thinks that Arendt's human rights problem is best addressed this way. Our second group of writers, the pragmatists, respond to Arendt at a more down-to-earth level.

This brings us back to Samantha Power, the first of our two pragmatists. Power was born in Ireland and moved to the United States as a child. In her mid-twenties she travelled to Bosnia to cover the war there. After returning to the United States she served as the founding director of the Carr Center for Human Rights Policy, a research and teaching institute based at Harvard. In 2005–06 she took a leave of absence from academia to work as foreign policy adviser to Senator Barack Obama, whose interest in genocide she is credited with fostering (and whose presidential election campaign she resigned from after calling Hillary Clinton a "monster" in a newspaper interview).

Throughout all these guises, Power has approached human rights issues from a perspective that mixes idealism with a strong dose of realism. Such a cast of mind is evident in Power's account of her visit to Chad. The camps the Darfuris occupied, she notes, were "a stew of disease and malnutrition," not fit for animals, let alone human beings. As the refugees approached Power, they would discuss with her how they thought the outside world should respond. "They would come up to you," Power recalls, "and they would draw on their sense of what human rights are. It wasn't a formal sense of what the Universal Declaration of

Human Rights says, but a much more intuitive sense: 'Hey, we're people, and this is what they've done to us. Aren't you coming? Aren't you on the outside going to come and help?'"

Power had devoted her career to awakening politicians to the need to stop crimes against humanity, and she could not have agreed more strongly with the basic moral claim the refugees were making. Yet reading Arendt had also brought home to Power that moral claims often fail to motivate action. As Power puts it, "I was reminded [that] summer again of Arendt's large and prophetic point that when all you can draw upon is your humanity, on 'Hey, I'm a human being, help,' that that doesn't actually buy you very much. That it's very rarely enough to trigger outside action, to simply be a human being in need."

Although Power is an admirer of Arendt, she does not see human rights as an unenforceable concept. Instead, she points to the important role that non-government organizations now play in rights advancement. As Power notes, such groups have grown in size and scope, to the point that they are able to expose and oppose human rights violations around the world: "Arendt could not have envisaged a day when a non-state entity like Human Rights Watch would spend more than US$22 million per year, and would conduct its own rigorous field investigations to shame criminal officials, their abettors, and the world's bystanders. And far more important than international human rights groups are the hundreds of thousands of indigenous human rights groups—led by labor organizers, women's suffrage advocates, AIDS activists, fledgling independent newspaper journalists, and others—throughout the developing world. It is with these groups that hope lies."

For Power, an important reason to place our hope in the rights groups of the developing world is that they "see themselves not as 'human beings in general,'" but as members of particular communities, with a stake in how elections are conducted, in whether the police uphold the rule of law, and other local issues. For this reason, Power suggests, such groups are not vulnerable to the criticisms Arendt makes of human rights and their lack of effectiveness. When we look beyond states to civil society, we find a reason to continue to place our faith in the rights of humanity.

Power's view of NGOs is a refreshing contrast to Arendt's more cynical take on the subject. Arendt was dismissive of the "professional idealists" who formed such organizations. She wrote, "The groups they formed, the declarations they issued, showed an uncanny similarity in language and composition to that of societies for the prevention of cruelty to animals. No statesman, no political figure of any importance could possibly take them seriously." Arendt's negative view has not aged well. As we saw in the Haitian refugee crisis, it was a coalition of groups acting in the name of human rights that closed the Guantánamo HIV camp. This is only one example of what NGOs are capable of, and Power is right to stress the crucial role such organizations play in the advancement and protection of rights around the world.

But this still leaves the question of whether NGOs can address the particular problem we are concerned with, which requires the enforcement not of the rights of people in general, but of people seeking asylum. Power's remark that rights groups often see themselves as members of local communities first and foremost, rather than proponents of human rights in general, does not really address Arendt's criticism of human rights, as her criticism does not have to do with how human rights organizations see themselves, or what their motivations are. Rather, Arendt highlighted the problem of upholding enforceable legal rights for someone who is no longer a member of a political community and so no longer fully protected by the law of any country.

Once the nature of Arendt's human rights problem is recalled, it is sobering to note a less encouraging lesson of the Haiti refugee crisis. The Yale team was supported by one of the most distinguished coalitions of non-governmental groups ever assembled. Supporting briefs in its lawsuits were filed by Amnesty International, the Lawyers Committee for Human Rights, the International Human Rights Law Group, the American Immigration Lawyers Association, the United Nations High Commissioner for Refugees, the National Association for the Advancement of Colored People, the American Jewish Committee, the Anti-Defamation League and a half-dozen other organizations. These and many other dedicated NGOs also conducted extensive extra-legal advocacy work on the refugees' behalf. Yet in the end, even they were unable to overturn the Bush-Clinton policy of returning refugees to danger.

That such a distinguished coalition of NGOs was ultimately no match for federal administrations determined to violate the rights of refugees should cause us to recognize what NGOs can and cannot achieve on their own. What refugees need is shelter and protection, either from their own government or from some other powerful entity that is trying to do them harm. That is not something labour unions, AIDS activists or the other groups Power mentions can provide by themselves. Rather, it is something that can come only from another state, one that admits refugees and allows them to remain inside its borders. As important as NGOs are, they are not capable of enforcing the rights of refugees on their own. Stressing the importance of NGOs as Power does, therefore, although it is true as far as it goes, does not strike Arendt's human rights problem at its root.

An emphasis on the responsibilities of states is one of the defining features of the work of Matthew Gibney, our second pragmatist and final respondent to Arendt. Like Power, Gibney is himself a migrant. A native of Australia, he moved to the United Kingdom in the early 1990s to study at the University of Cambridge. While there he became interested in asylum and wound up writing his PhD dissertation on the subject. Almost as soon as Gibney started his research, Germany experienced its asylum crisis, and asylum shortly became a high-profile issue in other countries. "The topic was hot pretty soon after I picked it up and has remained so ever since," Gibney says. Today Gibney continues to work on issues related to asylum at the Refugee Studies Centre at the University of Oxford. "It is an area where the state can make an absolutely huge difference in an individual's life," Gibney says of his ongoing interest in the topic. In 2004 he published *The Ethics and Politics of Asylum*, the first book to examine both the political and ethical issues surrounding asylum.

Gibney's book opens with a quotation from Arendt, whom he goes on to criticize and praise. He points out that Arendt tended to see refugees in state-centric terms, as people persecuted by their own governments. The concept of a refugee is more coherent, Gibney argues, if it is broad enough to include someone like an Iraqi displaced by the U.S.-led invasion of Iraq, or a Zairean in flight from the Ebola virus. That is, anyone whose vital subsistence or security needs have been violated in such a way that their only recourse is to flee their home country. In redefining the very category of a refugee, Gibney displays his frequent willingness to go beyond Arendt's analysis. But when it comes to the difficulty of enforcing the rights of refugees, Gibney agrees with her. As he crisply summarizes her basic insight, "In spite of the lofty rhetoric of human rights . . . the implications of a lack of citizenship in a world carved up amongst sovereign nation-states were, as Arendt realised, absolutely devastating."

Gibney's approach to writing about refugees is reminiscent of Arendt's in that he puts forward a political theory that is richly informed by historical fact. His book is simultaneously an incisive critique of what contemporary thinkers have said about asylum issues and a magisterial documentation of the ways

Western states respond to asylum-seekers. But Gibney ultimately seeks to do more that diagnose and describe intellectual and political trends regarding asylum. He also makes recommendations regarding how governments should treat refugees and asylum-seekers. In doing so, Gibney hopes to avoid the otherworldly perspective that sometimes informs the recommendations of academic theorists. As Gibney puts it, "The detached perspective of the 'philosopher,' in which all or most obstacles to what is practically possible are removed, can give us a critical perspective that is simply unavailable to policy-makers."

This pragmatic perspective leads Gibney to eschew some of the more radical suggestions that other writers on asylum have made. As he notes, there is an academic school of thought that suggests the only way wealthy states can be fair to international migrants is to adopt open borders. Yet this overlooks the negative effect unfettered immigration could have on the welfare state: not only is it possible that a wave of recent arrivals might have short-term welfare needs that drain the receiving state's resources, but open borders could potentially result in such a huge influx that it erodes the population's willingness to provide public goods. Only slightly less unrealistic, Gibney argues, is the position of some refugee advocates that all measures states currently use to deter asylum-seekers from reaching their shores, such as imposing visa requirements and airline fines, are unjust and must be abandoned. It is a fact of life that economic migrants lodge false refugee claims, Gibney notes, and the question is not whether governments should put in place measures intended to stop them, but which particular no-entry measures are defensible.

What refugee policies does Gibney consider realistic? In outlining his answer to this question, we come to the core of Gibney's response to the asylum crisis. One thing politicians can do, he proposes, is to increase the number of refugees they admit—without raising the overall number of migrants they take in. Gibney notes that immigrants currently fall into three broad categories: economic migrants, family reunification cases and refugees. In no Western country do refugees make up one-third of the total immigration intake. This is the case even though refugees have a stronger moral case for entry than members of the other two categories. Were states to decide that they should take in more refugees at the expense of economic and family migrants, Gibney argues, it would "have profound implications for the distribution of protection."

This proposal is meant to avoid the backlash that might be expected if politicians were to increase immigration overall. Gibney's scheme is intended to be politically effective, given the constraints politicians currently face. But as Gibney points out, political leaders should not merely follow public opinion: they also have a responsibility to shape it. To that end, he proposes more long-term measures, designed to challenge the constraints politicians now operate within.

To foster that outcome, Gibney calls on politicians to pledge not to exploit popular anxiety over foreigners, as they sometimes do by playing off negative stereotypes about people seeking asylum (such as that they are all criminals, or prone to disease). As Gibney puts it, "Political leaders could attempt to establish greater political bipartisanship on asylum issues in order that the minimum requirements of humanitarianism can be met. The costs able to be borne for refugees are likely to be greater in a state where there is a political consensus not to exploit asylum for electoral gain than in one where it is seen like any other issue." Gibney also proposes government-sponsored public relations campaigns to increase awareness of the moral importance of asylum. Such efforts would see more resources devoted to combating racism and xenophobia, which sometimes colour public attitudes toward refugees.

In addition to these original proposals, Gibney also echoes a call that previous writers on refugee issues have made. It is that refugee-receiving states work together to create a new international system based on the principle of resettlement sharing. Right now, the United States, Canada and a few other Western countries individually seek out refugees from crisis zones overseas. But not only are these countries the exception, there are wide disparities in the overall number of refugees different countries admit. In 2004, for example, the United States, with a population of 292 million, took in 74,016 refugees, enough people to fill a modern football stadium. Japan, meanwhile, with a population of 127 million, found it in its heart to take in 24 people that same year, or about enough to fill a small bus. The disparity widens even more when we consider the millions of refugees in poor countries such as Pakistan and Iran. Gibney joins a long line of writers who call for an international system that would distribute refugees among receiving states in a more even-handed way. Various methods of doing so have been put forward, but each would see receiving countries work together to relocate refugees, either directly from crisis zones or from one receiving country to another, to counteract the wide disparities that characterize the current system.

Gibney's approach, like Power's, might be described as this-worldly idealism. It eschews radical or utopian visions for more practical and achievable outcomes. Although Power directs her attention to non-governmental organizations while Gibney focuses on politicians, their proposals are not mutually exclusive. There are many areas where NGOs and governments can work together. Consider Gibney's proposal to reshape public opinion. This has been a goal of groups such as the Refugees, Asylum-seekers and the Media Project, or RAM, a U.K.-based organization set up to counter the tabloid press's negative depiction of refugees by having British media outlets hire journalists who are themselves refugees (a project that has since evolved into the Exiled Journalists' Network). Politicians can provide groups such as RAM with financial and other forms of support. Similarly, Canada currently allows churches and other organizations to sponsor the resettlement of refugees from overseas, a process that often sees government working with non-government groups. Were European and other countries to adopt a similar program, it would harness the energy and creativity of NGOs in an area that has traditionally been left entirely to governments.

The measures Gibney recommends would all be welcome improvements on the way things currently stand, none more so than an international system of refugee resettlement. At the same time, however, his proposals come with built-in limits. Take his suggestion that one-third of the immigration intake of Western states be made up of refugees. From a humanitarian point of view, such an arrangement would certainly be an improvement over the current composition of immigration streams. But a key question this approach raises concerns how big the overall immigration intake of each country should be. Gibney's answer is that a country's existing immigration level should set its benchmark. In other words, refugees should make up one-third of however many immigrants any given country takes in right now. As Gibney points out, taking existing immigration levels as a standard gets around the problem of determining some objective international standard: "one can assume that these judgements provide a reasonable (albeit subjective) indication of the total volume of new entrants a state is capable at a minimum of integrating; it is, after all, the level that the government itself has chosen."

This reasonable-sounding proposal has a paradoxical element that becomes evident when we ask what its ramifications would be in places such as Japan, Israel and Germany, which do not see themselves as countries of immigration (or not a country of non-Jewish immigration in Israel's case). In Gibney's scheme, these countries would be allowed to take in low to negligible numbers of conventional refugees—because they take in few immigrants to begin with. Yet placing such policies beyond criticism risks legitimizing the same attitudes that the asylum-awareness campaigns and other measures Gibney proposes are meant to call into question. Similarly, if the international resettlement scheme Gibney favours is to come into being on a wide scale, the unreceptive attitudes of countries with tight models of citizenship must be up for re-examination. Challenging such attitudes, however, requires a degree of criticism of national policies toward immigration, something Gibney's approach consciously avoids.

Finally, there is Gibney's call for greater bipartisanship on asylum. There have been times when such an understanding did inform national debates. Malcolm Fraser, a former prime minister of Australia, once told an interviewer that during his time in power, in the 1970s and 1980s, there was such a consensus in place regarding refugees. Fraser, however, made this remark in 2004, after the Australian consensus had been replaced by the attitude on display in the *Tampa* episode. The timing of Fraser's comment illustrates how we tend to become aware of the value of a bipartisan consensus on asylum only after it has already broken down. As Gibney himself notes, anti-immigration politicians such as Pat Buchanan in the United States, Pauline Hanson in Australia and Jean-Marie Le Pen in France are all familiar products of democratic politics. The result would seem that bipartisanship regarding asylum will often be hardest to implement just when it is most needed.

This highlights the main problem with Gibney's approach. All of his proposals rely on elected politicians doing the right thing. As we saw in the case of Australia, where a group of backbench MPs ended mandatory detention, individual politicians can indeed bring about significant changes. But if Agamben goes too far in diverting our attention away from individual political actors, Gibney goes too far the other way in proposing solutions that ignore the structural factors that cause refugees to be mistreated. Often there are powerful incentives for politicians *not* to do the right thing, as when public opinion is genuinely against refugees. If we place our faith in politicians alone to uphold the rights of asylum-seekers, we are bound to be disappointed. We need to consider the possibility that some decisions, particularly those involving fundamental rights, should not be in the hands of elected officials. Yet precisely because Gibney's approach takes the exclusive authority of politicians for granted, it does not challenge the latitude they enjoy in dealing with asylum. Like Power's recommendations, Gibney's proposals are missing something. They are important and worth acting on wherever possible, yet not sufficient to safeguard the rights of refugees seeking asylum.

The philosophers and the pragmatists respond to Arendt in very different ways. Derrida and Agamben adopt a radical approach, asking us to rethink our sovereign institutions or our commitment to human rights. Power and Gibney take a more practical view, yet in so doing, they leave intact the structural features that make enforcing the rights of refugees so difficult in the first place. Neither approach, in short, mixes idealism with realism in quite the right measure. Could there be a third way that gets the balance right? I believe that there is, and that there is one country where such an approach has already begun. It is to that country that I now turn.

SEVEN

THE RIGHT TO HAVE RIGHTS

IT WAS RWANDA, 1994, and a genocide was unfolding. In Francine Peyti's village, the killers came in the morning. Members of her Tutsi ethnic group were marched into the village square and made to form two lines. Peyti, a young mother in her twenties, watched as Hutu militiamen set upon a row of Tutsis that included her parents and brother. The attackers used household machetes to hack at their victims' heads and torsos. After most of the village was dead, one of the younger killers rounded up Peyti, her husband, Paul, and their children. As the boy did so he quietly informed them he was a friend of the family. The teenager then turned to his accomplices and addressed them while waving his machete at Paul: "Go ahead and move on. I'll kill these ones myself, starting with him."

The boy brought his machete down on Paul's finger, separating it from his hand. Convinced of his intentions, the other militiamen left the square. Once they did so, the teenager motioned for Peyti and her family to run in the other direction. Eventually they found an abandoned house, in which they hid for ten days. When they emerged, the society they had known was gone. Throughout the countryside entire villages were empty. The bodies of their former inhabitants were strewn across the floors of churches and schoolrooms, or stacked in mounds every few hundred metres beside village roads.

The Peytis moved to a different part of Rwanda, where they lived in relative peace for three years. But in 1997 Tutsis who had witnessed the genocide were again targeted for violence. During this period, a group of armed men arrived at Peyti's door and took Paul away in an unmarked car. Two days later they returned with a message. Paul was dead, and Peyti would be next if she told anyone.

There was nothing left to do but run. Peyti and her remaining family made their way on foot and by minibus three hundred kilometres west to the border with Zaire (now the Democratic Republic of the Congo). Zaire was in the middle of a civil war, and Peyti's sister and other family members decided to stay at the border while Peyti sought a permanent refuge where the others could join her. After a harrowing journey through the countryside during which bandits shot at and nearly raped her, Peyti reached Kinshasa, Zaire's capital, where members of her extended family lived. After she told her relatives what had happened, they pooled their money to buy her a fake Dutch passport and a plane ticket. In May of 1997 she flew to Canada and filed a refugee claim. After it was accepted, Peyti still faced many challenges, including post-traumatic stress disorder. But she had managed to put the genocide and its aftermath behind her, and so could begin to live again.

Francine Peyti's story, like every refugee's story, is a testament to what Hannah Arendt termed the "violent courage of life": the insatiable will to survive that even genocide cannot snuff out. But Peyti's journey also symbolizes something about the country she fled to. Peyti arrived in Canada after it introduced a rights-based approach to asylum. Although Canada's approach is based on human rights, the rights it recognizes do not include a right to asylum. Canada thus holds out the possibility of enforcing human rights in a way that avoids the problems of the right-to-asylum approach. As such, Canada's experience points toward a means by which rights for refugees might be effectively enforced.

This is not because Canada's approach to refugees is perfect. As we will see, the country is an enthusiastic participant in the international trend of turning away refugees. Canada's shortcomings, however, are the same as most other countries', while its virtue is particular to it. That virtue is to suggest a means by which enforceable rights might finally be rooted in humanity rather than in citizenship, even in a world of sovereign states.

In 1984 Canada's Supreme Court decided the country's most important refugee case. The case was very different from the Team Haiti lawsuit that would preoccupy the U.S. Supreme Court nine years later. The actions of the Canadian government beyond its own borders were not at issue, nor was Canada accused of returning refugees to danger. Nevertheless, in Ottawa as in Washington, Hannah Arendt's ghost could be felt hovering inside the courtroom. In both cases a key issue was whether refugees are subject to legally enforceable rights. The Canadian government had recently enshrined in its constitution a Charter of Rights and Freedoms that contained some strong rights language. The Supreme Court was now being asked to determine how far those constitutional rights would extend. In the words of Barbara Jackman, one of the lawyers involved in the case, a fundamental question at issue was "whether or not the Charter of Rights and Freedoms are *human* rights. Does the rights part of our constitution apply to persons who are not citizens?"

The Ottawa case was set in motion in the early 1980s, when Canada received two thousand refugee applications by Sikhs.

The Sikhs stated that they feared persecution by the government of India (which was then clamping down on a Sikh separatist movement), only to see their claims universally rejected. The mass wave of rejections came just as Canada's asylum system was undergoing heavy criticism. Refugee decisions were made by officials who never met the people seeking asylum. Instead, an official would look over a transcript of an interview to determine whether the claimant's story was bona fide. This method was widely criticized on the grounds that credibility was not just a matter of what someone said, but how he or she said it. As one refugee lawyer remarked of his client, "You're asking him to place his life, his future, in the hands of a tape recorder . . . The sense of urgency in the voices of those who are attempting to describe torture or show scars and so on [is lost]." The same criticism was made by people who ran the system. One refugee official told a reporter that she had lost faith in Canada's approach after judging two thousand cases without meeting a single applicant. "You realize how big an element demeanor is in judging a claim."

The mass rejection of thousands of claims, coming as it did when Canada's system was in dispute, resulted in a battery of legal challenges. Brought forward primarily by rejected Sikhs, they all charged that the method Canada used to decide refugee claims was unfair. The Supreme Court case had begun as half a dozen such lawsuits which were eventually amalgamated into one. It involved Harbhajan Singh and five other Sikh men who all belonged to Akali Dal, a Sikh political party. (A seventh claimant, a woman from Guyana, was unaffiliated with Sikhism.) By the time the case reached the Supreme Court, it was no longer about any individual refugee claim. Instead, Canada's system was itself on trial. Did it give asylum-seekers a fair chance to tell their story?

As with the Haiti lawsuit, part of the case concerned how to read a single word. In Canada, it was "everyone." Canada's

Charter of Rights contains the following sentence: "Everyone has the right to life, liberty and security of the person and the right not to be deprived thereof except in accordance with the principles of fundamental justice." On one hand, "everyone" could conceivably be taken to mean every citizen of Canada. If so, then the asylum-seekers would have no case, as the right to life, liberty and security did not apply to them. On the other hand, if "everyone" was taken in a broader sense, to include literally everyone in Canada, citizen or not, then the rejected asylum-seekers would at least have a leg to stand on.

A surprising feature of the case is how much unanimity emerged on this point. Not only Jackman and the other lawyers challenging the government but the legal team defending it all eventually agreed that "everyone" meant literally everyone physically present in Canada. Several passages in the Canadian Charter restrict a given right to "Every Citizen of Canada." If the Charter's drafters had wanted to restrict the right to life, liberty and security to citizens, therefore, they could have said so. "Everyone" therefore had to include a wider class of people, including both citizens and non-citizens.

Given that the lawyers agreed on this point, it was perhaps unsurprising that the justices would take the same view when they decided *Singh v. Minister of Employment and Immigration*, as the case is called. What was at issue, however, was what a universal right to life, liberty and security amounted to in practical terms. Here there was no agreement whatsoever among the lawyers. But in the end the court sided with the appellants. In particular, it accepted their claim that people seeking asylum were entitled to an oral hearing.

It may not sound like much, the right to an oral hearing. To this day, however, it is rare for countries to extend constitutional rights of any kind to asylum-seekers. Germany and other states that have experimented with a right to asylum are exceptions to the predominant international trend. The mere fact that potential refugees were deemed to have constitutional rights was thus a breakthrough in itself. But the breakthrough was not just conceptual. The Supreme Court's decision resulted in Canada's entire asylum system being overhauled. In 1989 Canada replaced its old Kafkaesque approach with one that gave asylum-seekers a face-to-face interview as a general rule. The Refugee Convention allows signatory states to turn away dangerous individuals such as terrorists and serious criminals, and the *Singh* decision maintains the same exceptions. But violent cases are a tiny minority, and most people who sought a refugee hearing in Canada in the decade following *Singh* got one. Canada's asylum system during the 1990s was far from perfect: decision-makers were too often appointed on the basis of patronage rather than merit, among other problems. But unlike the experience of some societies, the criticism that a given right was respected in theory but not in practice does not apply.

Courts in other countries have recognized the rights of people seeking asylum. *Singh*, however, is the most important decision of its kind. Because of it, Canadian politicians cannot employ some of the no-entry policies that have been adopted by other countries. In Australia, for example, Christmas Island and other locations have been declared "excised offshore places" for the purposes of immigration law. This allowed the Australian government to decide asylum cases without any opportunity for appeal, a benefit refugee claimants have long enjoyed on the Australian mainland. Even though *Singh* does not say anything about appeals, it makes any sort of excised offshore place unlikely. This is because *Singh* applies the idea of a universal right to life, liberty and security to all Canadian territory. Attempts to "excise" parts of Canada for the purposes of refugee law risk being challenged in the courts. Politicians thus have a strong incentive to treat Canada as one seamless "rights zone."

Another measure *Singh* rules out is the cunning use of deadlines. Different countries currently impose time limits of varying lengths on refugee claims. In some countries the deadlines are extremely, even viciously, tight. For example, Turkey maintains a two-tier asylum system, in which Europeans seeking refugee status can do so at any time after arrival. Europeans are far less likely to seek asylum in Turkey than people from nearby crisis zones in the Middle East and North Africa. Non-Europeans seeking asylum, however, must do so within five days of entering Turkey, after which even the most well-founded claim is automatically rejected. Even leaving aside the double standard regarding European and non-European claims, the five-day deadline is an administrative weapon deliberately used to deter genuine refugees. In Canada, thanks to *Singh*, the whole issue of punitive deadlines is a non-starter.

No Kafkaism. No excision zones. No death by deadline. In each of these ways, *Singh* has functioned as a real law with real power. This brings us back to the central problem of this book. Hannah Arendt argued that so long as sovereign states exist, they will fail to uphold the rights of refugees. She argued that when extending protection to refugees conflicts with a nation's interests, or requires more than a token sacrifice, refugees will lose out. Hence Arendt's pessimistic conclusion that human rights were a mere abstraction. She thought it hopeless to believe that rights we acquire by virtue of being human could ever have the same force as rights we obtain as members of a political community.

Singh is a breakthrough because it does what Arendt said was impossible. In Canada we find a sovereign state that enforces a right of refugees seeking asylum with the same powerful tool, constitutional law, with which it upholds the rights of its citizens. Although asylum-seekers have fewer rights than Canadian citizens, that they have constitutional rights *at all* is enough to show that Arendt was wrong to conclude that it is impossible for states to uphold the rights of refugees in any meaningful way. In

Canada the condition of possessing effective rights is not that of being a citizen. Rather, it is that of being human.

Canada is only one country, and human rights are supposed to be universal. We should therefore hope that the *Singh* decision is studied and copied by rights advocates and lawmakers in other countries. This is not a utopian dream. Legal writers use the term "legal transplantation" to describe the process by which laws made in one country are adopted in another. Legal transplantation is increasingly common, but laws of different countries migrate with different speeds. University of Virginia law professor Frederick Schauer notes that Canadian laws and Supreme Court decisions have often served as inspiration for foreign lawmakers: "Canadian ideas and Canadian constitutionalists have been particularly influential, especially as compared with the United States. One reason for this is that Canada, unlike the United States, is seen as reflecting an emerging international consensus rather than existing as an outlier."

Singh may be even more transplantable than most Canadian Supreme Court decisions. This is because of the unusual role two influential traditions of law played in the court's thinking. This aspect of the litigation began eight months after Jackman's court appearance, when the justices sent her and the other lawyers a strange message. Could they all submit new briefs that re-argued the main issues, not in regard to the Charter of Rights and Freedoms, but in reference to Canada's confusingly similar Bill of Rights? ("That surprised me," Jackman recalls. "That was very unusual, for the court to come back with an entirely new argument that had never been raised.")

The Canadian Bill of Rights was a legacy of former prime minister John Diefenbaker. He had become a civil libertarian during the 1940s, when the revelation of a Soviet spy ring caused the Canadian government to employ secret interrogations and other draconian measures against espionage suspects. Diefenbaker said that his Bill of Rights, introduced in 1960, was designed to "curb the human tendencies of national governments to take shortcuts in ruling the people."

Diefenbaker has come to occupy a place in the Canadian imagination very different from that of Pierre Trudeau, who introduced Canada's Charter of Rights and Freedoms. Trudeau is remembered in legendary terms, the leader who arrived in office on a wave of Trudeaumania and vanquished Quebec separatists in a referendum. Diefenbaker, by contrast, is most famous for presiding over a badly divided Conservative Party and for cancelling production of a popular airplane, the Avro Arrow. Among Canadian prime ministers, Diefenbaker is a Rodney Dangerfield figure, one who never gets any respect (even if, in fairness, Diefenbaker was the name of the wolf-dog on *Due South*).

What is true of Trudeau and Diefenbaker the individuals is also true of the rights instruments they left behind. While every Canadian schoolchild is now familiar with Trudeau's Charter, the introduction of which is seen as a historic turning point, Diefenbaker's Bill is forgotten. In terms of understanding *Singh*'s international relevance, this is unfortunate, as Trudeau's Charter and Diefenbaker's Bill represent two distinct traditions of law, both of which influenced *Singh* and both of which remain influential abroad.

Trudeau's vision was in keeping with the liberal tradition, stretching back to the American and French revolutions, which sought to entrench rights at the constitutional level. In this view, fundamental freedoms need to be placed beyond the easy reach of elected politicians, who will often be tempted to curtail rights, particularly during times of crisis. Outlining a set of rights in the constitution is thus a way of giving courts the power to enforce and uphold rights when politicians will not.

Diefenbaker, by contrast, had no truck with constitutional rights. His view was similar to one still popular in the United

Kingdom and Australia, both of which lack a constitutional rights instrument at the national level (even though the U.K. is now a signatory to the European human rights charter). As Diefenbaker's view is summarized by his biographer, Denis Smith, "rights were only what parliament declared them to be . . . He genuinely rejected the belief that they should exist beyond parliament's power." Diefenbaker's Bill, therefore, was simply a normal piece of legislation, one that outlined the rights that in Canada "have existed and shall continue to exist," as the Bill's preamble put it. Not only could Parliament get rid of the entire Bill of Rights by simple majority vote, but the Bill also came with a giant loophole: lawmakers could disregard any right contained in it so long as they announced that they intended to do so.

Diefenbaker's critics pointed out, with some justice, that such allowances made his Bill less a binding legal document than a list of toothless suggestions, or what one critic dismissed as "a timid and tepid affirmation of a political and social tradition." But Diefenbaker always maintained that requiring Parliament to publicly declare when it was violating a right had value in itself. No longer could the government override rights through the use of little-noticed administrative decrees, which it had done during the war. Now Parliament would have to take responsibility in the full glare of public debate.

Singh is unusual in that it draws on both the liberal (via Trudeau) and the democratic (via Diefenbaker) conceptions of rights. In the first half of the decision, three of the justices evaluate Canada's asylum procedures by the standards set out in Trudeau's Charter. They conclude that the old paper-based system failed to live up to standards of fairness the Charter sets out. The second half of the decision represents the view of three other justices; they do not say anything about the Charter, but instead note that Canada continues to have a Bill of Rights, which still deserves to be taken seriously in the Charter age.

Today *Singh* is remembered as a Charter decision. It is not hard to see why. Diefenbaker's Bill had little influence before the Charter was introduced, and it is unlikely the case would have gone the same way had the Charter not existed. As McGill University law professor Julius Grey put it, the 1982 adoption of the Charter created a "new atmosphere favorable to the protection of basic rights." Without the revolution in thinking caused by Trudeau's Charter, Diefenbaker's Bill would never have been taken seriously enough to strike down Canada's old asylum laws. In this and other ways there is simply no comparing the liberal and democratic traditions of rights. To be serious about rights is to side with Trudeau against Diefenbaker, and place at least some rights beyond the everyday reach of elected politicians. This is why the great majority of industrialized democracies now enshrine rights at the constitutional level.

The role the democratic tradition of rights played in *Singh* is nonetheless significant. The Diefenbaker justices mounted a plausible challenge to Canada's Kafkaesque asylum system, pointing out that it was in violation of even the minimal safeguards of the Bill of Rights. Insofar as the Diefenbaker approach to rights is still influential internationally, *Singh*'s relevance applies even to countries that do not have charters of rights or written constitutions. Those countries include Australia, the U.K. and Israel, all of which commit ongoing injustices in their treatment of asylum-seekers. Against such a backdrop, it is worth stressing that the *Singh* decision is as compatible with the broad legal philosophy of these societies as it is with that of France, the United States or even Canada itself. *Singh* should serve as an inspiration for rights advocates in countries that have constitutional rights instruments as well as those that do not. Its relevance is truly global.

Arendt framed her argument in terms of what was and was not historically possible when it came to upholding human rights. As we've seen, the treatment refugees continue to receive around the world is often at odds with respecting those rights. For both these reasons, Canada's precedent is worth stressing. It shows that our civilization can do better than Arendt thought, and far better than is currently the norm.

This is the first lesson of *Singh*. But in addition to showing how universal human rights can be enforced, *Singh* is instructive in two additional ways. A second lesson concerns how rights are given force. Crucially, this is not something that depends on governments alone. Rather, *Singh* confirms the importance of background cultural attitudes and the role of non-governmental organizations. Both have a key role to play in making sure the rights of human beings seeking asylum are respected. *Singh*'s third and final lesson, by contrast, concerns the particular role of states, where the ultimate responsibility for enforcing rights lies. The *Singh* decision's breakthrough conception of rights provides a template for the enforcement of other rights for refugees, beyond that involving an oral hearing.

The importance of cultural attitudes in making rights a reality can be seen by recalling Arendt's experience as a refugee. When refugees of her generation poured into France, background attitudes about belonging and citizenship strongly influenced their reception. This remains true today, most obviously in descent-based societies, which accept fewer refugees than countries of immigration. In Canada's case, by the time *Singh* was decided, it had long embraced a different model of belonging, one that stressed the importance of multiculturalism. Not only was Canada where the term *multiculturalism* was coined, in a 1965 government report, but in 1971 multiculturalism became an official government policy.

What is important in understanding *Singh* is less the federal policy than the underlying attitude toward difference, what might be termed "unofficial multiculturalism," that made such a policy possible. Canada shares with other former settler societies such as Australia and the United States a self-understanding as a country of migration. This attitude is one that has long seen the arrival of British and European immigrants as a positive development. Unofficial multiculturalism extends the same thinking to include non-European immigrants, and embraces cultural pluralism as a fundamental social good. Such an attitude, which is increasingly common internationally, had already become prominent in Canada by the time *Singh* was decided, in a way that it is still not widely accepted in descent-based societies. The view of cultural difference as something not merely to be tolerated, but valued, has something to do with why *Singh* happened in the time and place that it did. We can grasp that indirect but nonetheless important influence of a pro-multiculturalism attitude by imagining a refugee lawsuit being brought forward by members of a foreign cultural minority in Japan, only to be rejected long before ever reaching the supreme court.

In addition to multiculturalism, *Singh* also confirms the importance of non-governmental organizations. Barbara Jackman was the attorney not for any of the asylum-seekers, who had their own lawyers, but for two intervenors that took an interest in the case, the Canadian Council of Churches and the Canadian Sikh Federation. Jackman's arguments, which were different from those of the other legal team, influenced the court's decision. Had the two religious groups not intervened, the case may well have had a different outcome. A key right was thus recognized, not due to a government or an NGO acting in isolation, but to the two rights-defining entities engaging in dialogue with one another. The power of NGOs in this regard is worth noting, given how few rights refugees enjoy around the world. Governments may not always listen to NGOs, but when they do the outcome can be a powerful form of progress.

If *Singh* highlights how rights for refugees can be possible, and how multiculturalism and NGOs can advance those rights, its third and final lesson is more forward-looking. There is a difference between asylum-seekers being able to exercise some rights, however minimal, and being able to exercise a fully adequate set of rights. As we have seen, governments exhibit much cunning in their treatment of refugees. In a truly just world, or at least one more just than ours, asylum-seekers would possess constitutional rights beyond that to an oral hearing. The question is, what particular rights would those be?

Here *Singh* helps us to better grasp how human rights can be enforced without being pitted against national sovereignty. As Giorgio Agamben and other critics of human rights have pointed out, whether someone's rights are respected has long been determined in part by a person's territorial location. We have seen that one of the most difficult places to enforce human rights today is on the ocean, beyond the borders of any state. Similarly, when Germany tried to extend rights to refugees, that took the form of a right to asylum within Germany. The *Singh* decision did not eliminate the connection between rights and territory, as someone has to be physically present in Canada before their right to an oral hearing is *recognized*. Nevertheless, the right in question is one that could potentially be *exercised* anywhere. And separating the place of recognition from the place of potential enforcement may be *Singh*'s greatest breakthrough of all.

Barbara Jackman brought this point home during the trial by drawing a handwritten chart to explain to the justices what was involved in the oral hearing process. It made clear that a right to an oral hearing would not prevent Canada from controlling its borders. As Jackman puts it, her chart showed how someone "could in fact be removed even if the person was recognized as a convention refugee. All it was, was a recognition that the person might be persecuted in their home country: it wasn't a guarantee that Canada would have to keep the person in Canada."

Singh says nothing about someone found to be a refugee having to stay in Canada. Rather, it says that people who make an asylum claim are entitled to an oral hearing, a procedure that does not necessarily have to be performed inside Canada. If Canada were to turn refugees away at the Canada-U.S. border, for example, and have them file their refugee claims in the United States instead, such a policy would be perfectly legal so long as the U.S. asylum application involved an oral hearing. Indeed, Canada and the United States implemented precisely such a policy in 2004. As we will see, the policy has hideous flaws, but the point to note here is that removing someone from Canada is in principle compatible with *Singh*, because the right to an oral hearing *Singh* upholds is "portable" in a way the right to asylum is not. And once we realize that a right can be portable, it should cause us to ask whether there are other rights that asylum-seekers should have enforced on their behalf, rights that can also be exercised beyond the borders of any particular state.

I believe justice for asylum-seekers entails recognizing at least two additional constitutional rights beyond that involving an oral hearing. The first is the right of all asylum-seekers to be represented at their asylum hearing by legal counsel. Today no one would deny that a person who cannot afford a lawyer is entitled to have one appointed for him even in cases where his life is not on the line. Given that a wrong asylum decision can potentially result in a refugee being returned to danger, the same principle should apply to people seeking refuge.

The second additional right is not to be subject to arbitrary detention. The mass detention of asylum-seekers as was practised in Australia until recently treats refugees like criminals. Immigration officers at ports of entry should have the power to detain individuals they consider suspicious, but long-term detention without a trial is even more wrong in the case of asylum-seekers than it is in the case of suspected criminal citizens. Anyone held for more than two or three days should be entitled to some form of judicial review, to ensure that there is a legitimate reason for the continued confinement.

That *Singh* says nothing about a right to legal aid or judicial review is testament to the fact that, well made as the decision was, the protection it offers refugees is ultimately limited. If the right *Singh* upheld is a breakthrough when viewed against the backdrop of historical reality, when judged by the standards of ideal justice that same right is laughably inadequate. Nevertheless, *Singh* provides a model of how additional rights might someday be enforced. Crucially, as with the right to an oral hearing, neither of the two rights just mentioned would have to take place in any particular territory. In that sense they both follow the underlying logic of *Singh*. And it is in its underlying logic, one that conceives of human rights as portable and procedural, that *Singh*'s ultimate significance may be found. Where Arendt began with history and soared into philosophy to argue that human rights are impossible, *Singh* allows the defender of human rights to reply at both levels, an existing framework of asylum-seekers' rights serving as a template for what a more fully adequate model of rights will someday look like.

We can call the *Singh*-plus model of refugee rights the portable-procedural approach. To see its advantages, it is helpful to imagine different approaches to asylum inside a scalene triangle, which has sides of three different lengths and angles of three different degrees. In the narrowest angle of the triangle, where there is the least room for human rights to be exercised, are clustered the asylum systems of most Western countries. Here people seeking asylum have no constitutional rights of any kind. In the second angle is a German-style right to asylum, where rights have slightly more room to operate, at least in theory. In the third corner, one with the most expansive room for rights to be exercised, is the portable-procedural model, one that includes a right to legal aid and judicial review alongside the right to an oral hearing. The great value of a portable-procedural approach is not that it would be perfect or flawless—it is not—but that it would have fewer shortcomings than either of the alternatives our civilization has yet produced.

The advantage of a portable-procedural, or *Singh*-plus, model over most existing systems is that it would enforce human rights at a constitutional level. One of the major problems with most asylum systems that currently exist is that they place few if any limits on the policies politicians can introduce. This was noted by former British cabinet minister Richard Crossman when, looking back on a package of British immigration reforms of the 1960s, he observed that they contained "plans for legislation which we realized would have been declared unconstitutional in any country with a written constitution and a Supreme Court."

Crossman's observation helps explain not only Britain's experience but also Australia's. Because both countries lack a charter of rights, politicians as less likely to face serious court challenges, and so have enormous latitude in how they treat refugees. Such an arrangement, however, is the exception, as most countries today regard some rights as so fundamental that they inscribe them in a constitution, a step that makes it maximally difficult for politicians to tamper with those rights. Yet the international norm is still for most countries' charters of rights to protect the rights of citizens with greater force than those of non-citizens. A portable-procedural model of rights would be a step forward because it would enforce three crucial rights of asylum-seekers in the same powerful way.

To see how important those rights are, consider the current situation in the United States. As in most Western countries, it is taken for granted that the right to a fair trial is a crucial legal safeguard, so crucial that someone who cannot afford a lawyer will have one provided to him or her. This is the case even when the person is accused of a misdemeanour that involves a relatively short prison sentence. But people making refugee claims do not enjoy the same right to legal aid. American lawyers often take on asylum cases on a pro bono basis, but inevitably, many cases are heard without legal advice. This has an impact on which claims are successful. A 1987 U.S. government report found that asylum claimants without legal representation had a 16 percent success rate compared with 36 percent for those with lawyers. More recently, refugee advocates have suggested that U.S. claimants in general are four to six times more likely to be accepted if they are represented by a lawyer. Surely this arrangement is upside down. Compared to people accused of a misdemeanour, the stakes for people seeking asylum are far higher. In their case, a wrong decision could potentially see them returned to a country where their lives are in danger. Yet the legal rights they enjoy are fewer than those of someone accused of a crime.

A similar situation holds in Australia. It is unimaginable that criminals there would be placed in indefinite detention en masse. Yet this was the fate of asylum-seekers such as Mohammad Al Ghazzi, who committed no crime by seeking refuge in Australia. Against the backdrop of the situation in the United States, Australia and so many other countries, the key advantage of a portable-procedural approach becomes clear. It would narrow the gap between citizens' and human rights. Asylum-seekers' rights would be enforced the same way crucial citizens' rights are: by being constitutionally enshrined and placed beyond the easy reach of politicians, who all too often tamper with the rights of refugees seeking asylum.

Turning to the other corner of the asylum triangle, a portable-procedural model of rights is also clearly superior to the right-to-asylum approach. Recalling the rise and fall of the right to asylum in Germany, and noting how things might have gone differently if a portable-procedural approach had been in place instead, highlights two key advantages of the procedural approach.

The first is that in a country that adopted it, the rights in question would not be as easily undermined by the restrictive policies of nearby states. As we saw, part of Germany's problem was that other EU states had no-entry policies that contributed to Germany's influx. In this way, the no-entry policies of Germany's neighbours contributed to the undoing of the asylum clause. The portable-procedural model would clearly require co-ordination between states. But had it been in place in Germany, lawmakers there would not have been quite so at the mercy of their neighbours' restrictive attitudes and policies. Rather they would have had greater flexibility to deal with the crisis as it was unfolding.

A key feature of Germany's crisis was that the asylum clause obliged officials to admit every asylum applicant to Germany's determination system. This created an incentive for an ever-increasing number of weak claims. With the portable-procedural model, by contrast, lawmakers could relocate asylum applicants to a sufficiently rights-respecting third country, and thereby break the vicious circle of unfounded claims and ever-lengthening determination times within a particular state. By granting politicians a greater ability to defuse asylum crises as they are happening, the portable-procedural model is less likely to create crises that can be resolved only by abolishing constitutional safeguards for refugees. A portable-procedural model may therefore be better able to survive at least some situations of mass influx than the right to asylum proved to be.

The portable-procedural model's second advantage over the right to asylum is that it would change the nature of safe third country agreements. Such agreements are now a fact of life across the Western world. That they result in refugee applicants being relocated from one liberal state to another is not in itself objectionable. What is of concern is the circumstances under which such returns are made. Germany's arrangement is typical in that its third-country agreements allow it to adopt an "out of sight, out of mind" attitude. If improper procedures were used or something went wrong after an asylum-seeker were returned to Poland or elsewhere, it was of no concern to German officials: Germany's responsibility for returned asylum-seekers ended once they left Germany territory. This approach risks seeing a refugee returned to a third country that in turn sends her back to a situation of persecution, a phenomenon known as chain *refoulement*. Even when this extreme outcome does not occur, returned refugees and asylum-seekers can suffer other negative results, including becoming so-called refugees-in-orbit, shuffled from one country to another without ever having their claims heard.

A portable-procedural model would reduce the likelihood of such negative outcomes occurring by attaching conditions to third-country agreements. They would now be better termed *fair* third country agreements, as the states in question would have to pledge to give asylum-seekers a fair hearing. States that adopted the portable-procedural model would be required to make sure that any third country to which they returned asylum-seekers would uphold the same procedural safeguards as the state from which they were being returned. Applied to the German case, an asylum-seeker would not lose the three rights outlined above upon being sent to Poland. Rather, those rights would "follow" him or her over the border. Even if Poland did not normally supply asylum-seekers with legal representation, it would be obliged to do so in the case of returnees. Where Germany's crisis was ultimately resolved by a severe reduction in refugee protection within Germany, a portable-procedural model could potentially see future crises resolved by improving asylum procedures for at least some applicants in countries to which applicants were returned. States with which Germany signed third-country agreements would have legally committed to an absolute minimum standard of treatment for returned refugees. Should those standards not be met, it could potentially result in a legal challenge to the agreement in a German court.

The re-imagined scenario I have just described leaves some important questions unaddressed. Who should administer the oral hearings to people knocked back to Poland from Germany? The Polish government? Agents of Germany acting abroad? The UN High Commissioner for Refugees? On the portable-procedural approach, there is no commitment in advance to any particular government or organization being involved. Just so long as the correct procedures are followed, any of the preceding three entities, or some entirely different one, would be acceptable. But more important than re-imagining every particular of the German situation is to highlight the twofold advantage of the portable-procedural approach over a right to asylum. It would not create the same incentive for false claims that Germany was faced with, as there would be no obligation to hear every asylum case within the borders of one country. And it would attach conditions to safe third country agreements of the kind Germany eventually introduced, and which now define the situation of refugees around the world.

A portable-procedural model of human rights would achieve these goods without calling into question a country's ability to police its borders. In addition to sending asylum-seekers to appropriate third countries, it would allow refugee-receiving countries to deny work permits to asylum-seekers. The current international trend is for states to be much too quick to deny asylum-seekers the right to work. (Many governments also seem not to realize that it is in their own interest to allow people to work while they are waiting to have an asylum claim decided, as doing so costs less than welfare.) Nevertheless, withholding the right to work may occasionally be among the measures that policy-makers need to use to discourage false claims. Nothing in the portable-procedural model rules it out.

A third disincentive the portable approach allows is selective detention. The United Nations has stated that detaining asylum-seekers is "inherently undesirable," particularly when asylum-seekers are housed with criminal offenders, a wrong that is only exacerbated when the asylum-seekers are children. But as the UN also points out, there are cases when adult detention can be justified. They include situations in which there is a need to verify a refugee's identity, cases in which people have destroyed their travel documents, or to incarcerate a genuine terrorist or war criminal who has made an asylum claim. As is the case with withholding work permits, detention is currently overused by many countries, and often administered in a cruel and humiliating way. Yet given that detention can be justified in selective cases, it is worth noting its compatibility with the portable approach, on the crucial condition that detention decisions are subject to judicial review. By permitting these and other forms of immigration enforcement, the portable-procedural approach would leave intact a country's right to control its borders. It thus represents a better reconciliation of national sovereignty with human rights than has been the case to date.

The framework of rights advanced here does not address all the ways states currently mistreat refugees. In the United States, for example, people seeking asylum are forbidden both from receiving welfare and from seeking employment for six months after filing a refugee claim. This places them among the truly destitute. Yet this and other forms of hardship are not addressed by the portable-procedural model. Some critics may thus ask, in what sense can it be justified in the name of human rights?

In response I would make two points. I am arguing for a model of refugee rights to be enforced at the level of constitutional law.

Constitutional rights place limits on the measures elected officials can implement. The experience of Germany, however, suggests that one cannot always anticipate the consequences of constitutional rights for non-citizens. I have not argued for constitutionalizing additional rights beyond the three bedrock universal safeguards—the rights to an oral hearing, counsel and judicial review—in order to reduce the risk of creating a system with perverse incentives and unwanted consequences of the kind Germany experienced.

It does not follow, though, that no other safeguards should be put in place for asylum-seekers. At the level of ordinary rather than constitutional law, they should normally enjoy a right to welfare, employment and many other entitlements. Meeting these and other needs through ordinary law would allow politicians more flexibility should a mass influx occur, and some ordinary entitlements need to be modified. Taking three core rights out of the hands of elected politicians in no way implies that refugees should be stripped of other legal rights at a non-constitutional level.

Some critics might then reply by asking what is so special about the three rights singled out above. Why should a right to welfare not be regarded as equally worthy of constitutional protection? Perhaps I am wrong to focus on only three rights. But if that is the case, the portable-procedural model can be modified to take the overlooked right into account. It could be adapted so as to state that a refugee can be relocated to a third country where his or her right to welfare would also be respected alongside the three rights highlighted above. This type of criticism is thus not a rejection of the portable-procedural model so much as a possible grounds on which to modify it. I would welcome its expansion to include as many rights as are feasible for it to contain. I have focused on just three partly because it is difficult to say in advance what all the necessary constitutional rights might be. But guaranteeing the three rights at hand is a necessary condition of extending justice to asylum-seekers, whether or not it is a sufficient one.

A model of asylum-seekers' rights based on the principles I have outlined could be implemented in a variety of ways. In Canada the Supreme Court found that the Charter of Rights and Freedoms entitles asylum seekers to the right to an oral hearing. Human rights jurists in other countries could potentially initiate similar litigation bringing their constitutional rights instruments to bear on asylum law. Less likely but still possible is that when liberal states introduce new rights instruments or amend existing ones, procedural safeguards for refugees could be inserted. In situations where asylum seekers have no legal protections at a constitutional level, the portable-procedural model could inform the work of non-government organizations that lobby legislators on behalf of refugees. Non-government organizations could take the portable-procedural model as one of their goals to work toward at the level of ordinary of administrative law. Portable-procedural rights would serve as a standard by which to judge refugee protection regimes which fall short of this model. Even where it is not legalized, popularizing it would put paid to the widespread view that controlling the border requires not even hearing the claims of desperate men and women seeking asylum.

A positive view of *Singh* is in keeping with how refugee advocates regard the decision. In Canada the decision's anniversary, April 4, is marked by human rights groups as Refugee Rights Day. Some critics, however, regard *Singh* not as a great breakthrough but as a step backwards. Even before September 11, critics charged that *Singh* was an unjustified erosion of Canada's sovereignty. It is worth examining those criticisms, not only to determine if they are correct but also to see if they highlight problems with the model I have argued for, which goes far beyond *Singh*.

Singh is unpopular with advocates of reduced immigration. In the Canadian context the most prominent representative of this view is Daniel Stoffman, a distinguished journalist and author. For Stoffman and other advocates of low immigration, the problem with Canada's *Singh*-based refugee policy is that it does justice neither to the claims of sovereignty nor to rights. Instead, they say, it offers the worst of both worlds. Canada's border control is compromised in the name of a refugee system that does little to help actual refugees.

Stoffman asks us to consider what a truly humanitarian refugee system would look like. To that end, he holds up Norway as an example. In 2001 the country gave $84 million to meet the needs of people living in refugee camps in the developing world—a remarkable amount for a country with a population of less than 4.5 million. This is in noticeable contrast to Canada, which donated only $51.2 million to the same cause, even though its population was seven times that of Norway's. When it comes to people who make refugee claims inside the two countries, however, the relationship is reversed. Canada accepts the majority of claimants while Norway rejects all but a handful. As Stoffman puts it, "Norway's acceptance rate for people who show up at its doorstep and ask for sanctuary within Norway itself is a minuscule two per cent, compared with Canada's lofty 58-per-cent approval rate of in-Canada refugee claims."

Stoffman argues that Norway does the most good for the greatest number of deserving refugees, who are found in camps in the developing world. Canada, by contrast, focuses its resources on the much smaller group of people—amounting to forty-four thousand in 2001—who make refugee claims inside Canada. Stoffman notes that on an international level, only 15 percent of people who make refugee claims within Western countries are accepted. He takes this to show that the majority of claimants are really economic migrants trying to move from a poor country to a rich one. The primary effect of Canada's high acceptance rate, therefore, is to create a "pull factor" that encourages non-refugees to make refugee claims. Hence Stoffman's conclusion that Canada has things backwards. "We are spending too much on refugee claimants in Canada and not enough on the real refugees in the camps."

What would a better approach look like? Stoffman does not object to the court's central conclusion in *Singh*, saying, "Anybody who claims their life is in danger is at the very least entitled to an oral hearing." But Stoffman argues that Canada has gone further than *Singh* obliges it to. In the late 1980s, the Canadian government set up a refugee tribunal that hears refugee claims months after claimants have entered the country. Stoffman argues that such an approach is not the only way to implement oral hearings.

"The issue is, what sort of an oral hearing?" Stoffman says. "The way that it's been interpreted subsequently is that it's a full-blown hearing that anybody, even from a non-refugee-producing country, even from a democratic country—even if his claim is transparently absurd—is entitled to a full-blown oral hearing."

Stoffman believes it would be better to screen out manifestly unfounded claims at the border. He points to the fact that Canada has received refugee claims from democratic countries such as Costa Rica, which hardly fits the profile of an oppressive state. Not only has Costa Rica long followed the rule of law, but in 1949 it became the first country in the world to abolish its military. Yet in 2002 and 2003, Costa Ricans made 3,357 refugee claims in Canada, which caused the Canadian government to impose a Costa Rican visa requirement (which reduced claims to a trickle). Stoffman argues that rather than let Costa Ricans and other unlikely refugees go through the full hearing process, it would be better to interview all refugee claimants when they first arrive.

"At the border there would be a qualified refugee hearing officer who would weed out the transparently fraudulent cases," Stoffman says. "The non-serious ones would be asked to leave, and the serious ones admitted to the system." Many other critics have also endorsed border screenings, an approach that is now used in the United States and many European countries. Like Stoffman, these critics argue that it would create a "refugee dividend" that could be diverted to refugees in camps overseas.

What are we to make of Stoffman's criticisms? Much more than the particular experience of Canada is at stake. If Stoffman and other critics are correct, an approach to refugees that stresses the procedural rights they should enjoy upon arriving in the West is misguided from the start. It would be much more sensible to focus on turning away unfounded asylum claims and devote more energy to helping refugees in camps overseas, who are more deserving of our help. I believe that Stoffman's argument is based on good intentions. Nevertheless, his analysis has serious problems, the first of which recalls Mark Twain's quip that there are three kinds of mendacity: lies, damn lies and statistics.

In regard to Norway's acceptance rate, Stoffman's 2 percent figure refers to the tiny group of refugee claimants who receive permanent residency. But Norway offers a second type of protection, involving what are known as temporary protection permits. These were introduced across Europe after the civil war in Yugoslavia, when European countries were reluctant to take in thousands of displaced Bosnians. For the purposes of classifying someone as a refugee, people who receive temporary protection are fleeing persecution just as real as that experienced by other refugees. This is why the United Nations and other observers usually include both groups when calculating how many people have received humanitarian protection in a particular country. And when the figures for both groups are combined for Norway, its total recognition rate climbs from 2 to 33 percent.

That is still lower than Canada's 58 percent acceptance rate. However, this figure is itself misleading, as it does not include claims that are abandoned. Every year, a few thousand people make a refugee claim in Canada, only to disappear. In Norway, by contrast, asylum-seekers are normally housed in government-run reception centres, which makes it much harder for someone who has filed a claim to drop out of sight. The fact that so many people disappear might be a good reason for Canada to set up its own system of reception centres. But for the purposes of comparing Canada's acceptance rate with that of Norway, not including abandoned claims means that claims that are especially weak, as abandoned claims are thought to be, are included when determining the acceptance rate of one country but not the other. To correct for this, it makes more sense to use the Canadian government's official figure, which includes abandoned claims, and which gives the acceptance rate for 2001 as 47 percent.

Needless to say, 47 versus 33 percent does not suggest quite the dramatic imbalance as 58 versus 2 percent. But even the revised statistics do not take account of the fact that Canada's and Norway's asylum systems operate in different political contexts. As we've seen, a country's refugee acceptance rate is influenced by its background attitude toward immigrants. Norway has not traditionally seen itself as a country of immigration. In 2001 the third-largest party in Norway's Parliament was an anti-immigration faction, the so-called Progress Party, whose supporters told pollsters that Norway should slash its refugee intake. This cultural backdrop has an effect on Norway's asylum system, which few observers other that Stoffman see as one worth celebrating. The Norwegian Refugee Council, for example, has spoken out against "the extremely low level of [permanent] refugee recognition in Norway and the serious loss in moral consistency that this represents."

The approach Stoffman endorses involves more than giving

asylum-seekers a chilly Scandinavian welcome. Stoffman also believes that diverting asylum budgets overseas will ensure that political considerations do not undermine humanitarian ends, as aid will no longer be wasted on the bogus claimants he sees as clogging up Canada's asylum system. Instead, resources will reach the real refugees in camps. This view of humanitarianism, which sees it best practised at arm's length, is one that has also been vigorously championed by advocates of stronger border enforcement in other countries (including Australia's Philip Ruddock). Such critics are right to suggest that the situation of refugees in camps is very different from that of refugees seeking asylum in the West. Among other contrasts, people in camps often want to return home, and doing so frequently requires a regional peace settlement. Stoffman and other critics are also correct that we could do far more to help people living in such situations, who can be trapped in camps for years or even decades. Nevertheless, his proposal fails as a serious form of humanitarianism.

The main problem with Stoffman's proposal is that it risks making the situation of overseas refugees even worse. This is because of the negative message it would send to governments in the developing world, who host most of the planet's refugees. As we saw, after the U.S. Supreme Court legalized the forced return of Haitians, the governments of Thailand and Tanzania were both quick to make their refugee policies less welcoming. That restrictive entry policies in the West have a ripple effect across the globe is now a well-documented trend. In the words of Arafat Jamal, a former analyst with the United Nations High Commissioner for Refugees, "Nations that absorb the most refugees in Africa will often cite the EU or U.S. tightening their policies as a rationale for them to tighten their own policies." If we really want to help people warehoused overseas, the last thing we should do is demonstrate that we are not serious about admitting refugees ourselves.

The second problem with Stoffman-style proposals is that they exaggerate the differences between people who seek asylum and those who are trapped overseas. Stoffman argues that most asylum claims are fraudulent, and so the people who make them are far less deserving of aid than the legitimate refugees stranded overseas. This view overlooks the fact that asylum-seekers like Francine Peyti are often fleeing the same conflicts that drive hundreds of thousands of people into camps in East Africa and elsewhere. The only evidence Stoffman cites for his assertion that asylum claims lodged in Western states are overwhelmingly fraudulent is the 15 percent international acceptance rate. But this figure does not include refugees granted temporary protection, a common outcome across Europe. It also overlooks the no-entry policies put in place by Western states. Stoffman has a narrow focus on Canada and never critically examines the asylum programs of the United States, Australia, Germany or other countries. Yet as we've seen, the asylum programs of these and other countries have devastating drawbacks from the point of view of human rights. Averaging the acceptance rates of the asylum programs that currently exist, with no notice given to how they reflect background conceptions of belonging and other factors, is not a plausible way of determining how many genuine refugees seek asylum. Francine Peyti and other genuine refugees manage to reach the West with greater frequency than Stoffman and other critics allow.

There is a flip side to the similarity between asylum-seekers and camp occupants. Just as asylum-seekers include many deserving refugees, administering aid to refugees overseas involves its own political challenges. This point has been vividly brought home by Fiona Terry, who in 1994 was working in Tanzania as the head of the French section of Médecins Sans Frontières (MSF), the well-known humanitarian organization. In the wake of the Rwandan genocide, hundreds of thousands of ethnic Hutis and Tutsis poured into refugee camps in Tanzania and Zaire. As Rwandans filled up tent cities such as Camp Benaco, a massive lakeside encampment in Tanzania, they brought the killing campaign with them. With dawning horror, Terry and her colleagues realized that the same camps they were working in had become mass murder zones.

"The genocide against the Tutsi and those who were seen as supporting them had continued in the camps, and bodies were frequently dragged from the lake," Terry has written. "In the MSF hospital we strongly suspected that Tutsi children were given minimal care, or left to die, when we were not around to supervise." As Terry and her colleagues conducted daily battles against disease and malnutrition, they pushed away doubts about the consequences of administering aid to people carrying out a genocide. "[But] they would reappear around the table at night, after a couple of beers, and divide the team." Eventually Terry's section of MSF withdrew from the camps, a controversial decision that has been widely debated ever since.

MSF's experience in Tanzania highlights a problem that has occurred in other crisis zones. Because refugee camps are often close to the conflicts that created them, they can be tempting locations for combatants to operate from. Camps in Mexico, Thailand and different parts of Africa have been drawn into regional wars. Moreover, the issue of "refugee warriors," as camp-based combatants are known, is an extreme illustration of a broader phenomenon—namely, that overseas aid efforts come with their own political challenges. According to Terry and other humanitarians, this means that administering to the needs of people in refugee camps requires more than airlifting in medicine and food, as urgent as that goal is. We also need to make careful judgment about the way the aid is administered, to ensure that it does not advance goals diametrically opposed to humanitarianism.

The existence of refugee warriors and similar political challenges illustrates the false nature of Stoffman's division between

fraudulent asylum claimants who reach the West and easily iden-
tifiable refugees in tent cities in the developing world. The truth
is that in both contexts humanitarianism needs to be informed
by careful judgment to make sure that genuine refugees are the
ones who benefit from our efforts. In refugee hearing rooms in
industrialized countries, the challenge is to separate refugees
from economic migrants. In the camps, it is to avoid creating
refugee warriors, among other pitfalls. Advocates of low immigration are therefore wrong to suggest that redirecting a dollar
away from a domestic asylum program to overseas camps will
mark a clear gain in humanitarian efficiency.

Finally, Stoffman never explains why an increase in overseas
humanitarian aid has to come at the expense of helping people
seeking asylum. The amount of money Western states spend on
asylum claims is typically less than 1 percent of total spending.
The much larger sums we lavish on ourselves is surely a more
promising source of new dollars. To take but one example,
Western states are often criticized for their huge agricultural sub-
sidies, which price farmers in the developing world out of the
international market. Redirecting some of that money abroad
would seem an especially effective form of international aid. It
is an artificially limited form of humanitarianism that suggests
we can only help refugees abroad at the expense of helping those
who manage to make it to our shores.

Stoffman's attempt to fly under a humanitarian flag is not
convincing. What about the idea of conducting refugee screenings at the border? It would seem a separate proposal, independent of his discussion of refugee camps. Again, Stoffman
is putting forward a proposal that many other observers have
called for, and again, his argument has problems. Yet unlike
his argument for redirecting aid abroad, Stoffman's discussion
of border enforcement does contain a kernel of truth. He correctly highlights a genuine cost of Canada's refugee system,

a cost that I must admit the *Singh*-plus model also bears.

Critics who support border screenings often make it sound as though fraudulent claimants can be identified by their nationality. Take claimants from Costa Rica, for example. It is true that the overwhelming majority of them are not refugees. That is why 98 percent of them were rejected in the two years leading up to Canada's visa change. But 98 is not the same as 100. Countries like Costa Rica can on rare occasions fail to protect their own citizens, which is why countries other than Canada sometimes determine Costa Rican refugee claims to be genuine. In 2002, for example, twenty-three such claims were recognized in the United States. The risk of border screening is that it can cause the small number of genuine refugees from unlikely source countries to be turned away amid all the false claimants. Admittedly, there is a financial cost to allowing people in this situation access to a refugee system. But the cost at issue is a manageable one, and not worth the moral loss of a compromised commitment to human rights.

Nevertheless, it must be admitted that the approach I have defended has a political cost of its own. An open system can be accessed by almost anyone. When divisive or controversial individuals are permitted to make refugee claims, the system itself will become embroiled in controversy. A notorious example of this occurred in 2003, when a refugee claim was filed in Canada by Ernst Zundel. Zundel was a Holocaust denier who had long been familiar to Canadians. During his four decades living in Canada he published pamphlets such as *The Hitler We Loved and Why* and *Did Six Million Really Die?* which resulted in a number of high-profile trials. Zundel's legal battles eventually drove him to the United States, but in 2003 he was found guilty of immigration violations there and returned to Canada. Although he had lived in Canada for many years, Zundel had never been allowed to take out Canadian citizenship. This meant that at the time of his return he was eligible to be deported to Germany, where he was wanted on hate crime charges. To avoid this outcome, he filed a refugee claim.

For many observers, the thought of a Holocaust denier being allowed access to the refugee system was too much to bear. "If Ernst Zundel is a refugee, Daffy Duck is Albert Einstein," wrote columnist Rex Murphy. "If we in any degree take this 'claim' of his seriously . . . then the last thread of credibility that attaches to our real refugee system is snapped forever." The editorial board of the *Toronto Star* took a similar view: "Every time he has a hearing, he gains a platform for his bottomless well of hatred. Every public appearance is an excuse for his smirking, misguided followers to gather." The basic concept of a refugee is often illustrated by reference to Jews fleeing Nazi Germany. For many people sympathetic to human rights, there was something obscene in the thought of an apologist for Nazism being granted the due process of refugee law. The Canadian government soon adopted the same view. It declared Zundel a security threat and employed a rare legal measure that allowed suspected terrorists to be pulled from the refugee queue. Zundel was imprisoned and eventually sent to Germany.

The Zundel case forces us to ask where the final boundary of an open refugee system should lie. Refugee law has always made an exception for violent individuals such as war criminals or terrorists. But Zundel's case was clearly different. Murphy and other observers said they did not believe that Zundel, who had always been non-violent, was really a terrorist (and the process used to declare him one was later struck down by the Supreme Court). It was his hateful ideology, they argued, that should have disqualified him from a hearing. Thus, whether or not Zundel was actually a threat to public security, he represents a type of individual many people would rather see turned away than granted a refugee hearing, because of his repellent political views.

To argue against border screenings is to support an arrangement that would allow Ernst Zundel and other offensive individuals to receive an oral hearing. As the *Toronto Star* pointed out, the resulting media coverage could generate publicity for some nefarious causes. Any honest defender of an open refugee system must therefore admit that there is a cost to not having screenings at the border. Non-violent individuals who are demonstrably not refugees cannot be turned away, no matter how manifestly fraudulent their claims.

This is a real cost of the system I am defending. The case for an open system, however, does not depend on its having no costs. It depends on its having fewer costs than any realistic alternative. When it comes to the rights of citizens, we grant even obviously guilty people the right to a fair trial, on the grounds that it is better that the guilty walk free than an innocent person be imprisoned. Extended to human rights, the same logic should cause us to recognize that it is better that the most fraudulent and offensive claimant be granted a full hearing rather than risk turning even one real refugee away. This is confirmed by examining the experience of the United States, where border screenings were introduced in the mid-1990s, and where they have been shown to come with significant moral costs of their own.

The first cost is symbolized by a well-known case involving a woman named Fauziya Kassindja. Kassindja grew up in the African nation of Togo, where her father protected her from the local custom of female genital mutilation. But when Kassindja was sixteen, her father died, and she was forced to marry a man who demanded that her clitoris be removed. She fled first to Germany and then the United States, where one of her cousins lived. After Kassindja made a refugee claim at Newark Airport in New Jersey, she went through a long ordeal in detention, during which she was beaten and tear-gassed, and her refugee claim was rejected. But Kassindja was able to appeal the decision, and by the time she did so a law professor named Karen Musalo became involved with her case. At Kassindja's appeal hearing, Musalo set a precedent by arguing that Kassindja represented a new type of refugee. For the first time, female genital mutilation, a cultural practice rather than a government policy, was recognized as a form of persecution.

Kassindja arrived in the United States in 1994, two years before border screenings were introduced. Human rights advocates have since pointed out that had she been subject to an airport interview upon her arrival, the correct legal decision would have been to put her on the next flight back to Togo. In the words of Philip Schrag, a law professor at Georgetown University, "An interviewer at the airport would certainly have deported Kassindja to be mutilated in Togo, because even if he believed her, the Board of Immigration Appeals had not yet declared that the threat of genital mutilation was a valid ground for asylum." Border screenings are based on the false assumption that there will never be another asylum-seeker who sets a precedent and requires a receiving country to re-examine its refugee laws.

A second problem with border screenings is highlighted by the case of Libardo Yepes. Yepes was a cattle farmer in Colombia, which has long been the site of an armed conflict in which insurgent groups fund themselves through extortion. He was terrorized on his farm for two years by left-wing guerrillas who made him pay them US$250 a month. After members of a right-wing paramilitary squad discovered Yepes was paying the leftists, they intervened—by trying to assassinate him. Caught between two rival factions, in November of 2000 Yepes flew to Florida. Upon his arrival at Miami International Airport he tried to make a refugee claim, only to be interviewed and deported within twenty-four hours.

Yepes, however, was both lucky and determined. Lucky, because he managed to avoid being killed upon his return to Colombia. Determined, because he soon fled again. This time he made a three-month journey through Central America to the Texas border, where he floated across the Rio Grande on an inner tube. After Yepes was picked up by border agents he again lodged an asylum claim. Rather than a quick interview at the airport, this time he was allowed to make his case in an unhurried asylum hearing. And this time he was found to be a refugee.

Yepes's case should cause us to recognize the higher likelihood of mistakes being made when refugee cases are heard at the border. This is hardly surprising, given that claimants subject to turnaround decisions upon arrival do not have time to speak to a lawyer, obtain documents from their home country or take similar steps.

Not having border screenings reduces the risk of committing a supreme injustice against the next Fauziya Kassindja or Libardo Yepes. Although there are also moral costs to not having screenings, they are borne primarily by the receiving state rather than the refugee, and do not involve a matter of life and death. This moral cost-benefit analysis should be enough to rule out border screenings, regardless of whatever financial benefits they might bring. Yet it is worth pointing out that the amount of resources border screenings would actually save is itself a matter of some debate.

In the United States, border screenings for refugees are part of a larger system known as expedited removal. It allows border guards to turn away people who do not make refugee claims with even less formality than those who do ask for asylum. After expedited removal was brought in, Immigration officials in California were surprised to find that the new arrangement seemed to result in more border crossing attempts. People who were subject to instant turnarounds, it turned out, made more attempts at entry than people deported under the old system, which involved a judicial hearing. Immigration officials concluded that being denied entry due to a hearing was a stronger deterrent against trying again than being summarily rejected at a border post or airport. As one government report put it, "It appears that an order issued by an immigration inspector does not have the psychological force of an order issued by an Immigration Judge. What is gained in expediting by the new statutory process may be lost in increased recidivism." Until we know the relationship between border screenings and repeated refugee claims, it seems premature to conclude that screenings will necessarily bring significant savings.

None of this, however, is to deny that there are shortcomings either with Canada's approach to asylum or the *Singh*-inspired model I have defended. To see those shortcomings, though, we have to look in places that advocates of low immigration rarely do.

Romero House is a refugee shelter in downtown Toronto. Its storefront office faces out onto an old industrial neighbourhood that now has a multicultural feel, Eastern European delis and Asian restaurants mixed in with movie-art dealers and hockey supply stores. Visitors to Romero House are greeted by its director, Mary Jo Leddy, who has a gravity-defying bouffant of grey hair. Leddy, a former nun in her sixties, has been at Romero House since she more or less fell into working there in 1992. ("I was on the board of a Catholic newspaper. We were looking for a new editor and we found someone we liked. She said she had a job at a shelter. I said I'd take her job at the shelter.") Today Leddy and a changing group of volunteers live with refugee claimants in a network of four houses Romero operates, where more than two thousand people have stayed over the years.

Leddy wrote a PhD dissertation on the philosophy of Hannah

Arendt. As an illustration of the enduring value of Arendt's work, Leddy describes a hearing she once attended with a successful refugee claimant who was seeking landed immigrant status.

"I have some rights here in Canada," the refugee said at one point.

"No, you don't," the Immigration officer replied. "You don't have any rights until I *give* them to you."

In such moments Arendt's diagnoses of human rights are vividly brought to Leddy's mind. "Human rights, she was saying, are an empty concept, unless they are enforced through public institutions," Leddy says. "I see this every day, as I go to Immigration offices and refugee hearings."

Leddy is an admirer of the *Singh* decision, which she calls "an incredible piece of [law] that should stand as a model for the world." Yet Leddy also says she has seen a great falling-away from *Singh* and what it represents. "We have made administrative decisions that effectively shut the door . . . in a very Canadian way, quietly, all on paper."

Leddy points to the Canada-U.S. Safe Third Country Agreement, which allows Canada to turn back refugee claimants who arrive at a land border crossing and have their claims heard in the United States instead. The agreement does not apply at airports, where it was thought it would be impossible to enforce (someone who arrived by air could destroy all her documents in the airport, effectively hiding the fact that he had arrived via the United States). The agreement was widely taken to account for the immediate drop in the number of refugee claims filed in Canada; they fell from 25,500 in 2004 to 19,740 the next year. But since then the total has climbed, reaching 28,340 in 2007, although it is impossible to know how many more claims might have been made had the deal not been signed.

A shortcoming of the third-country agreement is personified by Gustavo Neme, a Colombian refugee who now works for

Romero House as an administrator. With his neatly pressed white shirt, short black hair and outgoing personality, Neme could be the maître d' at an expensive restaurant. In reality, he is the former director of the Bogotá parks system, a government position that brought him to the attention of the Revolutionary Armed Forces of Colombia, a Far Left rebel group known by its Spanish acronym, FARC.

FARC controls large portions of the Colombian countryside and has pockets of support within various Bogotá neighbourhoods. It has for years targeted members of the Colombian middle class for extortion. Neme believes they singled him out because of his job: "Sometimes they think, you're working for the government you're working against them, so . . . you can become a target. That happened with me. So I have a couple [threats] happen with me, against my life."

Neme fled to another part of Colombia, only to realize it was not safe before fleeing again, this time to the United States. His first asylum hearing occurred in the wake of September 11, during which time the American government widened its definition of a terrorist. Under the so-called material support doctrine, anyone who provides money to terrorist groups is also considered a terrorist, and so ineligible to make a refugee claim. The law made no distinction for money extracted through extortion, with the result that thousands of Colombians were classified as terrorists, even though they themselves are victims of terror.

Neme spent four years trying to make his case to American Immigration officials, only to be repeatedly denied. "The two hearings I had in the States, it was bad. I feel like I was the most biggest terrorist in that country. They treat me so bad I was ready to tell them, 'I don't care. I don't want to be in your country. Just forget it, I would like find another country.'" In 2004 Neme moved to Canada, where he was finally accepted as a refugee.

"The treatment was much better," he notes. "The judges and everything, the systems, they have big differences."

Mary Jo Leddy says that before the Third Country deal was signed, many of the refugees she dealt with were middle-class Colombians like Neme. They are still targeted by rebel groups in their home country. Yet they are no longer eligible to make refugee claims in Canada and are sent back to the United States instead, no matter how unreasonable the procedure they can expect to face there. In 2008 the situation of Colombians seeking asylum in the United States improved when the government changed the law to permit exemptions for people in Neme's situation. Exemptions, however, have been granted in a halting and piecemeal fashion, such that the material support doctrine still sees asylum seekers undergo extended detention, separation from their loved ones and other deprivations.

In addition to posing special problems for Colombians and several other nationalities, the American asylum system has other drawbacks—such as the lack of legal aid for people making refugee claims—that have caused Canadian refugee advocates to call for the Safe Third Country deal to be scrapped. As Leddy describes the deal, "There's somebody clawing at the door in desperation, and we have slammed it in their face."

In 2005 the same Barbara Jackman who argued *Singh* worked with three other lawyers to file a legal challenge to the Safe Third Country Agreement. In 2007 a Canadian judge accepted their arguments and issued a 126-page decision that noted a wide range of areas in which American asylum procedures fell short of human rights standards. The judge's criticism of the material support doctrine, in particular, was scathing. He called it "a significant departure from both international law and Canadian law. The absence of the defence of duress turns child soldiers, those forced (often at gunpoint) to support terrorist groups, and those coerced to pay revolutionary taxes, into terrorists in the

U.S. system and subject to *refoulement*." The judge's decision was so favourable to Jackman's legal team that they could not believe the scope of their victory. "We are somewhat surprised," one of Jackman's colleagues admitted. "This is a vindication of the rights of refugees that we haven't seen around the world in a while."

But the victory was short-lived. The Canadian government appealed, resulting in a second decision that could not have been more different from the first. Whereas the original judge had addressed the material support issue and other questions on their merits, the appeal judge focused on technicalities. One of them was whether Canada had considered American asylum practices in good faith before signing the deal. The main issue, in other words, was not U.S. policies, but whether Canada had taken reasonable steps to look into them when it signed the agreement.

Here the appeal court noted that before the Safe Third Country Agreement went into effect, the Canadian government had received testimony from the Canadian representative of the United Nations High Commissioner for Refugees, Jahanshah Assadi, who said, "We consider the U.S. to be a safe country." In the view of the appeal court, that was enough to show that the Canadian government had met the good faith test when it signed the Third Country deal. "Given the position of the UNHCR, the main supervisory body in relation to refugee protection, it cannot be suggested that the [Canadian government] was not acting in good faith, when it designated the United States as a country that complies with its Convention obligations."

A point that was overlooked during the trial was that UNHCR is often criticized for being too dependent on the goodwill of the American government. Critics point to a shift UNHCR has undergone since the end of the Cold War, transforming from an agency that focuses strictly on refugees to one that attempts to help anyone affected by humanitarian crises, whether or not they are refugees. This expanded mandate required more extensive fundraising efforts to address crises in regions such as the Balkans and East Africa. Yet these same crises also saw UNHCR fail to live up to its new mandate, causing its donors to actually slash their funding. The result is that in recent years UNHCR has become heavily dependent on a small handful of governments, particularly the United States, which has long been its biggest donor. As Gil Loescher of Oxford University and two co-authors have written, "While the scale of US support has enabled UNHCR to carry out many of its programs, American dominance has enabled Washington to determine many policy and personnel decisions within UNHCR." According to Loescher and other critics, UNHCR goes to excessive lengths "safeguarding the confidence of donor governments" such as the United States.

Such an arrangement calls into question the reasonableness of letting UNHCR testimony regarding the safe third country be decisive. At a minimum, the Canadian government should have also been expected to give weight to the views of Amnesty International, the Canadian Council for Refugees and the Canadian Council of Churches—three NGOs directly involved in the legal challenge—as well as Human Rights First, Immigration Equality, the World Organization for Human Rights USA and the American Civil Liberties Union, all of which submitted affidavits on the Canadian NGOs' behalf. In his testimony, Assadi presented no evidence to defend U.S. policy from the many criticisms levelled against it by these and other groups. Yet despite his testimony's shortcomings, it was taken to show that Canada had done due diligence before signing the agreement.

The result of the Safe Third Country Agreement is that Canada has taken a major step backwards in the protection it offers refugees. Colombians have been denied a much-needed avenue of escape. Moreover, while 85 percent of asylum claimants in

Canada have legal representation, the percentage is much lower in the United States. Even non-Colombians, therefore, are sent through an inferior system when they are turned back at the Canadian border. These limitations infringe on the rights of people seeking asylum in Canada. The deal, as we have seen, makes an exception for people who arrive by air, and so does not completely destroy Canada's refugee rights framework. But it does violence to that framework nonetheless.

Canada's agreement with the United States is one reason why it is important to distinguish between the *Singh* decision and Canada's approach as a whole. If the *Singh* decision is inspiring, Canada's system as a whole is not. As we've seen, interdiction measures against refugees are employed everywhere from the Windward Passage to the northwest coast of Australia. And the *Singh* decision, it bears noting, has not prevented Canada's enthusiastic participation in this sad international trend.

This fact is often brought home to Howard Adelman of York University who specializes in refugee issues and who regularly travels to East African and other international crisis zones. "I haven't studied this, so I must admit, it's impressionistic," Adelman says, "but Canada probably has one of the best systems of interdiction at airports abroad."

Adelman points to events he has witnessed many times while standing in line in airports in the developing world: "I travel all the time, especially to Africa, and I can't tell you how many times I've seen people pulled out of the line. [Immigration or airline officials] have various clever devices. They ask you where you live. Your telephone number is a good clue. And if the telephone doesn't correlate with where you live very quickly, or your postal zones, or things like that—and these guys really know their numbers—they catch you."

We can imagine how this arrangement would have worked had it been in place in Zaire in 1997, when Francine Peyti was trying to get to Canada on a fake Dutch passport. Standing in line to board a plane at the Kinshasa airport, Peyti would have been asked where she lived in the Netherlands and what her phone number there was. If she had even thought to make up a number, the officials questioning her could have simply dialled it and seen that it was not hers. Peyti would thus have been unable to escape Zaire, where she had been shot at and been the victim of attempted rape. That Zaire was a dangerous place for someone like Peyti would be of no concern to the airline personnel involved, whose chief concern is to avoid a fine for bringing in travellers who don't have the right documents.

That Canada conducts its own forms of interdiction highlights the fact that whether the right at issue in *Singh* will be enforced crucially depends on whether the asylum-seeker involved has reached Canada. The scope of this limitation becomes apparent when we recall how much interdiction is now done at sea. *Singh* would have no relevance to someone intercepted on the high seas before reaching the shores of Nova Scotia or British Columbia. *Singh*, therefore, does not represent an adequate solution to all the problems refugees now face.

It is difficult to think of what a fully adequate solution might be to the problem of human rights enforcement at sea. When Japanese ships harpoon whales off the coast of Antarctica, members of Greenpeace sail after them to record and denounce their every move. There may be no solution to interdiction at sea short of human rights groups adopting a similar approach in regard to the U.S. Coast Guard. Either that, or international trade deals should be made to include human rights clauses, as rights advocated have long pushed for. But so far as current reality is concerned, Arendt's criticism of human rights remains nowhere more powerful than in regard to the high seas.

In addition to the Safe Third Country Agreement and interdiction, Canada's refugee system has a third problem. As it happens, it is one emphasized by low-immigration advocates, but is one human rights advocates should take seriously as well. It concerns deportation. The number of people actually removed from Canada has long trailed behind the number of deportation orders. In 2008, for example, there were 66,000 people slated for removal (a group that includes not only rejected refugee claimants but tourists, students and other temporary residents who overstay their visas); the whereabouts of 41,000 of them were unknown.

Canada's experience is not unique. Many other countries also fail to follow through on deportation orders. Officials in both Paris and London have estimated that when failed asylum claimants are not detained, they disappear 70 percent of the time. In London alone, failed asylum claimants and their families are thought to make up a significant portion of a total underground population estimated at 100,000. If Western states have a border-control problem, therefore, it is due not to an inability to control who enters their territory, but to who exits. Or as Howard Adelman puts it, "The big problem that no one has solved is not the problem of intake, because that works more or less effectively and fairly with all kinds of little problems in management. The real problem is no country knows how to deport people effectively."

Some rights advocates might ask whether a failure to carry out deportations is really so bad. If some people are able to stay in Canada after their paperwork expires, who really is hurt? The answer is, refugees. The fact that many people are not removed after arrival has been a major incentive to the creation of no-entry policies for asylum-seekers. As Matthew Gibney puts it, "The restrictiveness of the liberal state's policy towards asylum seekers can be seen as flowing from the liberalism (intentional or otherwise) of its policy towards foreigners [illegally] inside the state. Inclusion and exclusion are two sides of the same liberal coin." Given the diminished likelihood that failed claimants will eventually be deported, not admitting them in the first place is now seen as the only way to prevent their long-term residency.

Many states today turn away genuine refugees, so we should hope that they improve their asylum programs before addressing their deportation problem. Nevertheless, over the long term no-entry policies are unlikely to disappear without swift deportation becoming a more likely outcome for people who are fairly found not to be refugees. In that regard, it is encouraging to note that Canada has recently increased the number of deportations it carries out. Deportation, however, remains a neglected spending area, and more resources still need to be devoted to it in Canada and elsewhere.

The *Singh* decision was concerned only with one narrow right, and it does not prevent interdiction abroad or at sea and other injustices. Despite these limitations, the principles underlying *Singh* show how the rights of refugees can be enforced, and provides a model of what a more adequate list of asylum-seekers' rights will someday look like. If the portable-procedural approach were adopted it would make the human rights to which asylum-seekers now appeal more similar to citizens' rights. Arendt thought it was impossible to bridge the gap between these two understandings of rights in a world of sovereign states. The model of asylum-seekers rights outlined here, however, does not call a state's prerogative to control its borders into question. Rather it seeks to extend to asylum-seekers three procedural entitlements that we take for granted when it comes to the rights of citizens, who enjoy all three safeguards defended here when they are accused of a crime. Were the portable-procedural model adopted, I believe it would represent our civilization's best chance of reconciling the existence of sovereign states with the aspiration of human rights. That no state currently follows this model should remind us how far our world is from justice for refugees. Two centuries after the Declaration of the Rights of Man, human rights is still a radical creed.

EIGHT

THE LEGEND OF AHMED RESSAM

PETER SHOWLER IS A SQUAT MAN with a ruddy complexion and a protruding jawline. Looking at him might call to mind an athletic director or a National Football League coach. His careful manner of speech, however, gives away his training in the law. In 1999 Showler was appointed head of the Immigration and Refugee Board, or IRB, the Canadian government agency that decides refugee claims. As chair of the national tribunal, Showler worked on the twelfth floor of a glass office tower in downtown Ottawa. One day in 2001 he was in his spacious corner suite overlooking the Gatineau Hills, discussing refugee issues with a visiting official, when his assistant appeared at the door and told him there was something on TV he needed to see.

Showler didn't keep a TV set in his office. Years earlier, another official at the board had authorized an expensive office refurnishing; the bill had been leaked to the press, creating a minor media scandal. Showler deliberately kept his furnishings spartan to avoid a similar fate. After his meeting wrapped up, therefore, Showler walked over to his executive director's suite, which was on the other side of the building. When Showler arrived a group of staff members were standing around her TV, watching American Airlines Flights 11 and 175 fly into the World Trade Center. It was the morning of September 11, and as Showler recalls, he and his colleagues reacted to what they saw with "visceral shock and horror."

Several of Showler's staff had friends or family in New York whose whereabouts were unknown. Others were made ill by what they were watching. Showler spent the next several hours pacifying distraught employees, some of whom had to be sent home for the day, and trying to keep on top of what was happening. The anxious mood inside the refugee board mirrored that of the Canadian government as a whole. As Showler says, "Ottawa was frozen in panic at the time. Nobody knew *what* was going on."

It would eventually become clear that Mohammed Atta and the other hijackers executed their plan from within the United States. In the nervous days following the attacks, however, rumours and false leads swirled everywhere. On September 13, Boston newspapers reported that investigators were examining whether the terrorists had entered the United States through Canada. "The cause of that rumour was that two of the terrorists actually started their flight from Bangor, Maine," Showler says, referring to Atta and another hijacker who transferred onto American Flight 11 in Boston. "It was a means of surreptitious entry onto the flight without attracting attention. Because it was Bangor, Maine—well, for a lot of Americans, Maine is almost Canada."

The Boston papers had reported on a lead authorities were investigating. Follow-up stories that appeared elsewhere were not so restrained. "Foreign terrorists bent on wreaking havoc in the United States have found the path of least resistance into our country—Canada," *The New York Post* told its half-million readers. "At least four suspects in last week's attack on the World Trade Center crossed into the United States over our porous, 3,987-mile border with Canada." Similar stories quickly appeared in both Canada and the United States under headlines such as "Canada: A Club Med for World Terrorists."

Fear that Canada might be implicated in the attacks was soon felt inside the refugee board, when Showler and his colleagues began to hear rumours that the hijackers not only had come through Canada but had come through the refugee system. As the names of Atta and the other attackers trickled out in the media, Showler had his staff search the board's files to check whether any of them had ever made a refugee claim. Each search came back negative, but Showler remained on edge. There was still the possibility that they might have used false names, which would take longer to rule out. The hijackers, moreover, were not Showler's only problem. Amid the stream of stories portraying Canada as a staging ground for September 11, one name kept reappearing: Ahmed Ressam.

Ressam, also known as the Millennium Bomber, had made a Canadian refugee claim before plotting to blow up the Los Angeles airport in 1999. His plan made headlines at the time of arrest, but in the days following September 11, it generated a fresh thunderclap of publicity. "What really made [Ressam] significant was 9/11," Showler says. "When 9/11 happened, within three days you heard nothing but 'Ahmed Ressam, Ahmed Ressam, Ahmed Ressam,' both in the American and Canadian media."

Several days after the attacks, Showler assembled two files on Ahmed Ressam. One was a list of media talking points noting the key dates in his refugee claim. The other was an internal legal document tracking Ressam's passage through the wider Canadian immigration system, of which the refugee board was only a part. After sitting down in his office to go over this

material, Showler was brought up short. Ahmed Ressam's journey through Canada's refugee system was indeed a troubling
affair. Yet as Showler turned the pages, he could see that there
was a second Ressam scandal. Only this one, unlike the failed
bomb plot, had not yet been stopped.

Ahmed Ressam was born in 1967 in Bou Ismail, Algeria, a
poor town on the Mediterranean Sea that offers its residents
little in the way of prospects. As a boy he displayed an aptitude
for numbers, and his family hoped that he would do well on the
exams that guaranteed good students a university education.
When he was sixteen, however, Ressam developed an ulcer. "We
found him all the time holding his stomach," a boyhood friend
recalled. "We would ask him what's wrong, and he would say
that his stomach ached." The teenage Ressam went to Paris for
an operation and a long recovery. When he came home he had
missed so much school he had to repeat a year. When he finally
took the university exam but did poorly it proved to be the first
of many things he would fail at.

With university now unlikely, Ressam tried to join the police,
only to be told he lacked the right qualifications. Eventually he
settled into a menial job serving tea and lemonade at his father's
café. The town's largest mosque was across the street, but Ressam
never crossed its threshold. He and his friends were too interested in drinking wine, smoking hash and hitting on women at
the local seaside nightclub. "He was a handsome young man.
He was cool and had no problem finding the *jeunes filles*," a
friend of the family said. "Ahmed liked to dress himself well and
go search for women. He had nothing to do with Islam."

Islam, however, would have something to do with Ressam. In
the early 1990s Algeria experienced a moment of hope when it
carried out the first round of an election that was among the
freest in the history of the Arab world. The election, however,
was marked by the strong performance of the Islamic Front for

Salvation, a fundamentalist party. Members of the Front were known to patrol the streets with cudgels, enforcing their own version of Islamic law by attacking cafés that served alcohol and knocking cigarettes out of smokers' hands. In Bou Ismail the Front issued death threats against the local imam, whom they considered insufficiently observant, forcing him to flee. On a national level, the party's rise caused the socialist government to cancel the second round of voting scheduled for 1992. Islamic radicals armed themselves and took to the hills, vowing revenge. Algeria soon descended into civil war, the same conflict that triggered the formation of the International Parliament of Writers, and which would eventually see over 100,000 people killed.

Algerians who survived the bloodshed faced a stark choice. If they stayed in Algeria they could support either an authoritarian military regime or an equally authoritarian Islamism. Ressam, like many, chose to leave the country. In 1992, when he was twenty-five, he bought a ticket for the ferry that ran from Algiers to Marseilles, France. He arrived with a thirty-day visa but stayed on illegally after it expired and drifted to Corsica, a French island in the Mediterranean, where he found work picking grapes and painting at a tourist resort. His only real concern now was to evade Immigration authorities, but this proved to be beyond his abilities; he was arrested and scheduled for a deportation hearing. Rather than go home, Ressam bought a fake French passport and flew to Montreal, a city that had recently seen a dramatic increase in its Algerian population. France, the traditional home of Algerian expatriates, had tightened its visa requirements just as the civil war was intensifying, forcing Algerians who wanted to escape the bloodshed to look farther abroad.

When Ressam arrived in Montreal in February of 1994, the situation in Algeria was highly repressive. Yet Ressam himself had never been persecuted. As he would later admit, his primary motive in moving to Canada was to "improve my life in general." When he landed at Mirabel Airport he had a cover story prepared, according to which he was a French citizen with a different name. Upon reaching the front of the immigration line, Ressam held out his passport with the glued-in photograph and inwardly held his breath. Customs officers immediately pulled him into a small room where they looked at his passport through a microscope and passed it under ultraviolet light. The glue and ink used to doctor it began to glow.

"Is this a fake?" an Immigration officer asked. After Ressam admitted that it was, he was detained, at which point he said he wanted to file a refugee claim. His passport exposed as a forgery, he dropped his story about being a French citizen and filled out an immigration form, accurately listing his name, nationality, date of birth, marital status, lack of religious affiliation and French proficiency. He also included the address of the YMCA where he would stay after leaving the airport. On a separate form he indicated his grounds for claiming asylum. It contained a tissue of lies. Ressam made up a story about being falsely accused of selling weapons to a childhood friend before being arrested and coerced. "I was tortured with ribbons, soap, chlorinated water, a system of scales and even the drawer of an office desk," he wrote in one imaginative passage.

Ressam was given a hearing date for his asylum claim, five weeks hence, and released. As of yet he had no connection to terrorism, and was just another asylum claimant with a made-up story living on welfare down at the Y. Perhaps it was because he knew his story would be found out that Ressam did not show up for his refugee hearing. (When his lawyer called and angrily asked, "Where the hell were you?" Ressam claimed he forgot.) His failure to appear meant that he now had to demonstrate some compelling reason for his absence, such as a car accident on the way to the hearing, to prevent his claim from being automatically rejected. He was scheduled for a so-called abandonment hearing at which he could explain himself, but he put little effort into assembling a credible case. As in Algeria, Ressam's main interests after arriving in Canada revolved around meeting women in nightclubs. It was hard to look good on what welfare provided, however, so he soon turned to petty crime.

In August of 1994 Ressam tried to steal a security guard's wallet at a shopping mall. That resulted in an arrest, but the charges were dropped. Five months later an Eaton's store detective watched Ressam and an accomplice make a clumsy attempt at stealing an Armani suit. Ressam's friend managed to get rid of the stolen merchandise before being stopped by police, but the less adroit Ressam was caught with another suit stolen from the Bay. At his criminal trial Ressam claimed the bag he was carrying belonged to his friend, but the justice ridiculed his story. Ressam was fined $100 and placed on two years' probation. This was typical of his time in Montreal, during which theft, along with fifteen months of welfare payments, was his main means of supporting himself. Ressam would steal purses on his own, or snatch luggage from downtown hotels while working with different Algerian accomplices. He would rummage through their contents for money or credit cards. If they held passports, he knew where to sell them.

By the time of his sentencing for shoplifting, Ressam had a bigger problem than his scrapes with the law. A month earlier, in May of 1995, his refugee claim had been rejected. In a disastrous ruling for Ressam, the government declared that he abandoned his claim by not attending his hearing. As a result, he was now scheduled for a third and final hearing, which would concern the details of his deportation. When he once again failed to appear he was arrested, detained and given a deportation date.

Ressam's lawyer, however, pointed out that his refugee file was being reviewed by a federal judge. Canada's asylum system at the time did not allow for appeals in the normal sense of the term, as mistaken facts could not be corrected, but claimants could seek a review of how the law was applied in their case. Ressam's lawyer had sought this kind of review, and Ressam could not be deported until it was concluded. After his August arrest, therefore, Ressam was released on the condition that he present himself to Immigration officials once a month, while everyone waited for the outcome of his legal review.

The wait lasted six months. Finally, in February of 1996, two years after his arrival in Canada, the justice upheld the rejection of Ressam's refugee application. Immigration officials now had a green light to carry out his deportation. Yet they failed to do so. As we will see, there were several reasons why, but the most immediate one was the Immigration Department's lack of resources. At the time, Canada devoted an even smaller budget to executing deportation orders than it does now, and Immigration officials had to choose which removals to prioritize. Failed refugee claimants with shoplifting convictions were low on the list. "They're not our top priority, that's for sure," an Immigration spokeswoman said of Ressam in 1999. "We make sure that people who are considered dangerous or [serious] criminals get out first." Ressam thus lingered in Canada in the legal equivalent of limbo. He continued dutifully reporting to Immigration every month, and they just as dutifully continued working on other deportations that struck them as more pressing.

Ressam's economic prospects now were even bleaker than they had been in Algeria. There at least he could work in his father's café. In Canada, by contrast, no restaurant could legally hire him after his refugee claim was rejected. Having his claim rejected also saw his welfare payments cut off. With no income and nothing left to lose when it came to his immigration status, Ressam had little incentive not to keep breaking the law. He eventually committed thirty or forty crimes altogether, a spree that saw him arrested on two further occasions. They included an October 1996 charge for pickpocketing, which netted him a $500 fine and more probation, but still no movement on his deportation.

It was now eight months after his final brush with the refugee system. Ressam was a petty criminal eking out a marginal existence while Immigration officers worked their way through the many deportation orders that, unlike his, seemed important. If Ahmed Ressam failed to amount to much in the eyes of Immigration officials, it was in keeping with the rest of his time in Canada, during which he had failed at everything. He had failed to pass himself off as a French traveller at the airport. Failed to lodge a successful refugee claim. Failed to avoid arrest as a thief and an illegal immigrant. To outside observers he was not so much a fearsome figure as a pathetic one.

There was still one area, however, where Ressam could excel. Even though he had little interest in religion, shortly after his arrival in Montreal he began attending mosque as a way to meet other North Africans. Ressam frequented Assuna Annabawiyah, a combined mosque and bookstore that operated out of a downtown storefront and attracted fifteen hundred worshippers, predominantly Algerians, for Friday prayers. It was through Assuna that Ressam met the accomplices with whom he committed his string of petty crimes. And it was through the same Assuna contacts that he met two individuals who would have a fateful impact on his life.

The first of these was a fellow Algerian named Fateh Kamel. Kamel was the person who bought the passports and other documents that Ressam and his friends filched. Unlike Ressam, Kamel had made a successful life in Canada. After immigrating from Algeria in 1987, he married a Canadian woman and opened a craft store. Whereas Ressam had no valid travel documents and so could not leave Canada, Kamel was a jetsetter who often flew off to Europe and the Middle East. Kamel told people his frequent travel was for business, but that was untrue. The real reason was his extremist political views. By the time he met Ressam in the mid-1990s, Kamel was a veteran of Afghanistan and Bosnia, and a fixer for a diffuse network of Islamist terrorist groups. Italian intelligence agents once recorded Kamel boasting about his dedication to the cause: "I do not fear death . . . because the jihad is the jihad, and to kill is easy for me."

The second transformative figure in Ressam's life was Abderraouf Hannachi, an immigrant from Tunisia in his forties. Like Kamel, he was both a Canadian citizen and an extremist who had trained at a military camp in Afghanistan, in Hannachi's case one operated by Osama bin Laden. At the Assuna mosque Hannachi was the muezzin, the official who calls worshippers in for prayers, which is a position of respect among mainstream Muslims. The people who really looked up to Hannachi, however, were the tiny cluster of local Arabs who shared his violent ideology. Among Kamel and other Islamists, Hannachi's status as an associate of al-Qaeda gave him a special cachet.

It is not hard to imagine the impression Hannachi and Kamel would have made on Ressam. As his thirtieth birthday drew closer, Ressam had no legal status in Canada, had no career prospects and was thousands of miles away from his family. The two older men, by contrast, were players, "important brothers" in the local Arab community. Ressam and a half-dozen of his Algerian accomplices, several of whom were also failed refugee claimants, gradually fell into the jihadists' orbit. As an Italian prosecutor once said of an al-Qaeda network that formed in Milan, "These are people with a lot of problems. Adapting to this country is devastating to them. In radical religious activity they found rules, a structure. It's not just religious, it's psychological and personal." The same process occurred with Ressam and his displaced criminal associates. By the summer of 1997,

Ressam was asking Hannachi how he might make his own trip to Afghanistan and be inducted into a full-time terror career.

A major barrier to Ressam's goal was his lack of a passport. Here, however, Ressam finally succeeded at something. Quebec had an unusual law at the time that allowed residents to obtain a passport by presenting only a baptismal certificate. Ressam obtained a blank certificate from a local parish, found out the name of the priest who ministered there in 1971—the birth year he would provide—and forged the priest's signature. A few weeks later, he had a perfectly legal Canadian passport under a false name, Benni Norris, and was free to travel wherever he liked.

This was true even though Canadian intelligence knew about Ressam. After being warned about Fateh Kamel by European intelligence agencies, the Canadian Security Intelligence Service (CSIS) bugged the apartment Ressam shared with three other Algerian thieves-cum-jihadis. The eavesdropping operation was focused on Kamel and his "right hand," a fellow Bosnia veteran named Said Atmani, who came to Canada in 1995 and later moved in with Ressam. Over the course of two years, CSIS recorded hundreds of conversations in which the residents of Ressam's apartment and their visitors denounced the West and plotted its destruction. They would refer glowingly to the Armed Islamic Group, an Algerian terror organization known by its French initials, GIA. The CSIS agents eavesdropping on Ressam's apartment used a similar acronym for Ressam and his crew. Only in was BOG, short for "Bunch of Guys." Rather than a lair of cold-blooded terrorists, Ressam's dumpy apartment struck the CSIS agents as the home of a group of bumbling amateurs. With the exception of Atmani, who had seen combat, the rest seemed marginal types, their big talk a way of covering up their obvious failures and inadequacies.

By the time Ressam left for Afghanistan in March of 1998, CSIS had overheard where he was going and why. They therefore put his name on a watch list that would prevent him from re-entering Canada. Some time afterwards CSIS also passed Ressam's details on to American intelligence. But what CSIS had not been able to overhear was that Ressam had obtained a valid passport under a different name. So despite his presence on the watch list, he would be able to travel without attracting suspicion.

Up until his departure, Ressam had continued to report to Citizenship and Immigration Canada every month. But leaving the country meant he missed an appointment, triggering an Immigration warrant for his arrest. Ressam was also wanted by the Montreal police on some outstanding criminal charges, but neither type of warrant had much effect once Ressam arrived in Afghanistan. Over the course of nine months he received combat training at two al-Qaeda camps, covering everything from knives to rocket launchers, as well as instructions in bomb-making. By February of 1999 he was in Pakistan, from where he flew via Seoul and Los Angeles back to Canada. When he presented his passport to an Immigration officer at the Vancouver airport, the false name allowed him to breeze through.

After Ressam returned to Montreal a month later, acquaint-ances said that he was more confident. That was not the only change. Before his trip, CSIS had managed to record hundreds of Ressam's conversations. After visiting Afghanistan, where he was taught to avoid detection, CSIS would never catch Ressam on tape again.

Ressam's training marked a turning point. He was now a genuinely dangerous individual. In autumn of 1999 Ressam began to seriously work toward bombing the Los Angeles air-port, which he had passed through on his way back from Afghanistan (and which was why it was chosen as a target).

By this time the authorities were closing in on the Bunch of Guys. Ressam's former roommate Atmani was the first to go. Like Ressam he was a failed refugee claimant and a petty criminal. But after he was picked up in Ontario for credit card fraud, he made a much stronger impression on authorities than Ressam had. Firefights in Bosnia and Afghanistan had left him with bullet wounds across his torso and an open wound on his buttock that still required padding. Monthly reporting would clearly not do in his case, and Atmani was swiftly deported to Bosnia. Soon afterwards the BOG suffered an even bigger blow when their ringleader, Fateh Kamel, was arrested in Jordan and taken to France on terrorism charges. Ressam's name came up during Kamel's interrogation with French intelligence, and they pressured Canada to bring in Ressam next.

The Royal Canadian Mounted Police complied by raiding a Montreal apartment where Ressam was sleeping. Ressam, however, managed to escape down a back alley. Undeterred by his near arrest, he recruited an untrained fellow Algerian to fly with him to Vancouver, from where they would try to execute their Los Angeles plan before the millennium. By this point Ressam had built an entire identity around his fake passport, making it difficult if not impossible for the authorities to catch him.

Ressam and his rookie accomplice checked in to the 2400 Motel on the outskirts of Vancouver and asked for the bungalow farthest from the road. During their two-week stay, they struck the cleaning lady as a strange pair. They asked her to clean their cabin as infrequently as possible. When she came by they insisted she leave the clean sheets outside and forbade her from ever entering the rear bedroom. Their habit of leaving the windows open during November also seemed suspicious. Passersby could smell a strange chemical odour, like some overwhelming and toxic cologne.

Inside the bungalow, the two men were using notes Ressam had taken in Afghanistan to build a bomb. Their mixture of hexamine, citric acid and hydrogen peroxide could be set off by an accidental jolt, and the process they were using gave off toxic fumes, which the pair tried to ward off by sucking on lozenges. The splitting headaches the chemicals caused, though, were something they simply had to endure. Ressam was also suffering from malaria, caused by a mosquito bite in Afghanistan, and this sometimes made it difficult for him to get out of bed. As if that were not bad enough, he also spilled some chemicals on himself. After burning through his jeans, they left a scar on his thigh. Finally, after the two men decided that one person would attract less attention going over the border, Ressam's accomplice returned to Montreal. It was now left to Ressam to travel by rental car and ferry into the United States.

Al-Qaeda had trained Ressam in bomb-making, but he had to sort out the logistics of his trip on his own. Here the old bumbling Ressam returned with a vengeance. His operation was premised on the strange idea that rather than drive into the United States and assemble his explosives there, it would be best to drive through customs with a bomb kit in the trunk of his car. A second problem was Ressam's belief that he would attract less attention travelling alone: solo travellers receive more scrutiny from border guards than people in pairs. His decision to take a ferry has likewise been termed "a serious intelligence error," insofar as ferry passengers receive more attention from customs than drivers at land crossings. Among other drawbacks, Ressam would have to go through two inspections rather than one.

The route Ressam took was a roundabout one that involved three separate ferries, one inside Canada, one across the border and one inside the United States. When he arrived at his second ferry terminal, on Vancouver Island, an American pre-inspection agent asked where he was going. Even though his circular itinerary was clearly impractical, Ressam told the agent that he was on a short business trip, a discrepancy that resulted in his car being searched. After his trunk turned out to contain only some luggage with clothes, Ressam was waved on board, free to try his luck with the second inspection that would occur when he got off the ferry.

Here Ressam's mistake was to hold back until he was the last car, not realizing this would only heighten suspicion. By the time he rolled up to the female customs agent waiting onshore, Ressam was sweating and fidgeting, causing her to wonder if he might be a drug smuggler. After she asked Ressam to step out of the car, two other agents went through his trunk. This time they unscrewed the fastener on the spare tire well and looked inside. "Hey, we've got something here," one of them called out. Ressam took off, followed by border agents who captured him several blocks away. He has been in prison ever since.

What are the lessons of the Ahmed Ressam affair? How we answer this question depends on which period we have in mind—before or after his transformation into a terrorist. In regard to the pre-terrorist Ressam, he spent two years passing through Canada's refugee determination system before he became the responsibility of Citizenship and Immigration Canada, which carried out deportations. The amount of time it took to officially reject his refugee claim is a reminder that refugee systems, like legal systems, often grind slowly. During the same period Ressam was in Canada, for example, it took Western European countries an average of three years to decide refugee claims. The handling of the pre-terrorist Ressam is a reflection of the bureaucratic nature of most asylum systems, of which Canada's is no exception.

Being bureaucratic is one thing. But failing to deport Ressam after he left the refugee system was a serious breakdown. With an under-resourced Immigration Department, violent types like Atmani took priority, and a petty hoodlum like Ressam could all too easily fall through the cracks. Yet even if Canada had adequately funded deportations, it is unlikely that Ressam would have made a swift exit. Undemocratic regimes like the one that ran Algeria in the 1990s sometimes refuse to take in nationals who have committed crimes abroad. They can stonewall deportations through various means, such as demanding proof that the person in question is in fact a citizen. As the proof often involves documents that only the same regime can provide, the possibility arises for a country to drag out a deportation. According to Elinor Caplan, Canada's minister of immigration at the time of Ressam's arrest, this happened with Ressam. "Bottom line, we couldn't get travel documents," she said in 2001. "We have a number of countries [where] it takes a lot of time to get travel documents unless the information and identity documents are clear."

In 1997, a third factor emerged that prevented Ressam's deportation. In March of that year, Canada placed a moratorium on deportations to Algeria. The moratorium, which was later adopted by Germany, the United Kingdom and other countries, was invoked after violence in the Algerian civil war reached a new level of horror. As Amnesty International noted in 1997, "This year alone Algerians have been slain in their thousands with unspeakable brutality—decapitated, mutilated and burned alive in their homes . . . We can think of no other country where human rights violations are so extreme." Amnesty pointed to a massacre in Ressam's hometown of Bou Ismail, where a family of twelve were murdered with the seeming approval of local authorities.

In their different ways, then, Immigration officials in Canada and Algeria were both responsible for the failure to deport Ressam the petty criminal before the moratorium took effect. Ressam's transformation from common criminal to bomber, however, confirms the adage that terrorists are made, not born. And if there is one institution implicated in Ressam's metamorphosis, it is the Canadian passport office. Having a passport in a false name is what allowed Ressam to travel to Afghanistan for terrorist training. Having a passport is what allowed him to sail through customs at Los Angeles airport and re-enter Canada, even though CSIS had given his name to Federal Bureau of Investigation and despite his presence on the Canadian no-entry list. And having a passport, finally, is what allowed Ressam to live under a new identity after warrants were issued for his arrest.

Ressam was able to obtain a legal travel document because of the lax procedure that allowed Quebec residents to obtain passports with no more than a baptismal certificate. "This is the kind of thing we would see all the time from Third World countries," Peter Showler says, referring to documents presented to him during refugee hearings. "There's no standardized state-issued document: all you've got is this little wrinkled piece of paper, all written in ink, signed by the parish priest." When Quebec law was changed in October of 2001 to make passport requirements more stringent, it was an appropriate response to the major institutional shortcoming that had allowed Ressam the terrorist to operate.

Ressam did not receive terrorist training until the spring of 1998, two years after his final brush with the refugee system. It is therefore a gross distortion to portray his case as one in which an extremist used the refugee system to try to execute a terror plot. Such a false view is potentially damaging, as it risks spreading hysteria about refugee applicants being terrorists. A false understanding might also divert attention away from the institutional failures that did enable Ressam's journey into terror. Whether we are concerned with protecting refugees or with preventing national security risks, therefore, we should hope to see the facts of Ressam's case correctly recorded and the right lessons carefully drawn.

Unfortunately, one of the primary lessons of Ressam's case is how easily the truth can be replaced by a legend. The real Ahmed Ressam has long since disappeared and been replaced by a destructive myth, one in which the passport office features only intermittently, if at all, in Ressam's transformation. The revisionism began at the time of Ressam's capture, when conflicting reports appeared in Canadian newspapers. Among the most significant was a story on the front page of the *National Post* under the headline "Algeria Considered Suspect a Terrorist: Despite Admission, Canada Did Not Deport Ressam."

According to the *Post*, Ressam had been a terrorist from the moment he landed in Canada: "[Ressam] admitted to Canadian immigration authorities more than five years ago that he had been arrested in Algeria on suspicion he was an Islamic terrorist . . . Despite the admission in his refugee form, it appears Mr. Ressam, described by U.S. authorities as a serious terrorist threat, was not under police investigation."

The *Post* took at face value the false story of persecution Ressam had included in his old asylum application. That application contained the following sentence: "To them [the Algerian government], I was but an Islamist terrorist, even though I had no ties to the Islamist movement." Re-examined five years after it was submitted, Ressam's asylum sheet seemed to show that he had a connection to Islamism when he first landed in Montreal. It is not hard to see why such a connection would have seemed plausible in the aftermath of Ressam's bombing attempt. And yet the *Post*'s version of events was based on dubious assumptions no one thought to check. One was that terrorism allegations made by the Algerian government, a perpetrator of major human rights violations, did not require corroboration. The other assumption was that a real terrorist trying to sneak through the refugee system would not keep his membership in an extremist group a secret, but advertise it upon arrival.

When Ressam had written in his refugee application that he was suspected of selling weapons in Algeria, he had been making up a story. Now that story was taken as fact. Ressam's terrorist career was effectively backdated. It was this revised image of Ressam that would define subsequent retellings of his story. Certainly such was the case eight days after Ressam's capture when the *Globe and Mail* editorialized against Canada's becoming a staging ground for terrorists. "The wisdom of allowing people with fake passports into the country to make refugee claims is at best dubious," the *Globe* argued, proposing a policy change many other commentators would echo.

Shortly thereafter, the U.S. Congress held hearings to determine what factors had allowed Ressam to operate. David Harris, a former CSIS official turned Ottawa consultant, travelled to Washington to offer testimony. "Absurd refugee laws," Harris told the committee, "commonly see ostensible applicants disappearing underground in Canada and the U.S." Harris seemed unaware that Ressam had been reporting to Immigration before he acquired a passport, or that Harris's own former agency had been monitoring Ressam during the same period.

Eight months after Harris's testimony, September 11 happened. The backdated version of Ahmed Ressam was suddenly everywhere. The Canadian Broadcasting Corporation aired a documentary about Ressam, "Trail of a Terrorist," that took it for granted that he arrived in Canada as a terrorist. It also introduced a new twist. Narrator Terence McKenna noted that Ressam's asylum application had been turned down, yet he still referred to Ressam as an "Algerian refugee," confusingly (and contradictorily) suggesting that Ressam's claim was bona fide or had been accepted. The Canadian Press would express a similar idea in a more straightforward way when it flatly declared, "Ressam was accepted in Canada as a refugee."

It was the original myth, the one that backdated Ressam's involvement in terror, that would have the most legs. In October 2001 the Public Broadcasting Service rebroadcast "Trail of a Terrorist" in the United States. An extensive website accompanied the program under the title "Is Canada a Safe Haven for Terrorists?" Politicians, security analysts and low-immigration advocates were asked about the mythical Ressam's arrival in Canada. An exchange with Texas congressman Lamar Smith was typical:

> When Ahmed Ressam came to Canada, he claimed refugee status, and he admitted apparently that he had been in jail in Algeria and had been convicted of weapons offenses and accused of terrorism. Nothing apparently happened. What should have happened?
>
> . . . I know what the United States would have done, and that is conduct a background check to make sure that he was eligible for entering the United States and that he was not going to be a threat to the American citizens. I am not sure he would have even gotten in our front door, to tell you the truth.

Smith was a long-time proponent of slashing immigration. For him, Ressam's case merely confirmed the problem with "lax" immigration laws. When Elinor Caplan, the Canadian immigration minister, was interviewed for the same program, it provided an opportunity to correct the impression that Ressam arrived in Canada as a terrorist. That Caplan never did suggests that even she thought it was true.

"Trail of a Terrorist" and its website were used as sources for *The 9/11 Commission Report*, the U.S. government inquiry into September 11. The report described how Ressam first entered Canada: "Following a familiar terrorist pattern, Ressam and his associates used fraudulent passports and immigration fraud to travel. In Ressam's case, this involved flying from France to Montreal using a photo-substituted French passport." When the 9/11 report's version of events was quoted in the media, the backdated version of Ressam's arrival became self-perpetuating, with media reports citing a government document that had itself sourced its version of events from the press.

The Ressam myth was widely taken to highlight a problem with Canada's policy of official multiculturalism. Such was the conclusion of the *New York Times*, for example, when it reported on the factors in Canada that had allowed Ressam to thrive. The *Times* explained Ressam's attempt to kill thousands of Americans by reference to "the rich ethnic mix and the loose immigration controls that have made it possible." For years afterwards, Canadian commentators would draw a similar connection between multiculturalism and terror. The same David Harris who had denounced "Canada's absurd refugee laws" in Washington later acknowledged to an interviewer that Ressam's passport played a role in his transformation. But Harris went much further than calling for changes to the passport application procedure. "We need a gigantic cultural shift in this country," he said:

> We are not used to seeing ourselves at the front line of any major struggle. But there is a war on. It's a global, terrorist-based war that we are all going to be facing, and it is increasingly going to become home here to Canada. We have got to get our laws and our attitudes into line to meet the threat before it's too late. . . . Above all, all of us have got to be more aware that no matter what kind of emphasis we want to place on multiculturalism and the benefits of diversity, some of those issues open us to struggles that are going on around the world, and that we don't want to have to come home.

Harris was drawing the same connection between Ressam and multiculturalism that the *New York Times* had drawn, one that would continue to be reiterated for years afterwards. In 2008, for example, a report by the Vancouver-based Fraser Institute argued that "high immigration compromises security" and invoked the legendary Ressam to make its case. Canada's immigration and multiculturalism policies had always had critics. But the legendary Ressam provided the critics with a new talking point that had a powerful resonance in the wake of September 11. Multiculturalism. Immigration. Refugees. *These things are all dangerous.*

The Fraser Institute report came out a decade after Ressam had left for Afghanistan. Accurate accounts of his activities had long been available, including a twenty-part *Seattle Times* series that documented his transformation in painstaking detail. Yet it did not seem to matter. It was as if the legend of Ahmed Ressam had become indestructible. In real life Ressam had combined professional training with personal incompetence. After the legend took hold, his ill-conceived border crossing was taken to show he was "no amateur," while he himself was promoted to a terrorist "all-star." The central image of Ressam's arrival was not that of a run-of-the-mill economic migrant with a false story of persecution. It was rather of a terrorist who had not only waltzed through Canada's asylum system but had been allowed to do so after he "all but volunteered to immigration officials that he was a terrorist," as *60 Minutes* put it.

The real Ahmed Ressam was gone. The failure and petty criminal who drifted into terrorism years after arriving in Canada had been replaced by a far more ominous figure. One who used Canada's refugee system as a means of executing a major terror operation and was only narrowly averted from causing great carnage in the United States. His actions showed that Canada's refugee system was a gaping weakness in the North American security perimeter. The only thing to do now was to overhaul that system from top to bottom to make it far less welcoming.

Columnist Diane Francis drew the lesson of the Ressam affair most bluntly. "There should be a complete moratorium on immigration." Canada was admitting too many dangerous foreigners. Something had to be done to stanch the flood tide. It was time to slam shut the door.

Peter Showler put the Ressam file down on his desk. He could not quite believe what he was reading. It was as if there were two Ahmed Ressams. The real one, who had his final brush with the refugee board in 1996 and flew off to Afghanistan two years later, and the very different figure being described in the press. "The media conception of him was that . . . he was a terrorist when he entered, which is false," Showler says. Showler would do what he could to counter the myth, in interviews and elsewhere, but it was like a household fan blowing into an airplane engine's exhaust. There was too much misinformation coming the other way.

Showler left the refugee board in 2002 to teach refugee law at the University of Ottawa. The Ressam legend bothered him for years afterwards. It was not because Showler thought Canada's asylum system of the 1990s was perfect. Far from it. In late 2001, Canada introduced a new security review for refugee claimants. They would now have their personal data sent to CSIS immediately upon filing a claim. This reasonable step, which had previously been planned but received funding only after September 11, was one Showler approved of. As he says, "Some changes were appropriate."

Showler's concern had to do with the timing of the Ressam legend and the lessons that were drawn from it. There was something surreal, he thought, about so much criticism being directed at Canada's refugee program in the wake of September 11. What did the terrorist attacks have to do with refugees? After all, the attacks had not involved any refugee claims, in Canada or anywhere else. "None of them actually came through the American asylum system either," Showler says. "But you didn't see huge headlines: '[Terrorists] coming in on student visas,' '[Terrorists] coming in on business visas.' But the fact of the matter is that these people, most of them entered the country legally: primarily through business visa programs, student visa programs. Some of them overstayed and became illegal, but you didn't see this treated as the leak in the system. Instead you saw endless replays of the case of Ahmed Ressam."

To Showler it was as if someone had determined in advance that Canada's refugee system was a danger to the public, and the legend merely reinforced a view that was never really up for examination.

There was something else. The introduction of the front-end security review, alongside other safeguards that had been in place when Ressam arrived, meant that the Ressam myth took off just when Canada's refugee system became one of the *least* effective ways for a terrorist to enter North America. Showler describes the process refugee claimants go through: "The first thing that happens is they're photographed, they're fingerprinted, and [scheduled for] an intensive interview. Well what self-respecting terrorist would do that, when most terrorists have the money and the means to obtain false passports, false visas? Or even obtain legal visas and enter the country through legal means? Why would they bring themselves to the attention of authorities, knowing that they would immediately be put into Interpol scans?"

Showler's reference to terrorist resources is borne out by *The 9/11 Commission Report* and other sources, which note that al-Qaeda maintained its own passport office in Afghanistan. As for Ressam himself, it is worth noting that he did not file an asylum claim when he attempted to enter the United States, for precisely the reason Showler states. It would have attracted unwanted attention.

This brings us to one of the most misleading aspects of the Ressam myth. It was widely taken to show that if Canada's refugee system were harder to enter, fewer terrorists would try to reach Canada. Showler's remarks about terrorist resources, however, suggest that this view is naive. More likely is that that they would continue to arrive through other means, such as business and tourist visas. The terrorist's choice, in other words, is not whether to travel at all but between different means of doing so. Given this reality, it is worth asking whether Canada's refugee system is really a fatal weakness terrorists can exploit, as the legend would have it, or whether it is in fact an underappreciated counter-terrorism tool.

In order to answer this question we need to know two things. How frequently do terrorists arrive in Canada via asylum fraud compared with other means of travel? And what is the capture rate of terrorists who enter on a refugee claim compared with those who come in other ways? I am unaware of any study counting the number of terrorists who have tried to enter Canada through the refugee system. But by looking through media and think tank reports, and using a broad definition of "terrorist," it is possible to generate a rough count of twenty-six asylum claims made by individuals involved with extremism (see Postscript). Statistics on the number of terrorists active in Canada are even harder to come by, for obvious reasons. But in 2000 a rough benchmark was provided by Ward Elcock, then the head of CSIS, who said that his organization was aware of 350 terror suspects in Canada. (As Elcock pointed out, this is not a large number for a country of 33 million.) They belonged to about fifty organizations working for overseas causes, such as radical Sikh, Tamil and Islamist groups.

Elcock's figure was a snapshot of groups active in the year 2000, whereas the twenty-six refugee claims were made between 1988 and 2001. If we were to speculate about the number of terrorists present in Canada during the same thirteen-year period, it would possibly be larger. But the limited information that is available suggests that terrorists intending to exploit the asylum system represent a small minority of those who attempt to reach Canada.

What is even more striking about terrorists who pose as refugees in Canada is their overwhelming failure rate. There have been a few cases characterized as terrorists twisting the system to their own ends, but they are ambiguous. Essam Marzouk, for example, was a member of al-Jihad, an Egyptian organization that later merged with al-Qaeda, when he filed a refugee claim in Vancouver in 1993. Marzouk, whose claim was eventually accepted, was later rumoured to be indirectly involved in the 1998 bombing of two American embassies in East Africa, although his involvement in the bombing has never been conclusively established. He was captured by the Central Intelligence Agency shortly after the embassy attacks, but was not included in the list of suspects brought to the United States for indictment. (The CIA handed him over to Egyptian authorities instead, who convicted him of the separate charge of belonging to al-Jihad.) More importantly, during his time in Canada Marzouk was either in jail or under investigation by CSIS, frustrating whatever terrorist designs he had while in North America.

Marzouk, in other words, did not use the refugee system to carry out a successful terrorist operation. In this way he is typical of extremists who file refugee claims in Canada. In two or three cases they lived quietly for a few years before engaging in non-violent crimes, such as passport forgery, for which they were eventually caught. In others they were arrested on arrival by the RCMP or later placed under CSIS surveillance. In only one case, involving a fundraiser for Hezbollah who fled to Lebanon after CSIS began following him, was a documented terrorist able to avoid arrest. Contrary to the Ressam legend, in none of the twenty-six instances was someone plotting a terrorist attack able to use a refugee claim as a means of avoiding detection.

Said Atmani, Ressam's former roommate, provides a better example of what happens to terrorists' refugee claims than the Ressam legend did. Atmani did not actually use asylum fraud to enter Canada. Rather, he smuggled himself into the country by sailing as a stowaway on a cargo ship that docked in Halifax, and then filed a claim a month later. Nevertheless, at the time of his refugee claim Atmani was unambiguously a political extremist and while living in Montreal he forged documents for Islamic terror groups.

Filing a refugee claim, however, did not allow Atmani to evade detection by authorities. CSIS bugged the apartment he shared with Ressam precisely because they knew Atmani lived there. This is quite common with extremist refugee claimants, who often provide valuable intelligence to CSIS without knowing it. More to the point, Atmani's dual status as a terrorist refugee claimant made him the easiest member of the Montreal cell to deal with.

Unlike Kamel and Hannachi, who had Canadian citizenship, Atmani had no legal right to stay in Canada. Unlike Ressam, who was not a terrorist at the time of his criminal arrests, Atmani's history of political violence was obvious when he was picked up for credit card fraud. As a result, the moment Atmani found himself in police custody it was all over for his North American terror career. He was on a plane to Bosnia three days later.

The reason Atmani could be summarily deported was because he was both a terror suspect and a refugee claimant. In this way he symbolizes what may be the most overlooked fact about terrorists who pose as refugees: rather than being especially dangerous, such terrorists are the least likely to be effective, as they are the easiest to prosecute. This is evident in the fact that the most common outcome for terrorists who enter Canada's refugee system has been not merely to be arrested but to be subject to what are known as security certificates.

Security certificates, which can be used against any non-citizen, grant the government sweeping powers of detention. Refugee claimants can be pulled out of the refugee system and incarcerated, a step that is consistent with both the *Singh* decision and the Refugee Convention (neither oblige Canada to grant oral hearings to terrorists or other violent individuals). Security certificates are by far Canada's most powerful national security tool. They are also controversial, on account of the extraordinary measures they allow the state to employ. Prosecution lawyers have been able to present evidence that is withheld from an alleged terrorist and his lawyers, giving rise to allegations that the certificate process is itself a form of lawlessness, or what critics have termed "Guantánamo North."

In 2007 a Supreme Court of Canada decision modified, but did not eliminate, the secret-evidence provision of security certificates. Even in their revised form, certificates are arguably inconsistent with the principle of human rights, as they permit procedures that would be illegal in any legal context involving Canadian citizens. But what is not in doubt is the certificates' effectiveness as counterterrorism tools. As of 2009 fifteen terrorist asylum claimants have been dealt with through certificates. In each case, whatever threat they represented was instantly neutralized. Thanks to certificates and conventional arrests, no terrorist who has come through Canada's refugee system has been able to carry out an act of terror in North America.

The overwhelming capture rate of terrorists who make refugee claims is in noticeable contrast to terrorist operations that do not involve asylum fraud. The September 11 hijackers, as we've seen, used student tourist/business visas, while the largest terrorist attack in Canadian history, the 1985 Air India bombing, involved alleged or convicted prepetrators who were all long-time Canadian citizens. Perhaps a successful operation involving the Canadian asylum system will someday occur or come to light. But the evidence to date suggests that terrorists who attempt to enter North America through Canada's refugee system are making a huge mistake, one that dramatically increases their chance of being caught.

If the alternative is terrorists not coming to North America at all, we should obviously hope no extremist ever makes another asylum claim. But the more likely alternative is that terrorists will continue to arrive. Given this reality, we may actually prefer that they come in through Canada's refugee system. Because during the 1990s it was the means of entry that functioned like flypaper: nearly every terrorist who touched it was stopped dead in his tracks.

The strong emotions the Ressam myth tapped into caused many observers to associate Canada's refugee system with a higher level of fear than was warranted. In this way the myth illustrated a phenomenon known as "probability neglect." This term, which was coined by American legal scholar Cass Sunstein, describes responses to emotionally charged events, such as terrorist attacks and natural disasters, that do not take note of the low probability of such events occurring. The aftermath of low-probability catastrophes often sees people calling on governments to undertake major policy responses, even though the event in question is less likely to happen than other risks the public is familiar with. "Hence an act of terrorism will have a large number of 'ripple effects,'" Sunstein writes, "including a demand for legal interventions that might not reduce risks and that might in fact make things worse." Sunstein gives the example of extensive security precautions at airports causing more people to drive, even though driving is more dangerous than flying.

The Ressam myth had two negative ripple effects. The first was to advance a flawed view of the best way to respond to terrorism, one that, if acted upon, would only make life worse for people whom terrorists target. Terrorism is a form of universalism. This much, at least, it has in common with the doctrine of human rights. When a bomb goes off in a public place such as an airport or subway car, it does not discriminate on the basis of nationality or religion or race. As in the case of September 11, when victims of fifty-two nationalities died inside the World Trade Center, everyone within the radius of a bomb blast is equally its victim. If we are truly opposed to terror, we will not wade selectively through the carnage and express remorse only for some who have suffered. Rather, we will oppose terrorism at the same level at which it operates by exhibiting sympathy for all victims.

Many people who make refugee claims are running from terror. They do not always speak the same language as us or practise the same religion, but they are terror's victims nonetheless. Imposing harsh measures on refugee claimants as a class, let alone choking off their only means of escape, is not a measure that can plausibly be justified in the name of opposing terrorism. Of the many harmful aspects of the Ressam myth, the worst was the support it lent to the vicious thought that we should strike a blow against terror by punishing its victims.

Consider the suggestion, put forward by mythologizers, that people who travel on fake passports should be denied entry. As we saw in the case of Francine Peyti, a fake passport is what allowed her to reach North America from Zaire. According to Peter Showler, this is common with genuine refugees. "Fifty percent of claimants do not have documents when they make their claim. [But] virtually all of them have some form of identity document by the time their claim is heard. Because after they can get legal counsel, they find ways to get documents, whether it's birth certificates, driver's licences, school graduations." Rejecting refugee claimants who arrive with false papers would have devastating consequences for people like Peyti who have no other way to escape unspeakable violence.

Another proposal mythologizers made concerned appeals. As the *National Post* editorialized, "Even when refugees are turned down, they often are permitted to remain in Canada through the seemingly interminable appeals process permitted under existing legislation. A prime example is Ahmed Ressam." It is true that Ressam's lawyer asked for a review of his case that drew out his deportation by six months. But this is not what really allowed Ressam to remain in Canada. Canada could have not permitted any review of refugee decisions whatsoever, and Ressam would still have remained, for all the reasons outlined above. Canada at the time had no appeal process for refugee decisions based on factual mistakes. It is reasonable to ask how such an appeal might be structured so as to discourage false claimants from indefinitely drawing out their claims (perhaps appeals and deportation hearings could be combined). But claiming that the review Ressam's lawyer sought is what allowed a terrorist to almost blow up the Los Angeles airport injects propaganda into the debate over an important legal safeguard.

The myth's second ripple effect concerned not the needs of refugees, but the nature of terrorism. Here the legend's pernicious effect was to reinforce a widely held but mistaken view of what drives people to extremism. The view holds that foreign-born terrorists, particularly those from the Middle East, are invariably extremists from the moment they arrive in the West. As *National Post* columnist Lorne Gunter sums up this view, "It is recently arrived Muslims who are the most likely to be filled with the hateful, anti-Western teaching that is booming in the Middle East. Long-standing Canadian Muslims are largely as peaceful as they claim to be." There is no question that long-standing Canadian Muslims should not be stigmatized by association with the tiny handful of terrorists who somehow claim to act in Islam's name (given the Koran's prohibition on all forms of suicide, being an Islamic suicide bomber is as contradictory as opening a Catholic abortion clinic). Gunter, however, is wrong to suggest that recently arrived Muslims are the group most likely to be hate-filled ideologues.

This can be seen by comparing the terrorist cell that formed around Ahmed Ressam in Montreal to one that coalesced around Mohammed Atta in Hamburg. Atta flew the first plane into the World Trade Center, and Hamburg is where he met the accomplices he would work most closely with, including the pilot of the second plane. Atta was much more successful and self-possessed than Ressam. Rather than an uneducated economic migrant, he was a professional urban planner who moved from Egypt to Germany to obtain a graduate degree. Atta was the leader of the Hamburg group, the other members of which all went to Germany as students. (One of the four, Ramzi Binalshibh, had applied for asylum in Germany in 1995 but was rejected. He returned to the Middle East and re-entered Germany as a student.) Like Ressam, none of the Hamburg hijackers were terrorists when they landed in Germany.

Even more so than the Montrealers, members of the Hamburg cell were typical of the thousands of young Middle Eastern men who trained in terror camps in Afghanistan. As Lawrence Wright notes in his prize-winning history of al-Qaeda, "What the recruits tended to have in common—besides their urbanity, their cosmopolitan backgrounds, their education, their facility with languages, and their computer skills—was displacement. Most who joined the jihad did so in a country other than the one in which they were reared . . . Alone, alienated and often far from his family, the exile turned to the [fundamentalist] mosque." The Bunch of Guys in Montreal were not as sophisticated as the average al-Qaeda cell (and were technically freelancers rather than sworn al-Qaeda members). But like their Hamburg colleagues, most of them adopted extremism during a time of displacement.

Displacement, crucially, is a phenomenon of migration rather than of immigration as such. This is why Atta and his cell members could experience it even though they entered Germany on student visas, and even though Germany is not a country of immigration. We should therefore be skeptical of explanations of Ressam's conversion that automatically ascribe a central role to Canada's immigration and multiculturalism policies. Such explanations overlook the fact that displaced extremists are found in countries of low and high immigration alike. They can potentially arise in any state that allows human beings to cross its borders, whether as asylum-seekers, students or guest workers. It is thus not clear how any immigration policy short of a North Korean–style ban on entry can prevent their occurrence. Canada could scrap all its multiculturalism programs tomorrow and still not stop the rise of terrorist cells.

Very well, some might say. If Canada reduced its immigration intake, it might not keep out every potential terrorist, but it would surely reduce their number. This, however, does not necessarily follow. In Canada a commitment to high immigration and official multiculturalism have gone hand in hand. While it is possible in theory to embrace both low immigration and multiculturalism, on a political level they usually rise and fall together. This is important to note, because there is a view that suggests combating terror requires *more* multiculturalism, not less.

This theory holds that multicultural policies make migrants feel welcome, and so reduce the sense of alienation that usually precedes a would-be terrorist's trip to Afghanistan. If this theory were correct, it would explain why the terror cell that formed in Germany was made up of individuals who were more accomplished and capable than Ressam and the Bunch of Guys. Members of the Hamburg cell would have had their inclination to reject mainstream opportunities reinforced not by a personal lack of talent and potential, but by the comparatively unwelcoming attitude of the society around them.

Mentioning the "more multiculturalism, less terror" theory is not the same as endorsing it. Many facets would need to be examined before we could fully understand the relationship between multiculturalism and terror-cell formation. The reason Germany's experience as an extremist breeding ground is worth mentioning is to note what is at stake in getting that relationship wrong. It is possible to have the worst of both worlds, after all. A country can fail to do justice to the needs of refugees and immigrants while simultaneously incubating terror. In Germany's case, it tore apart its asylum system in 1993, yet still gave rise to a terror cell far more lethal than any that has come out of multicultural Canada. Lethal enough, it turned out, to bring down the twin towers.

The fact that two September 11 pilots took up extremism in Germany should cause us to see the dogmatic assumptions at work in blaming Ahmed Ressam on multiculturalism. Making Canada's immigration regime more like Germany's will not necessarily make North America safer. Such a view simply takes it for granted that slashing refugee and immigrant intakes will ensure that no foreign terrorist ever again attempts to drive a car loaded with explosives across the Canada-U.S. border. There is, however, a second possibility. It is that there could in fact be a next time. But rather than a failure like Ahmed Ressam, someone with Mohammed Atta's dark talents will be the driver.

Ultimately, the real lesson of the Ressam affair is not that we should turn away refugees or abolish multiculturalism. It is that more resources should be devoted to deportation. In 2001 Canada increased its budget in this area by $48 million, but there is still room for improvement. The failure to promptly deport Ressam and his cohort likely created an atmosphere that made extremism more attractive. "If you're in a situation where you're not removed, but you're subject to a deportation order, it's very difficult to find work," Showler points out. "So [when] you're sitting there in a kind of impoverished situation, and you're also primarily relating only with members of your expatriate community, it creates a kind of hothouse situation. It makes it ripe if recruiting is going on." Increasing the budget for deportations would decrease the possibility of further hothouses arising, without jeopardizing the protection Canada extends to genuine refugees.

Three weeks after September 11, the Ressam myth collided with the foundation of Canadian refugee policy. Tom Kent, a former deputy minister for immigration, released a report slamming the *Singh* decision. Kent wrote his paper before September 11, but its release at a time when the rubble was still smouldering saw him give interviews in which he invoked terrorism to bolster his case. "It becomes particularly significant now, I think, because these people who make these claims to be refugees because they've got here—well, they can be here for all sorts of reasons," Kent said. "It's an easy entry for people with other motives, including those with terrorist intentions."

Kent was a highly respected public servant. He had been a key architect of Canadian immigration policy during the 1960s. Someone with his credentials attacking the *Singh* decision was a bit like Pierre Trudeau coming out against rights or Ronald Reagan saying he wanted to bring back communism. For this reason the media gave Kent's report big play. Unfortunately, Kent's comments did not reflect a detailed grasp of what *Singh* actually said. Perhaps this was because it had been several decades since Kent had been required to look at migration law closely. Whatever the cause, Kent had entered the debate without realizing that both international and Canadian refugee law permit exceptions for terrorists. He therefore argued that the so-called notwithstanding clause in the Charter of Rights and Freedoms needed to be used to overcome *Singh*.

The notwithstanding clause was the result of a political compromise at the time of the Charter's introduction. Pierre Trudeau originally conceived a document similar to the U.S. Bill of Rights, in that it would give the Supreme Court the final say in applying rights. The Charter that Trudeau was eventually able to bring in, however, made a significant concession to the Diefenbaker tradition of law. If Parliament did not like a court decision involving certain Charter rights—including the right to life and liberty on which *Singh* was based—Parliament could decree that the court's ruling would have no effect for five years (at which point Parliament could extend its override for another five years, and still again five years later, ad infinitum). A majority vote in Parliament would be enough to overrule the court. Trudeau reluctantly accepted this arrangement as the price of having any rights instrument at all. To this day, there are Trudeauites who regret the existence of the notwithstanding clause, regarding it as a steaming pile of Diefenbaker law in the middle of an otherwise pristine document.

The Trudeauite critique of the notwithstanding clause raises an issue that is also central to Hannah Arendt's critique of human rights. Arendt judged human rights according to what we might think of as a hyper-Trudeauite standard. A right is insufficient, or not really a right at all, according to the ease with which it can be overridden. Hence, the frequency with which European border guards turned away refugees caused Arendt to conclude that refugees had no rights whatsoever. Trudeauism is also concerned with how easily rights are disregarded: this is why it is reluctant to give carte blanche to politicians. Whereas for Arendt a concern with enforcement leads to a rejection of the whole idea of human rights, for Trudeau and the broader liberal tradition a concern with enforcement leads to a Charter that takes at least some rights out of the hands of Parliament.

A consistent application of Arendt's argument would suggest that any right that can be overridden with the ease that the notwithstanding clause allows—a category that includes the right to an oral hearing enshrined in *Singh*—is not really a right at all. It is, rather, a privilege that can be revoked whenever Parliament chooses. Fully assessing this criticism would require a lengthy detour into the debate over Canada's notwithstanding clause, which is a bit like flying into the Bermuda Triangle: those who do so have been known to disappear into an ambiguous no man's land of constitutional law, from which they do not always come back alive. But defending the inner logic of the *Singh* decision does not require taking a stand on the separate matter of the notwithstanding clause. *Singh* is worth copying, whether or not the notwithstanding clause is.

Tom Kent was not the first person to portray *Singh* as a legal disaster. Preston Manning, leader of the 1990s-era Reform Party, had also called for the notwithstanding clause to be used, as had former officials in the Department of Immigration who tended to see their job as keeping people out rather than letting them in. Kent's high-profile report gave new life to this long-standing view. It also made a special contribution of its own. This was to associate the *Singh* decision with terror. Kent's report was brandished in Parliament by Canadian Alliance MP Stockwell Day, then the leader of the Opposition. "Why does the Prime Minister not overturn this decision," Day demanded, "which is a threat to our security and of no help whatsoever to true refugees?"

Against this backdrop, it was only a matter of time before Ahmed Ressam was blamed on *Singh*. As a *Calgary Herald* editorial put it, the "Singh decision extended charter protections to non-Canadians. That allowed rule-breakers, queue-jumpers and frauds with sinister intentions—would-be LAX bomber Ahmed Ressam, for instance—access to welfare, legal aid and numerous appeals." It did not matter that welfare, legal aid and appeals were subjects that *Singh* did not mention. It did not matter that *Singh* extended no protection to suspected terrorists. It did not matter that the one right *Singh* did uphold, the right to an oral hearing, was one that Ahmed Ressam never exercised. The threat of terrorism was in the air, and refugee claimants had to be stripped of the one slender right they possessed.

Calls to invoke the notwithstanding clause against *Singh* are now a routine part of Canada's refugee debate. Large swaths of the media are opposed to *Singh*, as are many politicians. Given the controversial nature of the notwithstanding clause, it is difficult to imagine its ever being used to overturn *Singh* outside the context of a national emergency involving a huge influx of refugees. But that the anti-*Singh* voices have not yet succeeded in destroying Canada's great contribution to the tradition of human rights does not make the anti-*Singh* position any less destructive. Take away *Singh*, and we take away human rights. The Ressam legend did lasting damage by falsely associating *Singh* with terror. It triggered a debate about how *Singh* might be abolished, when the real question is how the principles underlying *Singh* might be broadened and extended.

Peter Showler will never forget the legends that sprang up in the wake of September 11. "To this day," he says, "there are Americans, including members of the U.S. Senate, who still believe that some of the terrorists came through Canada." But it was not just Americans who spread myths, and not just the September 11 hijackers who were their subjects. Ahmed Ressam became the subject of a myth in a classical sense. His legend made a larger point through the recounting of apocryphal events. It was put forward by a chorus that recounted an epic journey and a passage through the underworld. Ressam was the myth's warrior-protagonist. Like Odysseus, he is always ever-returning.

NINE

IN THE TRACKS OF LEVIATHAN

THIS BOOK HAS OFFERED a response to Hannah Arendt's diagnosis of the conflict between human rights and national sovereignty. Throughout the preceding chapters, I have often had occasion to explicitly address the subject of human rights, and I have tried to show how the rights of refugees might be enforced in a world of sovereign states. The solution I have proposed, however, is currently the law in no country, and the tension Arendt diagnosed continues to define the treatment of many refugees seeking asylum. Precisely because I have stressed the enduring nature of the conflict between sovereignty and human rights, some observers might conclude not that my proposed solution is worth adopting, but rather that it is ultimately a problem without a solution. From this pessimistic point of view, sovereignty is a monolith of brute power, against which a moral concept such as human rights is forever doomed to beat its gossamer wings without effect.

It is not hard to see why someone might adopt such a stance.

Our world is so dominated by sovereign states that there is an understandable temptation to view them as natural phenomena, institutions that have always existed and will always be there, unchanged and enduring. In reality, however, the sovereign state is an institution created by human beings. Like other institutions, it arose in a particular place at a particular time, and it has changed in response to new challenges and needs. The best way to see this is to approach the sovereign state in historical terms. Charting its rise and spread, and the way different aspects of sovereignty arose in different periods, should make us optimistic that states may someday exercise their sovereignty in a way that exhibits greater respect for human rights than is currently the norm.

The history of sovereignty I am about to offer will leave out many things. The rise of international entities such as the European Union and the International Court of Justice, the deregulation of financial markets and the global spread of the Internet; these and other trends others have all been held up as evidence that the sovereign state is on the wane. I will not try to outline every different area in which sovereignty is contracting or expanding. For however much state sovereignty may be reduced in other areas, when it comes to the situation of refugees, it remains a force of some power. For this reason, charting how we came to inhabit a world in which sovereignty poses a challenge to the enforcement of refugee rights will speak to a problem we still face.

Before offering a history of sovereignty, however, there is another question that needs to be addressed, one that I have left in the background until now. The question has to do with the fact that it is possible to understand sovereignty in more than one way. The form of sovereignty I have been most concerned with is a property of states. Sovereignty, however, can also be understood as a property of peoples. When sovereignty is understood in this way, it calls into question the relevance of a response to Arendt that offers a new model of constitutional law, let alone a history of sovereign states. For from this point of view, human rights are undone by a force more powerful than any government.

State sovereignty is associated with the system of international relations in which governments are recognized as ultimate legal authorities within their borders and only within those borders. Popular sovereignty, by contrast, refers to the right of a population to exercise self-determination, most obviously in areas such as electing leaders or deciding which outsiders will be allowed to join the political community. These two forms of sovereignty, one possessed by an institution, the other by a group of people, do not refer to the same thing. This is evident in the fact that they can potentially come in conflict, as when a population seeks to participate in an election which an undemocratic government forbids (as was the case, for example, in Algeria in 1992).

Which understanding of sovereignty does Arendt have in mind when she says national sovereignty is the undoing of human rights? Most often she refers to states, as when she speaks of "the very institution of a state, whose supreme task was to protect and guarantee man his rights as man." There are moments, however, when she appears to have populations in mind, as when she characterizes the Right of Man as the view that rights "should be guaranteed by humanity itself," humanity being a group of people rather than a state. Arendt scholars have often noted she does not always distinguish between state and popular sovereignty, or clearly indicate which one she has in mind as the final source of the problem she diagnosed.

By proposing constitutional safeguards that would rule out certain government actions, my primary focus up to now has been on state sovereignty. I have taken such an approach because it seems in keeping with the argument Arendt makes most of the time. But once we have in mind popular sovereignty, we are faced with a different question. Is there a way to prevent human rights violations caused by the exercise of the power of people rather than of states?

This question reiterates Arendt's critique of human rights in an even more acute form than she presented it. For while it is difficult to safeguard the rights of asylum-seekers against exercises of state sovereignty, doing the same in regard to popular sovereignty is more difficult still.

To see the scope of the problem, it is helpful to imagine a hypothetical scenario taking place thousands of years ago, before any state ever existed. Imagine that in a state-free world, a group of people are travelling by boat and come across someone treading water in distress. The person in the water desperately wants to be taken on board. The people in the boat can determine who joins their group, which in this case involves being admitted onto their vessel. They thus enjoy the equivalent of popular sovereignty. Seeking to enforce the rights of asylum-seekers against polities truly determined to exclude them is like asking if there is a rule that can be implemented on the boat that would make its operators pick up the person in the water, even when everyone on board was firmly opposed to doing so.

In both cases, the answer is no. It is no more possible to implement an internally enforced rights mechanism that will guarantee the rights of outsiders against a population universally opposed to admitting them than it is possible to implement a rule on the boat that will make its unwilling pilots stop for the person in distress. Although there are many differences between ancient seafarers and modern polities, in both cases the underlying problem is the same. In both cases, we have conceived of the group in question as not being subject to any external authority. In both cases, therefore, a rule to admit outsiders can only be enforced by the same group determined to violate the rule in question. But there is no rule that we can expect to be upheld when its enforcement is left up to the people who give rise to the need for the rule in the first place.

Either sovereignty can be exercised by a group determined to exclude, or such a group can have its sovereignty compromised by having an admission rule enforced from outside. But both outcomes cannot obtain at once. The model of refugee rights I have put forward is no more able to get around this problem than is any other legal mechanism enforced by an autonomous polity. Even though that model involves procedural rights rather than a right of admission, it suffers from the same underlying problem. For in a society where everyone is determined to violate the rights of refugees, any law to the contrary will go unenforced, regardless of what it says.

This may sound like the worst possible outcome from the point of view of human rights. What is the point of a portable-procedural model of refugee rights, someone may ask, if it does not defuse the tension between human rights and national sovereignty when sovereignty is understood in popular terms? What is the point of constitutional rights for refugees if they do not solve the problem Arendt's skeptical argument ultimately presents us with?

Conceding that popular sovereignty is a more powerful force than human rights would indeed be devastating if it highlighted a problem particular to human rights. This, however, is not the case. If constitutional rights instruments cannot force a hostile and truly sovereign populace to respect the moral claims of outsiders, such rights instruments are equally ineffective in upholding the rights of *insiders* in similar circumstances. Applied to the boat scenario, the same problem would apply if the issue in question concerned whether the people on board were going to throw one of their members overboard. (We might wonder if an especially small group was capable of doing so, but our discussion concerns cases where their ability to exclude someone is not in question: this is part of what it means to be sovereign). Arendt's argument was meant to highlight a problem unique to human rights. This was why she thought it "much wiser" to rely on the rights of citizenship. The boat scenario, however, highlights a theoretical problem for *any* moral concept, whether it is organized around the principle of human rights, civic rights or some different ethical notion altogether, not involving rights at all, and whether the potential subjects of injustice are refugees, citizens or anyone else.

This problem at hand will exist where any group of human beings enjoys popular sovereignty and is determined to violate the moral claims of some minority, whether they be insiders or outsiders. This is the case whether the larger group live in a territorial state, a nomadic band or even an anarchist polity without political structures of any kind. This is because popular sovereignty is ultimately rooted in human plurality rather than any particular political institution. An inability to restrain a popular public determined to exclude is thus not a singular weakness of human rights in a world of sovereign states. It is, rather, a problem no theory of justice can rule out in any political universe in which one or more polities are truly sovereign.

From the perspective of our political universe, the problem of a sovereign public united in a project of exclusion is one that resides at a high level of abstraction. The boat scenario forces us to admit that no law can prevent human rights violations in situations where entire polities are committed to violating the rights in question. A framework of rights enforcement, however, does not need to meet this standard to have value. The civic rights Arendt considers it wise to rely on, for example, have often failed historically to ensure justice for all citizens, yet she correctly does not take this as grounds to reject the very notion of civic rights. Similarly, although the portable-procedural model I outlined may not serve as an absolute guarantee in the case of universally hostile polities, this is not grounds to reject it.

In modern liberal states it is rare to encounter entire polities that are monolithically committed to exclusion. More common is to find a range of views within a given population, with some sections committed to excluding refugees, others favouring inclusion and still others oblivious or indifferent. It is equally common for modern polities to be influenced at least to some degree by outside entities such as international NGOs or the United Nations. Against the backdrop of a plural and divided population in dialogue with outside forces, which is the typical polity we find today, constitutional law remains a powerful enforcement mechanism. That constitutional law may not be sufficient to uphold rights in all possible worlds does not call into question its power as an enforcement mechanism in this world. For this reason, switching our focus to popular sovereignty does not highlight a special problem for human rights and does not call into question the value of the portable-procedural model. Although such a model cannot prevent every form of exclusion the human condition gives rise to, it will solve many of the problems asylum-seekers currently face, which is sufficient testament to its worth.

What a focus on popular sovereignty should cause us to do is reiterate the value of multiculturalism and other inclusive models of belonging. This is especially true in regard to descent-based societies. Strictly speaking, a descent-based society could scrupulously uphold human rights by resettling asylum-seekers in other societies after ensuring fair procedures are used to hear their cases. But realistically, Germany, Japan, Israel and other societies with tight models of citizenship are unlikely to be scrupulously fair to foreigners without popular attitudes changing first. Other societies devoted to multiculturalism may have a head start in this regard, but their own treatment of refugees seeking asylum suggests they also have considerable room for improvement.

Popular sovereignty poses a general problem for any moral claim enforced through law. The exercise of state sovereignty poses a particular problem for the enforcement of refugee rights. For this reason, it is reasonable to focus on how human rights might be better reconciled with state sovereignty. Once we do so, what immediately becomes noteworthy about this form of sovereignty is how omnipresent it is. Few ideas command such overwhelming unanimity today as the notion that lines should be drawn in the earth to separate one country from another. As the political scientist Daniel Philpott has observed, "a generation ago, the sovereign state captured nearly the entire land surface of the globe when European colonies received their independence. Sovereignty has come closer to enjoying universal explicit assent than any other principle of political organization in history." To better understand the future of state sovereignty, it is worth asking how we got to this point. How did we come to inhabit a world in which nearly every major land mass on the planet is claimed by a state?

To answer that question, consider the plight of John Toul. As a thirteenth-century vassal in what is now northeastern France, his life involved political problems we can only dream of today. In keeping with the custom of his time, Toul received land (his "fief") from a local noble, in return for which Toul pledged to serve the lord in battle. It was common for vassals such as Toul to offer their allegiance to more than one lord, but Toul must have been especially ambitious, because he offered his services to four masters. Toul's popularity among so many nobles, however, created a problem. What if two or more of his lords went to war with one another?

In order to deal with this possibility, Toul swore out an oath saying what he would do if his lords ever faced each other on the battlefield. The resulting arrangement was fantastically complicated:

If it should happen that the count of Grandpré should be at war with the countess and count of Champagne for his own personal grievances, I will personally go to the assistance of the count of Grandpré and will send to the countess and count of Champagne, if they summon me, the knights I owe for the fief which I hold of them. But if the count of Grandpré shall make war on the countess and count of Champagne on behalf of his friends and not for his own personal grievances, I shall serve in person with the countess and count of Champagne, and I will send one knight to the count of Grandpré to give the service owed from the fief which I hold of him. But I will not myself invade the territory of the count of Grandpré.

There is no record indicating whether John Toul ever had to charge his own knights in battle. What is significant about his oath today is that it crystallizes how political power operated before the rise of the sovereign state. We take it for granted that political power should be allocated along territorial lines, and that within such territories there should be one final source of authority. Both of these ideas, however, were missing from John Toul's world.

Start with the absence of territorial borders. This does not mean that people in the Middle Ages somehow did not occupy particular places. It means, rather, that there were no lines on a map that everyone acknowledged as separating one political jurisdiction from another. The idea of mutually recognized frontiers actually arises fairly late in history. Early nomadic tribes based their authority on clan membership rather than location, and two tribes could occupy the same place during different times of the year. As more formal political entities such as ancient city states and empires arose, they put down geographic roots, but without coming to formal agreements among themselves as to where one jurisdiction's boundary ended and another's began. In the case of powerful entities such as the Roman, Byzantine and Chinese empires, their borderlands were wherever their armies came to rest. As international relations scholar Friedrich Kratochwil has put it, "the Roman Empire conceived [its frontier] not as a boundary but as a temporary stopping place where the potentially unlimited expansion of the Pax Romana had come to a halt." Something similar held true of John Toul's lords. Although they were named after different parts of France, their authority over their domains was contingent upon their military power rather than vice versa. Local political authority was something that could vanish and be replaced overnight, depending on the outcome of a single battle.

The medieval world's lack of mutually recognized borders went hand in hand with the absence of a clear political hierarchy. Local political power was fragmented, shifting and often in dispute. Some lines of authority, like that connecting John Toul to his quartet of lords, were based on personal ties. As Toul's oath shows, the resulting arrangements could be fiendishly complex. But that was not the only source of confusion. There was the additional presence of the king, who for hundreds of years in France and elsewhere was less powerful than prominent lords. Indeed, the king himself was often something of a vassal, in that he would frequently receive land from bishops, lords and other supporters. The political arrangements kings came to among themselves only added to the complexity. In the twelfth century, Henry II not only was king of England but held the separate office of duke of Normandy. In the latter capacity he was obliged to pay homage to Louis VII of France, which he did even though the French monarch was weaker than Henry in his capacity as English king.

The result of feudalism's emphasis on oaths of obligation was that there could be complicated arrangements between lords and vassals, lords and lords, kings and vassals and kings and kings. Trying to keep track of the overlapping network of personal ties would be like staring into a kaleidoscope. Yet as confusing as all this was, it does not do full justice to the complexity of medieval politics. There were also political institutions that made sweeping claims to authority, which only added to the confusion Toul and his contemporaries had to contend with.

The most prominent such institution was the church. The pope's claim to religious leadership was based not on where people lived, but on their status as believers. For John Toul and his neighbours, this would sometimes mean that there was a clear division of religious and political authority, at least when the church decided to leave worldly matters to kings and lords in order to focus on spiritual concerns. But it was more common for secular and spiritual jurisdictions to overlap. Not only did political rulers decorate themselves with holy insignia and claim divine authority, the church was heavily involved in education and other aspects of daily life, and it needed secular monarchs' armies to deal with Lombards, Muslims and other threats.

The church, however, was not the only institution that claimed universal authority. There was also its great medieval rival, the Holy Roman Empire. Being a medieval institution, it strove to be as confusing as possible, and so was located not in Rome, but in what is now Germany. The emperor purported to represent the coming together of many ancient kingdoms, a claim of unlimited jurisdiction symbolized by his imperial orb, which was said to contain soil from the four corners of the earth. Yet emperors such as Otto the Great (912–973) and his descendants did not stop at sweeping political claims. They also styled themselves as God's political representatives on earth—a claim to spiritual power that did not endear them to the church. An emperor's claim to universal rule, however, was usually no more secure than that of the pope. The emperors' rule over German dukes, for example, was often precarious, and this forced them to turn to church officials for help. Bishops and priests, however, resented the empire's spiritual pretensions, and so were conspicuously unreliable.

For someone in John Toul's era, then, political authority could be based on particular ties to a lord or a king, or it could be owed to a universal institution such as the church or empire. Either way, however, power was wielded over people rather than land. Lords, kings, the church and the emperor frequently claimed simultaneous jurisdiction, making the occupants of any given region subject to more than one source of authority. This way of organizing political life meant that, among other differences with our own time, there was no distinction between domestic and international politics, no national embassies, passports or border guards. In addition, what we now think of as public power was often held in private hands, and political life was a source of confusion and constant conflict, much of it violent. These and other distinguishing characteristics were a result of the fact that, as the political historian Hendrik Spruyt puts it, "the logic of feudal organization lacked a sovereign, a final source of authority and jurisdiction."

By the beginning of the fourteenth century, France and England were home to recognizably sovereign states. Of the two, France's road to sovereignty was more gradual, and so more typical of how states would arise elsewhere. In France, the process began in the tenth century, when Hugh Capet was chosen by a group of powerful nobles to occupy a precarious kingship, one that in geographic terms amounted to little more than a dot on the map outside Paris. Three centuries later, after a protracted civil war and much political manoeuvring, Capet's descendants had vanquished the dukes, expelled the English from most of France and forced a reluctant church to recognize the supremacy of the crown. That supremacy was now based on written Roman law, which had fallen out of use under feudalism. This shift transformed the king into a new type of ruler: one whose authority was partly based on his status as representative of the interests of the realm as a whole. This meant that obedience to the king was no longer based primarily on personal ties. Nor did he make claims to authority beyond France's borders. Of course, there would still be disputes as to where precisely those borders should be drawn and many other issues. Nevertheless, the foundations of a territorial state had been laid. As Spruyt writes, "The first notions of sovereign authority develop in this period. The French king was regarded as emperor in his own kingdom."

Looking back from the perspective of today on the spread of a territorially sovereign government across France, it is tempting to see the new principle of organization as an inevitable response to the chaos and confusion of feudalism. But there was nothing inevitable about it. The rise and spread of sovereign states was not a matter of a new form of political organization springing up and immediately displacing feudalism. It was a contested and long-term process, one with many ups and downs, sudden expansions and dramatic setbacks. This is evident in the fact that just as France was evolving into a sovereign state, other parts of Europe were giving rise to two other forms of political organization, both of which existed alongside sovereign states for hundreds of years.

The first was the city state, which existed in Italy between the tenth and sixteenth centuries. Historians have long pointed out that, despite the name, city states were not just smaller versions of sovereign states. When a city state conquered a smaller town, it would often allow the annexed region to maintain some independence (if only because the town's occupants resented being taken over). As a result, there was no mutually agreed-upon single source of authority.

But an even more important contrast comes to light when we recall that the French king gradually spread his authority over his rivals, and eventually came to represent the interests of the kingdom itself. He was in a sense above politics, in that he could mediate disputes among his subjects. This never happened in city states such as Venice or Milan, where political life was defined by constant factionalism. Rival noble families, made up of both biological relations and people who adopted a family name for political reasons, would form armed guards known as *consorterie* to do battle with one another. An entire family would live in adjoining houses around a tower, into which they would retreat when attacked, and from which they would launch projectiles onto invaders below. Blood feuds between families were frequent, a feature of city-state life Shakespeare immortalized in *Romeo and Juliet*, with its depiction of Montagues and Capulets fighting in the streets of Verona. When one family obtained the political upper hand, its rivals would regard it as a temporary setback and continue to scheme. Thus, when one faction came into power, it was always at the expense of another, unlike in France, where the king occupied an independent office above factional interests. In the city states, with their constant disputes over authority, an echo of feudalism always remained.

A political institution even more different from the sovereign state was the city league, which arose in the twelfth century around the North and Baltic seas. Merchant seamen from what are now Germany and Scandinavia found it easier to ward off pirates by sailing in convoys, and when they arrived in foreign ports they would work together in order to receive better treatment from customs agents and other authorities. The same merchants were often politically influential in their hometowns, and when they returned home the guild-like organization they used at sea became a new form of government on dry land. A group of towns would band together by pledging to come to each other's aid and by electing a league council to make collective decisions.

City leagues could grow to become quite powerful. In 1385, for example, the Swabian-Rhenish League was capable of mustering an army of ten thousand soldiers. More powerful still was the Hanseatic League, which eventually swelled to include almost two hundred towns. It was strong enough not only to control Baltic and North Sea trade but to depose a foreign king when it had to. As in other city leagues, Hanseatic laws often reflected the monopoly-seeking interests of merchants. Any citizen of a Hanse town who struck up a business venture with a non-member, for example, would lose two fingers for the privilege of doing so.

The Hanseatic League did many of the things we now associate with national governments. It signed treaties, collected revenues, raised an army, passed laws and regulated social life. Yet it was not organized around a single supreme authority. Although member towns deferred to the league council on many matters, they could act independently when it came to local affairs. (In practice this meant that some towns were autonomous while others were under the partial control of a larger town from the same league, or of a local lord.) Moreover, city leagues had no borders. Member towns were often separated by large tracts of land that were not subject to their control, an arrangement that has caused them to be termed "islands of urban law in a feudal sea." Towns that displeased the league council could also be threatened with expulsion, while others might be invited to join. This made the leagues in some ways similar to empires, in that they acknowledged no formal limits on how much they might expand.

Chronicling the rise of the state system as a whole would require recounting the history of many different states and the influence of everything from broad historical trends such as the rise of Protestantism to the particular decisions of individual rulers. That is not a story I can do justice to here. Instead, I will merely note that in addition to all the historical contingencies that brought an international system of states into being, there were two general considerations that help explain why sovereign states squeezed out both non-territorial forms of organization, such as feudalism and city leagues, and the territorially based but fractured form of authority represented by city states.

The first consideration has to do with life inside a sovereign state. Take something as seemingly unremarkable as weights and measures. If John Toul ever travelled outside his home region, he could expect to encounter hundreds of different types of measurement with thousands of local variations. All across Europe, units of measurement were set by local lords, who did so as both a form of social control and a money-maker. (Among other perks, lords could charge for the use of the right scales.) The result was that every town had its own way of measuring and weighing goods, based on countless different criteria: human body parts such as the foot, the size of a barrel or even the space between the knees of a statue outside a town hall. This chaotic arrangement was typical of medieval life as a whole, during which local authorities minted their own coins, imposed their own tolls and administered their own (often idiosyncratic) laws. Among other problems, the lack of standardization was a nightmare for travelling merchants, who were easily cheated in every new town.

A major advantage of living in a sovereign state was that it brought an end to the chaos of localism. As far back as the thirteenth century in France, Louis IX decreed that royal coins would be good throughout his realm. After that only a few powerful nobles continued to produce their own currencies, which were now confined to their own lands and had to be equal in value to royal tender. French kings also gradually made the law less arbitrary. Louis IX, for example, abolished trial by combat, and his successors began to enforce written property rights. The spread of uniform weights and measures took longer, but by the time of the French Revolution, although localism still ruled the countryside, standardization had caught on in towns. Slowly, local customs and tolls also began to disappear, as the kings developed a centralized system of tax collection. The result was that domestic and foreign merchants knew what to expect across France. The interests of kings and merchants formed a virtuous circle: as the crown's authority spread, it made commercial life more predictable and profitable, which increased taxes and contributed to the king's coffers.

This never happened in city states or city leagues. In Italy, conquest by larger cities meant that the two to three hundred city states that existed in the thirteenth century had shrunk to a dozen by the fifteenth. A powerful city like Venice would treat its conquered regions as a resource to be plundered rather than a fully integrated territory. The hinterlands resented the authority of the *Dominante*, or dominant city, and this made it impossible to standardize laws or anything else. Moreover, whenever a new faction of nobles came to power in the dominant city, they would issue decrees designed to advance their own short-term interests rather than that of the city state as a whole—regulations that would stay in effect only until the next family took over. Similar problems were evident in the Hanseatic League, whose member towns continued to apply their own measurements and laws. If the league council wanted to introduce uniform standards, they would need to be enforced by the same town councils that were dominated by local merchants—the group that often gained the most from localism and so had the least incentive to change.

This, then, was a major reason sovereign states gradually displaced other forms of government: on both a political and economic level, they represented a more efficient form of internal organization. As these benefits became clear over time, it provided people living outside sovereign states with a model to imitate. Why put up with the confusion of localism when there was new way of doing things emanating from the neighbouring kingdom? The appeal of sovereignty was obvious to merchants who did business over long distances, and who became one of sovereignty's early constituencies. They were hardly the only ones to note sovereignty's advantages, however. So did political elites across Europe. "Political entrepreneurs copy institutions they perceive to be successful," Spruyt notes. "Copying thus increases one's chances at relative success. It also enables such elites to be recognized as equals with the state system." As these groups and others became aware of the potential benefits, the principle of state sovereignty slowly began to spread across the continent.

But there was a second factor behind the rise of a system of sovereign states. It had to do with the way sovereign states related to other states. Crucially, sovereign states have always found it easiest to conduct foreign relations with other sovereign states.

The reason for this preference can be seen by recalling what it was like to sign a treaty with a city league. Because member towns had so much autonomy, it was often difficult for a central council to enforce its decisions. A particular town might not honour a pledge to send troops, or ignore a league decree concerning trade, or even go so far as to negotiate its own treaty with a foreign commercial power such as England. The constant threat of individual towns disregarding league decisions meant that just who the Hanseatic League represented eventually became something of a mystery. In the sixteenth century, for example, England repeatedly demanded a list of Hansa cities so it could know which ships were entitled to special customs duties in English ports. The league refused to supply the list, because it feared the English government would seek out its own arrangements with individual towns. Needless to say, this hurt the league's ability to function as a cohesive unit. A different version of the same problem occurred when league towns eventually came to occupy territory inside sovereign states. After some Hanse towns came to be part of Denmark, for example, it only exacerbated the inability of the Hanseatic council to make Danish member towns obey its decrees.

Signing a treaty with a sovereign state was a dream by comparison. For starters, representatives of foreign governments knew who to negotiate with, namely, the sovereign, and did not need to worry about side deals with sub-national entities. Moreover, because states had set borders, it was clear where the treaty would apply. But perhaps the biggest advantage was that sovereign states had the power to domestically enforce the treaties they signed. Although individual states would sometimes fail to honour a treaty, in general they were more stable and reliable partners to negotiate with compared with feudal lords, city leagues or even city states. Sovereign states thus preferred to deal with other sovereign states, resulting in what has been called a "process of mutual empowerment," as states reciprocally recognized each other's sovereignty while withholding recognition from non-states.

The external recognition that early states bestowed on one another is worth stressing, as there is a natural temptation to associate the rise of states with the triumph of military might. But that is not really why they triumphed. At different times city leagues and city states were capable of mustering armies more powerful than those of contemporaneous countries. Moreover, there has always been wide variation in the size and power of states, evident today in the vastly different resources of China and Liechtenstein. Entry into the state system is based on a sovereign government's recognized ability to exercise authority over a particular territory, regardless of that territory's size, and whether or not that government can crush its neighbours on the battlefield.

It has long been common to point to a single year, 1648, as the key turning point in the rise of the modern state system. This was when European diplomats signed two treaties collectively known as the Peace of Westphalia, which brought an end to the Thirty Years War, one of the most devastating European conflicts of all time. Before Westphalia, England, France and Sweden already functioned as sovereign states, and the Peace contributed to Denmark and Switzerland's soon achieving the same status. Westphalia is significant because it was the first time states recognized each other as formal equals. In so doing, they brought an end to the constant religious interference and war that had long occurred between Catholic and Protestant rulers (war between Christians and Muslims, as we know all too well, would prove to be a different story). This more or less marked the beginning of international relations as we understand it today, as a sphere in which political power is exercised by territorially autonomous governments.

The flip side of Westphalia's significance is that it marked the beginning of the end for non-state entities. This was perhaps clearest in the case of the Holy Roman Empire. Although the empire was not formally abolished until 1806, for practical purposes, Westphalia marked its epitaph. As historian John Gagliardo has observed, "The empire after 1648 was never again to function to any significant extent as a real supraterritorial government." When the treaty's negotiators refused to recognize the political authority of the church, it caused the pope to angrily denounce the Peace as "null, void, invalid, iniquitous, unjust, damnable, reprobate, inane, empty of meaning and effect for all time"—but all to no effect. As for the Hanseatic League, its entreaties to be recognized as an equal at Westphalia were simply ignored (as one diplomat sniffed, "One does not really know what the Hansa in essence is"). German princes, sensing the dawn of a new order, soon began to present themselves not as feudal lords, but as rulers of tiny sovereign principalities.

The international lawyer Leo Gross once described Westphalia as "the end of an epoch and the opening of another. It represents the majestic portal which leads from the old world into the new world." Such a high-flown description is misleading if we take it to suggest that the theory and practice of sovereign statehood arrived simultaneously. In reality, the lawyers and ambassadors who negotiated the Peace did not so much consciously design a system of sovereign states as stumble into one. Their treaties never mention sovereignty as a general principle, and instead consist of a long series of settlements regarding the rights of religious minorities, various territorial squabbles and other issues of local concern. This gradually led to a change in the practice of politics that was given theoretical expression only much later, in the eighteenth and nineteenth centuries, when philosophers such as Emeric de Vattel began to put forward non-intervention and the equality of states as principles of international relations.

At a practical level, moreover, there also continued to be considerable variation in how sovereignty was implemented after Westphalia. It was not until the nineteenth century, for example, that European states formally recognized the sovereignty of a non-Christian entity, the Ottoman Empire. There would also be new forms of government still to come that defied the logic of sovereignty. During the era of colonialism, parts of Africa, the Middle East and elsewhere became "protectorates" of European powers, which would control the colony's foreign, but not domestic, policy. This was a break from sovereignty in that authority was divided between two equally ultimate sources. Although other colonies, those that were not protectorates, technically upheld the logic of sovereignty in that they were under the control of one (overseas) authority, it was not until the 1960s and the rise of decolonization that sovereignty really became a global institution. Only now sovereignty's trappings were enjoyed not merely by white Europeans and their descendants and neighbours but by the peoples of Africa and Asia as well.

What is the point of this long swim through the past? It might seem far-fetched to conclude a book about the rights of refugees with a historical discussion mentioning Hugh Capet and the Swabian-Rhenish League. In reality, however, the history of the sovereign state has valuable lessons to teach us that are relevant to the situation of modern refugees.

The first lesson has to do with what historians call the invention of tradition. There is a universal human tendency to project arrangements we approve of back into the past. An example relating to migration is supplied by Jean-Marie Le Pen, the founder of France's National Front, a Far Right party that opposes non-European immigration. Le Pen has claimed that his party represents "the French people born with the baptism of Clovis in 496, who have carried this inextinguishable flame, which is the soul of a people, for almost one thousand five hundred years." Needless to say, Clovis would have been baffled by Le Pen's nationalistic conception of belonging, let alone the idea that France should exist as a territorial state within set borders. We can better immunize ourselves against the claims of Le Pen and other nativists by recognizing that the historical claims they make are often based on myths.

In addition to peoples, invented traditions also spring up around states. As institutions of authority they bedeck themselves in symbols that make appeal to the "sanction of perpetuity," as one historian of tradition puts it. When a people or a state's claim to timeless authority is taken at face value, it is easy to think of the rejection of refugees as a natural occurrence, as inevitable as a pack of animals protecting their territory. In reality the history of the sovereign state shows it to be a product of culture rather than of nature. States are something that human beings created and have changed considerably over time. Given this past, we should be hopeful that they might change again in the future, in a manner that makes the world safer for refugees than it currently is.

This brings us to the second reason to take note of the history of state sovereignty. That history has bearing on how we will judge Arendt's own solution to the enforcement problem human rights face in a world of states. "Solution" may be something of a misnomer. Unlike her detailed discussion of the problems refugees face, Arendt's remarks about how those problems might be solved are often brief and elliptical. A typical example concerns her remark that "human dignity needs a new guarantee which can be found only in a new political principle, in a new law on earth, whose validity this time must comprehend the whole of humanity while its power must remain strictly limited, rooted in and controlled by newly defined territorial entities."

There is now a long tradition of Arendt scholars citing this and other passages, including one in which she cryptically refers to "a possible law above nations," as evidence for an Arendtian alternative to the system of sovereign states. One thoughtful interpreter of Arendt, for example, has attributed to her a belief in "regional and global federation." In regions such as the Middle East, Israelis and Palestinians would not occupy separate states. Rather they would co-occupy a "binational, confederate state," a form of power sharing that would also apply to global institutions. "Rejecting national sovereignty as a recipe for disaster, she envisioned a political community with multiple and overlapping levels of authority," Jeffrey Isaac writes, "in which national identities would be respected but in which they would not be the exclusive basis of political power and citizenship."

If Arendt's scattered remarks about what might replace or supplement sovereignty do amount to a "vision of regional and global federation," it is a puzzling position for her to hold. Arendt, as we saw, was scathing on human rights because they lacked an institutional framework that could guarantee they would be respected. Her problem with human rights was that they had inadequate force in law. When it comes to "human dignity," by contrast, she is sympathetic to this notion, even though it too lacks a reliable enforcement mechanism. (This absence explains the need for a "new law on earth" devoted to upholding it.) But if a commitment to human dignity is not called into question by its lack of force in existing law, it is not clear why the same is not true of human rights. In her discussion of dignity and rights, Arendt appears to employ two weights, two measures.

The deeper problem, however, has to do with the idea of a global political order "with multiple and overlapping levels of authority." The sovereign state arose in part as a reaction to this kind of system. As we've seen, prior to the rise of the state, multiple and overlapping levels of authority resulted in multiple and overlapping problems. It was often unclear who was in charge and the overall system was conflict-prone, inefficient and confusing. There are good reasons why the territorial state is the most widespread and enduring form of political organization. Casual invocations of a less territorial alternative that do not take those reasons into account have an air of unreality. How might an alternative to sovereignty avoid the chaos of feudalism? How might we transition to such an arrangement in a world where states prefer to bestow recognition on each other? These are only some of the questions a "confederation of communities" gives rise to.

It is debatable whether Arendt really wanted to do away with sovereignty. Her reference to power controlled by "territorial entities," for example, sounds similar to the power of the territorial state. But visions like the one Isaac asks us to consider exhibit a problem, whether or not it is a problem shared by Arendt. That problem is sometimes referred to as utopianism, but the real failing is not how much such visions challenge the status quo, but how much they support it. If justice for refugees has to wait for a change on the scale of getting rid of national sovereignty, justice will be a long time coming, if it ever comes at all. It is both more realistic, and more radical, to seek justice for refugees in a world of states.

Make no mistake, there is a real role for international law and international organizations. The Refugee Convention and UNHCR are important developments in the history of refugee affairs. But it is possible to be both an internationalist and a realist, and the reality is that sovereignty is unlikely to vanish overnight. States, I have been at pains to show, are cultural artifacts with evolving histories. But that same history suggests that the international system of global order is unlikely to evolve into a system like the one which the state system originally arose to displace. A framework of refugee rights that at least has the potential to be implemented in a world of states in no way limits the future direction that evolution might take. It rather gives us a tool of judgment and action that we can apply to the political institution we currently find everywhere on the face of the earth, the same institution that currently exacerbates the situation of so many refugees.

Call this the Goldilocks view of state sovereignty. Inventors of tradition go too far one way and characterize the state as eternal and unchanging. Contemporary Arendt scholars go too far the other way and envision unlikely alternatives to the global state system. Where one approach is too hot, the other too cold, an emphasis on the possibility of change within the existing state system, or something very much like it, is just right.

As late as the nineteenth century, sovereignty posed no threat to the rights of refugees. The primary reason for this was that there were no refugee crises of the kind we are familiar with today. Although people were often driven from their home by religious persecution and war, most lacked the means to travel very far, let alone sustain themselves for long periods. The existence of a "refugee problem" also presupposes that local officials feel some obligation to care for impoverished migrants. This wasn't the case before the nineteenth century, when agricultural societies often could barely support their own populations. Thus, rather than occupying a special category, people fleeing political persecution before the 1800s would quickly become indistinguishable from local vagabonds and beggars who sought scraps of charity. Often they met the same fate. Historian Michael Marrus has noted of pre-modern refugees that they "would quickly succumb to hunger, disease, or exposure. Large masses of people simply could not move from place to place supported by meagre social services. Winters, generally, would finish them off."

Things began to change during the first half of the nineteenth century. This was the Era of Revolutions, when national liberation movements challenged a host of repressive governments all over Europe, from Ireland and Italy to Poland and the Austrian Empire. When many of these movements were defeated, thousands of revolutionaries, agitators and rabble-rousers fled to western Europe (a wave of displaced radicals that included Karl Marx, who washed up in England in 1849). Yet this "flotsam of revolution" was not quite identical to the refugees we know today. Not only were the numbers in the thousands as opposed to the millions, they were primarily men. (When women were driven to take flight abroad, it was usually because they had married a revolutionary.) The Era of Revolutions was thus less an age of refugees than an age of exiles. As Marrus describes them, these were "individuals who had chosen their political path, rather than large masses of people torn loose from their society and driven to seek refuge."

The reception these exiles received is difficult to imagine now. Suppose you were a Polish revolutionary who had participated in the failed uprising against the tsar in 1831 and then fled to England. You didn't worry about showing your passport to a border guard when you docked. You simply strolled down the gangplank, and that was it. You were free to go wherever you liked and stay for as long as you wanted. Legal barriers on migration certainly existed in the nineteenth century, but they tended to single out particular groups of people, and they varied widely from one frontier to another. In different parts of Europe, Jews and Gypsies were seen as especially undesirable, while in Northern American states, laws were passed restricting the movement of free blacks. And absolutely no country wanted migrants deemed "liable to become a public charge," that is, paupers and the handicapped. Overall, however, governments did not take the same degree of interest in border control that they do today. Enforcement measures tended to involve things like fines against shipping companies, to prevent them from granting passage to paupers or other unwanted groups. Not only did this mean it was harder to stop anyone who was determined to reach foreign shores and had the money to do so, but when it came to travellers who were wealthy and white, there were hardly any restrictions on their movement at all.

One might think that political revolutionaries would be among the groups singled out for exclusion. Surprisingly, this was not the case. One reason was that western Europeans did not regard the refugees in their midst as a threat. Partly this was because taking up the cause of revolution and flight into exile were both expensive undertakings: refugees of the day thus tended to be well-to-do and had an aura of nobility (albeit one that would fade the longer they stayed abroad). Moreover, the causes that animated groups such as "Young Italy" or "Young Germany," as European revolutionary movements were called, was often that of making their homeland more like the liberal states in which they now found themselves. This was a cause that their host societies often regarded with sympathy, even admiration. When the Italian revolutionary Giuseppe Mazzini fled to Switzerland in 1848, the local population treated him like a visiting dignitary. During the same decade, France went so far as to issue political exiles a living allowance, rated according to their military rank and social background.

But there was another reason why nineteenth-century exiles were comparatively well treated: governments lacked the means to keep track of them. Police and other officials did not have access to fingerprints, photographic ID and other forms of surveillance technology. As a result, it was often simply not possible to stop people from crossing the border or to monitor their whereabouts after they arrived. Such enforcement measures as did exist were not hard to evade. When the Russian radical Alexander Herzen travelled through Italy in 1847, he was obliged to produce his passport for a Neapolitan soldier who made a show of examining it, only to reveal that he was illiterate. A year later, in Switzerland, Mazzini sent out letters to local newspapers poking fun at the inability of Swiss authorities to catch him. "You are looking for me everywhere. You are wearing out your telegraph operators. . . . You do me the honour of buying my portraits."

The border regime that we know today took shape roughly between the mid-1880s and the mid-1920s. As with the spread of sovereignty itself, there were many particular causes that varied from country to country. But an important general cause was the rise of nationalism. In the nineteenth century, shared language and ethnicity came to be the prisms through which large numbers of people defined themselves. In many ways, this represented a more inclusive conception of belonging. With the rise of mass democracy, often a shared language was the only thing Germans, Italians or members of other national groups had in common. People who were part of the linguistic or national group thus became part of a new "welfare community," and so were entitled to the benefits of the developing welfare state.

The flip side of this positive development, however, was that governments now had a reason to separate citizens from non-citizens. As the historian John Torpey puts it, "In part as a result of the nationalization of welfare provisions and the increasing assumption by political leaders of responsibility for economic well-being, the distinction between 'national' and 'foreigner' . . . [grew] sharper. An international system of states comprised of mutually exclusive bodies of citizens was taking firmer shape." Whereas in the 1800s France and Prussia could extend welfare relief to foreigners, and Prussia could also supply non-citizens with passports, neither practice survived the beginning of the twentieth century.

The change in attitudes toward outsiders was perhaps starkest in England, which had traditionally held one of the most liberal attitudes toward migrants. It had no restrictions on entry of any kind before 1793, and even after such laws were introduced, they were laxly enforced, to the point that between 1823 and 1905, England neither expelled nor denied entry to a single foreigner. The seeds of a new understanding were planted in the 1880s, when waves of Jewish people left eastern Europe, seeking to escape pogroms, poverty and tsarist persecution. After many Jews settled in East London, they received a hostile welcome from their new neighbours, who pre-judged them as disease-ridden and prone to criminal activity. The darkening anti-Semitic mood caused East End members of Parliament to propose restrictions on immigration. By 1903, a public commission was recommending a law that would cut off the flow from eastern Europe and require mandatory police registration for all foreigners.

The law was opposed by a young Winston Churchill, who denounced it for violating "broad, general principles, long held in veneration in this country." Speaking in the voice of a nineteenth-century liberal, the future prime minister brought forward three central objections. "It endangered the right of asylum to political offenders and the poor and unfortunate. It allowed a police officer or Customs House officer to pronounce on matters of opinion, and it created a different status for people living together in this country. All should be free and equal before the law." But Churchill's opposition was a lost cause, and in 1905 the British Aliens Act came into effect. When Canada and the United States introduced their own restrictive immigration laws in 1919 and 1924 respectively, it marked a turning point in North Atlantic history. There would be later changes, as when racial quotas were dismantled in the 1960s. But the foundation of the border-control regime we are familiar with today had effectively been laid. When refugees appeared in great numbers in the aftermath of World War I, the stage was set for them to experience the new form of rightlessness Hannah Arendt so powerfully described.

The late arrival of border control illustrates that sovereignty is an institution with different parts. Usually when we speak of sovereignty, what we have in mind is the idea that there is one single source of authority over a particular territory. But as we saw in chapter 3, sovereignty also refers to a form of recognition that is bestowed on states by other states and outside entities. This was the quality that the government in exile of Somalia possessed and the government of Taiwan lacked. Sovereignty in the first sense has to do with power. Who controls a given territory? Sovereignty in the second sense has to do with legitimacy. Who should control that territory, whether or not they currently do? In addition to these two aspects, sovereignty has a third dimension, that involving a state's ability to control which people or goods come across its borders. This is also a form of control, but one that is distinct from a government's ability to police the area within its borders. (It is possible for a government to administer the rule of law internally yet not be able to stop people from coming across its border.)

Analysts of sovereignty now use the terms domestic sovereignty, international legal sovereignty and interdependence sovereignty, respectively, to identify these three different aspects of sovereignty. The history of sovereignty shows that they each arose at a different time for a different reason. Domestic sovereignty is the oldest, arising originally in western Europe. It spread because it is a politically and economically efficient form of organization. The curse of localism was the problem, and domestic sovereignty was the solution. Centuries later, the Peace of Westphalia brought the innovation of states formally recognizing each other's authority in the wake of the Thirty Years War. Endless religious war was the problem, to which international legal sovereignty was the solution. Centuries later still, in the early decades of the twentieth century, states introduced methods of border control that were stricter than those that existed in the nineteenth century. Foreigners arriving en masse was the problem, at least in the eyes of Western governments, to which interdependence sovereignty was the solution.

These forms of sovereignty are obviously related. When a new state comes into being, as the Czech Republic and Slovakia did after the breakup of Czechoslovakia, and as Quebec sovereigntists hope Quebec might by seceding from Canada, recognition of the new state by other governments can influence its ability to take out international bank loans, which can be used to fund the police and army. That border control is also carried out by an institution with the resources of a state is only one of the reasons it is as effective as it is. A second consideration that makes border guards effective is that they are widely seen as exercising a justified form of authority. Just as people in countries under military occupation will withhold co-operation with the occupiers when they do not think their presence is legitimate, forms of social control are often more powerful the more widely they are regarded as valid and reasonable. In the case of border control, its legitimacy has something to do with the fact that it is done in the name of states. If airports and other entry points were policed by vigilantes and members of private clubs, no matter how overwhelming their numbers, they would lack this important kind of power. It is not quite right, therefore, to see interdependence sovereignty as completely detachable from the other two aspects of sovereignty that long preceded it.

Nevertheless, the fact that the third aspect arose much later than the first two should give us hope. It should open us to the idea that the practice of sovereignty and human rights can be brought into better balance without eroding the goods that were created by the first two forms of sovereignty, goods having to do with efficiency, predictability, security and, at least some of the time, peace. Border control arrived late in the history of the state, and has undergone many changes since it began. It is not idle fancy to think that it might change again, in a manner that makes it less deadly for refugees. But just as the recognition states bestow on each other reinforces the overall state system, the fact that most industrialized states enforce their borders makes it less likely that any individual state will completely abolish border controls on its own. A framework for refugee rights that can be phased in, gradually spreading from one state to another without requiring early adopters to make themselves radically more open than their neighbours, is a framework that at least has a chance of coming into being. Because the portable-procedural model allows states to extend justice to refugees even as they police their borders, it is the framework more compatible with the evolving and enduring history of border control.

This brings us to the final lesson of the history of sovereignty. It may be the most encouraging lesson of all. The refugee upheavals of the twentieth century did not mark the first time human rights came in conflict with national sovereignty. The same two principles came in conflict in the nineteenth century—only to see sovereignty give way to rights.

This is borne out by the abolition of the transatlantic slave trade. In the nineteenth century, public opinion gradually turned against slavery. This was especially so in Britain, which outlawed the transportation of slaves on British vessels in 1807. Over the next dozen years, the United States and many European countries followed suit, while others signed treaties with Britain giving its warships the right to search and seize vessels suspected of carrying slaves.

Two significant holdouts to this trend were Portugal and Brazil. Portugal's colonies in Africa were major sources of slaves, while Brazilian agriculture was heavily dependent on slave labour. After years of trying to persuade Portugal to stop trading in slaves, Britain in 1839 unilaterally authorized its navy to seize suspected slave vessels sailing under the Portuguese flag and to release any slaves on board at the nearest British port. This was the case even though Portuguese law deemed trafficking in slaves perfectly legal everywhere south of the equator. Similarly, after decades of unsuccessful attempts to make Brazil stop its part in the slave trade, in 1850 Britain sent its warships into Brazilian waters. While under fire from Brazilian forts, the British vessels seized and burned a number of Brazilian ships suspected of carrying slaves, an intervention that ultimately proved decisive in finally ending the transatlantic slave trade.

Stephen Krasner, a historian of sovereignty, has remarked of Britain's aggressive actions in Brazil that "it is difficult to imagine a less ambiguous violation of the norm of non-intervention." Britain's efforts to stop the slave trade were not motivated by material interests. When those efforts began, British plantations in the Caribbean at the time were themselves dependent on slave labour. Rather, the British government's actions were influenced by the pressure of groups that opposed slavery on religious and moral grounds. There was thus a conflict between the cause of abolition, which we would now describe in human rights terms, and the claims of Brazil and Portugal to do as they pleased as sovereign states. In the end, human rights won out.

Closer to our own time, something similar happened in South Africa. By the 1980s its policy of racial apartheid had put it in a position like Brazil's a century before: a pariah state with few international advocates willing to defend it. Unlike in the nine-teenth century, however, this time the pressure to abolish a racist institution came from more than one foreign power, as govern-ments in Africa, North America and Europe all subjected South Africa to a variety of sanctions. Eventually, in the face of both foreign and domestic pressure, apartheid came to an end. Once again a cause animated by human rights won out over a state's claim to ultimate authority. In Krasner's words, "This transition was an extraordinary accomplishment, and one that took place with little bloodshed. But it was not consistent with Westphalian or international sovereignty. The pressure on South Africa was a denial of the right of its rulers to establish a race-based regime within their country."

The image of British warships invading Brazilian waters cap-tures something enduring about the history of sovereignty. As we all know, states have interfered in the affairs of other states many, many times since the Peace of Westphalia. This makes sovereignty a slightly curious principle of authority. On the one hand, international diplomats and the governments they repre-sent constantly affirm the importance of domestic and interna-tional legal sovereignty, which both support the view that states should not meddle in the domestic affairs of other states. On the other hand, one of the primary activities of states in general and powerful states in particular has been to constantly intervene in other states' internal affairs. This has happened so often that when a powerful state invades a smaller one, even when we are strongly opposed or recognize it as a clear wrongdoing, we are not so naïve as to be surprised that it is happening.

Krasner captures this aspect of sovereignty with the term *organized hypocrisy* (a term that, as we saw, Matthew Gibney borrowed to describe Western states' commitment to human rights). This memorable phrase is meant to capture the fact that the core notions of sovereignty relating to non-intervention are both widely affirmed and also routinely violated, sometimes by one and the same entity. "Rulers might consistently pledge their commitment to non-intervention," Krasner writes, "but at the same time attempt to alter the domestic institutional structures of other states, and justify this practice by alternative norms such as human rights or opposition to capitalism."

The reference to a state's violating another state's sovereignty because of opposition to capitalism conjures up images of Soviet tanks rolling through the streets of Prague and Budapest. This example of organized hypocrisy is hardly inspiring. But there have also been cases when sovereignty has been violated in the name of effective and genuine human rights enforcement (however much it has also been violated in the name of fraudulent human rights actions). In our time, the international boycott of South Africa provides one such example, as does Britain's role in the abolition of the transatlantic slave trade a century before. These cases are worth recalling not because they precisely parallel the conflict between sovereignty and human rights as it applies to refugees. Brazil, Portugal and South Africa were engaging in practices that were exceptions to the international norm. Britain, the United States and other countries had stopped trading in slaves and abolished segregation before they turned their attention to the south Atlantic slave trade and apartheid. In the case of refugees, by contrast, all Western states now employ measures that overemphasize border control at the expense of human rights.

Nevertheless, the end of the transatlantic slave trade and apartheid are encouraging in that they show that sovereignty can be made to give way to human rights when enough people want it to. In neither case did the triumph of human rights come easily, as both involved decades of sustained pressure. But both episodes are encouraging nonetheless, the peaceful way human rights triumphed in South Africa especially so. Rather than an unmovable force, sovereignty is a principle that at times has been disregarded in the name of a greater good.

This continues to be the case in our own time, when we hear calls for states to acknowledge a "responsibility to protect." The phrase, which is commonly invoked in debates about genocide intervention, makes the authority of states conditional upon them upholding the rights of populations inside their borders. Reasonable people can disagree as to where and when any form of military intervention in justified. But the fact that there is even debate about the legitimacy of human rights interventions captures something about sovereignty in our time, something that was not true in the age of territorial kings. It is that sovereignty is no longer just a kind of authority, but also a kind of responsibility. It is a principle not merely of power, but also morality.

In the modern world the state is not defined only by its part in an international order of organized hypocrisy. The liberal democratic state is also a central pillar of welfare and justice, arguably *the* central pillar, the growing importance of international institutions notwithstanding. A double wrong occurs when an institution of justice itself becomes an agent of injustice. The liberal state's role as a dispenser of justice makes it not only reasonable, but necessary, to judge the state itself by the highest standards of morality. Only when liberal states exhibit the same respect for the rights of refugees as they do the rights of their own citizens will the expectation that the liberal state generates about itself be met.

The lessons of sovereignty should make us far more optimistic than Hannah Arendt was about the long-term future of human rights. Arendt saw sovereignty as a monolithic force that consigned the idea of human rights to the realm of irrelevant abstraction. This pessimistic view, however, is not borne out by sovereignty's history. Sovereignty has changed in the past in order to address felt human needs. The more the situation of refugees is seen as a problem, the greater the likelihood that the exercise of sovereignty, if not its very nature, may someday change to address their needs also.

I have tried in this book to outline a way that this goal might be achieved in our lifetimes. But even if my particular proposal is wrong, the changing history of sovereignty should make us optimistic that some new arrangement can come into being that will reconcile sovereignty with the rights of human beings in general and refugees in particular. In a world of injustice, calls for human rights are like water dripping on a stone. One drop by itself explodes on the rock. But if water keeps falling long enough, eventually the stone will erode. An awareness that sovereignty has changed before and can change again should cause us to keep bringing water to this rock, until it too gives way.

POSTSCRIPT: REFUGEES AND TERROR

WHAT HAPPENS TO TERRORISTS who attempt to use Canada's refugee system as a means of covertly entering North America? The accompanying chart is meant to shed empirical light on this question. It examines refugee claims in Canada by people associated with political extremism. All of the individuals made a refugee claim between 1985 and 2005. Once I began compiling their names, however, it became clear that whether someone is a terrorist is often difficult to determine. For this reason, the names on the list and the considerations behind their inclusion require some explanation.

The purpose of the chart is to document the outcome of individuals who match the widespread image of Ahmed Ressam, namely, terrorists who have tried to use Canada's refugee system to facilitate a terror operation. Given this purpose, the chart does not include three types of refugee claimants. The first are those, like the real Ressam, who were not affiliated with terrorism at the time of their arrival and only became extremists years later.

Refugee Claims in Canada by Political Extremists 1985–2005

NAME	ARRIVAL IN CANADA	REFUGEE STATUS	OUTCOME
MANSOUR AHANI	1991	Accepted	Security Certificate 1993
HASSAN ALMREI	1999	Accepted	Security Certificate 2001
SAID ATMANI	1995	Rejected	CSIS monitoring, deported 1998
WAHID BAROUD	1991	Withdrawn	Security Certificate 1994
MOHAMAD DBOUK	1998	Fled before decision	CSIS monitoring, returned to Lebanon 1999
AHMAD FANI	1992	Accepted	Deportation proceedings 1999, deported 2004
MOHAMED HARKAT	1995	Accepted	Security Certificate 2002
MOHAMMED HUSSEIN AL-HUSSEINI	1991	Accepted	Security Certificate 1993
MAHMOUD JABALLAH	1996	Arrested before decision	Security Certificate 1999
MURALITHARAN NADARAJAH	1998	Rejected	Arrested 1998
MOHAMED ZEKI MAHJOUB	1995	Accepted	Security Certificate 2000
ESSAM HAFEZ MARZOUK	1993	Accepted	Arrested 1993; CSIS surveillance; left Canada 1998
EFFAT NEJATI	1995	Arrested before decision	Security Certificate 1996
PIRAKALATHAN RATNAVEL	1996	Rejected	Arrested 1997
PARMINDER SINGH SAINI	1995	Accepted	Arrested 1995, deported 2010
HANI ABDEL RAHIM AL-SAYEGH	1996	Arrested before decision	Security Certificate 1997
AYNUR SAYGILI	1996	Arrested before decision	Security Certificate 1996
LOGANATHAN SABANAYAGAM	1988	Accepted	Arrested 1992
DJAFAR SEYFI	1995	Arrested before decision	Deported 1996
BACHAN SINGH SOGI	2001	Excluded	Preventative detention 2002, deported 2006
IQBAL SINGH	1991	Accepted	Security Certificate 1997
TEJINDER PAL SINGH	1995	Excluded	Deported 1997
MAHMOUD ABU SHANDI	1991	Arrested before decision	Security Certificate 1991
MANICKAVASAGAM SURESH	1990	Accepted	Security Certificate 1991
KUMARAVELU VIGNARAJAH	1989	Accepted	Arrested 1996
NOURDDINE ZENDAOUI	1998	Rejected	CSIS monitoring left Canada 2004

AFFILIATION	POLITICAL VIOLENCE WHILE IN N. AMERICA	COUNTRY OF LEGAL DESICION	NOTES
Iranian Intelligence expert	No	Canada	—
Bin Laden network	No	Canada	—
Bin Laden network document forger	No	France	Ressam roommate and criminal accomplice; arrived as stowaway in cargo ship
Force 17/Palestinian Liberation Organization (PLO)	No	Canada	Disclosed PLO membership on arrival
Hezbollah fundraiser	No	Unconvicted	Spent nine months in Canada
Mujahedin-e Khalq (MEK)	No	Canada	MEK violently opposes the Iranian government
Bin Laden network	No	Canada	First CSIS interview 1997
Hezbollah	No	Canada	—
Al-Jihad	No	Canada	—
Tamil Tiger leader	No	Canada	Arrested again 2004; deportation to Sri Lanka halted due to torture concerns; released from prison subject to conditions
Osama bin Laden employee	No	Canada	First CSIS interview 1997
Al-Jihad training camp instructor	No	Egypt	Arrested for passport fraud upon arrival in Canada, filed refugee claim from jail; CSIS investigation involved 300 interviews
MEK	No	Canada	—
Tamil Tiger enforcer	No	Canada	Released from prison in 2001 subject to conditions
All India Sikh Students Federation	No	Canada	1984 plane hijacker; pardoned by Pakistan 1998
Saudi Hezbollah	No	Canada	—
Kurdistan Workers Party	No	Canada	—
Tamil Tiger	No	Canada	Arrested for 1975 assassination in Sri Lanka, later pardoned; involved in passport forgery ring in Canada
Iranian government torturer	No	Canada	—
Babbar Khalsa International (Sikh extremist)	No	Canada	Government case involved use of secret evidence
Babbar Khalsa International (Sikh extremist)	No	Canada	CSIS monitoring from 1991
Dal Khalsa (Sikh extremist)	No	Pakistan	—
PLO Colonel	No	Canada	—
Tamil Tiger fundraiser	No	Canada	—
Tamil Tiger and Sri Lankan government operative (double agent)	No	Canada	Caused scandal in 1996 by working as RCMP translator and stealing intelligence materials; RCMP launched investigation against CSIS for not sharing knowledge of his Tiger membership
Alleged member of Salafist Group for Call and Combat	No	Unconvicted	Fled Canada following "confrontation interview" with CSIS

Such cases should not be dismissed, but they represent a separate problem from a terrorist exploiting the asylum system as a means of travel. The second group I excluded were individuals associated with extremism who filed a refugee claim after living in Canada for over a year. (The four individuals, Tre Arrow, Bittor Tejedor Bilbao, Haig Gharakhanian and Mahmoud Mohammad Issa Mohammad, were all fighting deportation or extradition.)

Finally, I did not count four people who disclosed their former affiliation with an extremist group at the time of their refugee claim, and subsequently lived for years in Canada without engaging in any sort of extremist activity. This category included two former members of the Irish National Liberation Army, Malachy McAllister and Francis Patrick (Paddy) Ward, who were both on the run from their former organization. It also included two supporters of Basque Homeland and Freedom, an armed separatist group in Spain. The two Basque nationalists, Gorka Perea Salazar and Eduardo Plagaro Perez de Arrilucea, had been convicted in Spain of setting fire to several bank machines. Like the former INLA members, they disclosed their prior association with an extremist group at the time of their refugee claim, and lived for years in Canada without engaging in any sort of extremist activity. For these reasons they were not regarded as active terrorism supporters at the time of their deportation.

Deciding which categories to exclude was the easy part. The more difficult question was which particular individuals to include. What makes someone a terrorist? Once we get past people who set off bombs in public and other obvious cases, putting forward an uncontroversial definition becomes difficult, as reflected in the cliché that one person's terrorist is another person's freedom fighter. Rather than attempt to offer my own definition that finally settles the issue, I began by compiling cases of people who at some point had the terrorist label attached to them. My primary means of doing so was looking through newspaper databases and, to a lesser degree, government documents and think tank reports. All of the individuals on the list, therefore, have this much in common: they were at some point labelled a "terrorist" in the press.

Scrolling through media coverage of accused terrorists proved to be an eye-opening experience. Particularly since September 11, there have been many cases of someone being identified as a terrorist only for the allegation to prove false. (Stories making the initial allegation also travel much farther than follow-up reports correcting the record.) In order to avoid this problem, I added as a second criterion that the person in question must have been subject to a legal decision that determined them to be involved with extremism during or before their refugee claim. Most of the legal decisions were convictions on terrorism charges, but I also counted security-related deportation orders or, in one case, the conditions of release from detention (Pirakalathan Ratnavel).

Focusing on legal decisions, however, raises its own issues. The first is whether every conviction should be treated equally. This question is forcefully posed by the case of Mourad Ikhlef. Ikhlef arrived in Canada from Algeria in 1993 and successfully filed a refugee claim. While he lived in Montreal he was a political extremist close to Ressam and other convicted terrorists. Ressam testified during the trial of another co-conspirator that in 1999 he discussed with Ikhlef his plan to bomb the Los Angeles airport, and that Ikhlef helped him fix a circuit tester he was planning to use in his bomb. When a security certificate was issued against Ikhlef in 2001, it was an unsurprising outcome for one of Ressam the terrorist's enablers.

But was Ikhlef involved in terrorism back in 1993, when he filed his refugee claim? Most analysts have taken it for granted that he was, on the basis of a 1993 terrorism conviction in Algeria. Ikhlef, however, was tried in Algeria's so-called Special Courts, which the country's military dictatorship established to combat "subversion" during the civil war. The Special Courts were widely condemned by groups such as Human Rights Watch for "fall[ing] far short of internationally recognized standards for a fair trial." Sentences in the Special Courts overwhelmingly relied on evidence extracted through torture. Testimony was obtained from witnesses who were beaten by security agents until they could no longer stand, or from defendants who signed confessions after having their genitals destroyed. The most common sentence was death, which was handed down for "acts of terrorism" that included making a speech or distributing a leaflet.

Ikhlef was sentenced to death *in absentia* by a Special Court in 1993, when the violations were at their worst and the courts amounted to chambers of "summary or arbitrary executions," as Amnesty International termed them. These procedures cast Ikhlef's original conviction into doubt. In addition, Ikhlef was deported to Algeria in 2003, by which time the Special Courts had been abolished. He was then retried on the original charges and acquitted. There is therefore no legal basis on which to connect him to terrorism during or before his 1993 refugee claim. For this reason I have left him off the list.

A second issue raised by focusing on convictions is that doing so could leave out genuine terrorists who were clever enough to avoid being caught. I came across three cases that could potentially be construed this way. As the circumstances in each instance were different, I wound up deciding whether to include each one on a case-by-case basis.

One that seemed to clearly involve a genuine extremist was Mohammed Dbouk. Dbouk fled Canada for Lebanon in 1999 while being wiretapped by CSIS. There is strong evidence from a variety of law enforcement agencies that Dbouk was a fundraiser for Hezbollah at the time he filed a refugee claim. In 2000 he was indicted in the United States on fundraising charges but never tried (because Lebanon does not extradite to the U.S.). Given how well documented his case is, Dbouk's name cries out for inclusion on any list of refugee claimants connected to terrorism.

A more ambiguous case is that of Nourddine Zendaoui. CSIS publicly stated in 2005 that Zendaoui was a member of the Salafist Group for Call and Combat and had, until recently, lived in Toronto. According to CSIS, the agency had at one point considered invoking a security certificate against Zendaoui but decided instead to subject him to "confrontational interviews," to let him know he was being closely watched. Zendaoui left Canada after one such interview in 2004. It is not clear whether CSIS decided against a security certificate for lack of evidence, and terrorism allegations against Zendaoui have never been proven. As I say, his case is ambiguous, but I gave CSIS the benefit of the doubt and included him.

The third case is Omar el-Sayed, who washed up in Edmonton in 1998. A month after arriving on a fake passport, he told Immigration officials his real name and that he had once belonged to Hezbollah. The officials soon discovered that el-Sayed was wanted in Germany on drug charges, and he was arrested and slated for extradition. After a judge released el-Sayed on bail, he disappeared, generating news stories about a dangerous terrorist being on the loose. It seems unlikely, however, that el-Sayed entered Canada with terroristic intentions. His disclosure of his Hezbollah affiliation, as well as the fact that he had been living in Germany for eight years, both suggest he was telling the truth when he claimed to no longer belong to the organization. The wiretapping of Mohammed Dbouk's Hezbollah cell in Vancouver also took place in the months before el-Sayed's arrival, and there is no evidence they were aware of el-Sayed or attempting to get an operative into Edmonton. For these reasons I excluded el-Sayed.

Controversial omissions may be inevitable with a list like this. The same is true of controversial inclusions. Consider Palestine

Liberation Organization member Wahid Baroud. He was subject to a complicated legal ruling that said although there was no evidence he had ever engaged in terrorism, he did once belong to a PLO commando unit that did, on which basis he was deported to Sudan. Baroud has since been held up as an example of someone classified as a terrorist according to an overly broad legal definition. But his case was found to be serious by Canadian courts, and so he is included here.

Focusing on individuals who were eventually convicted or escaped while under observation by CSIS makes it possible to generalize about cases where the terrorist label is least in dispute. Although I am not aware of other cases meeting this standard, some could easily turn up. Yet if they do, this list is still likely to offer a reasonable estimate of how frequently terrorists have tried to enter North America through Canada's refugee system. It therefore provides some indication of what the typical outcome is for terrorists who try to pass themselves off as refugees.

Putting aside doubts about any particular individual, the list shows that people associated with political violence, a category that includes not only terrorists but also supporters who aided extremist groups through fundraising, passport forgery and other means, have sought to enter North America through Canada's refugee system approximately twenty-six times during the period in question. The first case occurred in 1988, the last in 2001. Clearly, extremists did try to pose as refugees during this time. Several observations, however, should be borne in mind when determining how much of a threat they represent.

The first is that political extremists are a microscopic portion of the total number of refugee claimants. During the same thirteen-year period that the twenty-six individuals in question arrived, 325,280 refugee claims were filed in Canada. This suggests that in any given year, the odds of a proponent of political violence being present in a refugee stream are one in 13,000. By way of comparison, the annual chance of dying in a car accident is one in 6,500, or twice as great. As for the possibility of actually being *killed* by a terrorist refugee claimant, the odds to date are too small to measure. Ironically, the extreme rarity with which terrorists make refugee claims may only enhance their media profile. A terrorist nabbed in the refugee stream is a front-page story. The greater risks we all take in stride every day are too routine to generate the same interest.

The second noteworthy feature about the twenty-six cases concerns when the last one occurred. Cases may someday come to light of terrorists who sought to enter Canada through its refugee system in the years immediately following September 11. However, given that none have emerged by the time of writing, as well as the dramatic changes in security legislation that occurred in North America during this time, it seems unlikely that cases during the 2000s will reach the same level as the 1990s. This reinforces an idea mentioned in chapter 8, namely that the Ressam myth fostered panic about terrorist refugee claimants just when they were least likely to arrive.

Another point is that in none of the twenty-six cases was the refugee system used as part of a successful terror operation. As also mentioned in chapter 8, there has been speculation that after Essam Marzouk left Canada for Afghanistan he trained two suicide bombers who carried out the U.S. embassy bombings in Africa. If so, that would make Marzouk the one person on the list to have been involved in a successful terrorist operation after filing a refugee claim. But if Marzouk did train the bombers, he had to leave North America to do so. While in Canada he was subject to observation and interviews by CSIS, which radically curtailed his effectiveness. Marzouk's time in Canada was likely the one point in his terror career when he knew he was being watched, and so had to avoid acting on his beliefs.

Each of the twenty-six individuals was either investigated by CSIS or taken into custody. This suggests that Canadians—and, by extension, Americans—are well protected by Canada's law enforcement agencies. The role of CSIS in particular is worth highlighting. Canada's security service has been embroiled in its share of scandals over the years, but when it comes to would-be terrorist refugee claimants, the evidence suggests that the agency is effective at identifying and neutralizing them. CSIS may well be North America's most underappreciated counterter-rorism force.

Finally, it is noticeable that security certificates were used against fifteen of the twenty-six individuals. Security certificates are an absolutely devastating legal tool. They allow the Canadian government to use in court evidence that is never shown to the suspect. They also give the government sweeping detention powers. When Ressam was sentenced, the presiding judge said that his conviction showed that the United States can protect its national security without compromising its constitutional ideals. "All of this occurred in the sunlight of a public trial. There were no secret proceedings, no indefinite detention, no denial of coun-sel." The same cannot be said of security certificates, which attract criticism due to the extraordinary power they grant the Canadian government. The point at hand, however, concerns the frequency with which certificates have been used against terror-ists posing as refugees. This frequency, together with the eight conventional arrests, suggests that the widespread view of the refugee system as an easy means by which extremists can avoid detection is the opposite of the truth.

Indeed, without wishing to give advice to terrorists, it is dif-ficult to imagine a terror operation less likely to succeed than one involving Canadian refugee claimants. Security certificates can be used against people who make refugee claims because they are not Canadian citizens. An operation involving so-called home-grown terrorists, who have full citizenship rights, would be much harder to prosecute. Conversely, foreign operatives travelling on business or tourist visas, which do not require submitting fingerprints and life histories, would be much harder to detect. Missions involving refugee claimants represent the worst of both worlds from a terror chief's point of view, as they combine maximum disclosure requirements with minimum legal rights. In the end, what is most striking about terrorists posing as refugees is not how much fear they should strike in us. It is how much terror we should strike in them.

ACKNOWLEDGEMENTS

THIS BOOK WOULD NOT EXIST without the help of many people. It began in a long exchange about rights with my old friends Daniel Brandes and John Haffner. It was through Daniel's extensive involvement in that exchange that I first became aware of Hannah Arendt's critique of human rights. Daniel is a humanitarian in his own way, but is less attracted than I am to the idea of human rights. Had he not presented Arendt's argument with such force, I would never have become interested in refugees. John was receptive to my initial thoughts on refugee law. He also informed me of the situation of refugees seeking asylum in Japan and lent me his apartment for two months while I was working on the book. I thank them both for the different forms of inspiration they provided and for their friendship over many years.

Before it was a book, *Frontier Justice* was a radio documentary on the Canadian Broadcasting Corporation's *Ideas* program. I thank my producers, Lisa Hébert and Susan Mahoney, for their original interest and for making the radio project so rewarding. I also thank the people who submitted to interviews for the documentary, portions of which also appear here.

After the show became a book project, it benefited from three institutions. The first was the Canada Council, which provided me with a grant during the research phase. The second was the University of Western Australia, with which I was affiliated during most of the writing. At UWA I am particularly grateful to Keith Horton, Rob Stuart and Miri Albahari, without whose support I would not have been able to finish the book while studying and teaching. The third institution was Random House of Canada, where my editor, Amy Black, provided the perfect mix of patience and enthusiasm when I was working on the manuscript, and provided invaluable comments on it when I was done.

I am grateful to the many people who consented to be interviewed for this book. I owe a special debt to Mohammad Al Ghazzi, who graciously submitted to multiple interviews about a harrowing and heartbreaking period in his life.

A number of people read portions of the manuscript. They include Lisa Daugaard, Elizabeth Detweiler, John Haffner, Jeet Heer, Sue Hoffman, Ian Mason, Paul Saurette, Peter Showler and Joe Tringali. I am grateful to each for taking the time to do so.

My biggest thanks is to my wife, Kirsty. She helped me develop the ideas in the book and went over every sentence with me. More than this, she was my refuge while writing it. This book is for her.

PREFACE

p. 3 *At one of the meetings* Jacques Maritain, "Introduction," in *Human Rights: Comments and Interpretations* (Paris: Unesco, 1948), p. 1.

CHAPTER 1: The Philosopher in Exile

p. 5 *Among them were a young Jewish woman and her mother* The story of Arendt's escape from Germany and life in France in the 1930s is taken from Elisabeth Young-Bruehl, *Hannah Arendt: For Love of the World* (New Haven, Conn.: Yale University Press, 1982), in particular chapter 4, "Stateless Persons 1933–1941."

p. 7 *The arrival of the German refugees* This account of France's refugee crisis draws on Vicki Caron, *Uneasy Asylum: France and the Jewish Refugee Crisis, 1933–1942* (Stanford, Calif.: Stanford University Press, 1999). Caron notes that France's refugee policy took a "twisted road" during the 1930s, alternating between welcoming and anti-refugee policies, before culminating in the extremely harsh anti-immigrant laws of 1938.

p. 9 *"When some of us suggested that we had been shipped there"* Hannah Arendt, "We Refugees," in Marc Robinson, ed.,

Altogether Elsewhere: Writers on Exile (Boston: Faber and Faber, 1994), p. 113.

p. 11 *"The very immensity of the crimes"* Hannah Arendt, *The Origins of Totalitarianism*, new edition (London: George Allen and Unwin, 1967), p. 439.

p. 11 *Even travelling to a foreign consulate* See Reg Whitaker, *Double Standard: The Secret History of Canadian Immigration* (Toronto: University of Toronto Press, 1987). Whitaker's book opens with the story of Beatriz Eugenia Barrios Marroquin, who was killed in Guatemala in the winter of 1985–86 while trying to obtain a visa to travel to Canada.

p. 12 *"saturated with Jews"* Michael Marrus, *The Unwanted: European Refugees in the Twentieth Century* (New York: Oxford University Press, 1985), p. 157.

p. 12 *"Most important, however, was the fact that France"* Caron, *Uneasy Asylum*, p. 15.

p. 12 *Switzerland's policies were unremarkable* The immigration policies of Western countries in the 1930s are described in Marrus, *The Unwanted*, chapter 3. For an example of a country with an especially restrictive policy, see Irving Abella and Harold Troper, *None Is Too Many: Canada and the Jews of Europe, 1933–1948* (Toronto: Lester & Orpen Dennys, 1982).

p. 13 *"will soon constitute groups of discontented"* Caron, *Uneasy Asylum*, p. 20.

p. 13 *"an honour for our nation"* Caron, *Uneasy Asylum*, p. 21.

p. 15 *Many of the new countries' borders* My discussion of the refugee crisis after World War I draws on chapter 9 of Arendt's *Origins* and chapter 2 of Marrus's *The Unwanted*. Hungary's sealed borders are discussed on p. 72 of the latter.

p. 16 *in 1926 there were still 9.5 million refugees* Marrus, *The Unwanted*, p. 51.

p. 17 *"The Rights of Man, supposedly inalienable"* Arendt, *Origins*, p. 293.

p. 18 *"The conception of human rights"* Arendt, *Origins*, pp. 299–300.

p. 19 *"It was a problem not of space"* Arendt, *Origins*, p. 294.

p. 19 *"essentially wipes out asylum"* Austin T. Fragomen Jr., "The Illegal Immigration Reform and Immigrant Responsibility Act of 1996: An Overview," *International Migration Review*, vol. 31, no. 2 (1997), p. 443.

p. 19 *"to secure our borders"* Bill Clinton, Address to Nation on
Haiti, September 15, 1994, http://www.clintonfoundation.org/
legacy/091594-speech-by-president-address-to-nation-on-haiti.htm,
last accessed February 28, 2005.

p. 20 *15 million in the late 1940s* Marrus, *The Unwanted*, p. 355.

p. 20 *2.9 million by 1975 The State of the World's Refugees: Fifty
Years of Humanitarian Action* (New York: Oxford University
Press, 2000), p. 310.

p. 20 *The Hungarian crisis of 1956* The Hungarian refugee operation
is described in Marrus, *The Unwanted*, pp. 359–60.

p. 20–21 *over 11 million . . . 31 million* United Nations High
Commissioner for Refugees, Frequently Requested Statistics,
"Total Population of concern to UNHCR: Refugees, asylum-seek-
ers, IDPs, returnees, stateless persons, and others of concern to
UNHCR by country/territory of asylum, end-2007," UNHCR
Statistical Online Population Database, http://www.unhcr.org/
statistics/49a2c7ff2.html, last accessed May 8, 2009. Note that
UNHCR's global statistics do not include Palestinian refugees,
who have their own UN agency and occupy a unique position of
permanent displacement.

p. 21 *In the early 1970s . . . 412,700 asylum applications* Matthew
J. Gibney, *The Ethics and Politics of Asylum: Liberal Democracy
and the Response to Refugees* (Cambridge: Cambridge University
Press, 2004), p. 3.

p. 22 *"liberal democratic states publicly avow"* Gibney, *Ethics and
Politics*, p. 229.

p. 22 *"the very phrase 'human rights'"* Arendt, *Origins*, p. 269.

p. 23 *"No such thing as inalienable human rights"* Arendt, *Origins*,
p. 229.

p. 25 *"The legal distinction between 'refugees'"* Michael Kinsley, "An
Open U.S. Door for Both Political and Economic Refugees," *Wall
Street Journal*, April 3, 1986.

p. 25 *"in the case of victims of famine"* Gibney, *Ethics and Politics*,
p. 8.

CHAPTER 2: American Lavalas

p. 27 *"The downtown part of Guantánamo"* Harold Koh interview,
March 8, 2005. Unless otherwise indicated, all subsequent Koh
quotes are from this interview.

p. 29 *"There was no way you could go to that camp"* Michael

Ratner interview, March 9, 2005. Unless otherwise indicated, all subsequent Ratner quotes are from this interview.

p. 30 *"a rights-free zone"* Harold Hongju Koh, "Reflections on Refoulement and Haitian Centers Council," *Harvard International Law Journal*, vol. 35, no. 1 (Winter 1994), p. 4.

p. 30 *debate the idea of collective suicide* Victoria Clawson, Elizabeth Detweiler and Laura Ho, "Litigating as Law Students: An Inside Look at Haitian Centers Council," *Yale Law Journal*, vol. 103 (1994), pp. 2375–76.

p. 31 *Between 1946 and 1994 it admitted* Matthew Gibney, *The Ethics and Politics of Asylum: Liberal Democracy and the Response to Refugees* (Cambridge: Cambridge University Press, 2004), p. 132.

p. 31 *"Vacationers, slick with suntan lotion"* Thomas Powers, "The Scandal of U.S. Immigration: The Haitian Example," *Ms.*, February 1976, p. 62.

p. 32 *But in 1980 the number of Haitians arriving by boat spiked to almost 25,000* In 1979, 4,449 Haitians arrived; in 1980, the figure was 24,562. Josh DeWind and David H. Kinley III, *Aiding Migration: The Impact of International Development Assistance on Haiti* (Boulder: Westview, 1988), p. 9.

p. 32 *several thousand criminals and psychiatric patients* Matthew Gibney gives a figure of 8,000. See *Ethics and Politics*, p. 153.

p. 32 *"The refugee question has hurt us badly"* Quoted in Gibney, *Ethics and Politics*, p. 156.

p. 34 *"We have taken careful steps"* Quoted in Guy S. Goodwin-Gill, "The Haitian *Refoulement* Case: A Comment," *International Journal of Refugee Law*, vol. 6, no. 1 (1994), p. 107.

p. 34 *"ordinarily asked all of the questions"* Lawyers Committee for Human Rights, *Refugee Refoulement: The Forced Return of Haitians Under the U.S.-Haitian Interdiction Agreement*, New York, 1990, p. 22. The questions and answers given in the text can be found on pp. 21 and 34. Note that the committee is now called Human Rights First.

p. 35 *"Of these, the attorneys wrote, two had lived in the United States . . . at least hundreds of refugees"* *Refugee Refoulement*, pp. 23, 3.

p. 35 *3 to 5 percent of those interviewed each month* Susan Beck, "Cast Away," *American Lawyer* (October 1992), no page (database).

p. 35 *"It's no place to do an interview"* Beck, "Cast Away."

p. 36 "analogous to a fish-processing ship" "Furor Erupts over U.S. Policy on Haitian Boat People," *Interpreter Releases*, vol. 68, no. 45 (November 25, 1991), p. 1686.

p. 36 *"I'm Jewish and my father"* Michael Barr interview, June 9, 2005. All subsequent Barr quotes are from this interview.

p. 36 *"the most important refugee case"* Michael Ratner, "How We Closed the Guantánamo HIV Camp: The Intersection of Politics and Litigation," *Harvard Human Rights Journal*, vol. 11 (1998), p. 220.

p. 37 *"I saw bed sheets tied to masts"* Beck, "Cast Away."

p. 38 *"he talked about how Bush"* Laura Ho interview, March 9, 2005.

p. 39 *"We had personal ties to a number"* Ratner, "How We Closed the Guantánamo HIV Camp," p. 193.

p. 40 *Whispers that it had something to do with HIV* Clawson et al., "Litigating as Law Students," p. 2351.

p. 41 *"We were like, 'Yeah!'"* Elizabeth Detweiler interview, March 8, 2005. Unless otherwise indicated, all subsequent Detweiler quotes are from this interview.

p. 41 *The Refugee Center had access to only five lawyers.* Harold Maas, "Law Students Spend Break Helping Haitian Refugees," *Miami Herald*, March 16, 1992, p. 1B.

p. 42 *"suddenly we saw we were part of something"* Victoria Clawson interview, June 11, 2005. Unless otherwise indicated, all subsequent Clawson quotes are from this interview.

p. 45 *"They were keeping Haitians on the top"* Ira Kurzban interview, June 11, 2005. Unless otherwise indicated, all subsequent Kurzban quotes are from this interview.

p. 47 *"Under current practice, any aliens"* Haitian Refugee Center v. Baker page 23.

p. 47 *"Everybody thought it was a great thing"* Joe Tringali interview, March 16, 2005. All subsequent Tringali quotes are from this interview.

p. 48 *"Are there not enough homosexuals"* http://www.aids.org/atn/a-128-03.html, last accessed August 16, 2008.

p. 50 *"It was really a great feeling to get"* Lisa Daugaard interview, June 20, 2005. Unless otherwise indicated, all subsequent Daugaard quotes are from this interview.

p. 51 *"identical in form and substance, or as nearly so as possible"* Rees memo, quoted in Clawson et al., "Litigating as Law Students," p. 2352.

p. 52 *"was asking for something 'as American . . . '"* Ratner, "How We Closed the Guantánamo HIV Camp," p. 197.

p. 53 *"I am from Bed-stuy"* Daugaard interview.

p. 56 *"She sang about hurting"* Quoted in Clawson et al., "Litigating as Law Students," p. 2357.

p. 57 *"Our litigation manager"* Koh, "Reflections on Refoulement," p. 6.

p. 58 *"If there is anything you can do for your clients"* Clawson et al., "Litigating as Law Students," p. 2358.

p. 61 *"There's nothing more we can do"* Clawson et al., "Litigating as Law Students," p. 2359.

p. 62 *"a floating Berlin Wall"* Clawson et al., "Litigating as Law Students," p. 2345.

CHAPTER 3: A Floating Berlin Wall

p. 67 *"I am appalled by the decision"* Quoted in Harold Hongju Koh, "Reflections on Refoulement and Haitian Centers Council," *Harvard International Law Journal*, vol. 35, no. 1 (Winter 1994), p. 2.

p. 68 *"There was no reason why eye infections"* Michael Ratner, "How We Closed the Guantánamo HIV Camp: The Intersection of Politics and Litigation," *Harvard Human Rights Journal*, vol. 11 (1998), p. 206.

p. 68 *The National Coalition for Haitian Refugees* The organization is now called the Haitian Coalition for Haitian Rights.

p. 69 *It was the one inhabited by the refugees themselves.* In the years since their detention, the refugees housed at Guantánamo have repeatedly said through intermediaries that they prefer not to be interviewed about their experiences. For this reason, quotations from the refugees in my account are all from written sources or reconstructed from interviews with the legal team.

p. 70 *"Yon sèl nou fèb"* Victoria Clawson, Elizabeth Detweiler and Laura Ho, "Litigating as Law Students: An Inside Look at Haitian Centers Council," *Yale Law Journal*, vol. 103 (1994), p. 2365.

p. 73 *Refugee one: How can we trust you?* Daugaard interview, June 20, 2005.

p. 75 *"You're working with these people?"* Ronald Aubege interview, Spring 2005. All Auberge quotes are from this interview.

p. 76 *"I was hurt."* Ronald Aubege interview.

p. 77 *"My name is Harold Michel."* Clawson et al., "Litigating as Law Students," p. 2366.

p. 77 *Later, Lisa Daugaard speculated* Brandt Goldstein, *Storming the Court: How a Band of Yale Law Students Sued the President—and Won* (New York: Scribner, 2005), p. 168.

p. 84 *"Don't count on me anymore"* Clawson et al., "Litigating as Law Students," p. 2375.

p. 86 *"sick faggots"* Lybi Ma, "Susan Sarandon: Speaking Out," *Psychology Today,* May/June 2003, p. 30.

p. 89 *"Refoulement, by contrast"* McNary v. Haitian Centers Council, Brief for the Petitioners, p. 39, Westlaw database number 1992 WL 541276.

p. 89 *"Limited territorial scope"* McNary v. Haitian Centers Council, Brief for the Petitioners, p. 36.

p. 89 *"Well, before you sit down"* Sale v. Haitian Centers Council, Oral Argument Transcript, March 2, 1993, p. 12, Westlaw database number 1993 WL 754941. Note that the name of the case changed when Clinton took office and replaced INS Commissioner Gene McNary with Acting Commissioner Chris Sale.

p. 90 *"all stood up and started cheering"* . . ."*When you left the Haitians on the dock"* Quoted in Clawson et al., "Litigating as Law Students," pp. 2383, 2384.

p. 91 *"Each year many 'non-immigrants'"* Haitian Centers Council v. Sale, Eastern District of New York, 1993, 823 F. Supp. 1082, pp. 62, 65. This decision and the Supreme Court decision have similar names but should not be confused. In the Supreme Court case, the parties' names are reversed and Sale comes first.

p. 91 *A Hatian man named Jean* Jean is a pseudonym.

p. 93 *"an arcane and highly dubious interpretation"* Matthew Gibney, *The Ethics and Politics of Asylum: Liberal Democracy and the Response to Refugees* (Cambridge: Cambridge University Press, 2004), p. 163.

p. 93 *"disingenuous"* James Hathaway, *The Rights of Refugees Under International Law* (Cambridge: Cambridge University Press, 2005), p. 337.

p. 93 *"the Dred Scott case of immigration"* Thomas David Jones, "A Human Rights Tragedy: The Cuban and Haitian Refugee Crises Revisited," *Georgetown Immigration Law Journal,* vol. 9, no. 3 (1995), p. 523.

p. 93 *"Under [the government's] reading"* Office of the United

Nations High Commissioner for Refugees, "The Haitian
Interdiction Case 1993 Brief Amicus Curiae," *International
Journal of Refugee Law*, vol. 6, no. 1 (1994), p. 91.

p. 93 *"The Supreme Court's citations are often adrift"* Guy
Goodwin-Gill, "The Haitian Refoulement Case: A Comment,"
International Journal of Refugee Law, vol. 6, no. 1, pp. 104–5.

p. 94 *"necessarily looks 'to' the place"* Quoted in Office of the
United Nations High Commissioner for Refugees, "The Haitian
Interdiction Case," p. 87.

p. 95 *"The bar to repatriations was exacerbating"* McNary v.
Haitian Centers Council, Brief for the Petitioners, p. 5.

p. 95 *"Well, that's a worthy problem"* John F. Harris, *The Survivor: Bill
Clinton in the White House* (New York: Random House, 2005), p. 6.

p. 95 One person present at the Little Rock meeting Goldstein,
Storming the Court, p. 199.

p. 95 *"Some of the criticism on the Haitian issue"* Bill Clinton, *My
Life* (New York: Knopf, 2004), pp. 467, 463–64.

p. 96 *"a complete sham"* Bill Frelick, "In-Country Refugee
Processing of Haitians: The Case Against," *Refuge: Canada's
Periodical on Refugees*, vol. 21, no. 4 (2003), p. 68.

p. 97 it would be *"suicide"* Quoted in Frelick, "In-Country Refugee
Processing of Haitians," p. 67.

p. 98 *"Our complaint was not with Guantánamo per se"* Koh,
"Reflections on Refoulement," p. 19.

p. 99 a *"clever ploy"* and a *"Machiavellian device"* Iain Guest,
"Refugee Policy: Leading Up to Governors Island," in Georges
A. Fauriol ed., *Haitian Frustrations: Dilemmas for U.S. Policy*,
(Washington: Center for Strategic and International Studies,
1995), p. 80.

p. 99 *"Citing the example of the Haitian refugees"* Bonaventure
Rutinwa, "The End of Asylum? The Changing Nature of Refugee
Policies in Africa," New Issues in Refugee Research, Working
Paper no. 5 (UNHCR, May 1999), p. 20.

p. 99 *17,254 Haitians, slightly less than the 18,230 Cubans* United
States Coast Guard, "Alien Migrant Interdiction," available at
http://www.uscg.mil/hq/cg5/cg531/AMIO/FlowStats/FY.asp, last
accessed October 24, 2010.

p. 100 *Although the shout test purportedly allows* Bill Frelick,
"'Abundantly clear': Refoulement," *Georgetown Immigration Law
Journal*, vol. 19, no. 2 (2004), p. 246.

p. 100 *In 2005, when 1,850 Haitians were interdicted* Human Rights Watch, "Submission to the Committee on the Elimination of all Forms of Racial Discrimination: During its Consideration of the Fourth, Fifth, and Sixth Periodic Reports of the United States of America CERD 72nd Session," Volume 20, No. 2(G) (2008), p. 14. The same Human Rights Watch report notes on page 13 that the shout test is administered to interdictees of any nationality other than Cubans and citizens of China (who are given a written questionnaire that allows them to indicate a fear of persecution). "However, as a practical matter, Haiti is the only other county whose nationals seeking asylum arrive by sea in significant numbers."

p. 100 *I have made it abundantly clear* Frelick, "Abundantly Clear," p. 245.

p. 101 *"I want them on Guantánamo"* Quoted in Luiza Ch. Savage, "Could the Next President Be Even Scarier?" *Maclean's*, November 12, 2007, p. 38.

p. 101 *become purely "metaphysical"* Martin Puchner, "Guantánamo Bay," *London Review of Books*, December 16, 2004, p. 7. Puchner is echoing a phrase that came up in *Rasul v. Bush*, a Supreme Court case dealing with the rights of enemy combatants held at Guantánamo.

p. 102 *the writings of contemporary political scientists* The distinction between sovereignty as recognition and sovereignty as control is taken from Stephen Krasner, *Sovereignty: Organized Hypocrisy* (Princeton, N.J.: Princeton University Press, 1999), p. 4. Krasner's more precise terms for these two aspects of sovereignty are "international legal sovereignty" and "domestic sovereignty."

p. 102 *"We became aware of a right to have rights"* Arendt, *Origins*, 296-7.

p. 103 *"If you want a definition of this place"* Quoted in David Rose, *Guantánamo: The War on Human Rights* (New York: New Press, 2004), p. 22.

p. 103 *"for the purposes of protecting"* Sale v. Haitian Centers Council, Oral Argument Transcript, p. 7.

p. 103 *"This case presents a painfully common situation"* Sale v. Haitian Centers Council, http://www.law.cornell.edu/supct/html/92-344.ZO.html, last accessed August 21, 2008.

p. 103 *"their plight is not that they are not equal"* Hannah Arendt, *The Origins of Totalitarianism*, new edition (London: George Allen and Unwin, 1967), pp. 295-96.

p. 103 *"the scum of the earth"* Arendt, *Origins,* p. 269.

CHAPTER 4: The Fatal Shore

p. 105 *One night in 1994 Al Ghazzi was at home* Details of Mohammad Al Ghazzi's arrest and flight are taken from interviews with Al Ghazzi, November 12, 2008, February 17, 2009, and September 17, 2009, and Anne Buggins, "Still Drowning in SIEV X Horror," *The West Australian,* October 14, 2006. Unless otherwise indicated, all subsequent Al Ghazzi quotes are from these three interviews.

p. 109 *"the intimidating presence of all-powerful"* U.S. Committee for Refugees, "World Refugee Survey 2000—Syria," http://www.unhcr.org/refworld/country,,USCRI,,SYR,4562d8cf2,3ae6a8cb4c,0.html, last accessed September 11, 2009.

p. 114 *"People will come to maybe escape"* Michelle Dimasi interview, December 16, 2008.

p. 114 *Between 1992 and 1998 an average of 115 people* Joint Standing Committee on Migration, *Not the Hilton: Immigration Detention Centres: Inspection Report* (Canberra, 2000), p. 74.

p. 114 *At first they came from Vietnam* Andreas Schoenhardt, *Migrant Smuggling: Illegal Migration and Organized Crime in Australia and the Asia Pacific Region* (Leiden, Holland: Martinus Nijhoff, 2003), p. 148.

p. 114 *following the rise of an "Iran for the Iranians" movement* Human Rights Watch, *By Invitation Only: Australian Asylum Policy,* Section IV, "Why Refugees Flee Their Own Regions," http://www.hrw.org/legacy/reports/2002/australia/australia1202-03.htm#P416_91971, last accessed September 17, 2009; Sue Hoffman interview, November 12, 2008.

p. 115 *Curtin Detention Centre, as it was called* Details taken from Mohammad Al Ghazzi interview, November 12, 2008; Australian Human Rights and Equal Opportunity Commission, "Report on the Human Rights Commissioner's Visit to Curtin IRPC in July 2000," http://www.hreoc.gov.au/human_rights/immigration/curtin.html, last accessed September 11, 2009. See also "Conditions in Curtin Detention Centre, http://www.refugeeaction.org/inside/curtin.htm, last accessed September 11, 2009.

p. 116 *"You couldn't really design"* Quoted in Linda Briskman, Susie Latham and Chris Goddard, *Human Rights Overboard: Seeking Asylum in Australia* (Melbourne: Scribe, 2008), p. 189.

p. 117 *"By the time they have been in detention"* Quoted in Penelope Debelle, "What Happened at Curtin?" *The Age*, May 5, 2001.

p. 117 *"Where are human rights? Where is freedom?"* Peter Mares, *Borderline: Australia's Response to Refugees and Asylum-Seekers in the Wake of the* Tampa, second edition (Sydney: University of New South Wales Press, 2002), p. 10.

p. 118 *Curtin's "subhuman" conditions* Mares, *Borderline*, p. 13.

p. 118 *Conditions improved after the hunger strike* "Report on the Human Rights Commissioner's Visit to Curtin IRPC"; Mares, *Borderline*, p. 33.

p. 120 *a Norwegian cargo ship, MV Tampa* Details of the *Tampa* episode are taken from Mares, *Borderline*, pp. 121–23.

p. 121 *"We simply cannot allow a situation"* "High Stakes for Howard," BBC News, http://news.bbc.co.uk/2/hi/asia-pacific/1517183.stm, last accessed September 11, 2009.

p. 122 *a rotting old fishing vessel* Details of Raghed's voyage are taken from Arnold Zable, "Perilous Journeys," *Eureka Street*, http://eurekastreet.com.au/articles/0304zable.html, last accessed September 11, 2009, and Briskman et al., *Human Rights Overboard*, pp. 43–48. See also the collection of resources about the sinking at www.SievX.com.

p. 123 *as if the gate to hell had opened* Zable, "Perilous Journeys."

p. 123 *"I didn't see for seven days"* Buggins, "Still Drowning in SIEV X Horror."

p. 124 *"bored and fed up with accounting"* Sue Hoffman interview, November 12, 2008. All subsequent Hoffman quotes are from this interview.

p. 125 *"criminals" and "law-breakers"* Margaret Piper, "Australia's Refugee Policy," *The Sydney Papers*, vol. 12, no. 2 (2000), p. 88.

p. 126 *Many people have claimed they had relatives on that boat* The official actually said, "Many people have claimed they had relatives on SIEVX, more than the boat could carry." SIEVX was the government's term for Raghed's boat, an acronym for Suspected Illegal Entry Vessel number 10.

p. 128 *many of the most extreme policies were revised* For changes to Australia's asylum policies see Briskman et al., *Human Rights Overboard*, pp. 385–89.

p. 128 *turned away Jews fleeing Hitler's Germany* The MP was Petro Georgiou. See Margot O'Neill, *Blind Conscience* (Sydney: UNSW Press, 2009), p 171.

p. 128 "*I have been in detention*" Briskman et al., *Human Rights Overboard*, p. 100.

p. 128 the Pacific Solution was called into question See *Plaintiff M61/2010E v Commonwealth of Australia; Plaintiff M69 of 2010 v Commonwealth of Australia [2010] HCA41 (11 November 2010).*

p. 129 "*Even if he is penniless*" Hannah Arendt, *The Origins of Totalitarianism*, new edition (London: George Allen and Unwin, 1967), pp. 286–87.

p. 129 "*Australian-style annual limit*" Conservative Party, "Controlled Immigration," http://image.guardian.co.uk/sys-files/Politics/documents/2005/01/24/conservativesimmigration.pdf 2005, p. 3.

p. 129 "*Canada and the United States need only look*" Diane Francis, "Australia Fixed Its Immigration Problem, We Should Do the Same," *The Province* (Vancouver), October 28, 2001.

p. 130 "*I mean, it's called the doctors' wives syndrome*" O'Neill, *Blind Conscience*, p. 225.

p. 130 "*the minister swivelled around*" Mares, *Borderline*, p. 111.

p. 131 "*incentive pull factors*" "Transcript of the Prime Minister the Hon. John Howard MP Joint Press Conference with the Minister for Immigration the Hon. Philip Ruddock MP Sydney, 1 September 2001," http://www.sievx.com/articles/psdp/20010901HowardRuddockConf.html, last accessed September 11, 2009.

p. 131 "*People are forsaking opportunities*" Philip Ruddock, "Meeting the Basic Needs of Genuine Refugees," *Canberra Times*, December 14, 2001.

p. 132 "*a system combining mandatory, automatic*" Working Group on Arbitrary Detention, quoted in Briskman et al., *Human Rights Overboard*, p. 59.

p. 132 *fifteen instances in which rejected asylum-seekers were killed* Briskman et al., *Human Rights Overboard*, pp. 233–36.

p. 133 *A UNHCR office in Jakarta* Human Rights Watch, *By Invitation Only: Australian Asylum Policy*, Section VI, "Why Refugees Do Not Remain in Transit Countries," http://www.hrw.org/legacy/reports/2002/australia/Australia1202-05.htm#P589_136885, last accessed September 11, 2009.

p. 133 "*Indonesia unequivocally refuses*" Human Rights Watch, *By Invitation Only: Australian Asylum Policy*, Section VII, "Measures Used by Australia to Deter 'Uninvited' Refugees," http://www.hrw.org/legacy/reports/2002/australia/australia1202-06.

htm#P804_201317, last accessed September 11, 2009.

p. 134 *over eleven thousand were eventually recognized as refugees* Briskman et al., *Human Rights Overboard*, p. 20.

p. 134 *"Often refugees have come from situations"* Matthew Gibney interview, spring 2003.

p. 134 *"involves instrumentalising innocent people"* Quoted in Briskman et al., *Human Rights Overboard*, p. 12.

p. 135 *problem of the ethical state* Gibney interview.

p. 136 *111 children attempted to reach Australia* Sue Hoffman, "Temporary Protection Visas & SIEV X," http://www.sievx.com/articles/challenging/2006/20060206SueHoffman.html, last accessed September 11, 2009.

p. 137 *"free-market sea"* William Langewiesche, *The Outlaw Sea: A World of Freedom, Chaos, and Crime* (New York: Farrar, Straus and Giroux, 2004), p. 13.

p. 138 *"The people on the top deck"* Survivors Speak: Ahmed Hussein, http://sievx.com/archives/2003_07-08/20030705.shtml, last accessed March 26, 2009.

p. 139 *Australia reintroduced a version of mandatory detention* Hayden Cooper and staff, "Onshore Defence Base to House Asylum Seekers," ABC News, April 18, 2010; Emma Rodgers, "New Centres to House 2,000 Asylum Seekers," ABC News, October 18, 2010.

CHAPTER 5: Raising the Castle

p. 141 *"Deportation is murder"* Tamara Jones, "Bonn Vote OKs Strict Curbs on Asylum-Seekers," *Los Angeles Times*, May 27, 1993.

p. 141 *"We are one people"* Niklaus Steiner, *Arguing About Asylum: The Complexity of Refugee Debates in Europe* (New York: St. Martin's Press, 2000).

p. 142 *Neo-Nazi out of parliament* Steiner, *Arguing About Asylum*, p. 85.

p. 142 *"You will see: whoever votes today"* *Arguing About Asylum*, p. 85.

p. 143 *"a more rigid general version of the rule of law"* Peter Graf Kielmansegg, "West Germany's Constitution: Response to the Past or Design for the Future?" *The World Today*, October 1989, p. 176.

p. 144 *"anti-Weimar Constitution"* Kielmansegg, "West Germany's Constitution," p. 176.

p. 144 *"If we include limitations"* Quoted in Wolfgang Bosswick, "Development of Asylum Policy in Germany," *Journal of Refugee Studies*, vol. 13, no. 1 (2000), p. 44.

p. 145 *"Because national feeling developed"* Quoted in Matthew Gibney, *The Ethics and Politics of Asylum: Liberal Democracy and the Response to Refugees* (Cambridge: Cambridge University Press, 2004), p. 91.

p. 147 *they accounted for up to 70 percent of the refugee claims* Bosswick, "Development of Asylum Policy in Germany," p. 50.

p. 147 *"While the number of applicants"* Gibney, *Ethics and Politics*, p. 97.

p. 148 *"Their tradition of nationalism"* Quoted in Bill Schiller, "Germany Is Torn by Refugee Crisis," *Toronto Star*, November 21, 1992.

p. 148 *Don't stone foreigners* Alexandra Tuttle, "Germany's Bid for Normality," *The Wall Street Journal*, November 24, 1992, p. 6.

p. 149 *Heil Hitler* Stephen Kinzer, "Germans Hold Suspect In Firebombing That Killed Three Turks," the *New York Times*, November 27, 1992.

p. 149 *"Let's not wait until the immigration problem"* Quoted in Craig Whitney, "Bonn Hopes to Move More Quickly on Asylum," *New York Times*, November 17, 1992.

p. 150 *"We have the freest constitution ever"* Quoted in Henrik Bering-Jensen, "A Flood of Strangers in Estranged Lands," *Insight*, January 4, 1993.

p. 151 *98 percent of pre-1993 cases would be ineligible* Bosswick, "Development of Asylum Policy in Germany," p. 51.

p. 151 *"Granting asylum is always a question"* Quoted in Bosswick, "Development of Asylum Policy in Germany," p. 44.

p. 151 *"While applying for asylum"* Gibney, *Ethics and Politics*, p. 103.

p. 152 *"I was disappointed because this is the first step"* "Gunter Grass Says German Politicians Akin to 'Skinheads,'" Reuters, January 31, 1993.

p. 152 *"Kidnapped"* Antonio Cruz, "Carrier Sanctions in Four European Community States: Incompatibilities Between International Civil Aviation and Human Rights Obligations," *Journal of Refugee Studies*, vol. 4. No. 1 1991, p. 73.

p. 152 *"Increasingly reluctant to carry passengers"* Cruz, "Carrier Sanctions," p. 72.

p. 153 *"many asylum-seekers are refused asylum"* Asylum Aid, "Still

No Reason at All: Home Office Decisions on Asylum Claims," London, 1999, p. 1.

p. 153 *"Several asylum-seekers have been 'released'"* Amnesty International, "Belgium: The Death of Semira Adamu— Responsibilities Past and Present," December 10, 2003.

p. 153 *In 1999 a forty-year-old Algerian woman* Elisabeth Zimmermann, "Algerian Refugee Commits Suicide in Frankfurt Airport's Asylum Zone," World Socialist Web Site, May 24, 2000, http://www. wsws.org/articles/2000/may2000/asyl-m24.shtml, last accessed March 28, 2010; Action-Alliance against Deportation Rhein-Main, "Call for publicly putting up the commemorative plaque at Frankfurt Airport," http://aktivgegenabschiebung.drittewelthaus. de/010500call.html, last accessed June 9, 2013.

p. 154 *"Certain key aspects of Dutch asylum policy"* Human Rights Watch, "Fleeting Refuge: The Triumph of Efficiency Over Protection in Dutch Asylum Policy," New York, 2003, p. 31.

p. 154 *Ibrahim Zijad, a thirty-one-year-old Palestinian refugee* "Airport Refugee Gains Asylum After Seven Months," *International Herald Tribune*, November 2, 2004.

p. 155 *"contrary to the Universal Declaration of Human Rights"* Human Rights Watch, "Universal Periodic Review of Switzerland," May 4, 2008.

p. 155 *"manifestly well-founded"* U.S. Committee for Refugees and Immigrants, "World Refugee Survey 2010, Country Reports, European Union," http://www.refugees.org/countryreports. aspx?id=2138, last accessed March 21, 2010.

p. 155 *"European countries have crafted policies"* U.S. Committee for Refugees and Immigrants, "Worst Places for Refugees," World Refugee Survey 2008, New York, p. 5.

p. 155 *"Greece effectively has no asylum system"* Human Rights Watch, "Greece: Unsafe and Unwelcoming Shores," October 12, 2009, New York.

p. 156 *Anomalous Zones* Gerald L. Neuman, "Anomalous Zones," *Stanford Law Review*, vol. 48, 1996, p. 1197.

p. 156 *"People have said we have our own Guantánamo"* Linda Briskman interview, October 29, 2008.

p. 157 *an annual average of 150,000 refugee applicants* United Nations High Commissioner for Refugees, *The State of the World's Refugees 2006: Human Displacement in the New Millennium*, Annex Eight: Asylum Applications and Total

Admissions in Industrialized Countries, 1995–2004 (Oxford: Oxford University Press, 2006), p. 225.

p. 158 *over 1.5 million ethnic Germans* Merih Anil, "No More Foreigners? The Remaking of German Naturalization and Citizenship Law, 1990–2000," *Dialectical Anthropology*, vol. 29 (2005), p. 457.

p. 158 *Germany, whose average annual recognition rate* Philip Martin, "Germany: Reluctant Land of Immigration," in Wayne Cornelius, Philip Martin and James Hollifield, eds. *Controlling Immigration: A Global Perspective*, (Stanford, Calif.: Stanford University Press, 1994), p. 192. See also United Nations High Commissioner for Refugees, *The State of the World's Refugees 1997: A Humanitarian Agenda* (Oxford: Oxford University Press, 1997), chapter 5, Figure 5.5.

p. 159 *"the perversion of the state"* Hannah Arendt, *The Origins of Totalitarianism*, new edition (London: George Allen and Unwin, 1967), p. 231.

p. 160 *1.3 million people living in refugee camps* United Nations Relief and Works Agency for Palestine Refugees, "Statistics," http://www.unrwa.org/etemplate.php?id=253, last accessed March 28, 2010.

p. 160 *"Possibly, one of the reasons"* Anat Ben-Dor and Rami Adut, "Israel: A Safe Haven? Problems in the Treatment Offered by the State of Israel to Refugees and Asylum Seekers," The Public Interest Law Resource Center and Physicians for Human Rights, Tel Aviv, September 2003, pp. 27–28.

p. 161 *a group that amounted to sixty people during the 1990s* U.S. Committee for Refugees, "World Refugee Survey 2001—Israel, http://www.unhcr.org/refworld/type,ANNUALREPORT,USCRI,ISR, 3b31e1641b,0.html, last accessed March 28, 2010.

p. 161 *According to UNHCR over 26,000 asylum-seekers* Yonathan Paz, "Ordered disorder: African asylum seekers in Israel and discursive challenges to an emerging refugee regime," United Nations High Commissioner for Refugees, Geneva, March 2011.

p. 161 *forcibly returning Eritrean asylum-seekers to Egypt* Human Rights Watch, "Service for Life: State Repression and Indefinite Conscription in Eritrea," Part 3: The Experience of Eritrean Refugees, April 16, 2009.

p. 162 *"constructive refoulement"* Quoted in Ben-Dor and Adut, "Israel: A Safe Haven?" p. 39.

p. 162 *"Much of what attracted Japanese to Germany"* Quoted in John Haffner, Thomas Casas i Klett and Jean-Pierre Lehmann, *Japan's Open Future: An Agenda for Global Citizenship* (London: Anthem, 2009), pp. 44–45.

p. 162 *"He saw the people in the refugee division"* Saul Takahashi, "The Wall: Asylum-Seekers in Japan," *Refugee Participation Network 19*, May 1995.

p. 162 *Legal aid is "hopelessly inadequate"* Saul Takahashi, quoted in Haffner et al., *Japan's Open Future*, p. 215.

p. 163 *expected to meet an "unusually high standard of proof"* United Nations High Commissioner for Refugees, *The State of the World's Refugees: Fifty Years of Humanitarian Action* (Oxford: Oxford University Press, 2000), p. 182.

p. 163 *"it is practically impossible to get asylum"* Takahashi, "The Wall."

p. 163–164 *an average of 27 asylum claims per year* United Nations High Commissioner for Refugees, *2005 UNHCR Statistical Yearbook*, Country Data Sheet, Japan, p. 382.

p. 164 *an asylum system designed not to protect refugees from danger, but to protect Japanese people from refugees* I owe this phrase to John Haffner.

p. 165 *"Asylum is analogous to"* "The U.S.-Canada Safe Third Country Agreement: A Vital First Step," Statement of Mark Krikorian before the House Subcommittee on Immigration, Border Security, and Claims, October 16, 2002.

p. 165 *Japan received an average of only 174 applications per year* United Nations High Commissioner for Refugees, *2002 UNHCR Statistical Yearbook*, Country Data Sheet, Japan, p. 348.

p. 165 *while during the same period Israel averaged 150* United Nations High Commissioner for Refugees, *2002 UNHCR Statistical Yearbook*, Country Data Sheet, Israel, p. 342. UNHCR statistics for Israel include 6,000 members of the Israel-sponsored South Lebanon Army and their families to whom Israel granted permanent residency in 2000. SLA militiamen do not meet the international definition of a refugee, and so I have not included them in Israel's refugee statistics.

p. 168 *"In reality, constitutional asylum was never"* Hélène Lambert, Francesco Messineo and Paul Tiedemann, "Comparative Perspectives of Constitutional Asylum in France, Italy, and Germany: *requiescat in pace?*" *Refugee Survey Quarterly*, vol. 27, no. 3 (2008), p. 21.

p. 168 The UN Committee against Torture, Amnesty International and other groups Amnesty International, "France Amnesty International Report 2008" and "France Amnesty International Report 2009"; The European Court of Human Rights, *Gebremedhin [Gaberamadhien] v. France* (application no. 25389/05), April 26, 2007; *Adel Tebourski v. France*, CAT/ C/38/D/300/2006, UN Committee against Torture, May 11, 2007.

p. 169 *home to a total refugee population of 26,875 people* United Nations High Commissioner for Refugees, "2006 Global Trends: Refugees, Asylum-seekers, Returnees, Internally Displaced and Stateless Persons," p. 17.

p. 169 *"in the world of betrayed constitutional provisions"* Lambert et al., "Comparative Perspectives of Constitutional Asylum," p. 25.

p. 169–170 *via Libya in the thousands* BBC News, "UN seeks access to Italy migrants," October 4, 2004, http://news.bbc.co.uk/2/hi/ europe/3714922.stm, last accessed March 28, 2010.

p. 170 *"As part of his new pan-African policy"* Hein de Haas, "Trans-Saharan Migration to North Africa and the EU: Historical Roots and Current Trends," Migration Information Source, November 2006, http://www.migrationinformation.org/ USfocus/display.cfm?id=484, last accessed March 28, 2010.

p. 170 *Italy returned over 600 people to Libya* James Kanter and Judy Dempsey, "Italy Seeks E.U. Aid to Cope With Libyan Refugees," *The New York Times*, February 24 2011. See also Human Rights Watch, "Letter to the Italian Minister of Foreign Affairs, Mr. Franco Frattini," June 16, 2011.

p. 171 *a 78 percent asylum acceptance rate* Human Rights Watch, "Pushed Back, Pushed Around: Italy's Forced Return of Boat Migrants and Asylum Seekers, Libya's Mistreatment of Migrants and Asylum Seekers," New York, September 2009, p. 11.

p. 171 *"For the first time in the post-World War II era"* Human Rights Watch, "Pushed Back, Pushed Around," p. 4.

p. 172 *"We don't have an internationally agreed system"* Howard Adelman interview, autumn 2004.

CHAPTER 6: An Asylum Made of Thoughts

p. 177 *"Arendt's voice inside my head"* Samantha Power interview, autumn 2004. Unless otherwise indicated, all subsequent Power quotes are from this interview.

p. 180 *"beyond human rights"* Giorgio Agamben, "Beyond Human

Rights," in *Means Without Ends: Notes on Politics*, trans. Vincenzo Binetti and Cesare Casarino (Minneapolis: University of Minnesota Press, 2000), p. 15.

p. 180 "*With his collarless shirts and dark suits*" Daniel Binswanger, "Preacher of the Profane," Signandsight.com, October 17, 2005, http://www.signandsight.com/features/399.html, last accessed May 20, 2009.

p. 181 "*The battle [against terrorism]*" Quoted in Paul Ginsborg, *A History of Contemporary Italy 1943–1980* (London: Penguin, 1990), p. 379.

p. 181 "*instead of championing civil-rights issues*" Ginsborg, *A History of Contemporary Italy*, p. 380.

p. 182 "*The decree was never repealed*" Giorgio Agamben, *State of Exception*, trans. Kevin Attell (Chicago: University of Chicago Press, 2005), p. 2.

p. 183 "*truly sacred, in the sense*" Agamben, "Beyond Human Rights," p. 22.

p. 183 "*in which the normal order is de facto suspended*" Giorgio Agamben, *Homo Sacer: Sovereign Power and Bare Life*, trans. Daniel Heller-Roazen (Palo Alto, Calif.: Stanford University Press, 1998), p. 174.

p. 183 "*The paradox from which Arendt departs*" Agamben, *Homo Sacer*, p. 126.

p. 184 "*Fascism and Nazism*" Agamben, *Homo Sacer*, p. 130.

p. 185 "*By applying these techniques*" Quoted in Karen Arenson, "In Protest, Professor Cancels Visit to the U.S.," *New York Times*, January 17, 2004.

p. 185 "*Humanitarian organizations . . . maintain*" Agamben, *Homo Sacer*, p. 133.

p. 186 "*the perfume of the radical*" Binswanger, "Preacher of the Profane."

p. 186 "*the strange relationship of law*" Ulrich Raulff, "An Interview with Giorgio Agamben," *German Law Journal*, vol. 5, no. 5 (2004), p. 609.

p. 187 "*This is what, in our culture*" Giorgio Agamben, *The Coming Community*, trans. Michael Hardt (Minneapolis: University of Minnesota Press, 1993), p. 86.

p. 187 "*pornographic*" J. M. Bernstein, "Bare Life, Bearing Witness: Auschwitz and the Pornography of Horror," *Parallax*, vol. 10, no. 1 (2004), p. 3.

p. 187 *"ontological loathing for government"* Timothy Brennan, "The Empire's New Clothes," *Critical Inquiry*, vol. 29, no. 2 (2003), p. 341.

p. 187 *"These facts and reflections"* Hannah Arendt, *The Origins of Totalitarianism*, new edition (London: George Allen and Unwin, 1967), p. 299.

p. 188 *"so-called human rights"* Karl Marx, "On the Jewish Question," in *Nonsense Upon Stilts: Bentham, Burke, and Marx on the Rights of Man* Jeremy Waldron, ed. (New York: Routledge, 1987), p. 146.

p. 188 *"he preferred his 'Rights of an Englishman'"* Agamben, *Homo Sacer*, p. 127.

p. 191 *"Yet the evolving human rights system"* Samantha Power, "The Lesson of Hannah Arendt," *New York Review of Books*, April 29, 2004, p. 36. Power's essay is also the preface to a 2004 edition of Arendt's *The Origins of Totalitarianism* published by Schocken.

p. 191 *endorses a suggestion to make Jerusalem* Agamben, "Beyond Human Rights," p. 24. Agamben suggests that such an arrangement could be "generalized as a model of new international relations," but says little about how such an arrangement would work.

p. 191 *"the possibility of a nonstatist politics"* Giorgio Agamben, "Forms of Life," in *Means Without Ends*, p. 8.

p. 191 *Take him for an anarchist* See Brennan, "The Empire's New Clothes," p. 341.

p. 192 *"a thinker of great value"* Paul Virno, "General Intellect, Exodus, Multitude: Interview with Paulo Virno," generation-online.org, http://www.generation-online.org/p/fpvirno2.htm, last accessed May 20, 2009.

p. 193 *"writers and intellectuals can no longer"* Quoted in Lise Wilar, "Le Parlement International des Ecrivans," *écrits . . . vains?* http://ecrits-vains.com/mots_dits/willar46.htm, last accessed May 20, 2009 (my translation).

p. 194 *"a genuine innovation"* Jacques Derrida, *On Cosmopolitanism and Forgiveness*, trans. Mark Dooley and Michael Hughes (New York: Routledge, 2001), p. 4.

p. 194 *Casts doubt upon the The Oxford Companion to Literature*, Margaret Drabble, ed. (Oxford: Oxford University Press, 2000), p. 265.

p. 194 *"Toward the end of his life"* Roy Rivenburg, "A Philosophical View of Sex," *Los Angeles Times*, February 25, 2007 (online).

p. 195 *The 1993 Pasqua Law* Not to be confused with an earlier Pasqua Law of 1986.

p. 195 *sustained protest against the "mean-minded"* Derrida, *On Cosmopolitanism and Forgiveness*, p. 11.

p. 196 *"Since the Middle Ages"* Christian Salmon, "The Parliament of a Missing People," *Autodafe Vol. 1: The Journal of the International Parliament of Writers*, p. 13. Salmon does not indicate which cities and states he is referring to, and may be speaking slightly anachronistically. See chapter 9.

p. 196 *"Arendt was writing of something"* Jacques Derrida, *Cosmopolites de tous les pays, encore un effort!* (Paris: Editions Galilee, 1997), p. 23 (my translation).

p. 197 *"equipped with new rights"* Derrida, *On Cosmopolitanism and Forgiveness*, p. 7.

p. 197 *"At a time when we claim to be lifting"* Derrida, *On Cosmopolitanism and Forgiveness*, p. 13.

p. 197 *"could it, when dealing with the related"* Derrida, *On Cosmopolitanism and Forgiveness*, p. 9.

p. 198 *"this generous border city"* Derrida, *On Cosmopolitanism and Forgiveness*, p. 18.

p. 198 *"God orders Moses to institute"* Derrida, *On Cosmopolitanism and Forgiveness*, p. 17.

p. 198 *"unconditional Law of hospitality"* Derrida, *On Cosmopolitanism and Forgiveness*, p. 22.

p. 199 *"secularized theological heritage"* Derrida, *On Cosmopolitanism and Forgiveness*, p. 20.

p. 199 *"We have doubtless chosen the term"* Derrida, *On Cosmopolitanism and Forgiveness*, p. 16.

p. 200 *"the fifth largest port in the world"* Michael Marrus, *The Unwanted: European Refugees in the Twentieth Century* (New York: Oxford University Press, 1985), p. 180.

p. 201 *between fifteen thousand and seventeen thousand Jews* Shanghai refugee figures taken from Marcia Ristaino, *Port of Last Resort: The Diaspora Communities of Shanghai* (Palo Alto: Stanford University Press, 2001), p. 103; Marrus, *The Unwanted*, p. 181; David Kranzler, *Japanese, Nazis and Jews: The Jewish Refugee Community of Shanghai, 1938–1945* (Hoboken, N.J.: KTAV Publishing House, 1976), p. 90.

p. 201 *"took on the character of a universal conspiracy"* Kranzler, *Japanese, Nazis and Jews*, p. 152.

p. 201 *"Both American and British residents"* Ristaino, *Port of Last Resort*, p 112.

p. 203 *"obsolete privilege"* "A Bogus Brand of Sanctuary," *National Post* (editorial), July 27, 2004.

p. 203 *"facilitates lawlessness"* Chuck Baldwin, "No Sanctuary for Illegal Aliens at Our Church," newswithviews.com, May 15, 2007, http://www.newswithviews.com/baldwin/baldwin369.htm, last accessed May 20, 2009.

p. 203 *"the mindless view that conscientious disobedience"* Ronald Dworkin, "Civil Disobedience," in *Taking Rights Seriously*, second edition (Cambridge, Mass.: Harvard University Press, 1978), p. 206. For a similar view see John Rawls, "The Justification of Civil Disobedience," in *Collected Papers*, Samuel Freeman, ed. (Cambridge, Mass.: Harvard University Press, 1999).

p. 204 *A study of church sanctuary in Canada* Marina Jiménez, "Historic Crypt Becomes Sanctuary for Failed Refugee Claimant, 68," *Globe and Mail*, September 25, 2004.

p. 206 *the tens of thousands of asylum cases that the United States accepted during the same six-year period* In the early 1980s the United States did not keep national statistics for asylum claims made in the context of deportation hearings, which has traditionally been a substantial number. This means it is impossible to say how many refugees were granted asylum (as opposed to resettled from overseas) between 1981 and 1986. The American Council for Nationalities Service records 15,342 successful asylum cases filed with the Immigration and Naturalization Service for the limited period June 1983 through September 1985. As this figure includes many cases involving more than one person, spans only a 27-month period and does not include any successful claim filed before judges in deportation hearings, "tens of thousands" is likely a reasonable overall estimate for the five years in question. American Council for Nationalities Service, *Refugee Reports*, December 13, 1985, p. 3.

p. 206 *St.-Pierre United in Quebec City* Rhéal Séguin, "Churches No Longer Safe Haven for Refugees," *Globe and Mail*, March 9, 2004.

p. 206 *Paris's St. Bernard Church* See Teresa Hayter, *Open Borders: The Case Against Immigration Controls*, second edition (London: Pluto Press, 2004), pp. 142–48.

p. 208 *"Arendt could not have envisaged"* Power, "The Lesson of Hannah Arendt," p. 36.

p. 208 *"see themselves not as 'human beings in general'"* Power, "The Lesson of Hannah Arendt," p. 36.

p. 209 *"professional idealists"* and *"The groups they formed"* Arendt, *Origins*, p. 292.

p. 211 *"The topic was hot pretty soon"* Matthew Gibney interview, October 14, 2008.

p. 212 *"In spite of the lofty rhetoric"* Matthew Gibney, *The Ethics and Politics of Asylum: Liberal Democracy and the Response to Refugees* (Cambridge: Cambridge University Press, 2004), p. 2.

p. 212 *"The detached perspective of the 'philosopher'"* Gibney, *Ethics and Politics*, p. 260. Gibney does not have Agamben and Derrida in mind, but his remark nonetheless applies to them.

p. 213 "have profound implications" Gibney, *Ethics and Politics*, p. 243.

p. 214 *"Political leaders could attempt to establish"* Gibney, *Ethics and Politics*, p. 246.

p. 214 *a call that previous writers on refugee issues have made* See James Hathaway and Alexander Neve, "Making International Refugee Law Relevant Again: A Proposal for Collectivized and Solution-Oriented Protection," *Harvard Human Rights Journal*, vol. 10 (Spring 1997). For some provocative criticisms of Hathaway and Neve's proposal see Peter Nyers, *Rethinking Refugees: Beyond States of Emergency* (New York: Routledge, 2006), p. 128.

p. 214 *Refugees, Asylum-seekers and the Media Project* See www.exiledjournalists.net, and Mike Jempson, "Truth Can Find Asylum," *Red Pepper*, July 2004, p. 31.

p. 216 *"one can assume that these judgements"* Gibney, *Ethics and Politics*, p. 242.

p. 216 *Malcolm Fraser, a former prime minister of Australia* "Extended Malcolm Fraser Interview," *Letters to Ali*, Special Features (Madman Films, 2005), DVD.

CHAPTER 7: The Right to Have Rights

p. 219 *It was Rwanda, 1994* For the background to events in Rwanda see Linda Melvern, *Conspiracy to Murder: The Rwandan Genocide* (New York: Verso, 2006), pp. 133–36.

p. 219 *In Francine Peyti's village* Marta Young, "Responding to the Psychosocial Needs of Refugees," in M. Loughry and A. Ager, eds., *The Refugee Experience: Psychosocial Training Module*, revised edition (Oxford: Oxford University Press, 2001). Francine and Paul Peyti's names are pseudonyms.

p. 220 *strewn across the floors of churches and schoolrooms* "Rwanda Killers Leave a Village of the Dead," *New York Times*, May 14, 1994.

p. 221 *"whether or not the Charter or Rights and Freedoms"* Barbara Jackman interview, autumn 2004. All subsequent Jackman quotes are from this interview.

p. 222 *"You're asking him to place his life"* Victor Malarek, "Court Ruling on Refugees Wins Praise from Lawyers," *Globe and Mail*, April 5, 1985.

p. 222 *"You realize how big an element"* Barbara Fryer, "New Oral Hearings Offer Clearer View of Refugees' Status," *Globe and Mail*, December 5, 1983. Canada's system was also criticized for its slow processing times, with claims taking an average of three years to decide. As Fryer points out, this was partly due to the time involved in reviewing transcripts. See Victor Malarek, "Refugees Maze: Arrivals Face 3-Year Struggle through Choked System," *Globe and Mail*, December 19, 1984, and "Smear Tactics Cited: India Pressing Canada on Refugees, Sikhs Say," *Globe and Mail*, July 23, 1985. A general overview of the old system can be found in Ninette Kelly and Michael Treblicock, *The Making of the Mosaic: A History of Canadian Immigration Policy* (Toronto: University of Toronto Press, 1998), pp. 412–13.

p. 224 *There have been court decisions in other countries* After Germany introduced its asylum clause, German courts routinely recognized asylum-seekers as rights-bearing agents, but the practical effects of such decisions were minimal even before the asylum clause was amended. The closest American equivalent to *Singh* is *INS v. Cardoza-Fonseca*, a 1987 Supreme Court case that ruled that refugees can have a well-founded fear of persecution even when there is a less than 50 percent chance of that persecution occurring. The decision was an important win for refugees as it eased the standard of proof they had to meet to have a claim accepted. But even if *Cardoza-Fonseca* were applied to the letter, it would not rule out the use of deadlines or asylum applications being decided entirely according to paper evidence, two measures ruled out by Singh. As it stands, one of the lawyers who argued the case has suggested that it has subsequently been undermined by American asylum officers "who are not applying the deferential standard announced by the Supreme Court in Cardoza-Fonseca."

See Bill Ong Hing, "A Well-Founded Fear that INS V. Cardoza-Fonseca Has Been Circumvented," *Georgetown Immigration Law Journal*, vol. 14. no. 3, p. 849.

p. 224 *Appointed on the basis of patronage rather than merit* For a thorough overview of this and related problems, see Francois Crépeau and Delphine Nakache, "Critical Spaces in the Canadian Refugee Determination System: 1989-2002," *International Journal of Refugee Law*, vol. 20 no. 1 (2008): 50-122. In 2010 the Canadian government passed the Balanced Refugee Reform Act, which reformed the appointment process to the body that hears refugee claims, the Immigration and Refugee Board.

p. 226 *"Canadian ideas and Canadian constitutionalists"* Frederick Schauer, "The Politics and Incentives of Legal Transplantation," Working Paper No. 44, Center for International Development at Harvard University, April 2000, p. 12.

p. 227 *"curb the human tendencies"* Denis Smith, *Rogue Tory: The Life and Legend of John G. Diefenbaker* (Toronto: Macfarlane Walter and Ross, 1997), p. 343.

p. 228 *"rights were only what Parliament declared"* Smith, *Rogue Tory*, p. 347.

p. 228 *"a timid and tepid affirmation"* The critic is Bora Laskin. Quoted in Smith, *Rogue Tory*, p. 343.

p. 229 *"a new atmosphere favorable"* Julius Grey, "Immigration Law Combines Lofty Principles, Few Rights," *Gazette* (Montreal), May 27, 1985.

p. 230 *A 1965 government report* Report of the Royal Commission on Bilingualism and Biculturism, by A. Davidson Dunton and André Laurendeau.

p. 235 *"plans for legislation which we realized"* Quoted in Matthew Gibney, *The Ethics and Politics of Asylum: Liberal Democracy and the Response to Refugees* (Cambridge: Cambridge University Press, 2004), p. 117.

p. 236 *16 percent success rate compared to 36 percent* Government Accounting Office, "Asylum: Approval Rate for Selected Applicants" (Washington, D.C., 1987), p. 2.

p. 236 *U.S. claimants in general are four to six times more likely* Audrey Macklan, "The Value(s) of the Canada-U.S. Safe Third Country Agreement" (Toronto: Caledon Institute of Social Policy, 2003), p. 23.

p. 240 *detaining asylum-seekers is "inherently undesirable"* Office of the United Nations High Commissioner for Refugees, "UNHCR

Revised Guidelines on Applicable Criteria and Standards Relating to the Detention of Asylum Seekers," February 1999.

p. 240 *This places them among the truly destitute* U.S. Committee for Refugees, *Refugee Reports*, June 30 1996, p. 6.

p. 243 *"Norway's acceptance rate for people"* Daniel Stoffman, "Fixing the Refugee Mess," *Maclean's*, December 16, 2002, p. 26.

p. 244 *"We are spending too much"* Stoffman, "Fixing the Refugee Mess," p. 27.

p. 244 *"Anybody who claims their life is in danger"* Daniel Stoffman interview, autumn 2004. All subsequent Stoffman quotes are from this interview.

p. 244 *Costa Ricans made 3,357 refugee claims* Citizenship and Immigration Canada, "Facts and figures 2007—Immigration Overview: Permanent and temporary residents," http://www.cic.gc.ca/english/resources/statistics/facts2007/temporary/27.asp, last accessed December 31, 2008.

p. 245 *it would create a "refugee dividend"* John C. Thompson and Joe Turlej, "Other People's Wars: A Review of Overseas Terrorism in Canada," Mackenzie Institute Occasional Paper, June 2003, p. 132.

p. 245 *its total recognition rate climbs from 2 to 33 percent* United Nations High Commissioner for Refugees, *2005 UNHCR Statistical Yearbook: Trends in Displacement, Protection and Solutions* (Geneva, 2007), p. 446. In practice, temporary permits have often turned out not to be temporary. When recipients get married, enrol their children in school and put down other roots, they develop social networks that can apply pressure on politicians to have their status made permanent. Conversely, when temporary permits are genuinely temporary, they are often criticized because they can leave people in limbo for years, unable to make long-term plans for the future. See Jan-Paul Brekke, "The Dilemmas of Temporary Protection: The Norwegian Experience," *Policy Studies*, vol. 22, no. 1, pp. 5–18.

p. 246 *acceptance rate for 2001 as 47 percent* Benjamin Dolin and Margaret Young, "Canada's Refugee Protection System," http://dsp-psd.tpsgc.gc.ca/Collection-R/LoPBdP/BP/bp185-e.htm#appendix1tx, last accessed December 31, 2008.

p. 246 *The so-called Progress Party* See Tor Bjørklund and Jørgen Goul Andersen, "Anti-immigration parties in Denmark and Norway: the Progress Parties and the Danish People's Party," in

Martin Schain, Aristide Zolberg & Patrick Hossay, eds., *Shadows Over Europe: The Development and Impact of the Extreme Right in Western Europe* (New York: St. Martin's Press, 2002). There are also differences between Canada and Norway when it comes to the procedures they use to decide refugee claims (in Norway, for example, initial interviews are conducted by the police), which may also influence the two countries' acceptance rates.

p. 246 *"the extremely low level of [permanent] refugee recognition"* Philip Rudge, "The Need for a More Focused Response: European Donor Policies Toward Internally Displaced Persons (IDPs)," Norwegian Refugee Council, 2002, p. 33.

p. 247 *"Nations that absorb the most refugees"* Quoted in G. Jeffrey MacDonald, "Stranded in an Unwelcome Land: Millions of Refugees Fled Their Homelands Only to Find No Willing Host Country," *Christian Science Monitor*, July 22, 2004, p. 13.

p. 248 *Not a plausible way of determining* Another problem with averaging international acceptance rates is that receiving countries receive claims filed by people from different source countries.

p. 249 *"The genocide against the Tutsi"* Fiona Terry, *Condemned to Repeat? The Paradox of Humanitarian Action* (Ithaca, N.Y.: Cornell University Press, 2002), p. 3.

p. 250 *Help refugees abroad at the expense of those* Canada's commitment to helping asylum-seekers did not prevent it from also helping overseas refugees in 2001. That year it was the 14th largest donor to UNHCR on a per capita level. This was behind Norway, which was number one, but better than most other governments. See United Nations High Commissioner for Refugees, *UNHCR Global Report 2001*, (Geneva: UNHCR, 2002), p. 24.

p. 251 *twenty-three such claims were recognized in the United States* U.S. Department of Homeland Security, Office of Immigration Statistics, "Table 21: Refugees and Asylees Granted Lawful Permanent Resident Status by Region and Selected Country of Birth, Fiscal Years 1946–2003," *2003 Yearbook of Immigration Statistics* (Washington, D.C., 2004), p. 72.

p. 252 *"If Ernst Zundel is a refugee"* Rex Murphy, "Let's Try Zundel Denial," *Globe and Mail*, February 22, 2003.

p. 252 *"Every time he has a hearing"* "Show Zundel the Door," *Toronto Star*, April 3, 2003. For defences of Zundel's right to receive a hearing, see Alex Neve, "The Case Is Troubling, but the Principle Is Clear," *Globe and Mail*, February 22, 2003, and the remarks of Janet Dench of the Canadian Council for Refugees quoted in Allan Thompson, "Zundel Haunts Us Still," *Toronto Star*, April 21, 2003.

p. 254 *"An interviewer at the airport"* Philip Schrag, *A Well-Founded Fear: The Congressional Battle to Save Asylum in America* (New York: Routledge, 2000), p. 156. Schrag also discusses at length the introduction of deadlines in regard to American asylum claims and the problems this has resulted in.

p. 254 *the case of Libardo Yepes* Eric Schmidt, "When Asylum Requests Are Overlooked," *New York Times*, August 15, 2001; Alexander Greenawalt, attorney for Libardo Yepes, correspondence with the author, November 19, 2008.

p. 256 *"It appears that an order issued by an immigration inspector"* U.S. Commission on Immigration Reform, *Becoming an American: Immigration and Immigrant Policy* (Washington, D.C., 1997), p. 110.

p. 256 *"I was on the board of a Catholic newspaper"* Quoted in Joe Fiorito, "Celebrating 15 Years of Hope in Canada," *Toronto Star*, June 16, 2006.

p. 257 *"Human rights, she was saying"* Mary Jo Leddy interview, June 2005. All subsequent Leddy quotes are from this interview.

p. 257 *a great falling-away from Singh and what it represents.* See F. Pearl Eliadis, "The Swing from Singh: the Narrowing Application of the Charter in Immigration Law," *Immigration Law Reporter*, Second Series, Vol 26. (1995), pp. 130–47.

p. 254 *it would be impossible to enforce* Interview with Janet Dench, Canadian Council for Refugees, August 30, 2005. A side deal to the Safe Third Country Agreement commits Canada to accepting 200 refugees a year from the United States. The Canadian Council for Refugees has suggested that this is likely so that the U.S. can resettle Haitian refugees interdicted on the high seas. The CCR opposes this aspect of the agreement (as it does the deal overall). See Canadian Council for Refugees, "CCR Denounces Secret Side-Deal," July 12, 2002, http://www.ccrweb.ca//sidedeal.html, last accessed January 2, 2009. In my view, however, this aspect of the agreement is worth keeping, in order to provide an alternative to forced repatriation to Haiti for at least some refugees.

p. 257 *from 25,500 in 2004 to 19,740 the next year* United Nations High Commissioner for Refugees, "Asylum Levels and Trends in Industrialized Countries, 2007," Geneva, March 18, 2008, p. 38.

p. 258 *"Sometimes they think, you're working for the government"* Gustavo Neme interview, June 2005. All subsequent Neme quotes are from this interview.

p. 259 *Exemptions, however, have been granted in a halting and piecemeal fashion.* "Terrorism Related Inadmissibility Grounds Backgrounder," Refugee Council USA, July 28, 2009.

p. 259 *"a significant departure from both international law"* Canadian Council for Refugees v. Canada, 2007 FC 1262, p. 75.

p. 260 *"We are somewhat surprised"* Nicholas Keung, "Refugee Rights 'Vindicated' by Court Ruling," *Toronto Star,* November 30, 2007.

p. 260 *"Given the position of the UNHCR" Canada v. Canadian Council for Refugees,* 2008 FCA 229, p. 35.

p. 261 *"While the scale of US support"* Gil Loescher, Alexander Betts and James Milner, *The United Nations High Commissioner for Refugees (UNHCR): The Politics and Practice of Refugee Protection in the Twenty-first Century* (New York: Routledge, 2008), p. 95.

p. 261 "safeguarding the confidence of donor governments" Gil Loescher, "The UNHCR and World Politics: State Interests vs. Institutional Autonomy," *International Migration Review,* vol. 35, no. 1 (2001), p. 50.

p. 261–262 85 percent of asylum claimants in Canada Peter Showler, *Refugee Sandwich: Stories of Exile and Asylum* (Montreal: McGill-Queen's University Press, 2006), p. 228.

p. 262 *"I haven't studied this"* Howard Adelman interview, autumn 2004. All subsequent Adelman quotes are from this interview. In addition to the phenomenon Adelman notes, refugees have been prevented from reaching Canada due to interdiction efforts of other countries. For examples see "European Court of Human Rights, Jabari v. Turkey, Judgement of 11 July 2000," *International Journal of Refugee Law,* vol 12 no. 4, 597-607; and Richard Dunstan, "United Kingdom: Breaches of Article 31 of the 1951 Refugee Convention," *International Journal of Refugee Law,* vol. 10 no. 1-2 (1998), 205-213. Both articles describe cases of individuals seeking to travel to Canada to file a refugee claim, only to be stopped at a European airport. In both cases, the individual in question was later recognized as a refugee (by the UNHCR in Turkey and the British government respectively).

p. 264 *66,000 people slated for removal* For a general discussion of Canada's removal policies, see chapter 7, "Detention and Removal of Individuals—Canada Border Services Agency," in Office of the Auditor General of Canada, *May 2008 Report of the Auditor General of Canada* (Ottawa, 2008), p. 15.

p. 264 *they disappear 70 percent of the time* Matthew Gibney and Randall Hansen, "Deportation and the Liberal State: The Forcible Return of Asylum Seekers and Unlawful Migrants in Canada, Germany and the United Kingdom," UNHCR, February 2003, p. 11.

p. 264 *total underground population estimated at 100,000* Matthew Gibney and Randall Hansen, "Asylum Policy in the West: Past Trends, Future Possibilities," United Nations University/World Institute for Development Economics Research, Discussion Paper No. 2003/68, 2003, p. 4.

p. 264 *"The restrictiveness of the liberal state"* Gibney and Hansen, "Deportation and the Liberal State," p. 14.

CHAPTER 8: The Legend of Ahmed Ressam

p. 268 *Visceral shock and horror* Peter Showler interview, October 8, 2008. Unless otherwise indicated, all subsequent Showler quotes are from this interview.

p. 268 *Boston newspapers reported that investigators* "Seeking Trail of Terrorists Across Borders," *Boston Globe*, September 13, 2001; Maggie Mulvihill, Cosmo Macero Jr. and Tom Farmer, "Terrorists' Plot Planned for Months — Cops Swarm Hub Hotel in Search for Evidence," *Boston Herald*, September 13, 2001.

p. 268 *"Foreign terrorists bent on wreaking havoc"* Al Guart, "Canada Border a Terror Sieve," *New York Post*, September 16, 2001. For more detailed discussions of the Canadian connection and the story's persistence, see Doug Struck, "Canada Fights Myth It Was 9/11 Conduit," *Washington Post*, April 9, 2005, and Jake Tapper, "Blame Canada," *Political Punch*, ABC News, April 22, 2009, http://blogs.abcnews.com/politicalpunch/2009/04/blame-canada.html, last accessed May 23, 2009.

p. 269 *"Canada: A Club Med for world terrorists"* *Guelph Mercury*, September 17, 2001, p. A5.

p. 270 *"We found him all the time holding his stomach"* Quoted in Hal Bernton, Mike Carter, David Heath and James Neff, "The Terrorist Within, Chapter Two: The Fountainhead," *Seattle Times*, June 23, 2002. This article is part of a comprehensive twenty-part series on Ressam available in its entirety at http://seattletimes.nwsource.com/news/nation-world/terroristwithin/, last accessed December 11, 2008.

This series, along with testimony Ressam gave at the trial of Mokhtar Haouari, forms the primary basis of my account of his time in Canada. For the relevant testimony, see *United States v. Mokhtar Haouari*, No. S4 00 Cr. 15 (S.D. N.Y.), July 3, 2001 (transcript pp. 531–85) and July 5, 2001 (transcript pp. 587–662). I have silently corrected very minor errors in the *Times* account.

p. 270 *"He was a handsome young man"* Bernton et al., "The Terrorist Within, Chapter Three: Leaving Home," *Seattle Times*, June 23, 2002.

p. 271 *Tightened its visa requirements* Michael Collyer, FMO Research Guide: Algeria, Forced Migration Online, http://www.forcedmigration .org/guides/fmo023/. Last accessed December 10, 2008.

p. 272 *"improve my life in general" United States v. Mokhtar Haouari*, July 3, 2001, transcript p. 536.

p. 272 *"Is this a fake?"* Bernton et al., "The Terrorist Within, Chapter Four: Sneaking In," *Seattle Times*, June 24, 2002.

p. 272 *"I was tortured with ribbons"* Ahmed Ressam refugee claim form, English translation, available at http://seattletimes.nwsource. com/news/nation-world/terroristwithin/chapter4.html, last accessed December 9, 2008.

p. 273 *Ressam tried to steal a security guard's wallet* "Terror Timeline: Ressam's Sorry Montreal Record," *Gazette* (Montreal), May 15, 2005.

p. 274 *"They're not our top priority"* Allan Thompson, "Man never regarded as a terrorist threat," *Toronto Star*, December 21, 1999.

p. 276 *"I do not fear death"* Quoted in Evan Kohlmann, "The Afghan-Bosnian Mujahideen Network in Europe," p. 17, http:// www.globalterroralert.com/specialreports.html, last accessed December 11, 2008.

p. 276 *"important brothers"* Bernton et al., "The Terrorist Within: Joining Jihad," *Seattle Times*, June 27, 2002.

p. 276 *"These are people with a lot of problems"* Marc Sageman, *Understanding Terror Networks* (Philadelphia: University of Pennsylvania Press, 2004), p. 108.

p. 277–278 *They therefore put his name on a watch list* Stewart Bell, "CSIS Watched Ressam for Years Before Arrest," *National Post*, April 7, 2001, and "Ressam Trial Reveals Cracks in System," *National Post*, April 9, 2001.

p. 278 *he was now a genuinely dangerous individual* During this period Ressam and an associate discussed planting a bomb in

Montreal in "a predominantly Jewish neighbourhood." It is not clear how much care or planning they put into the idea: they had in mind the intersection of Laurier and Park avenues, which was not in a Jewish neighbourhood. See "RCMP Play Down Threat," *Gazette* (Montreal), December 1, 2001.

p. 280 *"a serious intelligence error"* Andrew Mitrovica, "CSIS Tracked Suspected Terrorist for Years," *Globe and Mail*, December 23, 1999.

p. 281 *"Hey, we've got something here"* Lawrence Wright, *The Looming Tower: al Qaeda and the Road to 9/11* (New York: Knopf, 2006), p. 297.

p. 282 *"Bottom line, we couldn't get travel documents"* "Is Canada a Safe Haven for Terrorists?" "Trail of a Terrorist," *Frontline*, PBS, interviews, http://www.pbs.org/wgbh/pages/frontline/shows/trail/etc/canada.html, last accessed December 9, 2008.

p. 282 *"This year alone Algerians have been slain"* Amnesty International, "Algerians: Failed by Their Government and by the International Community," http://www.amnestyusa.org/document.php?lang=e&id=DAE932F2EA6C7D7E8025690000693085, last accessed October 26, 2008.

p. 282 *Having a passport is what allowed him* Stewart Bell, "Passport Office Takes Blame in Ressam Case," *National Post*, December 4, 2003.

p. 284 *"Algeria Considered Suspect a Terrorist"* Stewart Bell, Marina Jiménez and Andrew McIntosh, "Algeria Considered Suspect a Terrorist," *National Post*, December 21, 1999. See also "Extremist Linked to Arrest," *Times Colonist* (Victoria), December 19, 1999; Paul Koring and Barrie McKenna, "Terrorist Bomb Plot Suspected," *Globe and Mail*, December 18, 1999; and "Police Fear Millennium Bomb Plot," BBC News, December 19, 1999, http://news.bbc.co.uk/2/hi/americas/571584.stm, last accessed October 30, 2008. The *Times Colonist* and the *Globe* both quote the RCMP falsely stating that Ressam's asylum application was denied because he was a member of the Armed Islamic Group. For a rebuttal of this claim see Allan Thompson, "Man Never Regarded as a Terrorist Threat," *Toronto Star*, December 21, 1999.

p. 284 *"To them [the Algerian government]"* Ahmed Ressam refugee claim form.

p. 285 *"The wisdom of allowing people"* "Another Wintry Day, Another Refugee Debacle," *Globe and Mail*, December 22, 1999.

p. 285 *"Absurd refugee laws"* Barrie McKenna, "Canadian Border Raises Few Hackles Outside Hearing," *Globe and Mail*, January 27, 2000.

p. 285 *"Algerian refugee"* "Trail of a Terrorist," *Frontline*, PBS, transcript, http://www.pbs.org/wgbh/pages/frontline/shows/trail/etc/script.html, last accessed December 9, 2008.

p. 285 *"Ressam was accepted in Canada, Canadian Press,"* "Terrorist Ressam's Confessions Helping Canadian Spy Agency, Says Post," April 9, 2002.

p. 286 *"When Ahmed Ressam came to Canada"* "Trail of a Terrorist," PBS, interviews, http://www.pbs.org/wgbh/pages/frontline/shows/trail/etc/canada.html. Last accessed December 9, 2008. Smith seemed unaware of the case of Ramzi Ahmed Yousef, an asylum claimant who participated in the World Trade Center bombing of 1993, which injured 1,000 people and killed six. Ramzi, who to my knowledge is the only person to have committed asylum fraud as part of a successful terror operation in North America, was caught upon arrival at Kennedy International Airport in 1992. He could have been detained had it not been for a lack of detention facilities. In the United States at the time, jail space for aliens was funded through a user fee charged on international plane tickets. According to Philip Schrag, the fee was also used to fund airport facilitation, "that is, for the [immigration] and customs inspectors who worked in airports. The traveling public and the airlines cared a lot about facilitation, which directly affected how long an arriving international passenger had to wait in line after a flight. The airlines, which had considerable political clout in determining how the fees they collected would be used, lobbied successfully for the government to use most of the money for facilitation, as opposed to . . . detention." This unusual funding arrangement contributed to a security arrangement that allowed Yousef to enter the United States. For the details of his case, and the many restrictive measures the U.S. added to its refugee system as a result, see Schrag's book *A Well-Founded Fear: The Congressional Battle to Save Political Asylum in America* (New York: Routledge, 2000). Yousef's arrival is mentioned on page 39.

p. 286 *"Following a familiar terrorist pattern"* The *9/11 Commission Report: Final Report of the National Commission on Terrorist Attacks Upon the United States* (Washington D.C.: U.S. Government Printing Office, 2004), p. 585.

p. 287 *"the rich ethnic mix"* John Kifner, "Terrorists Said to Hide in Canada's Melting Pot," *New York Times*, December 24, 1999.

p. 287 *"We need a gigantic cultural shift"* "Trail of a Terrorist," PBS, Interviews, http://www.pbs.org/wgbh/pages/frontline/shows/trail/etc/canada.html.

p. 288 *"high immigration compromises security"* Mark Krikorian, "Mass Immigration Defeats Homeland Security," in *Immigration Policy and the Terrorist Threat in Canada and the United States* (Vancouver: Fraser Institute, 2008), p. 45.

p. 288 *"no amateur"* Paul Koring, "Plot Carries Trademarks of bin Laden," *Globe and Mail*, December 20, 1999.

p. 288 *"all-star"* Robert Leiken, *Bearers of Global Jihad? Immigration and National Security after 9/11* (Washington, D.C.: The Nixon Center, 2004), p. 80. Leiken makes this remark in the course of listing Ressam as one of several terrorist all-stars who attended a mosque in London. In reality, Ressam never travelled to Britain.

p. 288 *"all but volunteered to immigration officials"* "North of the Border," *60 Minutes*, CBS News, September 7, 2003, transcript, http://www.cbsnews.com/stories/2003/09/04/60minutes/main571584.shtml, last accessed December 11, 2008.

p. 289 *"There should be a complete moratorium"* Diane Francis, "Ottawa Pursuing an Incompetent, Dangerous Policy," *National Post*, January 4, 2000.

p. 289 *received funding only after September 11* Janet Dench, "Anti-terrorism and the Security Agenda," Canadian Council for Refugees, http://www.ccrweb.ca/ICLMGforum.html, last accessed December 11, 2008.

p. 289 *"None of them actually came through"* Peter Showler interview, autumn 2004.

p. 290 *"The first thing that happens"* Showler interview, autumn 2004.

p. 290 *al-Qaeda maintained its own passport office The 9/11 Commission Report*, p. 169.

p. 291 *aware of 350 terror suspects in Canada* Jeff Sallot, "Canada Not Overrun by Terrorists," *Globe and Mail*, March 3, 2000.

p. 292 *Essam Marzouk* Marzouk's time in Canada is described in a three-part *National Post* series. See Stewart Bell and Jane Kokan, "Bin Laden's B.C. Helper," *National Post*, October 13, 2005; Stewart Bell and Jane Kokan, "Under Western Eyes," *National Post*, October 14, 2005; and Stewart Bell, Jane Kokan and Nagwa

Hassaan, "Mossad's Canuck Gets His Man," *National Post*, October 15, 2005. Marzouk's capture and rendition to Egypt are described in Michael Ross and Jonathan Kay, *The Volunteer: A Canadian's Secret Life in the Mossad* (Toronto: McClelland and Stewart, 2007), pp. 222–25.

p. 292 *a fundraiser for Hezbollah* For the case of Mohammed Dbouk, see Stewart Bell, "Hezbollah Uses Canada as Base," *National Post*, October 31, 2002, and "Hezbollah Assigned Kingpin to B.C.," *National Post*, November 27, 2002.

p. 295 *"Hence an act of terrorism"* Cass Sunstein, "Terrorism and Probability Neglect," *Journal of Risk and Uncertainty*, vol. 26, no. 2/3 (2003), p. 122.

p. 296 *"Fifty percent of claimants do not have documents"* Showler interview, Peter Showler interview, autumn 2004.

p. 297 *"Even when refugees are turned down"* "Three Ways to Fight Terrorism," *National Post*, March 3, 2006.

p. 297 *"It is recently arrived Muslims"* Lorne Gunter, "A Dutch Lesson for Canada," *National Post*, November 15, 2004.

p. 298 *"What the recruits tended to have in common"* Wright, *The Looming Tower*, p. 304.

p. 300 *In 2001 Canada increased its budget* Paul Koring, "Some Border Security Gaps Plugged, Many Remain," *Globe and Mail*, March 14, 2001.

p. 300 *"If you're in a situation"* Showler interview, autumn 2004.

p. 301 *"It becomes particularly significant"* Quoted in Jack Aubry, "Refugee Laws Far Too Lax: Expert," *Ottawa Citizen*, October 2, 2001.

p. 303 *"Why does the Prime Minister"* Canada, Parliament, House of Commons, *Debates*, 37th Parliament, 1st Session, Edited Hansard no. 105 (October 30, 2001).

p. 303 *"Singh decision extended charter protections"* "Gatecrashers Shouldn't Stay," *Calgary Herald*, April 24 2004, 2006. See also Rory Leishman, "A Court-Contrived Refugee Scandal," *London Free Press*, August 3, 2004.

p. 304 *Large swaths of the media* The editorial boards of *The Globe and Mail* and the *National Post* have long opposed Singh, as have marquee columnists at both papers and at the *Toronto Star*. See "There Is a Difference Between Everyone and Anyone," *Globe and Mail* (editorial), November 6, 1999; "Fighting Terrorism on the Home Front," *National Post* (editorial), October 4, 2001;

Jeffrey Simpson, "Speaking of Suckers . . . ," *Globe and Mail*, November 24, 1999; Diane Francis, "Canada No Help to Legitimate Refugees," *National Post*, March 2, 2002; Richard Gwyn, "A Visionary Challenges Our Policy on Immigration," *Toronto Star*, March 12, 2000.

In addition to Stockwell Day, prominent politicians who have opposed *Singh* have included former Reform Party leader Preston Manning and former Liberal leadership candidate John Manley. For media coverage of their respective views, see Stockwell Day, "Defence Policy a Shambles," *Calgary Herald*, February 2, 2002; "Make Charter Apply to Residents Only: Manning," *Record* (Kitchener-Waterloo), September 23, 1994; and Marina Jiménez, "Broken Gates: Canada's Welcome Mat Frayed and Unravelling," *Globe and Mail*, April 16, 2005.

For other calls to use the notwithstanding clause against *Singh*, see Christie McLaren, "Jammed at the Door: Refugees in Canada," *Globe and Mail*, February 27, 1991; Tom Kent, "How to Reform Immigration Policy," *Literary Review of Canada* (March 2000), p. 5; "Notwithstanding Clause Could Offer Some Safety," *Vancouver Sun*, October 3, 2001; Rory Leishman, "Some Sound Advice from a Liberal Icon on the Need to Invoke the Notwithstanding Clause," *London Free Press*, October 9, 2001, and "Court-Contrived Refugee Scandal," *London Free Press*, August 3, 2004; and Joe Easingwood, "It's Time to Overhaul Canada's Stupid Immigration Laws," *Times Colonist* (Victoria), May 5, 2002.

CHAPTER 9: In the Tracks of Leviathan

p. 307 *"The very institution of a state"* Arendt, *Origins*, 230.

p. 307 *"Should be guaranteed by"* Arendt, *Origins*, p. 298.

p. 307 *Arendt scholars have often noted* For an example, see Bridget Cotter, "Hannah Arendt and 'The Right to Have Rights,'" in *Hannah Arendt and International Relations: Readings Across the Lines*, Anthony Lang Jr. and John Williams, eds. (New York: Palgrave Macmillan, 2005), p. 97. "For Arendt, [national sovereignty] refers to two separate principles, although she does not always clearly distinguish between them. First it is 'state sovereignty' . . . Second, 'national sovereignty' also refers to 'people's sovereignty.'"

p. 312 *"a generation ago, the sovereign state"* Daniel Philpott, *Revolutions in Sovereignty: How Ideas Shaped Modern*

International Relations (Princeton, N.J.: Princeton University Press, 2001), p. 3.

p. 313 *If it should happen that the count* Hendrik Spruyt, *The Sovereign State and Its Competitors: An Analysis of Systems Change* (Princeton: Princeton University Press, 1994), p. 39. My account of the history of sovereignty owes a debt to Spruyt's excellent book.

p. 314 *"the Roman Empire conceived"* Friedrich Kratochwil, "Of Systems, Boundaries and Territoriality: An Inquiry into the Formation of the State System," *World Politics*, vol. 39, no. 1 (1986), p. 36.

p. 316 *"the logic of feudal organization"* Spruyt, *The Sovereign State*, p. 38.

p. 317 *transformed the king into a new type of ruler* See Ernst Kantorowicz, *The King's Two Bodies: A Study in Mediaeval Political Theology* (Princeton, N.J.: Princeton University Press, 1957).

p. 317 *"The first notions of sovereign authority"* Spruyt, *The Sovereign State*, p. 79.

p. 319 *"islands of urban law"* Spruyt, *The Sovereign State*, p. 124.

p. 322 *"Political entrepreneurs copy institutions"* Spruyt, *The Sovereign State*, p. 171.

p. 313 *"process of mutual empowerment"* Spruyt, *The Sovereign State*, p. 178.

p. 324 *"The empire after 1648"* Quoted in Philpott, *Revolutions in Sovereignty*, p. 87.

p. 324 *"null, void, invalid, iniquitous"* Quoted in Philpott, *Revolutions in Sovereignty*, p. 87.

p. 324–325 *"One does not really know"* Quoted in Spruyt, *The Sovereign State*, p. 170.

p. 325 *"the end of an epoch"* Leo Gross, "The Peace of Westphalia, 1648–1948," *American Journal of International Law*, vol. 42, no. 1, p. 28.

p. 325 *a change in the practice of politics that was given theoretical expression only much later* Philpott, *Revolutions in Sovereignty*, p. 84; Andreas Osiander, "Sovereignty, International Relations, and the Westphalian Myth," *International Organization*, vol. 55, No. 2, 2001, p. 281.

p. 326 *"the French people born with the baptism of Clovis"* Quoted in Patrick Geary, *The Myth of Nations: The Medieval Origins of Europe* (Princeton, N.J.: Princeton University Press, 2002), p. 7.

p. 326 *"sanction of perpetuity"* Eric Hobsbawm, "Introduction: Inventing Traditions," in Eric Hobsbawm and Terence Ranger, eds., *The Invention of Tradition* (Cambridge: Cambridge University Press, 1992), p. 2.

p. 327 *"Human dignity needs a new guarantee"* Arendt, "Preface to the First Edition," *Origins*, p. ix.

p. 327 *"A possible law above nations"* The Burden of Our Time, London: Secker & Warburg, 1951, p. 436. This is the first British edition of *Origins*. It contains a chapter "concluding remarks," found in some but not all American editions of the text.

p. 327 *"regional and global federation"* Jeffrey Isaac, "A New Guarantee on Earth: Hannah Arendt on Human Dignity and the Politics of Human Rights," *American Political Science Review*, vol. 90 no. 1, p. 70.

p. 327 *"a binational, confederate state"* Jeffrey Isaac, "A New Guarantee on Earth: Hannah Arendt on Human Dignity and the Politics of Human Rights," *American Political Science Review*, vol. 90 no. 1, p. 70.

p. 327 *"Rejecting national sovereignty as a recipe"* Isaac, "A New Guarantee on Earth," p. 70.

p. 328 *"confederation of communities"* Jeffrey Isaac, *Arendt, Camus and Modern Rebellion* (New Haven, Conn: Yale University Press, 1992), p. 222.

p. 330 *"would quickly succumb to hunger"* Michael Marrus, *The Unwanted: European Refugees in the Twentieth Century* (Oxford: Oxford University Press, 1985), p. 5.

p. 330 *"individuals who had chosen"* Marrus, *The Unwanted*, p. 15.

p. 331 *In different parts of Europe . . . while in Northern American states* For nineteenth-century immigration controls in Europe and North America, see Andreas Fahrmeir, Olivier Faron and Patrick Weil, eds., *Migration Control in the North Atlantic World: The Evolution of State Practices in Europe and the United States from the French Revolution to the Inter-War Period* (New York: Berghahn, 2003).

p. 332 *"You are looking for me everywhere"* Marrus, *The Unwanted*, p. 22.

p. 332 *In many ways, this represented a more inclusive conception of belonging* But of course, not in every way. As historian E. J. Hobsbawm has remarked of this period, "Darwinian evolutionism, supplemented later by what came to be known as genetics, provided racism with what looked like a powerful set of 'scientific' reasons for keeping out or even, as it turned out, expelling and murdering strangers." *Nations and Nationalism Since 1780: Programme, Myth, Reality*, second edition (Cambridge: Cambridge University Press, 1992), p. 108.

p. 333 *"In part as a result of the nationalization"* John Torpey, "Passports and the Development of Immigration Controls in the North Atlantic World During the Long Nineteenth Century," in Fahrmeir et al., *Migration Control in the North Atlantic World*, p. 83.

p. 333 *Whereas in the 1800s France and Prussia* On passports see Torpey, "Passports and the Development of Immigration Controls," p. 83. On welfare see Frank Caestecker, "The Transformation of Nineteenth-Century West European Expulsion Policy, 1880–1914," in Fahrmeir et al., *Migration Control in the North Atlantic World*, p. 132, note 3.

p. 333 *England neither expelled nor denied entry* Marrus, *The Unwanted*, p. 18; David Feldman, "Was the Nineteenth Century a Golden Age for Immigrants? The Changing Articulation of National, Local and Voluntary Controls," in Fahrmeir et al., *Migration Control in the North Atlantic World*, p. 167.

p. 334 *"broad, general principles"* Quoted in Randall Hansen and Desmond King, "Illiberalism and the New Politics of Asylum: Liberalism's Dark Side," *Political Quarterly*, vol. 71, no. 4 (2000), p. 403.

p. 335 *domestic sovereignty, international legal sovereignty and interdependence sovereignty* Krasner, *Sovereignty: Organized Hypocrisy* (Princeton, N.J.: Princeton University Press, 1999), p. 9. Krasner also refers to a fourth aspect, Westphalian sovereignty, referring to "the exclusion of external actors from domestic authority configurations" (p. 9). The difference between this form of sovereignty and domestic and international sovereignty is subtle, and I have left it out for the sake of simplicity.

p. 337 *This is borne out by the abolition of the slave trade* See Stephen Krasner, *Sovereignty*, pp. 106–9.

p. 337 *"it is difficult to imagine a less ambiguous"* Krasner, *Sovereignty*, p. 108.

p. 338 *"This transition was an extraordinary accomplishment"* Krasner, *Sovereignty*, p. 125.

p. 339 *"Rulers might consistently pledge"* Krasner, *Sovereignty*, p. 8.

Postscript: Refugees and Terror

p. 348 *"fall[ing] far short"* Andrew Whitley, *Human Rights Abuses in Algeria: No One Is Spared* (New York: Middle East Watch, 1994), p. 21.

p. 348 *"summary or arbitrary executions"* Amnesty International, "Algeria: Executions after Unfair Trials: A Travesty of Justice," http://www.amnestyusa.org/document.php?id=EED75BFB746E20A D802569A600603A36&lang=e, last accessed June 3, 2009.

p. 349 *"confrontational interviews"* Stewart Bell, "CSIS Breaks Up Terror Cell," *National Post*, November 3, 2005.

p. 350 *Baroud has since been held up* See, for instance, Reg Whitaker, "Refugees: The Security Dimension," *Citizenship Studies*, vol. 2, no. 3 (1998), pp. 428–29.

p. 352 *"All of this occurred in"* Associated Press, "Judge's Comments in Ressam Sentencing," July 27, 2005.

INDEX